D1285682

INTRODUCTION
TO REALISTIC
PHILOSOPHY

JOHN WILD

NORTHWESTERN UNIVERSITY

INTRODUCTION TO REALISTIC PHILOSOPHY

18 17

HARPER & ROW, PUBLISHERS

NEW YORK, EVANSTON, AND LONDON

Contents

Section 2. Philosophical Anthropology

Preface

THE present book is an attempt to provide the modern student and general reader with a sympathetic introduction to the basic concepts and principles of classical, realistic philosophy. There is, today, a widespread recognition of the critical importance of this movement of thought, which began with the Greeks, which was extended and developed in the so-called Middle Ages, and which has been further refined and clarified down to the present day. Without some grasp of its basic principles, it is impossible to understand either the history of modern philosophy or the present nature of our western culture. There is a wealth of critical treatises and commentaries on the great thinkers who have contributed to this growing body of doctrine, but there is a noticeable lack of general treatises available to the modern English-reading student which are capable of introducing him to the movement as a whole. This book is an effort to meet this need.

The method followed is critical and systematic rather than "historical," if this latter word can be properly used in such a way as to exclude the former. Many sound historical surveys are now in existence. But a college course based upon such a survey is apt to leave the student with a blur of disconnected opinions and with little understanding either of coherent philosophical argument or of the evidence on which it claims to be based. The great classic texts are now fortunately available to our students. But the translations of these texts are difficult and often loaded with antique illustrations and doctrines that have no vital interest for the modern mind. In this book I have tried to present the basic classical doctrines and arguments in simple language, and with modern illustrations, capable of being understood by the student of today.

These doctrines have been drawn from the greatest thinkers of the realistic tradition, including Plato, Aristotle, Augustine, and Aquinas. In certain sections, particularly that on social ethics (Part I, Section 2), theories are presented which are novel in the sense that they are not found precisely stated in any of the above

ix

authors—though not novel, I think, in the sense that they are inconsistent with the fundamental principles of this tradition. The book as a whole represents an attempt to acquaint the student with the living current of realistic thought in relation to theoretical and practical problems of modern life. It is intended for the use of teachers in systematic introductory courses who have a respect for classical philosophy and who would like to make the rich and basic content of this philosophy the point of departure for class discussion and criticism.

When used in this way, the book should be able to stand alone. But such a course may be given a greater or less historical emphasis. For the convenience of those who may wish to refer the student to historical works, a reading list has been appended to each chapter. The "recommended readings," wherever possible, include references to classic texts on which the chapter is based. The "suggested readings" contain references to ancient and modern treatises that discuss the same topics in ways which are related or opposed.

I have tried to avoid unduly abstract language and to achieve simplicity of expression. But it is impossible, I believe, to familiarize the student with classical thought without at the same time trying to make him at home with its technical terminology. Hence the use of some technical terms, especially in Part II, has been unavoidable. Any attempt to penetrate to the basic roots of a philosophical position is bound to have its complexities and obscurities.

For these reasons, I recognize that the demands made on the reader by this book and the recommended readings are perhaps somewhat above those now commonly expected of an introductory text. In my opinion, however, we have gone too far in the direction of talking down to the student, and I believe that the time is ripe for a more ambitious teaching program, armed with more ambitious weapons. After all, beginning courses in the other sciences make considerable demands upon the intellectual energy and acumen of the student. The reading recommended here is not easy. But I think that it can be done with profit by the ordinary student who is willing to devote a reasonable amount of time and energy to the task.

It has of course been necessary to select only certain portions of classical philosophy for treatment in an introductory work of this kind. Logic has been omitted because of its more special appeal and because classical logic is to some extent better known to us.

Metaphysics is omitted because of its greater abstractness and difficulty. Realistic epistemology has been touched upon in Chapters 17, 18, and 19. Realistic ethics and philosophy of nature have been chosen for special emphasis because the facts on which these disciplines are based are closer to the student, and therefore easier for him to grasp.

Ethics, being especially close to our everyday experience, provides us with an ideal starting point for philosophical reflection. Hence we have followed the pedagogic rather than the natural order of presentation, and have begun with ethics, though this discipline certainly presupposes a view of man and the whole world of nature. But in this case I think it is better to begin where the greater interest of the student lies and to allow him then to catch up with his presuppositions.

Nevertheless, it will be possible for those who prefer the natural order to reverse this procedure and to begin with Part II. The two parts are, in fact, sufficiently independent so that they may be used, together with the recommended reading, in separate semester courses if this is desired. I think that it should be possible, however, to cover both parts in a single-semester survey course. My hope for both college students and for the general reader is that this work may serve a modest, mediating function in leading them back to the great classic texts of philosophy, in helping them to understand these texts and the language in which they are written, and finally, most of all, in enabling them by these means to gain for themselves that clearer insight into man and the world he inhabits which is the precious gift of philosophy.

To my colleagues in the Harvard Department I am grateful for discussions which have helped me to clarify my mind on many points. I wish to express my thanks to Professor Henry Veatch of the Department of Philosophy of the University of Indiana, and to Professor Radoslav A. Tsanoff, of Rice Institute, for their criticism of this manuscript when it was in a formative stage. I am also grateful to Dr. Constantine Cavarnos, Dr. John Ladd, and Mr. Walter Wurzburger, my assistants in the elementary course from which this book has grown, for many helpful suggestions.

Cambridge, Massachusetts   J. W.
September, 1948

Historical Introduction

Chapter 1

REALISTIC PHILOSOPHY AND ITS HISTORY

PHILOSOPHY is the attempt to understand the most basic facts about the world we inhabit and so far as possible to explain these facts. This enterprise is not the exclusive concern of certain specialists, but one in which every human being is deeply involved, whether or not he is clearly conscious of it. What kind of world is this? Where is it going? What is knowledge? What is really right and wrong? Is there any living human being who has not at least occasionally raised such questions and at least hesitantly and confusedly attempted to answer them? Indeed, the different civilizations men construct and the very different lives they lead are based upon attempts to answer these questions. Every way of life is based upon a way of looking at life. The way you look at life is your philosophy.

Just as there are many ways of life, so are there many philosophies, some more true and some less true. So important is this basic enterprise of man, so much hinges upon the avoidance of confusion and error, that since the time of the ancient Greeks a certain discipline has been set aside for the concentrated consideration of philosophical problems and for the careful comparison and criticism of different ways of answering them. This discipline has survived many centuries of barbarism and bloodshed and is still pursued in our colleges and universities. It is called by the ancient name, philosophy (the love of wisdom), and those who attempt to cultivate it in a technically responsible way are called philosophers.

But this should not lead us to forget that all men are philosophers and that the academic discipline exists solely for the purpose of purifying and refining that natural philosophy of the common man which is a necessary part of human life. Medicine is pursued in a professional way by technical specialists. But this is done in order to improve the health of living men. In the same way philosophy is pursued as a technical discipline by specialists. But this is done in order to help men think more clearly and more truly about themselves and the world which they inhabit. This book will attempt to introduce the student to the discipline, or science, of philosophy.

Just as there are many different ways of life, so are there many different philosophies which have been carefully worked out and scrutinized by disciplined thought. This at once brings us face to face with an important question concerning the introduction to this discipline. Is it better to present the student with all the different systems which have been worked out, and then let him make his choice—the historical method—or to present him first of all with one way of thought to be more thoroughly grasped and mastered—the systematic method? Which method are we to pursue?

The first has been widely followed in recent times because of its seemingly greater inclusiveness and its seeming lack of dogmatism. These advantages, however, are apparent rather than real. As to the first, so many different philosophies have been developed in the course of human history that they cannot all be really "included" in a single book or a single college course. There is not sufficient time to think through any one of them very thoroughly or to think of the actual facts, the primary concern of genuine philosophy. Instead of helping the student to clarify his thought and to grasp more truth, the net result of such a quick tour through history is very often to bring him into such a state of confusion that he despairs of ever grasping any philosophical truth at all. Superficiality is punished by skepticism and distaste, which will be intensified in the student if he reflects that all these myriad doctrines cannot be true. So even at best a great deal of his time has been wasted, for the purpose of all philosophy is to attain the truth. Is it not the duty of any conscientious teacher to attempt a separation of the wheat from the chaff, to make a selection of what is best and truest, and then to give the student time for a careful, critical assimilation?

As to the second advantage, the lack of dogmatism, this also is only apparent. Philosophy is unfortunately a necessity for any man who thinks and speaks and lives, even for the teacher of a history of philosophy course. No matter how he may try to conceal it by the constant discussion of other positions, he also has a point of view which emerges at least indirectly in what he chooses to discuss and how he chooses to discuss it. Even if he is a skeptic and believes that truth is unattainable, this also is a philosophy which requires exposition, explanation, and defense, if it is to be anything more than a prejudice. So the teacher who conceals his point of view under the mask of "historical objectivity" is not really being undogmatic. Masked dogmatism is the most dangerous kind. The open defense of a stated position is one of two things, neither of which is dangerous. It is either a weak defense with unsound reasons— which is dangerous only to the stupid—or it is a sound defense with sound reasons—which is neither dangerous nor dogmatic, but a systematic statement of the truth.

Hence we shall not follow the historical method in this book. We shall make no effort to discuss every position that has ever been held, though we shall try to deal critically with certain important historical theses other than that which we are explaining. The historical method certainly has its legitimate place. But this place is not the introductory course in philosophy. In beginning his disciplined quest for philosophic truth, the student needs help in clarifying his own basic insights, in connecting them with one another, and in slowly and systematically comparing them with the facts. All this takes time and patience. Whatever his own way of thought may be, he will be most aided in really grasping what he already vaguely knows, by the careful and painstaking study of a single philosophic discipline. But this brings up a further question. Which one shall we choose?

We are choosing realistic philosophy for three reasons. First, it has been pursued and developed by great minds from the fifth century B.C. in ancient Greece throughout the whole of our western history down to the present time. This unique record of historic continuity gives it a certain advantage over other alternatives. It can be truly said that realistic philosophy has been adopted and cultivated by more great minds for a longer time and in more diverse cultural settings than any other philosophy available to us.

Second, this realistic philosophy, unlike idealism for instance, does not violate any basic insight of that vague, incipient philosophy which we know as common sense. True philosophy is a therapy for the common intellect of common men, and true therapy does not try to destroy what it is trying to heal and perfect. If the native, rational faculty is basically corrupt, there is no sense in trying to study philosophy at all. The case is hopeless. If, on the other hand, the rational faculty of man is basically sound, then its basic appre- hensions, though often vague and mixed with what is false, must be respected. Realistic philosophy does respect such apprehensions. It can be truly said that this philosophy, while extending, refining, and purifying these fundamental insights of common sense, never- theless maintains a vital contact with them at every point.

The third reason is the most important of all, though it can be stated here only in a preliminary manner. This philosophy contains an important core of truth which cannot help but enlighten the individual intellect as it starts out on its quest for understanding. Our aim is to present this core of truth in realistic philosophy. But we have not as yet explained what is meant by the term.

1. WHAT IS REALISM?

The undisciplined intellect of mankind clings to three basic opin- ions about reality which, though they may not be clearly formu- lated, actually underlie its thinking as long as this is not distorted by sophistic argument. Our "common sense" tells us, first, that we inhabit a world consisting of many things which are what they are, independent of any human opinions and desires; second, that by the use of reason we can know something about these things as they actually are; and third, that such knowledge is the safest guide to human action. For example, when men wish to cross the sea, they turn to those who have studied navigation. When they are sick, they go to those who have studied medicine. They do this because they believe that the world is made up of different kinds of things which must be understood in different ways, that knowledge may be won by disciplined study, and that such knowledge may lead men to safety.

These basic beliefs of mankind are also the three basic doctrines of realistic philosophy: (1) There is a world of real existence which men have not made or constructed; (2) this real existence can be known by the human mind; and (3) such knowledge is the only reliable guide to human conduct, individual and social.

This does not mean that realistic philosophy is nothing but "com- mon sense." They differ in the following ways. Common sense holds these opinions, it is true, but vaguely and confusedly without critical examination. Realistic thought precisely formulates these principles, analyzes their component concepts, and examines them in the light of the evidence. Common sense is largely unaware of the implications of these principles and their interrelations with one another. Realistic reflection has discovered many such implications and systematic connections. Finally, because of its uncritical acceptance of these doctrines, common sense is often unable to defend them against objections and thus is easily led astray into non-realistic modes of thought. Realistic philosophy, because of its more exact analysis and critical examination of the evidence, is able to undertake the arduous task of defending these insights against alien ways of thought and of answering critical questions.

The three basic insights to which we have referred determine three basic subdivisions of realistic philosophy—the study of being or first philosophy (including metaphysics and the philosophy of nature) ; the study of human knowledge (including epistemology and logic) ; and the study of the human good (including individual and social ethics). None of these subordinate realistic disciplines is a priori, in the sense that it speculatively constructs concepts or theories that have no basis in the original data of experience. Every realistic theory in whatever field must be checked by these original data as they are apprehended either by sense or by reason. In this sense, every realistic discipline is radically empirical.

The fundamental science of metaphysics examines the fact of existence which reason discovers in every empirical datum of whatever sort. This fact turns out to be more complex than our common sense supposes, including such related facts as unity, truth, and perfection which follow after being wherever it is found; and possibility, change, and causation which necessarily attach to finite being. The task of realistic metaphysics is to illumine this basic structure of existence which underlies all the more particular facts revealed by the special sciences. By focusing the concept of existence in its vast and limitless scope, this discipline enables us to avoid the fallacy of confusing being with some subordinate category such as mind or matter. In this way it helps us to maintain a truly empirical attitude toward new and surprising facts whatever they may be, without attempting to reduce them to more familiar categories.

Closely associated with metaphysics is the subordinate discipline of the philosophy of nature, which studies the material, changing being of human individuals and the other material things around us.

Human knowledge is a most mysterious and complex phenomenon. The function of epistemology, or theory of knowledge, as it is conceived by realism, is first of all to describe this process accurately, then to explain it, and finally to defend it against those skeptical doubts concerning its ability to know things as they are which are constantly raised by the inquiring mind. Epistemology is the study of how, by means of concepts and other mental representations, we know extra-mental objects.

Logic is the study of these concepts as such, and of how they must be arranged in propositions and arguments if they are to become the instruments of true knowledge in any field. When properly developed in a realistic manner, logic thus becomes the universal instrument or organon of human knowledge, because all science has to be achieved by means of concepts that are expressed by means of propositions and developed by means of argument according to the rules of formal logic. But these rules are ultimately derived from the structure of existence. Hence formal logic cannot be properly understood without a correlated understanding of metaphysics and epistemology as embodied in the closely related discipline of material logic which, together with metaphysics, has fallen into sad neglect in recent times.

Insight into basic truth is something intrinsically desirable. So theoretical philosophy is an end in itself. But it is not the final end of man, who also requires many other activities to realize his complex nature. The attempt to use reason in aiding these other faculties to reach their natural end is called practical philosophy, or ethics. This discipline, as the realist conceives it, is based primarily upon our knowledge of the nature of man. First of all, it studies those acts which are required by this nature for its perfection, the human good; and then the habits of choice, or virtues, which must be developed to produce these acts. Social ethics studies the common good of all individual men that is the final end of rational action, and the cooperative structures of habit and choice that are required for the attainment of this end.

Part I of this book will deal with practical philosophy, Part II with theoretical philosophy. In the first section of Part I, we shall deal with individual ethics; in the second section, with social ethics. Every human being has to face such problems in directing his own life, and almost everyone has reflected seriously upon them. Hence the study of ethics is the most concrete approach to the problems of philosophy. In Part I we shall present the student with a modern interpretation of realistic, moral philosophy. But an ethics cannot stand alone. It rests upon a view of the world and man. Hence in the first section of Part II we shall deal with the general structure of the changing world that we inhabit. At certain points, however, especially in Chapter 16, we shall enter into the field of metaphysics. In the second section of Part II we shall present a realistic account of human knowledge, the most distinctive activity of man. Certain problems of material logic will be considered in Chapter 19. Thus every branch of realistic philosophy will be at least touched upon.

Our primary aim will be to introduce the student to the best realistic thought in these fields. But at certain points we shall present the objections and criticisms of other opposed views such as naturalism and idealism. The student should therefore gain an understanding of the most important alternative types of philosophy and of the major issues between them. Before he embarks on this task, however, he needs to know, at least in outline, something of the history of realistic thought.

2. SOCRATES

The basic insights of realism, as unanalyzed assumptions of common sense, are probably as old as the human race. But the first important name in its history as a critical discipline is that of Socrates, the Athenian (470–399 B.C.) . He was a stonecutter by trade and lived the active life of a citizen and a soldier during the period of the great war between Athens and Sparta. Early in life he began to think about those basic opinions concerning life and politics which his fellow citizens took for granted, and began to question them in the streets and houses of the city. Many friends, especially among the youth, were attracted by his discourses and conversations, and he became well known.

Refusing to take any party line, he simply followed the argument wherever it led him, often toward conclusions which seemed strange and even revolutionary to his contemporaries. After the defeat of Athens by Sparta in 404 B.C., he refused to obey the commands of the tyrants who then came into power and tried to implicate him in their plots. After the return of a democratic government a few years later, he was accused of impiety and corrupting the youth by dangerous doctrines. At the trial described in Plato's *Apology*, he was condemned to death, and later executed in the city jail. The conversation on the subject of immortality the last day of his life, and the final scene of his death, are vividly described in Plato's *Phaedo*.

Socrates left no writings, but from the account of him given by Plato as well as from other sources, it is clear that he made two important contributions to philosophy. The first was his passionate search for universal definitions of knowledge, virtue, and other basic facts which men think they understand as obvious but which, on being subjected to Socratic questioning, they discover that they do not really know. Never satisfied with the sensible instances men kept pointing at, Socrates would refer to other equally genuine but radically different instances of the same concept. Never ceasing to raise the philosophic question—what is it *(ti esti)*?—he did not rest until he had at least approached an intelligible definition of the universal concept, which remains the same in all instances and which is based upon a stable structure of things, independent of human opinion and desire. This critical zeal for the illumination of reality by immutable concepts led to the first formulations of realistic thought by Plato and his followers.

Socrates himself was primarily interested in practical philosophy, and in this field he made many pregnant suggestions. He was convinced that the soul, or source of action in man, is more important than the body *(Apology* 30) . From this insight he drew certain inexorable consequences—for example, that tending the soul and educating it are even more important than tending the body and providing it with material things. He also held that genuine wisdom is the most precious possession of man, and the source of all virtue. Sickness and death affect the body, but ignorance and vice affect the soul. Hence he maintained that vice was worse than death *(Apology* 29) . From the same premise he argued that it is worse to do injustice than to suffer it, because the former is a disease of the soul (*Gorgias* 474 ff.). In addition he believed in a being higher than man to whom we owe our existence and our first allegiance (*Phaedo* 62, and *Apology* 30), though he made no claim to any special knowledge of this being, or of the physical structure of the world (*Phaedo* 96 ff.).

These doctrines were assimilated and further developed by Plato and his later followers. But even more important than the first statement of these essential insights was the clear and manifest way in which he actually lived and died in strict accordance with them. It was this which enabled him to exert an extraordinarily magnetic effect upon many of his younger contemporaries. He not only led them to philosophic truth but showed them the philosophic way of life being lived before them in the flesh. The most important of his younger friends was Plato, who, while still a youth, was led by Socrates to abandon a political career, to devote his life to teaching, and finally to lay the first, careful, critical foundations of realistic thought.

3. PLATO

Plato (427–347 B.C.) was brought up in a prominent Athenian household, saturated with the ideals of Periclean democracy. At an early age he decided upon a political career of public service, and this basic desire to aid in the establishment of a just social order dominated his thought and activity to the end of his life. His youthful acquaintance with Socrates intensified this desire, but led him to see the hopeless inadequacy of existent party programs. How could men establish a just social order unless they first understood what justice is?

Meditating on the discourses of Socrates, Plato devoted the succeeding years to writing those earlier dialogues in which he tried to preserve the probing Socratic spirit and so far as possible to undo the work of the hemlock. Then he conceived the idea of starting a school where the Socratic insights and discipline might be further applied and handed on to succeeding generations. Returning from a trip to Sicily in 390 B.C., he made up his mind and founded the Academy. Two of his greatest dialogues, the *Gorgias* and the *Republic,* were probably written at this time.

There were other schools of learning already in existence, but they tried to do little more than acquaint students with past literature and influential currents of opinion. Plato was not satisfied with this. Current literature and opinion were too fallible and distorted. The aim of the Academy was to discover and to teach the truth about the world and man, irrespective of prevailing points of view. Politics can be redeemed only through the guidance of true philosophy. Attracted by this revolutionary idea, many students flocked to Plato's Academy, among them Dion, brother-in-law of the heir-apparent to the tyranny of the great city of Syracuse. Returning to his home, Dion managed to have Plato invited to supervise the education of the young prince soon after the death of the latter's father. Plato had deep misgivings about this adventure but felt that he could not resist an opportunity of having his ideas put into practice. After completing the *Parmenides* and the *Theaetetus*, which give us some idea of the advanced teaching of the Academy, he left for Syracuse in 367 B.C.

The plan did not succeed. After a short time Dionysius became jealous of Dion, and Plato was banished. He returned to the Academy but kept in touch with the situation, trying to reconcile the two relatives. In 361 he made a third trip with this end in view, but again without success. As a matter of fact his own life was for some time in danger, and it was only with great difficulty that he was able to return to Athens and resume his work in the Academy with Aristotle, who had entered the school in 367, and other students. Plato devoted the last years of his life to teaching and writing the *Philebus, Timaeus,* and *Laws,* the last of his dialogues. In his written works Plato not only preserved the courageous life and probing mind of Socrates, but at the same time, though often by indirect suggestion rather than didactic statement, laid down for the first time in written form the basic principles of philosophic realism.

Plato certainly held that there is a fixed and stable world order which is in no way dependent on the opinions and desires of men, that this order can be known by human reason as it really is, and finally that such knowledge is the only reliable guide to human action (a doctrine which lay at the very heart of his philosophy). These are the three fundamental theses of realistic thought; and the threefold division of philosophy that is based on these insights

—into the science of nature, the theory of knowledge, and ethics—was first worked out by the later Platonists as a result of reading the dialogues. But Plato not only explained and defended these principles; he also illustrated them by vivid myths and analogies, poignantly suggested them by penetrating questions and dialogues, and finally developed them into the first great literary expression of realistic thought.

Plato's major aim was that of strengthening and guiding the ceaseless effort of men to establish a just social order. This predominant practical interest is apparent in most of his dialogues, from the earliest to the last, the *Laws*. In the field of individual ethics he held to the basic theses defended by Socrates; that the soul is more important than the body, that vice is worse than death, and that it is worse to do injustice than to suffer it. But he developed them in many ways.

He held that all men seek the good by nature.[1] Hence the most potent source of evil and corruption is to be sought rather in ignorance than in some original desire for evil as such. The worst acts are performed involuntarily, in the sense that those who perform them do not understand their nature and confuse them with what is good (*Gorgias* 467). The most important of the virtues is knowledge, not merely an abstract, theoretical understanding, but an insight into the difference between good and evil, and a knowledge of how to achieve what is good. The other three essential or cardinal virtues are justice, which seeks from each according to his natural ability and renders to each according to his natural need; courage, which persists in rational action through all difficulties; and temperance, which binds all the different parts of the soul into harmony with the decrees of reason (*Republic* 441–2).[2]

There are good pleasures as well as evil ones. But the good pleasures, which attend rational action in accordance with nature, are more satisfying than the vicious ones (*Republic* 586 ff.). There is no natural conflict between the real interest and the real duty of man. The duty of man is to realize his nature, to be what he really is. This is also his interest. The ultimate standard of moral action is the law of nature, the pattern of action that will best fulfill the

[1] Cf. ch. 2.
[2] Cf. ch. 5, § 1.

original nature of man with which we are endowed (*Republic* 444C ff., and *Gorgias* 504–5) .

Plato also extended Socratic principles to the field of social ethics and developed them into a complete and coherent social philosophy, expressed with many concessions to current practice in the *Laws,* but most clearly and radically in the *Republic,* the crowning dialogue of his early maturity. Cooperative social life is demanded by nature for the satisfaction of necessary needs (*Republic* 369) . These needs are noetic, political, and material. To satisfy them, three major functions must be performed in the human community: knowledge must be acquired and preserved by the "guardians"; plans must be devised and carried out for the common welfare by the "auxiliaries" or administrators; and material artifacts must be produced by the "artisans." These functions fall into an order of subordination.[3] Political policy should be guided by knowledge, and material production should be directed to the common good by wise administration. Of all the material arts, hygiene should have the ruling position. The greatest danger facing a human community is the loss of that overarching purpose which can be provided only by true philosophy and religion. Without such rational guidance the community falls into chaos and finally into tyranny, the most corrupt of all social forms (*Republic,* Book VIII) .

Plato's *Republic* is not merely a statement of abstract principles: it is full of comment on concrete social practice and revolutionary suggestions for concrete social change. Among these radical reforms are the selection of officials on the basis of examination and merit rather than hereditary status (*Republic* 415) , the right of every child to an opportunity for highest office (*Republic* 415C) , the right of women to participate in all the cultural activities of the community and to exercise political power (*Republic* 456) , the elimination of excessive poverty and wealth (*Republic* 421D) , and a communistic way of life for the guardians (*Republic* 417) .

But though Plato's primary interest was in practical philosophy, he did not ignore epistemology and metaphysics. Indeed, in his view, these subjects were bound up with ethics in a most intimate way. It is impossible to gain any clear conception of what men ought to do unless we understand the nature of man and the mys-

[3] Cf. chs. 10 and 12.

terious awareness which attends his action. But it is impossible to understand the nature of man without also understanding the structure of the world we inhabit, with every level of which our nature is connected in myriad ways. Hence Plato's *Republic* is much more than what we think of as a treatise on political science: it also includes a theory of man and an outline of metaphysics. The *Laws* was planned as the completion of a great tetralogy treating first the origin and general structure of the world as a whole (the *Timaeus*), then prehistoric history (the *Critias*), then actual history down to the present (the *Hermocrates*), and finally the establishment of a just society governed by rational law (the *Laws*). Only the first and the last were actually finished.

Realistic epistemology is indebted to Plato for the following insights: The faculty of sense is quite distinct from the faculty of reason.[4] By sense we apprehend something that is ever changing and relative to us. By reason we apprehend something changeless, as it is in itself (*Phaedo* 65 ff.). We attain this knowledge by concepts, or "ideas," which are universal, changeless, and invisible, and therefore quite different from material things, which are individual, ever flowing, and visible (*Phaedo* 79). These ideas must not only be clearly grasped, but also be combined and separated according to the necessary nature of things, if truth is to be attained. When they are combined and separated according to sensory appearance without reference to this necessity, the result is opinion, which may be true or false. Knowledge always seeks necessity and, when it is attained, must be true. False knowledge is a contradiction.

Many of Plato's theories about nature are tentative and mythical, but the following doctrines are clearly suggested in his writings, and they played an important role in the further development of realistic metaphysics: The universe we inhabit was not made by us; it remains what it is whatever we may think or desire. It is very complex and probably includes many things of which we have no knowledge at all (*Phaedo* 109).

Man is a composite being, consisting of a body with something which moves and animates it, called the soul (psyche). The soul lives in the body as a pilot lives in his ship, and uses the body as its instrument. Death is the separation of the soul from the body

4 Cf. ch. 19, § 1.

(Phaedo 64) . At this separation the body is destroyed, but the soul, especially that part of it which thinks, is deathless. So far as the soul unites itself with knowledge, which is changeless, necessary, and immaterial, it too becomes changeless and indestructible *(Phaedo* 79D ff. and 96E) . The body and all other material things are in a constant state of flux. Each of them is a "mixture" of two components: something vague and indefinite from which it emerged (the *apeiron*) and a definite form which makes it what it is *(peras)* *(Philebus* 23–7) . There must have been some external cause which put these two components together.

The world is also a similar "mixture" with a certain order or structure which is constantly sustained. Hence there must be a first, external cause of the world as a whole *(Philebus* 30) . This first cause is living and intelligent. Plato calls it God. God is independent of all external influences and is immutable *(Republic* 381). He knows all the intimate affairs of men and cares for them *(Laws* X) . By sustaining the order of nature, he sees that justice is always done in the end.

Plato left many important questions still unsettled. The status of external objects of knowledge, for example, is unclear. Where are these fixed and immutable forms? Are they in the changing things of nature or in a special world of their own? [5] This and other questions remain unsolved; indeed, Plato never constructed a fixed and final system. He was always criticizing his own ideas, refining and even modifying them. Some have interpreted this ceaseless fire of self-criticism as an all-consuming skepticism. It is rather a testing fire from which the insights we have mentioned emerged in a purified form for further scientific clarification and development. The first great realistic thinker to achieve this was Plato's student Aristotle, who read, meditated, and studied at the Academy for a period of twenty years.

4. Aristotle

During this long period of study, Aristotle (384–332 B.C.) thoroughly mastered the later teaching of Plato and played a very active role in the intellectual life and discipline of the school. He wrote for publication several dialogues in which he eloquently set forth

[5] Cf. ch. 19, § 3.

the ideals of the Academy and defended them against the attack of Plato's enemies. After Plato's death in 347 B.C., he was dissatisfied, as were other students of the Academy at the choice of Speusippus as Plato's successor, and Aristotle joined a small Platonic group at Assos which had been gathered together by Hermias, the ruler of a small city. Here, and a little later at Mytilene with other friends, Aristotle began to criticize the thought of Speusippus and to work out an interpretation of Plato which he felt was truer to the mature philosophy of his teacher as well as to the facts of nature.

Through the mediation of Hermias, a friend of King Philip of Macedonia, Aristotle was asked to act as tutor to the young Prince Alexander. He accepted this offer and moved to the capital. Was it not in accord with the life and teaching of Plato to embrace every possible opportunity for combining science and philosophy with political power? But Aristotle was unable to exert any lasting influence on his royal pupil. From the evidence we have, it is probable that he recognized the tragic separation of the small Greek city-states and the desperate need for political union. But he disapproved the means used by Alexander for achieving this, and his vast scheme of world conquest. So he left the Macedonian capital and returned to Athens.

Aristotle's own thought was now developing in a direction definitely opposed to that of Plato's successors; so instead of returning to the Academy he established a new school, the Lyceum, in the northeast part of the city. Like the Academy, this institution was devoted not only to the task of teaching the untrained, but to that of investigation and research. Aided by specimens and information sent in by assistants who accompanied Alexander on his distant expeditions, Aristotle and his associates made many important observations and discoveries which left a permanent mark on the history of the natural sciences. But at the Lyceum, Aristotle gave even more attention to the underlying disciplines of philosophy, and most of the writings which we now possess were written at this time.

These treatises were not meant to be read by the general public but were rather detailed notes for lectures to be given before advanced classes in the Lyceum. Hence they presuppose a great deal, and cannot be understood without some previous mastery of realistic concepts and terminology. When these writings were rediscovered by European thinkers in the 12th and 13th centuries, they had to be studied very thoroughly and patiently before a satisfactory interpretation could be worked out and expressed in philosophical commentaries. Without such a commentary the modern student will gain little from plunging directly into these works.

After the conquest of Greece, Aristotle's association with Alexander made his position at Athens untenable. He was finally forced to leave, and went to an old home of his family at Chalcis on the island of Euboea, where he died (322 or 321 B.C.).

Aristotle distinguishes three divisions of philosophy—ethics, logic, and natural philosophy. In each of them he further developed the Platonic doctrine, introducing many important clarifications and distinctions, especially in the fields of logic and natural philosophy (the study of changing being) which he distinguished from first philosophy, the study of being *qua* being. Here he clarified Plato's suggestive discussions of the basic concept of being and analyzed the structure of unity, perfection, and truth which always attend being, and hence underlie all intelligible discourse. He also listed the basic categories, or major modes of being, which are found in the world. The most important of these are: substance, quality, quantity, place, position, action, passion, time, and relation. In many pages of acute exposition he laid the foundations for an exact analysis of these fundamental structures.[6]

In the field of the philosophy of nature, he corrected Plato's analysis of process as the passage from non-being into being, which he showed could not account for the continuity of natural change.[7] In addition to the two factors of privation, which initiates the process, and form, which terminates it, Aristotle's analysis shows the necessity of recognizing a third factor—the material cause which underlies the whole change and remains at the end, though now under a new pattern.

This analysis also brings into sharper relief the two extrinsic causes of change which had been vaguely recognized by Plato, the efficient cause which imposes form on the underlying matter, and the final cause which directs the efficient cause to a determinate effect. The changing world of nature, ceaselessly evolving from an

[6] Cf. ch. 15.
[7] Cf. ch. 13, §§ 4 and 5.

REALISTIC PHILOSOPHY AND ITS HISTORY

indeterminate, potential state into definite forms or patterns, requires a first cause which is perfectly actual and changeless.[8] These concepts enabled Aristotle to give a more exact formulation of Plato's arguments for a first cause.

In the *De Anima*, Aristotle deals with man, whom he regards unequivocally as part of the evolving world of nature. He agrees with Plato on the immateriality of reason, but denies that reason exhausts the essential nature of man who, like other natural entities, has evolved from an original prime matter. Hence like other natural entities, man possesses a hylomorphic nature, composed of matter or potency on the one hand, and determined by a complex form or structure on the other.[9] Reason is no doubt the most important part, but still only a part of this structure, which includes vegetative and animal elements as well. All are necessary for the existence of a man. Hence Aristotle rejects the notion that the soul is a rational entity accidentally attached to the body like a pilot to a ship. This fails to do justice to the unity of human nature. The soul is rather the determining form of the body, as the circular shape is the determining form of the gold in a ring. But body and soul are formal elements in one being, not two beings attached together. The rational part of the soul, being immaterial, can survive the death of the body, but it must not be thought of as a complete man. To function adequately in a human way the faculty of reason requires physical organs of sense and a material body to support them.[10]

Aristotle is legitimately regarded as the founder of the science of logic. He was the first to identify the syllogism as the form of all deductive inference, and carefully and exhaustively to analyze its different modes. In the *Topics* he also described the process of induction by which the mind passes from the particular to the universal, and the nature of dialectical or probable argument. But his discoveries in the field of epistemology were even more significant. Here he brought to a definite conclusion certain tendencies in Plato's later thought. The immaterial faculty of reason is able to identify itself with the forms of natural entities without their mat-

[8] Cf. ch. 16.
[9] Cf. ch. 17, § 1.
[10] Cf. ch. 19, § 4.

ter. The geologist may mentally become the stone in knowing it, without being physically petrified. Knowledge thus gives a new mode of being to things, making them not physically present but noetically present before the mind.[11] This analysis of awareness enabled Aristotle to explain knowledge without supposing any peculiar world of universal essences apart from the world of nature. Universal concepts exist only in the mind. But these concepts are the forms of physical things which exist individually and materially in the world around us, universally and immaterially in the mind.[12]

In ethics and social philosophy, Aristotle's insights were less epoch-making. Indeed, his major interest was in theoretical philosophy, and he carried this attitude into his moral philosophy; he never attempted to construct a vast, practical synthesis, in the manner of Plato, to guide the practical activities of man. Nevertheless, he developed the basic Platonic doctrine in many important ways. The practical use of reason in planning and deliberating is sharply and clearly distinguished from its theoretical use in grasping and investigating. The important role of appetite in free deliberation and choice is accurately described. The process of habit formation is carefully analyzed, and the different types of habit, good and bad, are described and classified more exhaustively and with closer attention to the data of experience than in the writings of Plato.[13] In the field of social philosophy also, Aristotle made no revolutionary changes in Platonic thought. He paid more attention to the empirical phenomena of social change and the concrete possibilities of the Greek political scene. In the second book of the *Politics*, he made extensive criticisms of certain more extreme measures suggested in the *Republic*.

This great body of descriptive analysis and doctrine, once it has been culled from Aristotle's obscure and fragmentary lecture notes, constitutes a most important source for the recapturing of sound insight. We shall refer to it again and again in our exposition of realistic philosophy. But it was the last great expression of the Greek philosophic spirit which may be said to have universal significance of the first importance. Useful commentaries were writ-

[11] Cf. ch. 17, § 4.
[12] Cf. ch. 19, § 4.
[13] Cf. ch. 5.

ten, and the tradition was maintained, but no great insights or refinements were introduced.

5. THE DECLINE OF HELLENIC PHILOSOPHY

The Aristotelian school survived to the third century A.D. The Platonic tradition survived longer; and from the third to the fifth century A.D., in the so-called school of Neo-Platonism, it brought forth a group of original Platonic thinkers of historic importance. The greatest of these were Plotinus (203–269 A.D.) and Proclus (410–485 A.D.). They often succeeded in elucidating and developing genuine Platonic thought. But their more original attempts to develop certain mythical elements into fixed doctrine and to reconcile Platonism with religious cults are of dubious philosophic worth.

Throughout this period of cultural decay, the Stoics defended an ascetic, ethical doctrine which set up virtue alone as the final end of man, and scorned all sensuous appetite. They supported this by an eclectic, theoretical philosophy pieced together from various sources, including Plato and Aristotle. The Epicureans, on the other hand, set up pleasure as the supreme moral end and conceived of reason and virtue as instruments for the attainment of the maximum pleasure.[14] They supported this theory by a materialistic view of nature as the chance result of spontaneously swerving atoms.

As is the case in similar periods of cultural decline, skepticism became increasingly influential. It was represented in the second century A.D. by Sextus Empiricus, one of the greatest skeptics of western history, whose philosophic treatises have survived. In these, he very subtly summarizes most of the arguments that had been so far constructed against the trustworthiness of the senses (because of their relativity), the reliability of deductive argument (because of its circularity), the existence of God (because either he wills the good and cannot achieve it, or he can achieve it but does not will it, or he neither wills it nor achieves it), causal necessity, and indeed, against any doctrine asserted to be self-evident or demonstrable. The upshot of such skepticism is a deadening of purposive aspiration and a consequent falling back upon animal appetite, and the purposeless drift into cultural decay. These arguments have

[14] Cf. ch. 2, § 1.

been revived and further developed in modern times. The study of realistic thought is a powerful antidote. One cannot consider himself to be even an incipient realist until he is able to answer the arguments of skepticism.

6. Augustine and the Coming of Christianity

The oppressed proletarian masses of the Roman Empire found an answer in the Christian religion, and the important thinkers of this later time devoted themselves to theology, the clarification and explanation of religious dogma. The greatest of these thinkers was St. Augustine (354–430 A.D.), the Bishop of Hippo in northern Africa. His interest was primarily theological; but since this, as well as every other intellectual discipline, involves philosophical questions, he was forced to deal with them as a by-product of his central train of thought. Christianity cannot be reconciled with materialism or pantheism, and certainly presupposes a realistic outlook. The dogma of the Incarnation implies the existence of the human body and other material things. The dogma that man has been created in the image of God implies that he possesses a rational understanding of these things as they are. It also implies an understanding of natural law and the difference between good and evil. St. Augustine shared this realistic outlook as a Christian.

But his reading of the later Neo-Platonic writers, particularly Plotinus (in the Latin translation of Victorinus), played a crucial role in his conversion from Manichaean dualism and ¬materialism to Christianity. This retained a permanent influence on his thinking and diluted his realism in certain respects. Thus he followed the Neo-Platonists, rather than the later dialogues of Plato, in distrusting the bodily senses as purely unreliable and subjective. As a consequence of this, he tended to regard the soul as radically separate from the body. Instead of drawing its ideas from sensory data, he held that the intellect is directly illuminated by God without the intervention of sense. These dubious theories tinged his basic realism and led him to assert that our belief in the existence of external things, though necessary for action, is only probable.

But aside from these Neo-Platonic influences, he was guided by religious dogma to make important contributions to realistic thought in the fields of metaphysics and the philosophy of history.

He used purely rational arguments in working out a philosophic theory of the first cause which was really consistent with religious faith, and therefore radically opposed to polytheism. He argued that the existence of a first cause could be rationally inferred from the order of the universe, that this cause does not *possess* being (which would imply composition in his nature) but *is* being, and also intellect and will. He maintained against the Neo-Platonists that the world is not necessarily emanated from the substance of the first cause, but that it is rather created *ex nihilo* by a free act of God. These theories went beyond anything hitherto attempted by Greek metaphysics.[15]

In his most influential work, the *City of God,* he worked out an interpretation of the meaning of concrete human history on the earth. Plato had projected something of the sort but had not been able to achieve it. No other thinker had attempted to find meaning in this vast chaos of conflicting lives and events. Augustine rejected the prevailing Greek view that history was made up of a more or less meaningless series of cycles in which civilizations rose and fell. He defended the thesis that history has a beginning, a middle, and an end. It began with the creation and the fall of man through subjective pride in himself and his failure to recognize his limitations. It reached its mid-point in the Incarnation, which through divine help offers man an opportunity to escape the disastrous consequences of sin and, if he so chooses, to live a truly human life in accordance with nature.

As for the future, Augustine foresaw no earthly Utopia, but only a more intense and bitter struggle between the two cities: the city of God, made up of those who are led by reason and faith to accept the guidance of something greater than themselves, and the earthly city of Babylon, made up of those who are led by complacent opinion and self-esteem to accept only their own haphazard appetites. History will reach its end when the forces of good and evil have been manifested as clearly as they can be under the conditions of time and change. Then they will be brought forth from the shadows (as they eternally are) and revealed in final clarity.

[15] Cf. ch. 16.

7. THE EARLY PHILOSOPHY OF WESTERN CULTURE

These predictions were certainly not disproved by the succeeding events of history. Soon after Augustine's death the long-decaying Roman Empire went through its final agony, and with the irruptions of the northern barbarians our present-day western culture appeared upon the scene. The ancient forms of life and institutions passed away, with the exception of the Church, the one surviving link with the past which was capable of giving guidance for the future. The Church succeeded in preserving many important records and manuscripts, and through the whole dark period of transition to the new western culture it was the center of such intellectual life as there was. So far as philosophy was concerned, this life was dominantly Neo-Platonic and Augustinian. The works of Aristotle were not known, and theoretical philosophy (metaphysics, the theory of nature, and logic), although not entirely neglected, was nevertheless not pursued passionately as an end in itself. The emphasis of this medieval Augustinian tradition was on practical philosophy, culminating in theology. The sole aim worthy of devotion was the salvation of the soul. Theoretical problems should be pursued only as a means to this single end.

But in the Byzantine world and in the Arabian world the great texts of Greek philosophy, including those of Aristotle, had survived, and among the Arabs especially the study of these texts had produced a rich philosophical literature. Among these were the great Aristotelian commentaries of Avicenna and Averroes. During the 12th century these Aristotelian writings began to seep into western Europe by way of Sicily and Spain. They immediately stimulated important new developments. The Augustinians like Alexander of Hales (1175–1245) and John of Rochelle (1200–1245) attempted to reconcile the new knowledge with their Neo-Platonism. But others like Siger of Brabant, influenced by the Arabian commentators, proceeded in the 13th century to work out a naturalistic interpretation of Aristotle, according to which the world of nature acts by an intrinsic necessity, the will of man is not free, the soul—being the form of the body—is destroyed with it, and human acts are removed from the control of providence.

A third group, with the aid of the great Arabian commentators and qualified Greek scholars, devoted their lives to the task of working out a sound and exhaustive realistic philosophy which should do justice to all the truth then known, including that of theology. The first of these was Albert the Great of Bollstadt (1206–1280), who worked out a great intellectual synthesis which did full justice not only to the major insights of Aristotle but to those of Plato as well. He was followed by several students who further developed his doctrine. The most important of these was the Italian, Thomas Aquinas, who, guided by the thought of his master, succeeded in working out an even vaster and more penetrating realistic synthesis.

8. THE REALISTIC SYNTHESIS OF AQUINAS

Thomas Aquinas was born in 1225 at Roccasecca in southern Italy and educated at the Monastery of Monte Cassino. At the age of eighteen he joined the Dominican Order and on showing evidence of great intellectual talent was sent in 1245 to the school of Albert the Great at Cologne, where he studied for seven years. In 1252 he went to Paris, where he finished his training in 1256, becoming a professor the next year. During this period he wrote his short treatise *On Essence and Existence*. In 1259 he went to Italy, where he wrote the *Summa Contra Gentiles*. He lived at the court of Pope Urban IV for several years. There he met William of Moerbeke, a fellow Dominican and a linguistic scholar, who worked with him on the original Aristotelian texts and helped him to prepare his commentaries on Aristotle's *Logic, Metaphysics, Ethics,* and *Politics*. In 1269 he was chosen by his order to fill an important chair at the University of Paris, and to defend Aristotelian philosophy against the intensified attacks of the Averroistic naturalists and the Augustinian theologians. In spite of facing bitter attack and controversy he nearly finished his monumental theological treatise the *Summa Theologica* before his early death in 1274.

This work is one of the great classics of realistic philosophy and we shall often refer to it. It has the form of a sweeping practical synthesis in the manner of Plato, like the *Itinerarium mentis in Deum* of Aquinas' great contemporary, Bonaventura. Starting with God, the source of all being, it then deals with the material world and man, finally terminating in an account of those natural and supernatural means by which human salvation is to be achieved. Many of the basic insights are also drawn from Plato, such as the emphasis upon the cardinal virtues, the eternal ideas in the mind of God, and the temporal creation of the world.

But this vast Platonic framework is clarified and enriched by the more detailed theoretical insights of Aristotle. From this source are derived the analysis of being and the transcendentals, substance and the categories, causation and change.[16] The treatise on man (Summa Theologica, Part I, Qu. 75–88) is a carefully developed interpretation of the De Anima, and the second part on moral philosophy contains an illuminating and detailed interpretation of the Nicomachean Ethics.

The treatise on God (Summa Theologica, Part I, Qu. 2–26) includes a defense of the thesis that faith is a completion of natural insight, a criticism of a priori demonstrations of the existence of a first cause, a compressed statement of five forms of causal argument demonstrating the existence of this first cause, and then a thoroughgoing philosophical defense of Augustinian theology. God is absolutely simple, perfect, infinite, and eternal. He possesses intellect and will, and has created the world ex nihilo by an act of free choice.[17] But these philosophical portions are constantly brought into harmonious relationship with that exposition of revealed theology which is the dominant purpose of the work. Not only is a place found in this vast synthesis for all the major insights of his realistic predecessors, but these insights are grasped with a peculiar terse clarity and developed with a never-failing rigor which emanate from the genius of Aquinas himself.

Though it must be admitted that the philosophical parts of this masterly work constitute the most complete and accurate account of realistic thought that has been so far achieved, certain imperfections nevertheless must be noted, in the order of increasing importance.

First, certain portions of the work are marred for the modern reader by the intrusion of astronomical and physiological views which have been discarded by the further advance of science and

16 Cf. chs. 13–15.
17 Cf. ch. 16, § 9.

are now known to be false. This is the least important criticism, since philosophy is distinct from science, and the intelligent reader will have little difficulty in separating the philosophic argument from its antique scientific context.

Second, the subordination of philosophy to theology sometimes leads to a compression and condensation of rational argument which is dangerously close to dogmatism.

Third, there is no full account of the natural order of civilization and culture,[18] many basic matters of social ethics being simply ignored and left to executive "prudence" and theological guidance.

Fourth, the social philosophy is seriously warped by too close an orientation to ephemeral phases of medieval life and culture, for example, the defense of slavery.

Finally, in the fifth place, there is no attempt to deal with the concrete phenomena of history. Aquinas' work is an attempt to interpret the structure of events, not the events themselves. This is not so much a criticism of Aquinas, who did not try to do this, as of those who seem to regard the *Summa Theologica* as the final solution of every philosophical question. This is certainly not so.

9. SCOTUS AND THE DECLINE OF REALISM

Instead of proceeding further, in a realistic manner, to correct these defects in the great Thomistic synthesis, medieval philosophy after the time of Aquinas took a new turn. The doctrine of Aquinas after his death was officially approved and widely accepted. His followers were organized into a school, but they were able to do little more than to repeat realistic formulas and defend them against the attack of radically non-realistic modes of thought which now appeared upon the scene. These movements were led by two important thinkers: Duns Scotus (1270–1308) and William of Ockham (1280?–1350). Their theories led to the decay of realistic philosophy and laid the foundations for what we now know as the "modern philosophy" of the 17th, 18th, and 19th centuries.

Ostensibly a realist, Scotus nevertheless introduced critical modifications into his version of the doctrine. Holding to mathematics as the ideal for all exact science, he attacked the Aristotelian

[18] Cf. ch. 12.

view that being and other metaphysical concepts are analogous.[19] Being, he maintained, was a clear, distinct, univocal concept, just like ordinary scientific ideas. What is mentally distinct must represent something formally distinct in the extra-mental entity. Hence he held that the genus (animal) and the difference (rational) were really distinct in the individual man.[20] He denied the indeterminacy of matter and held that it possessed a positive actuality which could be grasped by a clear univocal concept. He also denied that matter was the principle of individuation, holding that each individual possessed a unique, determining quality called *haecceitas* which could be intuitively grasped by the intellect.[21] These doctrines tended to break down the distinction between logic and metaphysics, or the order of knowing and the order of being.

In ethics Scotus defended a voluntaristic theory, according to which reason is only a servant of the will in acts of choice.[22] This was reflected in his theology by the view that God does not will anything because it is good, but that it is good because God wills it. Scotus held that the divine acts were as a matter of fact rational, but it was only a short step from this to the later conception of the divine will as a purely capricious, tyrannical power which we find in Ockham. Many of these Scotist theories were later incorporated by the Jesuit philosopher and theologian Suarez (1548–1617) in his influential eclectic treatise, the *Disputationes Metaphysicae*.

William of Ockham attacked realistic epistemology from a nominalistic point of view which lies at the root of his skeptical philosophy. The exaggerated realism of Scotus, which placed the universal in the physical thing, was easy to attack. Where was the evidence? Every existent entity outside the mind, every quality and every property is individual. Concepts exist only in the mind, as realism also maintains.[23] But for Ockham the material identity of the concept with the extra-mental nature is broken. According to him, this would mean the absurd view of positing universals outside the mind. The so-called concept is itself an individual image

[19] Cf. ch. 16, § 2.
[20] Cf. ch. 17, § 1.
[21] Cf. ch. 14, § 6.
[22] Cf. ch. 20, § 4.
[23] Cf. ch. 19, §§ 4 and 5.

which may include or supposedly refer to many individuals, but which is in no sense identical with them or any aspect of them. Reality is thus dissolved into a chaos of individual entities with no stable causal structure open to our intelligence.

Such a philosophy provides no foundation for a realistic metaphysics or philosophy of nature. So Ockham devoted his energies primarily to details of formal logic. At least we can manipulate the symbols and intentions of intelligible discourse, though we can never be sure as to what they stand for. This inaugurated an era of verbalistic argument and logic-chopping which insidiously crept into all schools of thought and marked the final decay of medieval philosophy. Absorbed in these formal exercises, the philosophers of the time paid less attention to questions concerning the fundamental structure of the external world, abandoning this problem to the new mathematical sciences.

This was even true of the self-styled defenders of realistic thought. When the new sciences succeeded in showing that many conclusions of antique science which had been incorporated in the realistic classics were definitely false, they failed to distinguish between science and philosophy, but leaped to the defense of outmoded hypotheses. This, together with the sensational success of the new mathematical disciplines within their special fields, helped to bring the whole realistic position into discredit and prepared the way for the "new philosophy" of Descartes and his followers.

10. DESCARTES

Descartes (1596–1650) was educated by the Jesuits at La Flèche in the tradition of Suárez, who had grafted many Scotist doctrines into his eclectic system. In epistemology he was a representationalist, holding that the mental idea was not identical with, but only similar to, the extra-mental entity.[24] This conception deeply influenced Descartes and underlay the methodological skepticism by which he claimed to have made a new beginning in philosophy. Guided by this doctrine he found it possible to doubt the existence of his body and all extra-mental things. His own subjective states and ideas, however, he claimed he could not doubt. He thus placed the ultimate source of certainty in the individual subject and laid

[24] Cf. ch. 19, § 1.

the foundations for a subjectivism which, since his time, has become the most distinctive feature of modern philosophy in all its manifestations. It led Descartes at once to break with the three basic theses of realism.

Since we know only our own subjective states which are the direct objects of knowledge, the existence of an external world is at once called in question. Descartes, it is true, finally convinced himself that the world does exist. But he did this by a very indirect and dubious procedure which has convinced very few besides the author. This procedure involves the ontological argument for the existence of God [25] which uses the idea of perfection in the mind as its only premise—and certain causal arguments, though he does not explain how his subjective premises justify the causal principle.

Once having arrived at God by these devious channels, Descartes argues that an extra-mental world corresponding to our ideas must exist, on the ground that God would not deceive us. But this world is deprived of all basic structure except for those mathematical properties which are of scientific interest and subject to measurement. Descartes rejects and ridicules the Aristotelian concept of change as the actualization of what is potential and regards process as a simple quality which a thing either has or has not.[26] Potency, or matter in the realistic sense, is thus banished as a contradictory notion. According to Descartes, the physical world lacks all sensible quality and all intrinsic tendencies to act. It is a passive field of extension (geometrical space) which is not even able to endure, but which has to be recreated by the first cause at each succeeding instant. Its final causes are beyond our ken. It cannot be explained or understood in any way except by the exact measuring techniques of the new mathematical sciences.

In epistemology Descartes sharply separated reason from sense. On the whole, he is distrustful of the senses. Reason, on the other hand, so far as it arrives at clear and distinct ideas may be trusted. These ideas, however, are not gained by abstraction from sense and imagination.[27] They are innate in the mind and may be brought

[25] Cf. ch. 16, § 2.
[26] Cf. ch. 13, § 3.
[27] Cf. ch. 19, § 2.

to consciousness and developed into knowledge without the aid of experience, as in the case of the ontological argument. In ethics Descartes adopted the voluntarism of Scotus and Ockham. The will is the highest faculty of man and may act independently of reason. This is true of the divine will which might even have willed contradictions to be true if it had so chosen.

These non-realistic principles inaugurated a new period in the history of philosophy.

11. The Period of Modern Philosophy

This period no longer presents the picture of basic insights being gradually clarified, refined, and developed as in the history of an advancing science. What we find is rather a great number of different systems constructed without much relevance to one another. It was commonly assumed that knowledge, like art, was a process of making rather than one of apprehending something already there. Hence novelty was very highly prized and a philosopher was not held to be really worthy of his salt unless he produced a new system. Nevertheless these novel systems fall into certain major groups which are easily identified. We shall deal with them here briefly, since they made no direct contribution to realistic philosophy.

After Descartes modern philosophy divided into two separate channels, the "rationalistic" school of Spinoza (1632–1677) and Leibnitz (1646–1716) on the European continent, and the "empiricist" school of Locke, Berkeley, and Hume in England. Both followed Descartes in denying the basic principle of realistic epistemology—that human knowledge can be achieved only by a union of the two distinct faculties of sense and reason working in cooperation. Each school then selected one of these and attempted to work out a theory of knowledge based primarily upon this faculty alone.

The "rationalists" either dismissed sense altogether as a source of knowledge or viewed it as incipient reason. Basing their doctrines on what they claimed to be a priori insights of reason wholly independent of sense, Spinoza worked out a monistic system which viewed the world as one substance and denied time and change as illusory, whereas Leibnitz worked out a pluralistic system which viewed the world as a set of absolutely windowless monads, each completely independent of the rest but made to fit with them through a harmony pre-established by the first cause.

The "empiricists," on the other hand, denied the capacity of reason to apprehend external existence. Thus, according to Locke (1632–1704), "the knowledge of the existence of any other thing we can have only by sensation" (*Essay Concerning Human Understanding*, Book IV, ch. 11). In the early writings of Berkeley (1685–1753) this sensationalism is still more marked, through his attack on abstract universal ideas which he reduces to mere words, so far as they do not refer to a group of particulars. This nominalism [28] reaches its culmination in the skepticism of Hume (1711–1776) for which the world is reduced to a succession of atomic "impressions." Any concept, like substance, self, or causation, which does not refer to such a sensory item, is dismissed as either meaningless or a pure subjective construction. This view was the source of a widespread movement which is now known as positivism.

At the end of the 18th century a synthesis of these two tendencies was attempted by the German philosopher Kant (1724–1804). On the one hand, he attacked the rationalists, asserting that concepts without sense data are empty and incapable of justifying any fixed conclusions. But on the other hand, he also attacked the empiricists, asserting that empirical data without conceptual interpretation are chaotic and blind. Both sense and rational "categories" are required for human knowledge. But still influenced by the subjectivistic assumptions of Descartes, Kant conceived of knowing as a process of making or constructing in which the raw matter of sense is molded into something new.[29] On this basis he concluded that we can know only an ordered world which is relative to the organizing principles of our minds. We cannot know real things as they are in themselves, but only our own constructions. These are incapable of providing any stable guidance for the human will which is "autonomous" and must lay down its own moral laws upon itself. These doctrines lay at the root of that idealistic philosophy which dominated western thought until the time of the first world war.

Idealism was developed in modern Germany and its leading

[28] Cf. ch. 19, §§ 3 and 5.
[29] Cf. ch. 19, §§ 3 and 5.

representatives were the 19th-century German philosophers Fichte, Schelling, and Hegel. But it soon spread widely over the whole western world and exerted a powerful influence on thinkers in all western countries. These philosophers accepted the subjectivist premises of Kant, but rejected the "thing-in-itself." There is no stable order of existence independent of the constructive processes of knowing and willing. The world which we produce in this way is the only world there is. But it is not "we" as finite individuals who perform this awe-inspiring function. It is a great world soul that works in and through us.

In this way the idealistic philosophy has attempted to distinguish itself from other forms of subjectivism, like that of Berkeley, and to satisfy the obstinate realistic predilections of mankind. In Hegel this vast constructive power is conceived as a world spirit (*Weltgeist*) which expresses itself in larger rather than in smaller social units, but which constantly tears down what it has constructed to achieve a higher synthesis. Marching through history according to immutable laws of its own, it ruthlessly stamps out or uses individual choices and ideas for its own half-hidden purposes. This same deterministic conception is found in the Marxian philosophy of history.

12. CONTEMPORARY PHILOSOPHY

The undisciplined speculations of idealistic philosophers concerning supposed spiritual meanings and activities back of nature brought philosophy itself into widespread disrepute. When its association with totalitarian political movements in modern Germany became manifest, it collapsed and western thought entered a new phase of its history. Present-day philosophy, however, is still dominated by three tendencies called forth primarily by antagonism to idealism, namely, a movement toward radical skepticism and disillusionment, a search for irrational substitutes to replace reason, and an assertion of the self-sufficiency of nature—naturalism.

The first includes those contemporary attitudes widely known as *positivism, scientism,* and *existentialism*—all of which tend to identify philosophy itself with the excesses of idealism which they bitterly repudiate. *Positivism* holds that concepts and propositions which cannot be directly verified by sensory observation are meaningless. It is closely associated with another movement we may call *scientism*, which believes that the restricted methods of the special sciences alone are capable of yielding sound knowledge, and that we need only wait for the maturity of the social sciences, and especially psychology, in order to find a solution for all those problems which are capable of any solution at all.

Existentialism began with the bitter attack of a Danish thinker, Kierkegaard (1813–1855), on Hegelian idealism, whose logical atmosphere and conceptual necessity he sharply contrasted with the contingent material existence of the lonely individual. His ideas have been developed by keen observers of human experience who have carefully described many concrete moral phenomena which cannot be fitted into the grandiose systems of the 19th century. At the present time, all of these contemporary views are vaguely associated with a naturalistic outlook.

This is also true of the various tendencies which have tried to discover some irrational substitute for reason on which to base a positive philosophy. The most influential of these is *pragmatism*. This view despairs of the capacity of science and reason alone to yield philosophic knowledge, but in place of reason it falls back upon voluntary action. Even though the rational evidence is indecisive with respect to two hypotheses, we are entitled to regard that one as true which is capable of guiding action to a "successful" conclusion. At the present time this view is usually connected with naturalistic theses.

There can be little question that naturalism is the most widespread contemporary philosophic tendency with definite doctrines to defend. Nevertheless it is largely defined in terms of definite negations (of what is immaterial and supernatural) and covers a great variety of divergent views. At one extreme there are the strict materialists who insist that all natural processes may be reduced to elementary quantitative changes. At the other there are mitigated materialists, willing to recognize qualitative and relational structures of a different order.[30] All naturalists, however, agree that reality is to be identified with the natural evolving world of events in space and time. They deny the existence of any first cause, and most of them deny any strictly immaterial existence. These are

[30] Cf. ch. 15, §§ 3 and 8.

forced to deal with knowledge as a sort of complex, material process which leads them toward subjectivism.

In addition to these tendencies realistic philosophy is still alive and is once more arousing widespread interest and serious study. There are several reasons for this. One is that it shares with all the tendencies noted above, a basic and irreconcilable opposition to idealism and idealistic pantheism. In addition it shares with positivism a sense of the need for exact analysis and empirical verification; and with naturalism, a sense of the need for a philosophic understanding of the structure of the changing world. A second reason is the great cultural and social crisis of our time which leads many to recognize the need for a disciplined philosophy that is based upon sound insight and age-long reflection. A third reason is the greater readiness of scientists to admit the limitations of their disciplines and the need for the employment of other rational methods for revealing the structure of nature. A fourth reason is the weakening of that bitter skepticism which was called forth by the excesses of idealism, and a readiness once more to listen to the claims of philosophy.

For all these reasons men are once again beginning to study the great classics of realistic thought and to reflect about them critically. It is possible that such a critical process may be aided by this book to some slight degree; if so, its purpose will have been achieved.

We shall attempt to state the basic insights of realistic philosophy in simple language which can be understood by the student of today. We shall refer him to important texts in the great realistic classics and we shall also try to assist him in understanding them. We shall begin first of all with a study of ethics (Part I) in order to see what light realism can shed for the guidance of individual and social human action. Then we shall examine the structure of the changing world of nature (Part II).

REFERENCES

Recommended Reading
Plato, *Apology* and *Phaedo*.

Suggested Reading
1. Wild, J. D., *What Is Realism?* Journal of Philosophy, March 13, 1947.
2. Cornford, F. M., *The Republic of Plato,* New York, Oxford University

Press, 1941, Books I–IV and Book VIII; Wild, J. D., *Plato's Theory of Man*, Cambridge, Mass., Harvard University Press, chaps. 1–4 and 8.

3. Jaeger, W., *Aristotle*, New York, Oxford University Press, 1934, chaps. 1–4 and 12–15.

4. Oates, W. J., *The Stoic and Epicurean Philosophers*, New York, Random House, 1940; for an account of the breakdown of Hellenic civilization in relation to modern western culture cf. Toynbee, A. J., *A Study of History*, New York, Oxford University Press, 1947, pp. 36–39 and 260–261; for a penetrating study of the state of mind in a disintegrating civilization, cf. *ibid.*, pp. 440–482.

5. DeWulf, M., *History of Medieval Philosophy*, London, Longmans, Green, 1935, chap. 2, § 2; and Przywara, E., *An Augustinian Synthesis*, New York, Sheed and Ward, 1935.

6. DeWulf, M., *History of Medieval Philosophy*, vol. 1, chap. 4, and vol. 2, chap. 2, §§ 7, 10, and 12.

7. Gilson, E., *The Philosophy of St. Thomas Aquinas*, St. Louis, Herder, 1924.

8. Gilson, E., *The Unity of Philosophical Experience*, New York, Scribners, 1937, chaps. 3 and 4.

9. Descartes, *Meditations* I–IV; and Gilson, E., *The Unity of Philosophical Experience*, Part II.

10. Hoffding, H., *A Brief History of Modern Philosophy*, New York, Macmillan, 1912.

11. Carnap, R., *The Unity of Science*, London, Kegan Paul, Trench, Trubner, 1934; Harper, R., *Existentialism, A Theory of Man*, Cambridge, Mass., Harvard University Press; James, W., *Pragmatism*, New York, Longmans, Green, 1943; and Krikorian, Y. H., ed., *Naturalism and the Human Spirit*, New York, Columbia University Press, 1944.

PART I
The Perfection of Human Nature (Ethics)

THE BASIC MORAL FACTS OF LIFE

ANY material, finite entity includes an imperfection or potency in its essential nature. Hence the existence of any such entity is imperfect and open to further perfection by the gaining of additional accidents. The whole of material nature is dynamic, or tending to that which can complete its deficient nature. The lower, inorganic things are perfected by causes external to them. But as we rise in the scale of natural being we discover entities which are more autonomous, that is, more able to perfect themselves under the support of external sustaining causes. To some degree they contain within themselves the efficient causes of their own operations.[1]

Plants are able to grow of themselves. Animals are able to sense and to move from place to place. They also contain within themselves some formal principle which determines their operations, since no efficient cause acts of itself without such a directing principle. This formal principle is their nature, which directs them to a certain determinate end and, therefore, to the determinate means required to achieve this end. But since they lack the faculty of reason they are unable to understand this end or the further ends to which this is in turn directed. Hence they do not include within themselves the *complete,* final cause of their perfecting operations.

Human nature is the highest achievement of evolution. It includes within itself the *immaterial* faculties of reason and will. By reason it is capable not only of materially embodying its form, like other material creatures, but of immaterially assimilating it, together with the forms of *all* other beings, including that of the first cause to which it is ultimately directed.[2] By will it is able to strive not only for certain determinate goods, but for the good in

[1] Cf. ch. 15, § 2.
[2] Cf. ch. 19, §§ 4–6.

general—all good things.[3] Man, therefore, is the only creature who can possess *within himself* immaterially the *complete,* final cause of his own perfection and the efficient means of achieving this. As such he is the highest evolutionary being. Once his finite nature is in being, this nature requires nothing further to perfect it, but can perfect itself by its own *immanent* acts of reason and will.

This human process of self-perfection in the concrete is called *history.* Its formal structure can be studied and grasped by reason in the disciplines of moral philosophy. Subhuman nature can only be perfected from the outside: it cannot perfect itself: its nature dictates the operations and changes which complete it. But human nature perfects itself, and its operations are not only determined by its nature but by the energizing of those higher immaterial faculties which enable it to be determined by that which lies above its nature. Hence the disciplines of moral philosophy which study this self-perfection of man—that *second nature* which man himself develops on the basis of the *first nature* with which he enters the world—must be distinguished from the disciplines of natural philosophy which study only the determinate, original natures of things. Moral philosophy is divided into two branches: ethics, the study of the self-perfection of the individual, substantial man (Part I, Section 1); and social philosophy, the study of the self-perfection of the human community as a whole (Part I, Section 2).

That which perfects any imperfect entity as such is *good.* But since there are very diverse types of imperfect being, *good* has very diverse meanings. What perfects a fish will not be the same as what perfects a man, and what perfects one man will not be precisely the same as what perfects another. Hence the question arises as to whether we can attach any single meaning to the word *good.* Can it be defined or is it a purely "relative" term? The answer is that *good* is always "relative" and as such is definable and constant in meaning. The perfection of a fish is to the fish as the perfection of a man is to the man. This relation is always *similar,* even though the entities and their perfections are different. Hence the notion of goodness, or value, is not an ambiguous or equivocal notion. The study of goodness in general, so far as it applies to all existence, belongs to metaphysics and will not be further consid-

[3] Cf. ch. 20, § 3.

ered here. We shall turn our attention to one kind of good, namely, that which perfects human nature—the *human good*.

The individual man is an imperfect, material being with a stable form or nature. To be a man is to be a rational animal and, therefore, necessarily involves a living body, senses and sensory appetites, reason and rational appetite, or will. Unless these elements are present, the being before us is not a man.

Ethics is not a *theoretical* science which studies the abstract nature of what *is*. We shall subsequently consider human nature in this way (Part II). Ethics requires such a theoretical understanding, but goes beyond it, aiming to discover not merely what man is, but how this nature may be perfected, what it *ought to be*. Hence it is a *practical* science.

In pursuing this practical investigation we shall consider three subordinate topics in the following order: First, we shall direct our attention to the final goal, or end, which will satisfy all the needs of such a nature and beyond which it will need to seek no further. In the second place, we shall consider those free, or responsible, processes by which man either attains or fails to attain this end (Chapters 3 and 4). In the third place, we shall consider the order, or structure, of the good life and those rational habits or virtues which it must necessarily include (Chapters 5–8).

1. Happiness: The Natural End of Man

It is clear that this final end, for the sake of which a human individual ought to do all that he can do, must be the complete realization of his nature. If his aspiration can really rest in it, then it must be self-sufficient—or contain within it all that he really needs or desires. What is this final end?

Certainly it is not the bare existence of human nature, for men can exist in a very imperfect or evil condition. It must, therefore, be an *activity* or operation of this nature, which perfects or realizes it. What will this activity be? Clearly it will be determined in general by human nature itself, which has three distinct, essential phases.[4] First, there is the vegetative aspect of human life which demands growth and nourishment. Second, there is the animal aspect, which brings forth sense, imagination, and the sensitive appetites with

[4] Cf. ch. 17, § 1.

their material objects. Finally, there is the peculiar, distinguishing difference of man—the rational aspect—causing reason and will, which must be *self-perfected* by autonomous acts of understanding and voluntary action. Since the determining difference of any species is the most important, governing part of its essence, these rational and voluntary operations will be the most important and decisive of all the actions making up a complete or happy life. The *final* end of man is to carry on *all* the operations which perfect his nature *under the guidance of reason.*

But this is not all. There are very few acts which do not more or less perfect *some* aspect of our nature. As long as we go on living at all we are carrying on operations which to some degree at least, agree with a more or less confused dictate of reason. Our real aim is not merely to live but to live *well,* that is, to the maximum degree of effectiveness at the highest pitch, or according to *virtue.* This virtue, or a maximum effectiveness of life, will depend primarily upon the maximum clarity and precision of the rational operations and upon the dominance of these over all the other subordinate human acts. To live a happy life is to operate rationally *to the maximal degree,* or according to virtue.

But this is not all: it is not enough to operate virtuously and, therefore, with maximum rationality for two days or two months or two years and then to collapse into a second-rate mediocrity. No one could rationally set this up as his aim. To be happy one must operate with maximal proficiency *for the whole span of a human life* and, indeed, for the whole period of existence which is allotted to its principal parts. This gives us the final definition of happiness —*to operate rationally with the maximum proficiency or virtue throughout the whole time allotted to an individual human existence.*

At first sight this formulation, like most exact definitions, seems very abstract and remote from those more familiar factors which we commonly identify with happiness and set before ourselves as final objectives. But a more careful examination will show that this is not the case. Such ends as pleasure, virtue, money, power, and external possessions are all included in our definition, if we properly understand it, though it properly refuses to identify any one of them with the final and therefore self-sufficient end of man. Let us briefly examine them, starting with pleasure.

Hedonism is the view which attempts to defend pleasure as the legitimate *final* aim of human life. Most of us, so far as we think at all seriously about the matter, find that we have strong hedonistic tendencies. But a more careful examination will show that hedonism is really indefensible. Pleasure results from the successful accomplishment of *any* act. To solve complex mathematical problems is fun for the mathematician; to hit a home run is fun for the baseball player. We cannot gain pleasure without performing the operations which the pleasure crowns and bringing into play the fixed habits necessary to perform the operations.

If, like the hedonist, we *separate* the pleasure from the act which produces it, viewing the latter merely as an accidental means to the former, requiring no special concern, we shall end by neglecting the habits producing the acts which produce the pleasure. This is the reason for the so-called hedonistic paradox: no one is apt to end in such misery as the consistent hedonist who becomes so obsessed with the golden egg that he forgets the goose that lays it. Pleasure is caused by acts, and acts are caused by habits, which require time, attention, and intense effort to develop and maintain. Thus we may truly say that there is no better way to pleasure than to develop habits or virtues which really perfect our nature in accordance with reason. The active life, therefore, which we have defined, is the only possible pleasant life, though it includes much more (operations and virtues) within it than pleasure.

Radically opposed to hedonism is the contrary view of the Stoic and Puritan moralists who insist that pleasure is actually bad and that the acquisition of virtue is the final end of human life. But from the fact that pleasure is not the complete or final good, it does not follow that it is bad. Because evil men derive pleasure from the successful performance of their evil acts, it does not follow that really good men do not also derive pleasure from the successful performance of their virtuous acts. This is the mistake of the Puritan. The process of acquiring a virtuous habit involves pain. This is as far as many of us ever get on the pathway to the happy or rational life, which explains the widespread puritanical tendency to oppose interest and duty, pleasure and virtue. But once we have actually acquired the habit or ingrained tendency to virtue, the performance of virtuous acts *is* pleasant.

As long as a generous act can be performed only at the cost of psychic strain and anguish, we have not yet really acquired the habit of generosity and are not ourselves really generous, though we may have painfully performed several generous acts. A little virtue is a painful thing. But the full possession of virtue, and the rational activity resulting from it, are supremely pleasant. On the other hand, the fact that we find some mode of activity pleasant to us at the moment does not imply that it is really rational, virtuous, and, therefore, pleasant in the long run. Pleasure *alone* is not the end of life and is not mentioned by name in our definition. Nevertheless, it is implied by this definition and indeed to the maximum degree, because the objects which reason alone can recognize as perfecting our nature are those which are the most pleasant in the long run.

Should we not then follow the Puritans and the Stoics in the positive phase of their teaching, that virtue is the final end of life? This doctrine is certainly not far from the truth. Nevertheless, we can see that virtue alone is not self-sufficient and therefore is not the final goal we seek, because the virtues, such as generosity, courage, and self-control, are firmly ingrained *tendencies* to act in accordance with reason in certain situations. Without such tendencies we cannot really be virtuous, except by chance and for very brief periods of time. But in themselves they are not enough to constitute a happy life.

A man may possess all the virtues and still never be confronted with a situation in which he can ever really exercise them. Thus a man who possesses nothing to give cannot exercise the virtue of generosity, though he may be very generous. Those who are overcome by disease or misfortune, even though they retain their virtuous character and are not themselves overcome, are nevertheless deprived of the instrumental means of *exercising* their virtues. Hence, although we may grant that they still possess the more important part of happiness, we may not think of them as enjoying the fullest, most perfect happiness which comes only with the *actual exercise* and operation of the virtues. Being is good in so far as it is perfect. Hence virtue is *praised* as a necessary part of happiness, but it is not *prized* as the final and inclusive end. This includes not only the ability or tendency to live well, but the *fulfillment* of this praiseworthy tendency in *actually living well*.

It is easy to see the fallacy involved in the attitudes of those moral materialists who identify the human good with money, power, or external possessions which, unlike pleasure and virtue, are not intrinsic but only instrumental goods. Money, for instance, is of no value *in itself*, but only instrumentally as a means of obtaining other things. The same is true of power, which we often regard as a full-fledged actuality and, therefore, as something finally good. As a matter of fact, it is only imperfect or potential, as its name implies, and is only actually valuable in so far as it is *used* well. Many individuals and many nations have been hastened to ruin by the acquisition of power which has merely enabled them to realize vicious and unnatural tendencies. The actualizing of a virtue is better than the virtue, but the actualizing of a vice is much worse than the vice.

Many "interests" or tendencies which spring up in our characters are much better as mere potencies than as full-fledged actualities. External things and possessions, though in themselves fully actual and determinate, are not fully actual or intrinsic goods for us. In relation to us they are only instrumental goods which must be used virtuously or rationally to become actually good. Food is no good to a sick man who cannot use it properly, and to a man or nation lacking the intellectual and moral virtues all the good things on earth are of no real worth.

But though this is true we must not conclude with the Stoics and moral extremists that external power and possessions are of no good at all. They certainly have a genuine, *instrumental* value, for they provide us with certain tools required for the exercise of all the human virtues. As we have seen, an individual cannot exercise the virtue of generosity with nothing to give, and a community cannot exercise the virtue of distributive justice with nothing to distribute. In order to live well we must *live,* and life necessarily requires a certain control over things and possessions. To the extent to which reason determines that they are really needed, then, such powers are included in our definition of happiness—*human operations rationally directed throughout the whole span of a human life.*

This is the *final end* to which we are ordered by our finite, human natures. To the extent to which we misapprehend this final end, confusing it with some one of its parts or with what is not really but only apparently good, our whole lives become misdirected and we are apt to discover, perhaps too late, that what we thought right was really tawdry and commonplace, and that what we thought wrong and unimportant was really excellent and fine.

2. NATURAL LAW: THE ULTIMATE STANDARD OF MORALITY

In defining happiness as the complete fulfillment of man's nature we have appealed to *nature* as the supreme standard for human morality. This is in accordance with the soundest philosophy of the past. Indeed the first principle of any realistic ethics must be *natural law, moral law,* or as it was first called, *the unwritten law.* According to Plato: "the unwritten, moral laws (*agrapha nomima*) are the links which bind every community of men together; they lie at the root of all the particular, written enactments which ever have been set or will be set; and if they are clearly understood and well established, they will guard and preserve the whole order of life which is derived from them." (*Laws* 793 A.) According to Aristotle: "the things which are just not *by nature* but by human enactment are not everywhere the same, but there is only one justice which is everywhere *by nature* the best." (*Nic. Eth.* 1135 A3ff.) What then is meant by natural law?

All men know something of this law and its universal prescriptions for honesty, fairness, and courage. Thus different communities at different levels of cultural development have very different ways of expressing courage. But there are very few peoples or communities where flabbiness of spirit, for example, is set up as a human virtue or where the man who runs away from every major difficulty is admired and respected as a hero. People are constantly appealing to this law of nature in common life and constantly attempting to justify their conduct before it.

Thus when we hear one person saying to another: "Leave him alone, he isn't doing you any harm" or "What if I did the same to you?" or "come along, you promised" or "give me some of your candy, I gave you mine," we seldom hear a subjectivist reply which repudiates the standard. Outside academic walls and classrooms men are not relativists and subjectivists. Both parties know *something* of the law of nature and accept its real, obligatory authority over them as they certainly would not accept any merely human invention or construction. So nearly always what the other man does is to try to justify himself and to show that in his circumstances he did not really act against the standard. What he really promised was something slightly different. This is now the last piece of candy in his possession, so the case is not the same, and so on.

Even primitive peoples and children have *some* knowledge of the moral law. This law obliges us because the subjectivist thesis is wrong. It is based, not on any human opinion or desire or construction, but on the very nature of man and the universe he inhabits. Hence of all our faculties reason alone, which apprehends things exactly as they really are, is able to apprehend its prescriptions.

As soon as we understand the nature of any finite thing we also understand the general kind of activity or treatment which perfects that thing. What is good for one thing is not good for another. What perfects a fish will kill a tree, and vice versa. We can gain some general understanding of *the nature* of man, i.e., what a thing must be to be human. Hence we can also gain some general understanding of the pattern of activity which will perfect this nature and the instruments it requires. This understanding (the *lex indicans*) is purely theoretical and is accessible to any human mind. But when it is united with an uncorrupted, natural desire to perfect man's nature it is transformed into a set of practical principles for the direction of human action (the *lex praecipiens*) . These are the principles of natural law—a rational determination, founded on nature, of the end which perfects man and the necessary means to this end.

This law is not made up or constructed by any man or human group: it is rather discovered by reason as embedded in the very nature of things and caused by whatever causes have produced human nature itself and the natural world of which man is a part. This law is not a mere empty form of universality lacking all concrete content, for human nature possesses distinctive notes and demands a distinctive perfection by distinctive modes of activity. Hence this law is not a priori in the modern subjectivistic sense: it can be discovered only by an empirical examination of the real nature of man as he actually exists. Finally, this law is universal in the sense that it applies not merely to this group or that, but to all men whatsoever, whoever, and wherever they may be. It does not describe the way in which they must act or do act, but the way in which they *ought* to act; the way they *must* act *if* they are to perfect their nature.

a. SUBJECTIVE ALTERNATIVES TO NATURAL LAW. If natural law is rejected the only other alternative is to accept some law laid down by man as the ultimate standard. But then we are confronted by two basic moral facts which it is impossible to explain.

First, there is the moral fact of self-justification. Men recognize that their own decisions and enactments require justification before some higher court of appeal. Men argue with themselves and with one another concerning what they ought to do. If each man or if any one man were an ultimate source of moral law such argument would be meaningless.

Second, there is the fact of moral obligation. Human individuals and groups are bound by moral principles, not merely *after* they have laid them down for the sake of consistency, but *before* they lay them down and even when they do not lay them down at all. In such a case we still hold them responsible and say that they *ought* to have known and *ought* to have done what they did not do. But if man is the ultimate source of the moral law this fact is inexplicable.

In spite of these facts, however, many modern ethical theorists, influenced by subjectivist philosophy, deny any natural, extra-human standard for action. They are divided into two major groups: first, those who think that the ultimate standard exists only in the human mind; and second, those who think that the standard lies in some subordinate part of human nature.

The first group includes the German philosopher Kant and his followers. In the *Critique of Pure Reason* Kant attempted to destroy the claims of theoretical reason to know things as they are in themselves, and thus laid the foundations for later German idealistic philosophy as well as for many modern currents of skeptical thought.[5] Hence he disputed the basic thesis of realistic philosophy —that human insight and science can provide us with reliable guidance for human action. Reversing the realistic theory of the order of the highest faculties he maintained the unqualified su-

[5] Cf. ch. 1, § 11.

premacy of practical reason over the theoretical, and even held, in harmony with this irrationalist view, that knowing itself was a kind of making or creating.[6] These views led him to propound a very original and most influential theory of ethics.

This theory recognizes the existence of a moral law which places all men under obligation. But Kant's skepticism led him to deny that this law can be apprehended by reason as grounded in the nature of man and the world he inhabits. It is rather constructed or created by the human mind autonomously without the recognition of anything beyond itself. Hence the law must lack all actual content and must consist of the pure form of rational universality alone. "Act in conformity with that maxim, and that maxim only, which you can at the same time will to be a universal law." [7]

This is the supreme, moral principle, or "categorical imperative," to which men must subject themselves if they are to maintain their freedom and dignity. In spite of its lack of all concrete content Kant believes that he can deduce from this formal principle certain definite duties, such as that of always keeping a promise once made, for if everyone lied no one would believe another and promises would, as a matter of fact, be discounted.

Like the Stoics and the Puritans, Kant takes a wholly negative attitude towards "natural desires and wants." Indeed, "so far are they from being sought simply for themselves, that every rational being must wish to be entirely free from their influence." [8] Duty is completely opposed to all such natural aspiration. A moral act is performed solely from respect for the moral law which is willed for its own sake alone. Only such a will can be called good without qualification. Only such a will can be called free, for freedom means to be "independent of the laws of nature." [9] So far as any natural aspiration to what is good or beautiful or holy enters into an act, the will is determined by something outside itself and thus loses its freedom.

This theory of ethics has exerted a far-reaching influence on modern thought. It has joined with Puritanism to bring forth a

[6] Cf. ch. 19, §§ 4–6.
[7] *Fundamental Principles of the Metaphysics of Morality*, Sec. II.
[8] *Ibid.*
[9] *Op. cit.*, Sec. III.

widespread tendency to think of morality as something consisting primarily of "don'ts" and utterly divorced from the common life of man. But aside from these unfortunate effects it is subject to the following systematic criticisms.

First, how is the Kantian skepticism of the capacity of reason to understand anything as it really is in itself to be reconciled with the claim of the Kantian ethics to give us a trustworthy insight into what is really good in itself, right without qualification, and free? If we can know these things as they really are why not also other things? But if we cannot know other things as they really are, why, then, is it that moral entities are intelligible?

Second, how can any concrete, moral duties be deduced from a categorical imperative which contains nothing but the empty form of logical universality? Any content whatsoever, good or bad, can be put into this form without logical contradiction. There is no formal reason, for example, which can prevent me from universalizing the act of lying. There are reasons, of course, as Kant indicates, for not willing such a state. Men are, as a matter of fact, rational beings, capable of learning from experience. They will soon detect a liar and distrust him. Hence it is easy to see that universal lying would bring forth universal distrust and render rational communication, and hence human life, impossible.

But the inconsistency which is here pointed out is not a *formal* inconsistency, based on logic alone, but a *material* inconsistency, based on an observation of the basic facts of human nature. Throughout most of his treatise, Kant calls all action based upon such empirical principles "heteronomy" and the abandonment of freedom.

Third, it is highly dubious that any human being possesses the unlimited sort of freedom from "the laws of nature" which Kant attributes to man. It is quite clear that human nature is not an invention of man and that causes outside of him are responsible for his existence. He is not free to act in ways which are completely beyond the range of this nature. He cannot act like a fish or a purely immaterial being. Within these limits, man has a range of choice or freedom but he is not free, as Kant supposes, to abandon all natural inclination.

Fourth, the confusion of any such escape from natural aspiration with the moral aim of man, is not only impossible but morally misleading. He who tries to be more than human achieves only the bestial and barbaric. The aim of human morality is not to escape from natural inclination into an empty realm of pure rationality, but to use reason for the ordering and control of all aspirations to their highest natural objects.

Finally in the fifth place, holding to the idea that man is in a position to lay down the ultimate moral law for himself without any reference to the actual nature he possesses and the world he inhabits, is to be deluded by an unnatural and, therefore, immoral pride and *hubris* which has been the curse of human life and civilization.[10]

The second group includes a great variety of doctrines to which the name *utilitarianism* may be generally applied. All these doctrines have three things in common. First, they fail to distinguish voluntary aspiration, resulting from rational deliberation and choice, from sensory impulse, and thus tend to reduce all human striving to the latter category of "desire" or "interest." Second, they therefore deny that reason is the natural guiding faculty of man, and reduce reason to a slave of interest or passion. Third, they make some aspect of our sub-rational nature (like pleasure or interest or some combination of the two) the supreme criterion of moral value.

Thus Hume, who holds that "reason is, and ought to be only the slave of the passions," [11] belongs to this group. Bentham's hedonism and any other consistent hedonism must also be so classified. On this view pleasure is the only good and pain the only evil, no effort being made to distinguish between different kinds of pleasure. The pleasure of pushpin is to count just as much as the pleasure of poetry. The whole of ethics thus consists of the calculation of future pleasures and pains in terms of intensity, duration, certainty, propinquity, fecundity, and purity; and the choice of that mode of action which will provide the most units of pleasure for the greatest number.

John Stuart Mill should also be classified in this group, though

---

[10] Cf. Toynbee, *A Study of History*, ch. 16, especially Section 7.
[11] *Treatise of Human Nature*, Book II, Part III, Sec. III, Green and Grose, 2nd ed., p. 195.

the qualitative distinction between pleasures which he introduces in his treatise on utilitarianism,[12] is inconsistent with his basic position and must be avoided by any consistent utilitarian. This view, although very influential at the present time, is subject to the following criticisms.

In the first place, such a view gives no explanation of *intrinsic* goodness.[13] But unless their minds have become thoroughly confused by bad philosophy, all men recognize that certain things are good in themselves whether or not anyone happens to be interested or pleased in them. Would we abandon our view that knowledge and courage were good even though large numbers of men or even all men lost interest in these things? Take the case of a human infant abandoned on a doorstep. The parents obviously have no interest in the child. No one else knows of its existence. There is no human interest whatsoever in the child at this moment. Does this mean, then, that there is no intrinsic value in the child? If there is, then some things are good *in themselves,* independent of human interest, and we must abandon the subjectivist thesis.

Second, this view can give no explanation of human freedom. This is rooted not in mere appetite or interest, but in the power of the will to seek a universal good which is rationally apprehended by the agent himself and not imposed by chance or the conditioning of other men. But the utilitarian recognizes no such power of *rational* appetition (will) : only appetites or interests which are at the mercy of chance or external manipulation.

Third, this subjectivist theory can give no account of the fact that certain appetites which sometimes occur and the pleasures associated with them, are intrinsically bad, independently of their frustration of other appetites.

Finally, in the fourth place, these appetites without the guidance of practical reason, fall into no stable order of subordination. So far as the appetites themselves are concerned this order is a mere matter of chance or accident, and subject to constant flux. One nation may prefer death to slavery, while another prefers slavery to death. Which preference is correct? The utilitarian can give no stable, clear-cut answer to such basic, moral questions. His answer

---

[12] J. S. Mill, *Utilitarianism,* Everyman, pp. 6 ff.
[13] Cf. ch. 20, § 3.

must depend largely on the unstable nexus of appetites which happens to prevail in a given community at a given time. But we are all at least dimly aware that there *is* a stable, universal, moral order independent of what we or any human group, no matter how big, may happen to like or dislike.

These reasons together with the fundamental fact that man is not a self-sufficient being, but a contingent entity, not existing *necessarily*, but requiring external causes to account for his evolutionary origin and maintenance in the world of nature, require us, therefore, to seek beyond ethical subjectivism (whether it be called *utilitarianism* or *eudaemonism*) for some stable, ultimate, moral standard, existing independently of capricious, human interests, or even the higher faculties of man, subjectively considered and thus materialized or debased. This standard is the ancient conception of natural law. It is found in our Declaration of Independence and, indeed, wherever democracy is really alive. This concept is an integral part of the realistic philosophy first expounded by Plato and Aristotle on which our western culture is based.

Law is the ordering of action by reason to the natural good. Thus the human individual can understand his own human nature, that which can perfect this nature, rest in such perfection, and the necessary means to this end. So far as his action is directed by an understanding of these moral principles and laws, he does what he ought to do and achieves his natural end.

b. THE PRESCRIPTIVE AUTHORITY OF NATURAL LAW AND ITS SANCTIONS. Individual subhuman creatures possess their natures in an entitative or material manner without apprehending them in an immaterial way. Such entities always act in a uniform manner unless coincidentally obstructed by an external cause. Hence for the most part they do what they ought to do [14] and the laws describing their behavior provide us with a reliable basis for prediction. But the acts of human creatures are not predictable in this way. Men do not do what they ought to do. Hence we are very apt to conclude that what we call the natural law of human conduct, or the moral law, is only made up arbitrarily, or constructed by man himself, without having any basis in the actual nature of things. This conclusion is expressed in the currently widespread distinction between

[14] Cf. ch. 14, §§ 4 and 5.

descriptive laws (such as the laws of physics) which indicate the way things actually do happen, and *prescriptive* laws (such as the laws of morality) which only indicate the way we would like things to happen.

This distinction, however, is based upon a most vital misconception. In the first place, even subhuman entities, because of their material natures, do not act in an absolutely predictable and determinate manner. Their material natures are susceptible to the influence of other independent causes which modify the effect and sometimes obstruct it altogether.[15] Thus no stone falls *precisely* according to the laws of falling bodies and sometimes a sustaining cause prevents a body from falling at all. However, it is not *external* causes of this sort that produce the most startling and important deviations of human acts from the natural law of human nature; it is because men *themselves* are the *primary* cause of the operations of human acts.

The prescriptive laws of morality are just as natural as the laws of falling bodies. The difference is that the natural operations of man, prescribed by his nature, are not produced by stable, external causes, but must be voluntarily and deliberately carried out by the man himself. Nature has decreed that man freely perfect himself; hence his failure to carry out natural law is not to be explained by an external cause, but by a privative vice or sin within himself. Every man possesses some knowledge of his nature and the nature of his end. This knowledge, however, is in itself vague and indeterminate. In the first place, it must be confirmed by theoretical reflection to protect it against skepticism and confusion. In the second place, it requires to be supplemented by further determinations which bring it to bear on the special circumstances surrounding all action.

Thus the end of individual aspiration and its *necessary* parts (the virtues) are determined by natural law, but the *contingent* means through which this end is to be realized by this individual in his particular circumstances, must be freely deliberated and chosen as positive, individual maxims. In the case of the human community the general nature of the common good and the necessary cultural means of achieving it, are determined by natural law, but the

---

[15] Cf. ch. 14, § 4.

contingent means through which this end is to be realized by this or that community, must be freely deliberated and chosen by that community or its representatives as particular, positive law. This positive law, whether individual or social, is no mere arbitrary construction backed up by force alone (except when unnaturally and therefore improperly achieved), but rather a more precise determination or filling in of the general framework laid down by the natural law. An unjust or unnatural law is no law and carries with it no obligation for obedience. It rather imposes upon every moral man the duty of disobedience. The right of revolution is based upon this maxim of natural law.[16]

This brings us to the question of sanction, or obligation. What binds us to the natural law and obliges us to obey it? The answer is quite clear—the striving or tending of our nature toward its end; the natural love of good, without which we would not be human; and the sanctions imposed by our nature and the whole of which it is a part. If subhuman entities are forced by *external* coinciding causes to act or suffer in a way which is contrary to nature, they suffer either frustration or extinction, because they positively tend to another end. The same is true in the case of man. If from *internal* causes he freely fails to act in accordance with the law of his nature, he must suffer the punishment of frustration or extinction.

The individual who performs a bad act is punished by an increased tendency to perform a further bad act, which may become a permanent habit. If this habit continues to be indulged the punishment will be increased by the loss of all rational control, by frustration, and finally by the destruction of individual life. The state which ceases to act in accordance with the law of nature but instead follows purely arbitrary decrees backed up by force, is punished for its mistaken purposes either by military defeat in its enslaving enterprises or by the more terrible defeat of military victory. This not only causes the enslavement of its enemies, but the self-enslavement of itself to its own irrational obsessions and delusions which must finally end in rational torpor and the black night of cultural death. On the other hand, those with the courage to fight and rebel against the pseudolaw of tyranny are rewarded by

[16] Cf. ch. 9, § 7.

freedom from unnatural frustration, whereas cowards and collaborators are punished by a slavery which is worse than death.

These natural, *negative* sanctions are discernible in every phase of human conduct, individual and social. They are sure and inevitable because they are ingrained in the very nature of man and the world which he inhabits. A knowledge of these sanctions (rewards and punishments) can aid and strengthen the moral urge to the self-perfection of man, but they are not the ultimate, *positive* sanction. This is found only in the aspiration of our nature to that which can perfect it and bring it to happiness. Without this positive sanction, the negative sanctions would have no force. Unless we tended naturally to the good the failure to achieve this good would be no punishment. But we do tend naturally towards the good which perfects our nature, and this is the first and final sanction of all morality.

We must now ask ourselves how this good is to be attained and how we fail to attain it. The answer is through good habits and bad habits, for man is a creature of habit. Good habits are called virtues; bad habits, vices. Virtues are the primary, *internal* causes of happiness. Vices are the primary, *internal* causes of misery. Nature herself sees to it that the other living things are brought into activity by *external* causes, so that they attain such approximations to happiness as they are capable of. To man alone she has given the power of *bringing himself* into happiness through the acquisition of freely chosen habits. We must now examine this process by which man himself responsibly brings happiness or misery upon himself. We shall divide this examination into four parts: first, the general nature of virtue, the primary cause of happiness; second, the way in which virtue is acquired; third, the way in which vice is acquired; and fourth, the general nature of human responsibility and irresponsibility.

REFERENCES

Recommended Reading
Aristotle, *Nicomachean Ethics,* Book I.
Aquinas, *Summa Theologica,* Treatise on Law, Prima Secundae, Qu. 90–
97, especially Qu. 94 and 97.

Suggested Reading

1. For a classical picture of the good life in the concrete, and at the same time for an ideal introduction to philosophy, cf. Plato, *Apology, Crito,* and the beginning and end of the *Phaedo.* For Stoicism, cf. Epictetus, *Encheiridion,* Loeb Library. For the hedonistic view with important qualifications, cf. Mill, J. S., *Utilitarianism.*
2. For the concept of natural law in Plato, cf. *Republic,* Book IV, pp. 444 ff., and *Gorgias,* pp. 501–508.
3. For Kant, cf. *The Philosophy of Kant; As Contained in Extracts from his own Writings.* Selected and translated by Watson, John, Glasgow, Maclehose, 1901. For utilitarianism, cf. Hume, *Treatise of Human Nature,* Book III, Parts I and II; Bentham, *An Introduction to the Principles of Morals and Legislation,* Oxford, 1822; and Perry, R. B., *Moral Economy,* New York, Scribners, 1909.

Chapter 3

HOW MEN MAKE THEMSELVES HAPPY OR MISERABLE

1. THE NATURE OF VIRTUE AND VICE

VIRTUES and their opposites (vices) are the objects of praise and blame whether they occur in ourselves or in others. Hence they cannot be faculties which we inherit as necessarily derived from our human nature, or ephemeral acts which occur simply from chance. Thus we neither blame anyone for being born blind nor praise anyone for possessing sight, because this is a natural faculty. Similarly we do not blame a man for an accident or praise a man for an unintentional coincidence, like the Nazi official who saved a prisoner's life simply because it so happened that this was the only means of saving his own. Such facts as these show that virtue is neither an inborn faculty nor an ephemeral coincidence. We are not born courageous or temperate or scientifically reflective. Neither do we acquire such virtues in a moment by coincidence, but only by long training as fixed dispositions of character. Such permanent tendencies are properly called habits: they do not constitute our hereditary *first nature,* but our acquired *second nature,* or character. All virtues are simply good habits; all vices are bad habits. This is the first thing to see.

But now we must distinguish between two sorts of habit: the *intellectual* habits, which are determined wholly by the formal nature of an external object of thought; and the *moral* habits, which involve our own preference or choice. It is true that before we actually think, we must choose to think, but once we begin to think theoretically we have left all subjective choice and preference behind, abandoning ourselves completely to the object. A mathematician does not choose the theorem he finally succeeds in demonstrating: he simply discovers its truth. Thus false opinions or bad habits of theoretical reflection arise, not from wrong *choices,* but from intellectual dullness, and the intrusion of choices into our train of theoretical reflection. Any such preference is bad because the aim of pure theory is simply to understand the thing as it is. Once we apprehend such a theoretical truth a firm habit of understanding is established in us, and such firm habits of apprehension are precisely the intellectual virtues.

a. WHAT CHOICE IS. On the other hand, all the *moral* habits involve choice or preference, for here something more than mere apprehension is involved, namely, appetite. In this case the aim is not merely to assimilate the truth, but to seek the right end, and we cannot do this except through choice, exercised by our seeking faculty. If we abandon all our subjective preferences (*prejudices* from the theoretical point of view) we simply do not act at all, though we may be acted upon and conditioned by external stimuli. But such an abandonment of choice is the cause of moral vice and depravity. It cannot lead to moral virtue, or the perfection of our active nature, for this nature demands that it be *freely* perfected through internal causes. Man is not a robot or a machine which is meant to be governed by external controls, but a voluntary being that is meant to be governed by the internal control of reason. If we abandon all such internal control we fall under the sway either of mere chance or of unscrupulous human manipulators who strive, not for the proper perfection of human nature, but only for the realization of their own evil ends. All the moral virtues are habits involving *choice*. They are chosen by man himself for the moral perfection of his active nature. What then is meant by choice?

Choice is not the same as opinion, for opinion is simply true or false, whereas choice is right or wrong and molds our character. It is easy to change or even to forget an opinion we have held, but our ways of choosing one mode of action rather than another, such as clinging to money rather than spending it, eat into us and are very hard to change once they are acquired. An opinion is only a theoretical mode of action; hence it abstracts from any direct relation to the agent and his acts. In fact the more abstract and detached it is, the truer it is apt to be. This is why it is so notoriously possible for a man to hold very enlightened and edifying opinions about morality in general or even about himself, and yet to *choose* acts which are shoddy and commonplace. Opinion concerns reality so far as it is changeless and determinate; choice concerns reality so far as it is changeable and subject to modification by our action. Hence it must also be distinguished from imaginative interest or wish.

Since our appetites are ever present, it is impossible for us to indulge in imaginary daydreams and thoughts about objects, no matter how remote they may be, without at the same time stirring up positive or negative responses in our interests. Thus abstract matters of theory strike us as interesting or dull, and in a desultory manner we can wish for what may be utterly beyond our reach, as the genius of another man, or for what is altogether impossible, as to live forever. Such wishful thinking, if it becomes an obsession, may take the place of choice and interfere with our action or actually distort it, if it conjures up irresponsible and false images of what we can do. This kind of thinking must be distinguished from choice, which is always concerned with what is in our power and always involves a comparison of alternative modes of action. Hence we must also distinguish choice from the "strongest" appetite with which it is often confused.

According to a very widespread view the role of practical reason in human conduct is merely that of presenting different courses of action to our desires. One mode of action may appeal to one interest, another mode to another interest. In case of conflict the stronger interest or group of interests must win, and this victory of mere might is confused with preference. The task of reason in conduct is thus degraded to the slavish function of devising ways and means for the satisfaction of the most interests already in existence. It cannot really govern them by qualifying these interests or by developing new interests in keeping with the true nature and dignity of man. This instrumentalist view really eliminates human freedom and makes man the slave of interests, which have simply sprung up in him by chance or by external manipulation. There are clear reasons, however, within the grasp of all, from which we can see that this degrading view is wholly false, because choice is not the same as *any* kind of sensuous appetite.

For instance, choice is not a violent tendency of our irascible nature such as rage, for such tendencies overwhelm us all of a sudden, whereas choice develops only out of a long and arduous process of deliberation, though once fixed in our character, it can function in the flash of an eye. Furthermore it is not the same as any mere appetite or combination of appetites, whether violent or subdued. We shall be able to see this if we remind ourselves of the familiar phenomena of continence and incontinence, or what we call self-control and its lack. The instrumentalist can offer no explanation of these phenomena, for on *his* view choice can never be totally opposed to interest, for choice is nothing but the pressure of the greater mass of interest. But we all know that men do sometimes lose control of themselves, following interest rather than choice, and we sharply distinguish this condition from that of the self-controlled man, who can do what he chooses in spite of his appetites.

These facts show clearly that there is something in us which is capable of opposing and governing appetite. This is preference or choice. We may confirm this truth by reflecting on the evident fact that animals, though they possess appetites, do not exercise choice. We may also see that appetite is always followed by pleasure or pain arising from the presence of a sense object, but choice need not be followed by either. We must therefore conclude, as against the interest or appetite theory, that man is free and that his practical reason is no mere slavish schemer of clever plans for satisfying the most desires, but rather a rational governor that is capable of ruling and even of opposing them. Choice is the rational qualification or determination of action resulting from deliberation. But what is deliberation? What kind of reason is this?

b. WHAT PRACTICAL REASON IS. We commonly refer to practical reason by such terms as planning, plotting, and scheming, as distinct from purely theoretical thinking and reasoning. We do not naturally speak of a mathematician as *deliberating* about the truth or falsity of a geometrical theorem, and we generally recognize with the ancients that it is possible for a speculative genius like Thales to possess considerable abstract theoretical knowledge of the heavenly bodies, etc., without knowing how to find his own way home. What kind of knowing is this: *knowing how* as distinct from *knowing about*? First of all, we must convince ourselves that it is really a kind of knowing.

All knowing involves the apprehension of simple terms and their combination in a certain order (the order of truth) . Deliberation involves the apprehension of simple terms called means and ends, and their combination in a certain order (the order of natural law or rectitude). The man who *reasons theoretically* must know certain basic facts and principles to start with. He must then be able to connect some proposition, concerning which he is in theoretical doubt, with the first principles he knows already to be so, by certain middle terms of the demonstration. Similarly the man who *deliberates practically* must know the end he is aiming at to start with, otherwise he could not plan anything at all. He must then be able to connect some individual act concerning which he is in practical doubt, with this end he is already aiming at, by certain middle terms of deliberation,—the *means* to the end. Hence we may conclude that deliberation is a kind of reasoning process, or reflection.

Theoretical reflection is universal (not particular) both in premises and conclusion: it is abstract from any reference to the individual agent and his interests, and is concerned exclusively with what is already necessary and determinate, rather than with what is contingent and indeterminate. We do not strive for what is universal and abstract. We strive for an end which is particular and concrete: my end, or the common end of these particular men.

But every concrete reality, whatever it may be, has a universal, causal structure. Hence the first step in any sound deliberation is to analyze the universal structure of the end and its necessary causes or means. This will result in an understanding of what must be done in general if the end is to be reached. With respect to these *necessary* means there is no freedom of choice. If the end is to be achieved at all, these necessary means must be achieved. They constitute the morally necessary, first principles of deliberative syllogisms.

Thus if victory over the enemy is to be won, an adequate army must be organized, his army must be defeated, and his country occupied. But since it is not victory *in general* that is to be won, but a concrete and particular victory, these universal prescriptions must be further particularized by minor premises involving such material factors as degree, quantity, where, and when. Thus before I can act, I must decide how big an army is to be raised, where the enemy is to be fought, and when his country is to be occupied.

These particular specifications are not exactly determined by the general nature of the end. With respect to them, freedom of choice may be exercised. The enemy could be defeated with a greater or a lesser sized army, by this or that mode of invasion, by a longer or shorter war. With respect to such contingent means it is no longer a question as to what must be done if the end is to be achieved, but rather as to how the end may be *best* achieved by the particular agents in question, in their concrete circumstances.

Here two opposed factors must be mutually harmonized according to the general principle of the mean. On the one hand, the end must be achieved. On the other hand, it must be achieved at the *least* cost, or *most* effectively by the particular, active agents who are not yet at the end. Thus two extremes are obviously to be avoided: first, any plan which though fitting the particular circumstances of the agent, would jeopardize the victory; and second, any plan which, though insuring victory, would involve greater sacrifices than the victory was worth. Sound deliberation will always lead to the choice of a mean between these two extremes. The end will be achieved in a manner best suited to the particular situation and character of the agent. Every step of this process involves universal as well as individual aspects, but we must note a difference in the relative importance of these aspects so far as they attach to the end or to the agent.

In the case of the end, its particular and contingent circumstances matter much less and its universal or essential structure much more, for it is something possessing the essential structure of the end we desire to attain, and as long as we attain this, the particular circumstances do not matter. But in the case of the agent who must act, his particular and contingent circumstances matter much more and his essential structure much less, for he must carry out the action, and he cannot act or operate in general, but only as a concrete individual in particular circumstances. Thus a universal understanding of the general structure of what is to be done as well as a concrete apprehension of its particular means, is demanded by deliberation, but it is more important to have a general understanding of the end and a concrete judgment of the agent.

This explains the well-known fact that it is easier for people to agree on ultimate ends than upon immediate means; for different, concrete persons in different circumstances must choose different, immediate means to achieve the same universal end. Hence it is wise in any moral argument to consider first of all the ultimate end concerning which universal agreement can be reached, and then to work down from this through the necessary means to the more and more contingent means which must vary from one individual agent to another. Nevertheless it is also necessary to follow the opposite course, which represents the order of execution, beginning with the first individual act of the individual agent and then ascending through the instrumental means, or middle terms, to the ultimate end, carefully considering at each point whether such an act is really possible for the agent in question and is best fitted among all the alternatives for leading him to the end. In fact, the two opposite methods must be mutually combined according to a mean which avoids two very familiar extremes.

First, we must not fall into the error of the rigoristic or a priori deliberator who follows only the downward course, fixing his attention so exclusively on the end and the first principles as to ignore the means. Such reflection often advocates means that are impossible for a given agent in a given situation or unjustifiable means which involve a greater sacrifice than the end is worth. But secondly, we must also avoid the error of the opportunistic or pragmatic deliberator who follows only the upward course, fixing his attention so exclusively on immediate things to do as to ignore the end. Such reflection often advocates means simply on the ground of their possibility, irrespective of whether they actually lead to a worth-while end at all, sometimes monstrous means whose evil far outweighs the good of the end they achieve.

c. THE NATURE OF VIRTUE AS A WHOLE. Our nature cannot be perfected unless every phase of human life is voluntarized by this process of deliberation into rational activity. Such voluntary activity has twelve distinct phases.[1] There must be a natural aspiration for the end (2). This is the *subjective* foundation for all virtue and moral action. Second, there must be a clear understanding of the essential nature of this end and the necessary means this nature dictates (1). This is the *objective* foundation for all virtue and moral action. Pure, theoretical insight can contribute much

[1] For a further discussion of these twelve phases, cf. ch. 20, § 4.

to this. (1) and (2) mutually re-enforce each other. A keen natural desire for the end (2) disposes us to exercise our understanding on it (1), and a clear understanding of the end (1) tends to strengthen our desire for it (2). We recognize one who possesses these two guiding factors to a high degree as a man of character or of high principles and moral integrity.

In addition to desiring keenly and understanding clearly the nature of the ultimate end, the sound man must, in the third place, possess an accurate *judgment* of his own individual character and the circumstances surrounding him (3) as well as a definite intention to do what he can do (4). Without these he will never really do anything in the concrete material world where all action must take place. Then he must have a fertile faculty of moral invention that is capable of devising quickly alternative means for the realization of an end (5) and a willing consent to follow these means (6). Without these he will fall into a sluggish routine and lose his faculty of choice and freedom. Next, he must be able to judge accurately between alternative means, each of which is possible and suitable, as to what is really the *best* way of achieving the end (7), and must be willing to choose that which is preferred (8).

Finally, the sound man must be ready to command all his faculties (9) and then to act (10 and 11) in accordance with the results of such deliberation. The incontinent man might just as well not deliberate, for he has lost control of himself, and cannot do what he chooses. Last of all (phase 12), he must be ready to take satisfaction in the attainment of the end, to rest in it, and enjoy it. Indeed, if no practical error has been made and if he has really accomplished it, this crowning phase of the act must occur. If a man reaches an end which he cannot enjoy, this means either that it was a mere accident which he did not achieve by his efforts or that an error was made in deliberating and that the end was not worth attaining.

All of these twelve factors are necessarily involved in virtue, or what we call moral freedom, which becomes actual only to the degree in which our action is removed from the control of haphazard, external forces, and placed under the control of deliberation. Without a clear and accurate understanding of our natural end we misdirect all our efforts towards what is only apparently good, not really good for us. In this case the cleverer we are at devising and judging adequate means to a false end, the worse off we are, for we necessarily fall into misery and slavery to what is opposed to our very nature and, therefore, to our most basic desire, no matter how we misconceive it.

On the other hand, even though our basic aim is clearly grasped and keenly desired we can never actually achieve it without devising, judging, and performing the contingent means which will lead us there. If we do not do this we must necessarily fall into misery and slavery to what is against our nature. Instead of ruling ourselves in accordance with the law of nature and the highest faculty of reason, which alone is capable of knowing this law, our habits and acts will be determined either by external tyrants seeking only some good of their own or by the external tyranny of mere chance, which seeks no good at all.

Human freedom involves an element of determinism and an element of indeterminism. We are determined, not by external constraint or compulsion, but by our very nature to seek our happiness or perfection, in general. This perfection, however, involves a vast plenitude of goods, an embarrassment of riches, which must be further specified and ordered before it can function as the concrete end of a particular man or group of men. Our nature determines us to seek the good in general: it tells us nothing concerning the highest good or the proper order of subordinating the lesser goods. This can be discovered only by a broad philosophical knowledge of reality and human nature in general.

With respect to the end, we have no freedom of *exercise*. We must all will some good, either real or apparent. But we do possess a freedom of *specification* in determining this or that to be the highest good and this or that order of subordination. But with respect to the contingent means of achieving the good, we possess, not only a freedom of specifying what we shall will as a contingent means, but also a freedom of exercise, for such a means may either be willed or not willed at all.

This combination of natural determinism with respect to the end, and indeterminism with respect to the means, is not at all a contradiction, but rather an integrated structure in which each of the two parts re-enforces the other. The more our practical reason, aided by true theory, succeeds in specifying a truly highest good and the necessary means leading to it, the more our natural aspiration is quickened and confirmed. But the more firmly we become attached to our natural end, the more detached do we become from purely contingent, instrumental goods, and the more we are protected against slavish obsessions. The more clearly we can apprehend the highest good which perfects our nature and the more strongly we can cling to its pursuit in accordance with the necessity of this nature, the more freely we can then exercise our freedom of choice in laying down our own path to this good and maintaining it amidst the vast concourse of historical events.

We are now in a position to give a complete definition of *moral virtue*. As opposed to the *intellectual virtues,* which are habits of apprehension (either simple or complex), the moral virtues are habits caused by free choice, resulting from a process of deliberation in which the natural end of man and the necessary means to this end are theoretically specified, and the contingent means correctly judged in relation to the individual agent and his circumstances. We must now examine the manner in which such rational habits of freedom are acquired.

2.   How Virtues Are Acquired

Without permanent, ingrained tendencies of aiming at rational modes of action, the attainment of happiness is impossible. We are certainly not born with such habits or virtues, but must somehow acquire them through free choice. Hence the question as to how exactly we do acquire them is of the utmost importance, for it is precisely the question as to how we become free and happy. We are not born happy, nor do we become happy by a fluke. The law of nature lays it down that man can become happy only through his own choices and efforts. Nothing outside us can make us happy. If we are to become happy we must be the principal causes of our own happiness and *make ourselves happy* by our own activity. But what sort of a process is this? What sort of *making* is involved?

a.   THE THEORY OF CONDITIONING.   A certain mode of thought, which began with laboratory studies of the white rat and the guinea pig and which has now deeply influenced our common sense, is ready with what seems at first glance to be a most plausible answer.

Habit arises from the repetition of similar acts. Why are certain acts repeated rather than others? Well, in the case of the lower animals this is clear: It is due either to the association of certain natural stimuli with natural instincts, as certain odors become associated with certain foods and thus call forth acquired food responses, or to the association of certain artificial stimuli with natural instincts as, for example, psychological manipulators can *condition* animal food responses to different colored lights.

New human habits are often formed in the same way, as when by chance a fear response in childhood becomes associated with a dog or when by the clever, external manipulation of advertisers and propagandists, human likes and dislikes get associated with certain stimuli. If these were the only ways in which we could learn new habits we should all of us be the slaves either of chance or of unscrupulous human overlords who condition us from childhood to habits convenient for themselves. But surely man is in some sense free and able to induce new habits in himself by the use of his own intelligence. Here also the animal-habit school of thought has an answer which we must examine with some care. It runs like this:

Yes, man is clearly different from the other animals, for in addition to his slavish animal nature, he is endowed with a superior faculty of intelligence which, living apart from the rest of his nature, can intervene in the habit-forming process, like a skilled psychologist, and condition him to stimuli of its own choosing. According to this theory our animal habits are just as automatic as those of the white rat and as long as a stable environment is maintained, they can function smoothly and successfully without the intervention of intelligence. But when some environmental obstruction arises or when one habitual tendency falls into conflict with another, such intervention is required to avoid disaster.

At such times of crisis our human reason is able to devise convenient means of solving the environmental problem or of reconciling the opposed appetites. Working out some satisfactory plan for circumventing the difficulty, it conditions us to new habits in accordance with the plan, as a clever psychologist conditions a rat to new stimuli and then retires to his own office, where he remains otherwise occupied or at rest until some new emergency confronts the helpless habits, and he is called upon once more. Man is thus viewed as a sort of super white rat with a clever psychologist living in his brain, a self-conditioning animal. This theory of the process of human habit formation has achieved a widespread vogue. When closely examined, however, it is seen to be subject to at least two basic criticisms.

In the first place, this theory of habit fails to recognize the intimate union of reason and aspiration at every stage in the development of a human habit. It thinks of reason as a separate faculty which intervenes only at critical junctures to solve practical problems, and it conceives of human habit as an automatic tendency to an end which it is able to seek, to enjoy, and to attain over and over again without rational cooperation. All that is needed to see the falsity of this account is to focus clearly some definite segment of your own waking conduct. Take such a segment! Of course habits are involved. You are doing something resembling what you have done before. But is your action wholly automatic? Do you have no idea of the end you are aiming at? Does the act merely run itself off without your having any awareness of what you are doing? Are you wholly unconscious of reaching the end, and is your satisfaction wholly unmingled with any glimmering of intelligence? If not, there is something wrong with the white-rat theory of habit formation as applied to human conduct, for on this view reason intervenes only at certain moments when subordinate problems arise.

But why should reason intervene at all if it is a separate theoretical faculty with its own work to do? Of course, there is such a faculty, but its work is to discover the truth, not to solve practical problems. Why should it be concerned with the attainment of some particular, practical end? Why should it function at the call of habit unless it has itself become habitualized and united with aspiration as *practical* reason? But if this has occurred, why has this practical reason concerned itself only with a subordinate, *instrumental* phase of the habit and utterly neglected its mainspring—the end? Let us raise a further question. Why should the automatic habit allow itself to be altered by reason in an instrumental emergency unless it has been already rationalized from beginning to end? As an isolated faculty of desire, it cannot think or understand. Why then should it heed the advice of reason even with respect to a minor phase of the act? If it does do this, why not even more with respect to the end, the mainspring of the act?

A careful examination of human conduct will show that this artificial separation of reason from habit is incorrect. There *is* a separate faculty of theoretical reason whose concern is exclusively with the abstract truth. But in addition to this, fortunately for us, we possess a practical, rational faculty which plans and deliberates in cooperation with the peculiarly human form of appetite (will). As we have seen,[2] this practical reason is not restricted to the solution of instrumental problems, but is capable of attending to *every* phase of a human act, specifying the end, deliberating the means, commanding and governing the act itself, and participating in the final satisfaction. To deny this, is to distort the whole structure of the act of will and to regard man as a brute animal. This is the first major objection to this theory.

The second objection is derived from the first. If the two faculties of habit and reason are isolated into two separate compartments and if the rule of reason is restricted to that of solving instrumental problems, how are *new* habits ever to arise? How are we to explain *radical* movements of reform and revolutions? What account are we to give of human freedom?

The conditioners can only say that this must consist merely in our ability to satisfy the desires and impulses we already happen to have. But what if these desires are cruel, sadistic, and tyrannical? How is an individual or a group to free itself from the burden of corrupt and depraved habits? How do our human tendencies become attached to new ends? Not through rational choice, for reason is subordinated to a servile, problem-solving function at the behest of irrational drives. Only through chance or through some process of conditioning under the control of some benevolent tyrant who manipulates the so-called educational system. But what determines *his* end? Not reason, but once more, only chance or the process by which he was himself conditioned. So where is human freedom and the right of revolution guaranteeing human liberty? It is most difficult to see.

Fundamental abuses are not swept aside by mere chance or by the arbitrary fiat of tyranny. They must first be sharply focused by

[2] Cf. this chapter, § 1.

practical reason and subjected to a *radical* criticism in the light of natural law. Then means of correction must be devised and freely chosen. Finally, reason must give the command for action and real risks must be run, not by human guinea pigs running off automatic reflexes, but by deliberate men, aware of every step they take. Revolutionary reforms, whether individual or social, can be carried out only in this way by free men acting under the guidance of that sound understanding of their nature and the nature of things which has been preserved in the great tradition of western philosophy. They cannot be carried out by human white rats, with conditioning psychologists living in their brains.

Needless to say, these objections are based upon facts which even a brief examination should make evident. We must therefore attempt to develop a less inadequate theory of the habit-forming process. We shall be more likely to succeed in this if we accept the guidance of Aristotle and the classical psychologists who, in formulating their theories of conduct, paid more attention to men, and less attention to rats.

b. THE ARISTOTELIAN THEORY. An instinctive act is preceded by an instinctive capacity that is simply inherited as a part of our original nature. A virtuous act, which is done virtuously and does not simply happen by luck, is preceded by a habitual tendency to perform such acts, which is acquired as a part of our character, or second nature. How are such habits acquired? Clearly, they can be acquired only by the performance of virtuous *acts*. But how are we to perform such acts unless we are already virtuous?

This problem confronts us with a dilemma. If we are already virtuous or in possession of a firm tendency to perform such acts, then we have nothing to acquire, because we are already virtuous. But if we are not already virtuous and have no such settled tendency, how are we to perform such an act except by luck? Clearly, only by the intervention of some external human cause in the process of moral education or habit formation, which involves far more than the conditioning of a past response, already in existence, to a new stimulus that is decided upon by an external manipulator.

The acquisition of a human habit, whether individual or social, involves a radical revolution from one mode of response to another, from an *externally controlled* or conditioned mode of response to one that is freely or *internally controlled*. It is not enough that the proper act be brought forth. It must be brought forth in the proper way, with knowledge, with choice, with pleasure, and by the agent, *of himself*. The conditioned-reflex theory of learning regards only the objective act, disregarding *the way in which this act is done*. In animals this factor may be properly disregarded, for they are unable to act of themselves. But in men, who are able to act of themselves, this aspect is of primary importance in the moral learning process. Let us take a concrete example.

Children are not born generous. On the other hand they are not born stingy. Our original nature is neutral in this as in all other specific moral respects. If the child is to develop a habitual tendency towards generosity the first step in this direction must be taken by the family and community in which the child lives. Such steps are always taken by any community in which there is any trace of natural law and order. They are due neither to chance nor to arbitrary decree, but to rational deliberation on the necessary means of achieving the end which nature has decreed for man, the common happiness or perfection of all the citizens. Since this involves the use of external goods as instruments and since the supply of such goods is not unlimited, it cannot be achieved without a common willingness on the part of all the citizens to share such goods, rather than to hoard them up and cling to them at all cost. Hence rational laws and customs, by the appropriate bestowal of rewards and punishments from the earliest age, condition the child to the actual performance of generous acts.

But this conditioning is only the first beginning of the learning process. The child may actually perform generous acts at this stage, but as long as he has to be *externally* threatened or coaxed or bribed into performing them, he does not perform them virtuously and is not yet virtuous himself. Many mature individuals never advance any further than this along the road to virtue. Knowing nothing of the law of nature, they continue to regard the laws and customs of their country as mere accidents or tyrannical decrees, as they may of course be in a nation which has long suppressed the use of reason and has no understanding of the necessary connection between the virtues and the natural end of man. Such men may continue *under normal circumstances* to perform virtuous acts, not for their own sake, but only as the best policy, in order to avoid punishment or to achieve some reward. As soon as the external constraint is weakened, however, when left to themselves they will revert to their childish, irrational interests, and jeopardize not only their own welfare but the welfare of all by vicious and unnatural acts.

Such moral disaster can be avoided in three ways: first, by strong external control, especially during childhood, when the human character is still plastic, causing the repeated performance of the right acts; second, by the inculcation of *the habit* of deliberation before action, for the tendency to think before we act can be externally induced like any other habit of man; and third, by education of the rational faculty which deliberates, teaching the child how to specify the natural end of man and showing him the necessary means to this end (the virtues). Only the *first* of these is necessary for animal conditioning. All three are essential for the acquisition of a rational human habit.

When such a habit is really acquired, the habit of deliberation is also acquired as an essential *intrinsic* part. No *human* act can be performed without deliberation.[3] Such deliberation must involve *a rational determination of the end* and the necessary means to this end, an apprehension of the particular contingent means, and finally, a constant control over these during the performance of the act. *At every stage of such an act,* the man will know both *what* he is doing and *why*. In the second place, such an act, performed virtuously or habitually, will be chosen *for its own sake* as part of *the natural end,* and *never as a mere means* to a further end. As long as external threats or bribery is necessary the habit has not yet been fully acquired or internalized. Finally, in the third place, such an act (including both deliberation and choice), since it expresses a settled tendency of habit in conformity with nature, will be done *with pleasure* if no external hindrance arises. The learning of virtuous habits necessarily involves pain, especially when evil tendencies must be rooted out. Hence the Puritan view that pleasure and virtue are necessarily opposed. But this view is definitely false. It is only the incipient or partly formed virtue that is painful or un-

[3] Automatic reflexes like the secretion of the digestive juices are acts of man, not human acts.

pleasant. Virtue itself, when unobstructed by misfortune, is intensely pleasant—far more pleasant than vice, which in the long run frustrates our nature.

Such is the process by which good habits or virtues are acquired by man.[4] The first step is the actual performance of virtuous acts, not yet understood by the agent nor chosen by him nor pleasant in being achieved, and, therefore, not virtuously performed. This first step must be brought forth under external control which, though external, is neither accidental nor capricious, but deliberate and freely chosen. But this rational, lawful control must not only produce a continuous repetition of virtuous acts in those under its charge, until they become a settled routine. It must *also* induce in the agent a sound understanding of the natural law requiring such acts, and a firm habit of considering and deliberating the contingent means for carrying out this law in particular circumstances. With this understanding clearly in mind, the agent himself can cause the act and take pleasure in its performance. When a sound understanding of the natural law is obscured in a given community, the external control of law and custom is weakened, individual vices spring up unchecked, and the whole community sinks gradually into anarchy and the complete cultural inversion of tyranny. But we must not be content with such a brief reference. Let us now examine the opposite process by which human beings acquire *bad* habits or moral vices.

3.   How Vices Are Acquired

Just as men are themselves the primary causes of their own happiness, so are they the primary causes of their own misery. We must admit, of course, that men are sometimes made miserable by great external catastrophes of nature such as floods, famines, and earthquakes. But further reflection will convince us that these evils are almost as nothing in comparison with those which man brings upon himself through inertia, pride, greed, crime, and war. By his intelligence he can take account of the accidents of nature and at least greatly minimize their deleterious effects. His failure to do so and all that follows from this failure, are evils that he brings upon himself by his own stupidity and laziness. We cannot avoid

[4] Cf. ch. 8, § 5 for an account of how justice is acquired.

the conclusion, therefore, that man is primarily responsible for his own misery.

This truth, however, is greatly obscured by the white-rat theory of habit formation we have been considering. As we have seen, this theory involves a basic separation of habitual drive from reason. But it is only when the two are united in rationally directed action, or will, that we have a thoroughly self-originating source of good or evil. If the two are separated from each other, man of himself cannot be a primary, originating source of evil. First of all, we cannot blame the isolated faculty of reason for mistaken action, for the function of reason is merely to apprehend reality, not to act. But secondly, we cannot blame mere irrational impulse or drive, for this is due rather to chance or to external manipulation than to any purely internal source. By themselves they do not exercise any choice. How then can we blame them? Finally, in the third place, how can we find any radical evil in such a bifurcated view of man? Reason has nothing to do with the guidance of appetite towards any goal or end. All our appetites are directed to some particular goal either by chance or by some external agency. One such desire is as good as another. What then is evil?

We cannot conceive of it as anything but a failure on the part of reason to exercise its subordinate problem-solving function in achieving a synthesis or harmony of random interests. But since the interests themselves are all intrinsically good, this failure to realize as *many* as we might is rather a *faux pas* or a regrettable mistake than anything inherently vicious or wrong. Moral vice is really eliminated, and stupidity or inefficiency is called upon to take its place. But we do not blame a person for being stupid or inefficient unless he in some sense *chose* these things or brought them upon himself. But when reason and desire are radically isolated from each other, choice is impossible and man is reduced to a passive pawn in the hands of chance or environment. He thus becomes incapable of committing wrong choices and wrong acts.

But we are all aware of such wrongful acts both in ourselves and others. Hence the white-rat theory of human habit formation cannot be accepted as an adequate account of the learning process. We sometimes blame ourselves and others for wrong acts that we ourselves or they themselves have committed. How is this to be explained? How are human vices really acquired? The answer is: in the same way that the virtues are acquired. Hence we may now be more brief in giving the answer.

Human nature is endowed at the beginning with a number of general tendencies to act which are certainly not bad. They become bad only by being directed to the wrong ends in the wrong manner. In human life as it is at present, the first impetus towards the development of such vices comes from the social environment of the child. Certainly children are not born to be selfish any more than they are born to be generous. But if, in a given community, the possession of wealth is admired as an end in itself and the ability to look out for one's self in this way is encouraged both by law and custom, any child born into such a community will soon be led into habits of selfish acquisition. He will simply perform such ungenerous acts as a result of external conditioning, not as a result of his own deliberation and choice.

As long as this is the case the child himself is not ungenerous. If left to himself he might still perform generous acts. But the child is not left to himself. As he performs the acts, he will also be taught to deliberate about them so as to be able to perform them all by himself without constant external direction. He will also be taught some naïve view of the nature of human life according to which external possessions are a supreme object of human desire, capable by themselves of perfecting the life of man.

If he is acute enough to question his teachers and to think seriously and accurately about the matter, he may be able to avoid falling into error, but this is unlikely, for the human, apprehensive faculties are difficult to master and, while in a youthful state of vague indeterminacy, are easily led astray. The child can easily apprehend his material organism and the material objects satisfying his material needs by the external senses. He cannot see or even imagine his faculty of reason and the more valuable things that perfect the higher part of his nature. Hence he is easily led to believe that the acquisition of money and material goods is the highest possible object of desire. So he will come to seek them, not merely because his friends and those around him do, but because he himself chooses to seek them for their own sake.

At this stage he not only performs ungenerous acts, but he himself becomes selfish and ungenerous, understanding the end that he is seeking, choosing it for its own sake, and deliberating about the means, both those that are necessary and those that are contingent. At every stage of the act he will know not only *what* he is doing but also *why* he is doing it. As long as all this is painful and arduous, so that he constantly needs external stimulation and encouragement from those more vicious than he is, the habit is not as yet fully acquired or internalized.

But finally, if no further hindrances arise, the repeated performance of such deliberate acts will give rise to a settled habitual tendency or habit, and then its activity will produce pleasure and joy when unobstructed. Since such vicious tendencies are actually opposed to human nature, the learning process by which they are internalized will be longer and more arduous than that required for the acquisition of virtues in conformity with human nature. The Nazis certainly had to spend much more time and energy in the educational process of instilling their moral vices into German youth than the democratic nations in the educational process of instilling certain opposed virtues into their youth. Ideally speaking, it is easier to perfect human nature than to corrupt it. If we could compare a perfect society with a corrupt society we should certainly see that the former would have an easier time educating its youth than the latter. But of course there is no perfect society. All societies we know are at least partially corrupt.

In such a society the process of acquiring certain virtues is certainly most difficult, since it involves a constant struggle with deeply rooted customs and traditions. But society cannot avoid corruption and tyranny unless this struggle is constantly made by individuals who have been able to gain a clearer understanding of human nature and its end than that of their associates and friends. Every individual who succeeds in achieving such a revolution becomes a center for the formation of further habits, for everyone is constantly influencing the habits of others by thought and word and deed. Hence a single individual can inaugurate a new set of habits and a new mode of life, which may spread first of all to a small group of friends and then to others, until a whole society is turned upside down and revolutionized for good or for evil.

Sometimes a small and feeble tendency towards sound and natural action, when it is seen to be inconsistent with the ruling beliefs and attitudes of a corrupt society, will lead a person to question their ultimate theoretical presuppositions, and thus to arouse his drugged intellectual faculties until clarity is achieved and his whole life reorganized and re-established on a basis which is true and stable. The ruling tyranny, if it is to endure, must therefore be on its guard against even the slightest manifestations of such rebellious tendencies and ever ready to oppose them both by argument and force. The same principle applies to rational rule, which may be gradually broken down by lack of control or incontinence, in those evanescent, detailed, individual acts of which our life consists. But we have a fatal tendency to overlook and to neglect these fleeting particular facts and acts.

Thus we all know people who sincerely hold the loftiest general moral principles, but who act quite differently in the concrete. A man may have a perfect understanding of justice in the abstract, and even a deep and heartfelt admiration for it in the abstract, without being able to judge it correctly in the concrete. Such a man knows only the *major premise* of the practical syllogism. But without the particular, *minor premise,* no practical conclusion will be obtained. He knows that injustice *in general* should be opposed, but he cannot see that *this particular situation confronting him, with its confused array of concrete accidents, is a case of injustice.* Hence he will not oppose it. This may be because he lacks any power of concrete analysis or because some one of his appetites (which, apart from the influence of reason, never seeks the universal but always what is particular) has become attached to the situation. Hence he will want to regard the pleasantness of the situation rather than its injustice, and will acquiesce rather than oppose.

Having once acted in this way he will have aroused a permanent tendency to disregard injustice in the concrete, which will become more and more pronounced after repeated acts of lethargy, though his passionate adherence to the *general principle* of opposing injustice may be still untouched. Then he may be confronted with a peculiarly flagrant example which even he cannot fail to recognize as a clear injustice, crying to high heaven for correction at whatever cost. He may know that he ought to do something about it, but by this time his passion of greed, let us say, has become too strong. He can no longer control it.

He does the wrong thing, though he knows it to be wrong, no doubt soothing his conscience (moral judgment) by a great array of more or less irrelevant argument. What could he do? What good would it do in general, even though he did try to do something about this situation? Other injustices would arise anyway. What is the use? Why then should he deprive himself of his own satisfaction in other aspects of the situation? And so on.

Finally, if his passion remains unchecked and if it continues to attract an increasing array of supporting images and persuasive arguments, the weight of his disruptive tendency will begin to impede the momentum of his basic aspiration and to wear away the basic moral principles hitherto supporting it. Any slight confusion in the pattern of these principles will be suddenly brought into view; any slight tinge of moral skepticism concerning them will be reawakened and strengthened. How does he know what human nature is anyway? How does he know that there is anything which is absolutely right and absolutely wrong? Who is he to set himself up as an arbiter in such matters? How can anyone do any more than to live his own life, responding as best he can to the confused maze of situations confronting him?

At this point the skill of his educators in cogently presenting the basic facts of life, and his own grasp of these principles, will be brought to the supreme test. If they were not presented to him in a manner which was both sure and convincing and if he never really understood them in their whole, articulate structure, then they will now fall into shattered fragments. He will give them up and will simply decide to follow his interests wherever they lead him, as the best way of life.

At first the trace of his past upbringing will remain to bother him and give him a twinge of remorse now and then at vicious acts, but finally even this slight trace will be overcome by rationalization. He will seek vicious action for its own sake without the slightest qualm and will delight in achieving it effectively with the crown of a vicious pleasure. In the stage of incontinence his higher faculties of intellect and will were still intact. Then at least he knew what he ought to do, and even wanted to do this. But now he no longer knows what is really good, or desires to have anything to do with such figments. His higher faculties are distorted and demoralized. He is a completely bad or self-indulgent man, desiring vice for its own sake and delighting in it.

If such men become preponderant in a given community they will confuse the pattern of education and distort the structure of the law. The children who have the misfortune to be born into such a community will then have little or no opportunity of ever gaining a clear understanding of the nature of human life and its perfection. They will not have to go through any long process of learning vice. They will be taught materialism and mass brutality from the very beginning. The minute they begin to apprehend some stable truth by the exercise of their cognitive faculties, they will be refuted at once by a host of relatives and teachers. The minute they show any tendency to act in a just or friendly way, they will be severely punished and set upon another path. Such a rule of irrational tyranny is the lowest depth to which human life can reach.

In the 19th century, when men believed the great myth of automatic progress, no one thought that such a depth could be reached by modern man. We now know that the myth of progress is nothing but a myth. We now know that modern man has reached such depths and that they may even be reached by us. The only way we can avoid them is to steep ourselves in the great truths of philosophy, especially in those which concern the rational nature of man and the virtues by which alone this nature can be perfected. Then, once having understood them, we must struggle with all our faculties, first of all to love them and the ways of life which they prescribe, and then to realize this way of life so far as we can in the world which we inhabit.

REFERENCES

Recommended Reading

Aristotle, *Nicomachean Ethics,* Book II, chaps. 1–6, and Book III, chaps. 2, 3, and 4.

Suggested Reading

1. For a detailed discussion of the interaction of reason and appetition in deliberation and choice, cf. Aquinas, *Summa Theologica,* Prima Secundae, Qu. 11–17. For an opposed view which recognizes no distinc-

tion between voluntary action and sensory desire, cf. Hume, *Treatise of Human Nature*, Book II, Part III, §§ 1–3.

2. For a fuller discussion of the nature of voluntary habit and the process by which it is acquired and lost, cf. Aquinas, *Summa Theologica*, Prima Secundae, Qu. 49–53. For the theory of conditioning, cf. James, *Psychology*, Briefer Course, New York, Holt, 1905, chap. 10, especially pp. 139 ff.; cf. pp. 352 ff.; and Dewey, *Human Nature and Conduct*, New York, Holt, 1922, pp. 177 ff.

Chapter 4

IRRESPONSIBILITY AND ITS CAUSES

HUMAN beings know that they are responsible for their acts because they know that they are the *causes* [1] of their acts. The skeptic who says that he does not believe in causation can offer no intelligible explanation of responsibility, for when we hold someone responsible for an act we mean that the act was a necessary effect of causes within that man. Unless we did hold ourselves and others responsible in this way our legal system would be a mockery, praise and blame would be impossible, and human life would, indeed, be unlivable. So even the skeptic, when he rises from his armchair and starts to act with other men, cannot escape from the general sense of responsibility which necessarily attaches to every phase of the life of man.

There are two intrinsic causes of human acts: first, an understanding of the end and the means—the general pattern of the act; and second, a motive power, or appetite, which moves our bodies and subordinate faculties in the actual performance of the act. When these two causes are completely present within us, we *will* the act and are wholly responsible for it, whether it is good or evil. When these two causes are not completely present within the agent, then to this degree the so-called agent is not responsible, but some other external agent must be held responsible for the act. At first sight it would seem as though this were a fairly simple matter. Thus no one would hold a lunatic, who has no understanding of what he is doing, responsible for his acts. Also no one would hold a man responsible for what he does under the compulsion of some overwhelming external force. In neither of these cases is the agent, as he is here and now, responsible for his acts.

Causes have contemporaneous effects: they also have aftereffects or results. Our understanding not only grasps isolated fragments or segments of life but also the whole of life. Indeed, we cannot

[1] Cf. ch. 14.

really understand the part without understanding the whole, and we cannot act well at any given moment without fitting this act into a complete life, which is in a sense present at that moment. Men are not only responsible for the necessary effects of what they do but for the normal aftereffects as well. Hence the matter of responsibility is not so simple as it at first seems.

In the case of the lunatic we must inquire as to how the lunacy was acquired. Unless it was due to extrinsic, hereditary causes, it might have been avoided by prudent precautions of the victim. If so, the man may have been partly responsible for getting himself into this state. In the case of the man overwhelmed by external force we must also inquire as to how he came to be involved in such a situation. Unless it was due to wholly extraneous, unpredictable causes, like a cyclone, perhaps, or a tempest at sea, the man himself may have been partly responsible for getting himself involved. If so, he may be justly blamed.

In general we may lay down the principle that a man cannot be held responsible for ignorance and for weakness that are not the normal aftereffects of his own past acts and choices. This much is true. But what sort of ignorance and what sort of weakness is this, and how can they be distinguished from other kinds? Let us now turn to these problems, first that of ignorance and then that of human weakness, or external *violence*. If we can draw any sound conclusions concerning them we may be greatly aided in refining and perfecting our moral judgments.

1. IGNORANCE

The ultimate, final cause of human acts is the good that we understand. Hence, the most serious impediment to full responsibility is ignorance of human nature and its end. Now, it is true that the most evil acts are no doubt performed in a state of *partial* ignorance concerning the true nature of these acts and of their necessary consequences. The greatest of human archcriminals and tyrants might plead, if we could conceive of their being genuinely reformed, that they never would have done what they did if they had only known the real nature of what they were doing. They might say that they did what they did *in* ignorance, and thus claim indulgence for their crimes. Could any such indulgence be justly granted? Was their position like that of the hereditary lunatic? I think we can see that it was not. But why was it not?

If we think about this, we shall see that the answer of Aristotle (*Nic. Eth.* 1113B14–1114B) is correct. It was true that they performed their murders and tortures *in* a state of gross ignorance. They had no real understanding of human nature or of human happiness. But was this ignorance *the cause* of their acts? Were their vicious deeds actually produced by an invincible ignorance? If so, they must be excused. Or was their ignorance rather caused by mad passions of pride, power-lust, and greed, which made them oblivious to the feeble glimmerings of intelligence in them and thus produced a far from invincible ignorance, for which their own uncontrolled appetites were responsible, not any cause outside themselves?

Every normal human being has a faculty of reason which cannot endure in a wholly inactive state. If he fails to exercise it further to discover the basic first principles of good and evil, then he is himself responsible for this, and not any external cause. Ignorance of these things is no excuse, but an indication of culpable neglect and greater guilt. His reason must have told him that he was a man. It must have given him at least a general understanding of the difference between good and evil, and a general indication that good was to be done and evil to be avoided. These first principles are known by *synderesis* [2] to every child. Why then did he not exercise his reason further and obey its clear prescriptions? Why did he pay no attention to these things until they were engulfed in the mists of obscurity and neglect?

He did not care for these things. He had no interest in them. Why did he have no interest? Because he was *more* interested in money, power, and other things. Who was responsible for these tendencies? Surely no one else. He gave birth to these monstrosities out of himself. What other answer can there be? His acts, like all thoroughly vicious acts, were performed *in* ignorance, not *by reason of* ignorance. (Cf. *Nic. Eth.* 1110B 17–27.) Hence such ignorance cannot serve as an excuse. Since the man himself produced it by his own appetites and neglect he is responsible for it and, therefore, he

---

[2] This is the technical name given to that apprehension of moral first principles which underlies moral judgment or conscience.

must bear the guilt. Such ignorance was later called a *concomitant* ignorance, not a *causing* ignorance. It attends the vicious action, but is not in any sense its source. Some overwhelming appetite is the true source. As long as this passion is in control, the man will not care, even if the so-called evil of his ways is pointed out to him. So a man cannot plead ignorance of what he is and what he is doing as an excuse for vicious action. Every man is under a natural obligation to know these things, for nature has presented him with the faculty of knowing them with a minimum of effort.

He is also under a natural obligation to know the *normal* consequences of his acts. Thus a vicious man might admit that he willed the vicious act in a single instance, in this one case, but he certainly did not will to become thoroughly vicious himself. This in a certain sense is no doubt true. The man might not have done the act if he had realized the sort of habitual tendency this act would inaugurate and the ultimate misery to which it would lead. If he had been another sort of man, with a firmer control over his passions, he would not have performed the act. But who was responsible for letting his passions get out of control in the first place? Every man with the slightest grain of rationality knows the general law of nature that a vicious *act* produces a vicious *habit*. He must have had some understanding of this. In spite of this understanding he chose to follow his irrational passion. Therefore he is responsible for the dimly seen consequence which he did not will *for its own sake*. But this does not mean that he did not will it at all.

Take the analogous case of a man who chooses to walk on a hot summer's day. He does not will to sweat *for its own sake*. That is true. But nevertheless he wills to walk, together with its dimly seen normal consequences, including the sweat. Therefore it would be silly for him to say later on that he did not will to sweat and was therefore utterly non-responsible for this, but only for the walking. In the same way it is silly for vicious people to say that they did not will their own viciousness and were therefore utterly non-responsible for this, but only for their vicious acts, which was all that they willed.

Every human being with normal faculties must be held naturally responsible for knowing the basic principles of the law of nature.

But how about the child who is born in a socially diseased community, where these principles have been allowed to sink into confusion or where they have been distorted into warped and garbled patterns by ages of sophistic reflection? How can a weak and helpless child be expected to resist the suggestive power of a disordered, educational environment? Here we must remember that reason is an *immanent* faculty that cannot be influenced by external force. No one can force even the reason of a child to think what it does not see to be so. Even the unaided intellect can arrive at the first principles of rational reflection and can at least question what is opposed to these principles. Even immature persons in schools and colleges are not helpless pieces of clay to be molded at the will of the teachers. They can exercise their own faculties, and if they do not do so, they may be held responsible.

But although external agencies cannot *directly* influence the individual intellect, they can put all sorts of obstacles in its path. The senses and the imagination are subject to external manipulation, and through these channels warped influences may be transmitted to the younger generation, which may greatly impede the exercise of intellect and lead to the development of unnatural desires and appetites. It is, indeed, impossible to hold an individual child completely responsible for the spiritual torpor and moral aberrations in which such a process may result. But does this relieve the child from all responsibility?

We might examine each individual one by one and exonerate *him* of all blame. Must we then conclude that no one else is to blame? This would be fantastic. As individuals we are not only responsible for our individual lives, but also for the general pattern of life in the community of which we are members. We share a *collective responsibility* for the common good, some more and some less, depending upon the responsibility of their positions, but everyone has some responsibility for these things. Thus when the whole community sinks into mass obsessions, the whole community is responsible, not merely those of a single generation, but those throughout all the generations in which the degradation took place. No one escapes this responsibility.

Every individual who refused to protest against it when it might still have been corrected in an incipient stage, is to blame. He is *himself* responsible. Those who acquiesced in these things when firmly established are also responsible. Others have rebelled in such situations, inaugurating corrective movements in accordance with the natural right of revolution. Why did they allow themselves to be deprived of their natural rights? Why were they more afraid of death than of human degradation? They were responsible. All are *collectively responsible* for these things.

If the evil is one which I have brought upon myself by my own laziness and neglect, then I am individually responsible. If the evil is one which has been brought upon me by social neglect and degradation to which I have nevertheless acquiesced, then I am collectively responsible, together with my whole group. There is no evil affecting me for which I am not, therefore, in some sense responsible. Men are responsible for all the moral evils which afflict them. Either individually or socially they have brought them upon themselves.

We must conclude that ignorance of the basic, natural aims of human life is never invincible and excusable. We are all endowed with a rational faculty, and the slightest, serious cultivation of this faculty is capable of telling us these things. It is true that evil men act *in ignorance* of these things and do not at the time of choice clearly see the fearful consequences of their acts in all their naked horror. But they act *in* ignorance, not *by reason of* ignorance. They neither will the evil they commit for its own sake nor do they will its opposite. Hence they are said to act *non-voluntarily* rather than *involuntarily*. Some overwhelming passion of pride or greed takes possession of them with their own assent and leads them to choose their evil act in spite of all the terrible consequences which are at least dimly glimpsed. It is their own failure to pursue reason and rationally to moderate their passions, which has produced this ignorance, not the ignorance which has produced their state of slavery. Until their passions die they will not care about the evils they produce, even when confronted with them. Hence, either individually or collectively, they are responsible, and may be justly blamed.

But now suppose that the ignorance does not concern the *basic* purposes of life, but only some instrumental means by which these purposes are to be achieved. Such ignorance may, indeed, mitigate human guilt. It falls into two distinguishable kinds: (1) that produced by momentary passions to which we are naturally subject and (2) that produced by the accidental complexity of material events. Let us consider them in this order.

It is evident that we are naturally subject to *passions,* or appetitive tendencies, elicited by causes external to ourselves and sensuously apprehended. It is our duty to subject these tendencies to rational control through deliberation and choice. Otherwise we lose our freedom and become the slaves of chance or immoral propagandists and manipulators. But even though we have gained a fairly stable control over these tendencies, extraordinary stimuli of an unac customed sort will often, so to speak, throw us off balance and temporarily blind our practical reason, so that it misjudges the immediate situation before it. Thus in a sudden fit of fear or rage or jealousy inspired by some extraordinary cause, our practical judgment may be blinded, so that we see only the fearfulness, or the injustice or the unfriendliness of the immediate situation, ignoring many of its other aspects and their relation to our major purposes. If our irrational passion is sufficiently strong we may not deliberate at all but simply respond in blind terror or mad rage. We shall consider the moral status of such acts later.

But even though the passion is not strong enough to obliterate deliberation it may blind our deliberation to all but a few abstract aspects of a complex situation, so that we judge it only partially, and not as we would judge it in a cooler moment. Such ignorance may be partially excusable and mitigate our guilt, depending on the situation. Various factors are relevant in deciding the degree of responsibility. First and chiefly, to what extent was the act performed as a result of an *extraordinary, external* stimulus to which we are by nature susceptible, rather than as a result of internal habits? In judging such cases we must probe into the inner motives of the act. The act itself is not enough to condemn the man, for it may have been due to a passional weakness of our nature.

In acts like theft and kidnaping, we ask only whether the act was or was not committed by the agent, for such an act requires premeditation. Hence its very commission is enough to show guilt. But where a sudden storm of passion may have been involved we must ask *how* the act was done. If it was really due to the situation rather than due to the man, his ignorance may be excused by the weakness of nature. In deciding this, the following three factors must be taken into account.

Was *the act* an unusual one *for the agent* in question? If so, he is probably less to blame, for it may be explained rather as due to something outside the man than to a settled tendency within him. Hence we are more lenient with *first* offences. Second, was *the situation* an unusual and extraordinary one for the agent in question? If so, he is probably less to blame, for there was no opportunity for the agent to build up resistance to the temptation. It is for this reason that acts of cowardice are more excusable than acts of intemperance, for there is a greater opportunity to train ourselves to resist the latter rather than the former. Third, was the agent actually sorry for his act after it was committed? If not, then he is certainly more guilty to the degree in which he is not sorry or repentant, for anything really done against the firm purpose of an agent must eventually produce sorrow and remorse as soon as he recovers his faculty of judgment.

If such an examination shows that the individual judgment was partly blinded by sudden passion elicited by a to-him unprecedented situation, so that he performed a for-him non-habitual act for which he afterward showed *real* remorse, then such ignorance may act as a partial excuse. The act may be attributed to human weakness rather than to viciousness. Nevertheless it cannot altogether excuse the man, for our passions can be mastered by reason and will. Hence the breakdown of such control and the giving way to passion shows imperfection and at least incipient vice.

But we must now remember that we not only act for a general end by general means, but as an individual, in an individual situation, clothed with a welter of particular circumstances. Even though our deliberative faculties are clear and unclouded by passion it is possible for us to misjudge these circumstances so as to do something in particular which is against our general will. Of course, if this ignorance of the circumstances was due to carelessness or appetite, then it was carelessness or appetite that caused the will, not ignorance, and the act is worthy of blame. But sometimes, even though all due precautions are taken, we remain ignorant of crucial circumstances in the concrete case before us, which accidentally produce a coincidental result very far from our purpose. Such ignorance actually mitigates guilt, for the ultimate intricacy of the individual situation is opaque to our understanding.

It is impossible to give an exhaustive list of all the accidental characteristics of an individual situation which may have some bearing on a moral act. But Aristotle's list (*Nic. Eth.* 1111A 3–21) contains the most important kinds of moral circumstances which may deflect the course of a moral act. A human agent ought to know the general nature of the end he is aiming at. If he does not know this, he is surely guilty. But knowing this, he may be excusably ignorant of the precise nexus of individual means and end in the individual case before him. Thus a doctor, meaning to cure the particular patient before him and adopting the *universally* necessary right means, may kill him instead. Second, there may be an excusable ignorance of the precise nature of the individual object or person that is being acted upon here and now. Thus a soldier, rightly deciding to kill an enemy, may discover that in this particular case he has killed his father. Third, there are circumstances connected with the individual instruments used in performing the act. Thus a person, having no malicious intent, thinking that the spear is buttoned and perfectly safe, may stab his friend to death. Had he known this circumstance, he would have acted otherwise, and the tragedy would have been averted. Hence this is a *causal* ignorance which may excuse the act unless culpable carelessness was at work. Finally, in the fourth place, there are circumstances connected with the quantity of the individual act. Thus a boxer may have given what in most cases would have been only a harmless blow, but in this case it may have resulted in serious injury.[3]

Other circumstances, such as *where* the act is performed and *when,* may also have a bearing on the individual act. In fact, any coincidence of accidents in an individual situation is a circumstance. Owing to the indeterminacy of matter, it is impossible for the human mind to apprehend accurately or to anticipate all such

[3] The fifth kind listed by Aristotle—the genus or difference of the act itself, i.e., the secret character of the mystery—would seem to be essential to the act, and thus not a circumstance. Hence ignorance of the secrecy of the mystery, or of the essential nature of an individual situation, is certainly less excusable than ignorance of an accidental circumstance. Nevertheless, obscure and disguised situations doubtless arise when even such ignorance is not worthy of blame. For example, doctors have mistaken a living man for a corpse.

chance coincidences.[4] Hence the ignorance of such a coincidence, which influences the outcome of an act, may cause an involuntary act— *by reason of ignorance,* and thus be excusable. However, as Aristotle reminds us, if the act has *really* been involuntary and against the general purpose of the agent, he must show real repentence and remorse. If not, the act is something that he might have performed anyway without the aid of chance.

We have now completed our consideration of ignorance, the primary cause which *may* remove the responsibility of an agent for an act. Now let us turn to external violence, the secondary cause of this sort.

2.   VIOLENCE

Let us begin, as in the case of ignorance, with those cases in which responsibility is not removed, passing on then to those in which it is to some extent removed, and finally to those in which it is altogether removed. Violence is an external, efficient cause which overpowers our will and forces it to act against its purpose.

First, there is a type of response which we easily confuse with violence, but which is not really violence at all. To this type belong all the acts of sensuous appetite we have already considered. Thus we say that the overpowering strength of the invading army *forced* him to flee in terror and that the bitter insults of his enemy *forced* the quarrel upon him. But in reality it was his terror at the invading force that overpowered him and forced him to flee. It was his own rage at the insults that forced the quarrel upon him. But terror and rage are internal tendencies, arising within the man, and not necessarily against his will and purpose. Hence the acts of such tendencies cannot be attributed to violence, which is external and against our will. Our feelings and appetites are ours and we are responsible for them. If they overpower our reason and will we have allowed them to overpower us, and we are responsible, no matter what the provocation may be, for they are a part of our own nature just as much as reason and the higher faculties.

Nevertheless we must recognize that these sensual tendencies are aroused by something external, perceived by the external senses. We are terrified at the hurricane *we see.* We are enraged at the ag-

[4] Cf. ch. 14, §§ 4 and 5 for a discussion of chance and accident.

gressive blow *we feel*. Fear and rage belong to our nature, but they are aroused in the concrete by some cause external to ourselves. Our finite, material nature makes us subject to such external influences. Our reason knows about these and can take account of them. If our response is in accordance with reason and its demands, then our feelings are not subject to censure. In fact it is rational for us to feel terror at what is really terrible and to feel rage and indignation at what is truly unjust. Such feelings constantly aid us in acting virtuously or rationally, and when they occur we are justifiably pleased at them in ourselves and justifiably approve of them in others.[5] But if our response is not in accordance with reason, as often happens, then we are probably worthy of blame.

If our feelings have not been sufficiently disciplined, so that they take things into their own hands and lead us into some uncontrolled act which our judgment does not approve when it is able to function once more, then we must probe further. Two types of response must be distinguished. Was the situation a fairly ordinary one, which should have been adequately dealt with by a moderately disciplined character? If so, the agent was more to blame, and should feel sharper pangs of remorse. Or was the situation an extraordinary one and so difficult as to strain even a highly disciplined character? If so, then more responsibility for the final result must be placed rather in the external cause, and the agent himself must be rightly judged as less responsible and less guilty of the mutual act.

Our most terrible enemies are not sub-human forces, like storms at sea and hurricanes, which lack intelligence, but rather other men, like ourselves, who know about our appetites and can elicit them to suit their purposes. Thus if two men fall into a vicious combat in which both are mastered by uncontrollable rage, both are no doubt guilty. But he who took the first aggressive step and who was, therefore, guilty of the first injustice is more to blame. Indeed, if the other was seeking merely to defend himself he is not guilty at all.

Thus we are led to a three-fold conclusion. Passion acting in accordance with both nature and reason is laudable. Passion acting in accordance with nature, but going beyond reason, is guilty but

[5] Cf. ch. 20, § 2.

excusable, because of the weakness of our nature. Passion which is against reason is immoral and worthy of blame.

To argue that we are not responsible for acts of irrational passion, is to ignore the fact that we are essentially animal as well as rational in nature. We certainly take credit for our feelings and appetites when they are in accordance with reason. How then can we consistently disclaim responsibility for them when they are not? It is the duty of every community, therefore, to establish a system of law and education which will tend to a rational discipline of the passions of its members. It is the duty of every individual to carry out this discipline within himself, restraining his appetites until they are thoroughly tempered, always waiting to hear the results of deliberation and always following these to the last degree.

We cannot evade responsibility for our passions and the acts which they inspire. But there are other acts which are done deliberately and yet which we speak of as being forced upon us. Thus we say that the passengers were *forced* by the storm to cast their possessions overboard or that the conquered people were *forced* to collaborate with their brutal conquerors. Such acts as these are not called forth by internal passions, but are coolly calculated and deliberated. Nevertheless they are done against the will of the agent. Surely, therefore, they are *forced* upon him by overwhelming external force, and he cannot be held responsible for them.

Such a conclusion, however, is not correct. These acts, if not done in blind passion, are deliberately chosen by the agent in the concrete situation confronting him. Hence he *is* responsible for them. How can we explain the seeming inconsistency of these opposed conclusions?

There is some truth in the first contention. The sailors and passengers, it is true, did not choose the storm: this aspect of the situation was simply forced upon them. But there is an element of this sort in all our conduct: no one of us chose to be born nor did we choose the universe in which we live. If the mere presence of such an element as this were enough to remove our responsibility we should not be responsible for anything at all. Every situation confronting us contains an unchosen element of this sort. We are never responsible for the whole situation, but only for our own part in it. Most situations confront us with alternatives which foster our natural tendencies and thus enable us, if we so choose, to survive and to perfect ourselves. Otherwise our race would have vanished long ago.

But some situations confront us only with evil alternatives. The passengers on a storm-threatened ship are forced to choose between two evil alternatives: either to go down with the ship or to cast away their possessions. The conquered are forced to choose either to collaborate and to commit injustice or to risk the anger of the tyrant and the danger of death. But a choice between two evils is still a real choice, and the guidance of reason is even more necessary in such dangerous situations than in more favorable ones. The reasonable choice for the passengers is to cast their goods away, for the loss of them is a *lesser* evil than the loss of their lives. The reasonable choice for the conquered people is a more difficult one.

It is easier for our imagination to conjure up the evils of physical suffering, imprisonment, disease, starvation, and death, than the greater evils of slavery, mental inertia, and becoming accessories to the commission of injustice. Hence, without careful deliberation and rational judgment, we are apt to make the wrong choice. If we do choose to defy the threats of the tyrant and the lesser evil of physical suffering and death, this is our own choice for which we ourselves are responsible. It is true that *in the abstract* no one would choose this *in general,* but no one acts in the abstract. In the concrete situation confronting them, they chose this as the lesser evil and acted in accordance with their choice.

Such acts are therefore called *mixed* acts, since they contain a very strong element of force and constraint together with a deliberate element of free choice. But since we always act in the concrete and never in the abstract, and since this is what we choose to do in the concrete situation confronting us, such acts are rather voluntary than against our will, and are therefore rightly considered as voluntary and freely chosen. When the right choice is made, greater praise should be given, in view of the peculiar difficulty of the situation. When the wrong choice is made, less blame should be given for the same reason. It is, of course, much worse to collaborate with a tyrant when he exercises no threats and uses no force than when he marches in with an army and the Gestapo.

We are responsible for our appetites and feelings. We are responsible for our mixed acts, but to a lesser degree. It remains only to consider those acts of absolute outer constraint for which we are not responsible at all. These acts are much more rare than we commonly think, but of course they do occur. There are situations which confront us with no active alternatives at all but in which we are utterly overwhelmed by external violence. Thus no one would hold anyone responsible for being picked up and cast off the roof of a building. In such situations all control has been taken out of our hands. We cannot act at all except to exercise a rational moderation of our internal passions. For this, of course, we are still responsible.

In conclusion, we must point out that the range of human responsibility extends over a far wider range than is ordinarily supposed. A responsible human act is one whose final and efficient causes are within the agent in the modes of understanding and will. We are responsible for what we do so far as we understand what we are doing and achieve it by our own active power. Hence ignorance and violence are the two causes of irresponsibility.

Since nature has endowed us with a rational faculty capable, with slight effort, of understanding the proper end of man, we are either collectively or individually responsible for ignorance concerning our major general purposes and the *necessary* means which they demand. Ignorance of the basic aims of human life is not only immoral but unnatural. Man, not nature, is responsible for this. Hence if it occurs, we can blame only ourselves. Blindness to the nature of a concrete situation, inspired by passion, may be partly excusable if the passion itself is excusable by the weakness of our nature. Otherwise we are responsible for it, and it is worthy of blame. Ignorance of the chance coincidence in a given situation, which may deflect the course of an act, is excusable if reasonable precautions have been taken and the act is really repented.

As to violence, it is much more restricted in extent than we commonly suppose. Passions and feelings of great intensity do not exercise violence upon us, but rather grow up in us by our own permission. Hence, if they carry us off our course, we have only ourselves, either collectively or individually, to blame. Difficult situations that confront us with no choiceworthy alternatives nevertheless usually confront us with certain alternatives which are less evil than others. Hence they offer us opportunities for *mixed choices* and *mixed activity*. The only cases where our free will is utterly unable to function are those in which we are completely overwhelmed by external powers, though even here we are offered different alternatives of *internal* control between which we may still choose.

All in all, as we have said, the range of human choice and will extends much farther than we commonly suppose. Our reason extends to the farthest reaches of the universe and to its first and ultimate causes. It also penetrates into the deepest resources of our nature. It embraces the whole compass of human life. If we properly discipline our nature by the formation of the virtues, we can take account of all these things and act in such a way as to perfect our nature and to achieve its natural end. What then is such action like? Let us now turn to a consideration of the particular virtues, or habits, which we require in order to perfect our nature and thus to take advantage of that responsibility which we so richly possess.

REFERENCES

Recommended Reading

Aristotle, *Nicomachean Ethics*, Book III, chap. 1.
Aquinas, *Summa Theologica*, Prima Secundae, Qu. 6–7.

Suggested Reading

1. Aristotle, *Nicomachean Ethics*, Book III, chap. 1, 1110B 17–chap. 2; Aquinas, *Summa Theologica*, Prima Secundae, Qu. 6, Art. 8 and Qu. 7.
2. Aristotle, *Nicomachean Ethics*, Book III, chap. 1, 1110B 17; Aquinas, *Summa Theologica*, Prima Secundae, Qu. 6, Art. 1–7.

Chapter 5

INTELLECTUAL VIRTUE
AND MORAL VIRTUE

WE have now considered the general nature of moral virtue and how it is acquired. In the light of this analysis we can distinguish four aspects that must always belong to that responsible activity which primarily perfects our human nature. These distinct but inseparable aspects of all virtue have been traditionally called *the cardinal virtues* since the time of Plato.

1. THE CARDINAL VIRTUES

First, all virtuous action must involve an end and means that are specified by reason. All virtue must therefore be under the guidance of this supreme human faculty. All virtuous action must be *wise*. In the second place, it must actively carry out the commands of reason in the concrete, rendering to all objects what the end (as specified by reason) duly demands according to the law of nature and imposing the order of rational action on every particular phase of our conduct. All virtuous action must be *just*. In the third place, the tendencies to such action must be firmly ingrained in our nature by the arduous process of habit-formation, and therefore capable of withstanding frustrating obstacles and misfortunes. All virtuous action must be *courageous*. Finally, in the fourth place, such action must be in control of the whole of our nature, dominating and harmonizing every subordinate impulse or tendency. All virtuous action must be *temperate* in the sense of tempering or harmonizing the raw impulses to which we are subject.

These four so-called *cardinal virtues* are not really distinct virtues at all, but four distinct aspects of virtue in general, no one of which can be possessed without the rest. The virtuous life as a whole must be rational, freely chosen, and energized by the agent himself, firmly enduring in spite of obstacles through the whole of life and strictly imposed on all subordinate interests or appetites.

All these perfecting tendencies must be achieved to the most extreme degree, for virtue is itself an *extreme,* the most extreme, perfecting activity of which our nature makes us capable. But it is clear that this order has several distinct divisions, each with a distinct object and mode of perfection peculiar to itself. We must now turn to a more detailed study of each of these distinct, major divisions.

First of all, we cannot act virtuously unless the end of life is properly specified by reason. This requires purely theoretical or rational modes of activity, *the intellectual virtues,* to which we shall turn first of all. These virtues enable us purely and simply to understand our nature and the nature of the world in which we live. Unless these purely intellectual virtues are actualized all our activity will be misdirected. But more than the purely intellectual virtues are required for the perfection of our composite, human nature. We are required, not only to understand the general nature of the good, but also to carry it out in the concrete with the whole of our animal nature.

This involves another kind of virtue, moral virtue, which is concerned with: (1) the rational guidance of our sensuous appetites and (2) the rational guidance of our overt, public acts (justice). After we have considered the various *intellectual virtues* [1] we shall turn next to the *moral virtues.* It is of course true that every moral virtue must be just, in the general sense that it is actively carried out by the agent in accordance with reason; courageous, in the general sense of persevering; and temperate, in the general sense of moderating animal appetite as the rational end demands. But we can go further than this. A closer examination will discover that there are different kinds of moral, *passional* virtue, each concerned with the moderation of a distinct kind of appetite to which we are subject (Chapters 6 and 7), and different kinds of moral, *active* virtue or justice, each concerned with the moderation of a distinct kind of public act (Chapter 8).

The task of ethics is never completed with the discovery of glittering generalizations, for action is always concrete and individual, never general. Hence we must subdivide our practical concepts as far as we can, making as close an approximation as possible to the

[1] This chapter, § 2.

concrete, contingent situations in which all human action takes place. This we shall attempt to do in Chapters 6, 7, and 8, following the guidance of Aristotle and the practical science he founded.

2. THE INTELLECTUAL VIRTUES

We have seen that happiness is rational activity perfecting our human nature. But such activity cannot be restricted merely to a brief period of time. It requires *fixed tendencies to rational action,* or virtues. These firmly ingrained tendencies, or habits, are not fully realized. They are nevertheless *incipient* acts, an imperfect activity which constitutes an essential *part* of that full activity in which happiness consists. Hence we are trained for the sake of the virtues as *intermediate* ends. Once possessing these, and then given the requisite external powers and implements, we may achieve the ultimate end. This end, happiness (rational activity), is produced by virtue (rational tendency), and virtue is produced by individual, rational acts, not fully chosen or desired for their own sake, but induced in us by a proper moral education in accordance with the law of nature.

Such a proper moral education and the general structure of community life which this presupposes, rest ultimately upon that general understanding of what is good and that basic aspiration for the good that belongs to man by nature. Right reasoning *(orthos logos)*, therefore, is involved at every stage of the acquisition of virtue. It is, in fact, part of the very definition of virtue—a habitual tendency to act *in accordance with a correctly reasoned principle* or end, by particular means within our power. Moral virtue therefore involves right reasoning or intellectual virtue. Let us now turn to an examination of intellectual virtue and its kinds.

All acts of *will* are directed outwardly toward external objects in the environment. The moral virtues are habits of action. Acts of *understanding,* on the other hand, are inwardly directed, or assimilative.[2] They enable us to absorb something immaterially into ourselves. The intellectual virtues are habits of assimilation. First of all, they must be divided into two major kinds: (1) the theoretical virtues by which the *proper* activity of reason is attained, i.e., the abstract assimilation of the determinate, changeless, and universal

[2] Cf. ch. 19, § 1.

structural phases of the world and (2) the calculative virtues, by which the activity of reason is extended to the task of aiding another faculty, the will, in attaining its unrealized ends, i.e., the assimilation of what is indeterminate, changeable, and related to us as individuals. We shall now take up these two major kinds of virtue one by one.

a. THE THEORETICAL VIRTUES. The most fundamental of these is simple apprehension or insight (*nous*), without which no further acts of understanding are possible. If we do not have a clear conception of what it is we are thinking about, the whole of our thinking must be vague or confused. Hence it is necessary for us to be constantly on guard against vague assumptions or postulates and to define our terms clearly and truly before we begin to reason with them. A false definition will ruin the whole of a supposedly rational discourse, and vitiate its conclusion. Once we have abstracted the universal form from a concrete example with clarity and precision, we possess it from henceforth as a fixed, intellectual habit, but the process of acquiring this first act of apprehension may be long and arduous, involving the comparison of vague, half-formed concepts with many concrete instances.

In clarifying such an imperfect concept we must first apply our faculty to a single instance, paying attention only to what is essential in it, and abstracting from the many irrelevant accidents which attach to the sensible example. Then we must discern the composite structure of this essence, noting what it has in common with other forms and what distinguishes it, clearly apprehending the simple notes of the whole compound. This is the fundamental operation of our understanding (the highest natural faculty of man), which cannot be checked or verified by any higher faculty except only, so far as it is imperfect, by the continuous self-criticism of this faculty. In addition to these basic simple concepts, our reason also is immediately able to apprehend certain connections between them as soon as they are clearly understood—for instance, the law of contradiction, and the relation of whole to part. These basic insights are the units of which the whole reasoning process is composed. This process has two distinct phases: (1) judgment, or the expression of a fact and (2) demonstration, the expression of a reasoned fact.

Judgment is the combination or separation of simple apprehensions. For example, I may simply apprehend the change of what is before me, and then its being caused. Once I have grasped the simple concepts of change and causation to some degree of clarity, I may note that in this case, at least, they belong together. Then I may combine two simple concepts together in the positive judgment: *this change is caused,* or separate two simple concepts from one another in the negative judgment: *this change is not uncaused.* Judgment is the combination or separation of simple apprehensions. Each true judgment expresses a fact, one real existence joined with another. All facts are such existential entities. As such they can all be expressed by judgments.

But some facts are caused or necessary facts. We can only discover these by asking the question: why is *S* joined with *P* in the judgment? Perhaps it is only a material coincidence which merely happens to hold in this case before me. Or perhaps there is a real reason or cause why *S* is joined with *P*. What we call reasoning or demonstration is the search for some middle term connecting *S* and *P* necessarily. If I can discover such a middle term I have no mere fact, but *a reasoned,* demonstrated fact, a scientific fact. Thus if I desire really to *understand* the fact expressed by the judgment, *this change is caused,* I must look for a middle term capable of bringing these two apprehensions together necessarily.

Is there anything about change that *requires* a cause? All discursive reasoning is the seeking for a *cause* of this sort. When I see that change is essentially *composite,* the acquisition by matter of some form, I have found the middle term for a demonstration. The togetherness of form and matter is due neither to the form alone nor the matter alone—hence it requires an external cause. All composite things require a cause. Change is composite. Hence the discovery of this middle term enables me to draw the conclusion, *all changing things require a cause,* which is now no longer a mere fact, but a *reasoned fact* that is explained by reference to the formal and material cause. The efficient cause and the final cause also provide middle terms for demonstrations, which reveal necessary structures in the world around us and thus constitute science in the strict sense of this word.

The discernment of such a middle term, which enables us to see the necessary, causal connection between two entities that cannot be otherwise, is a scientific habit of demonstration. When we cannot discover any such middle term and therefore cannot demonstrate, we must rely exclusively upon sensory evidence. But such evidence, no matter how extensive it may be, can establish only the *fact* of a connection, never the *reasoned fact*. It justifies at best only a probable conclusion, not one that cannot be otherwise, though such conclusions make up the greater part of what we now call natural science in a broader and less strict sense of the word. The conclusion is never more certain than the premises, and premises resting on sensory evidence alone are never *objectively* certain and necessary: they are only *subjectively* necessary.

While I am confronted with a sensory object, I am, of course, certain that I am sensing, but the object is a changing cluster of accidents. Hence, when the sensations cease, I am no longer certain of the status of the object, though I can formulate guesses concerning it. But strict science can be achieved only by apprehending (through insight) some universal, essential cause in the sensory manifold, and using this as a middle term in a necessary demonstration. Such science is therefore defined as the habit of discovering *causal* middle terms and then of using such terms for the demonstration of necessary connections in the external world. Such connections, *which cannot be otherwise,* are not only *subjectively* but also *objectively* certain.

Some men possess the gift of keen and accurate insight. Others possess also the gift of discerning necessary connections—accurate judgment and rigorous reasoning through middle terms. This enables us to understand the supreme intellectual virtue of wisdom (*sophia*), the highest perfection of our rational faculty. If we apprehend the most fundamental and universal structure of things, using the most ultimate causes to demonstrate what is most important about reality as such, then to this degree we possess *wisdom*, the fully consummated understanding of the most universal and, therefore, most important matters. Each of these three virtues rests upon that which precedes it as a foundation which it perfects. Wisdom is impossible without demonstration, and demonstration, or science, is impossible without judgment of the facts. Finally, judgment is impossible without insight into the simple elements of such facts and the first principles. So much, then, for those three major intellectual virtues of insight, scientific demonstration, and wisdom, which concern the determinate, universal, changeless structure of the world.

b. THE CALCULATIVE VIRTUES.   As active agents, we are indeterminate, changeable, and individual, for we cannot act *in general* towards a purely universal object, but only *in particular* towards a particular object. The rational guidance of such action therefore must involve a calculative apprehension of particular objects and their relation to us. Since our action may be either a transitive flowing out into something external or an immanent action on ourselves, such calculative apprehension is divided into two calculative virtues, art or technique, the rational habit of changing something outside us; and prudence or sagacity, the rational habit of changing or energizing ourselves.

The various arts, crafts, and professions consist of trained habits of making useful, rational changes in natural objects outside the agent who is acting. The rational calculation governing such action involves two distinct but inseparable phases: first, a correct apprehension of the end and the *necessary* means to this end; and second, a correct apprehension of the particular, contingent means of achieving this end. The first is taken from theoretical science, the second from experience. The doctor's treatment of a given patient is ultimately governed by understanding of anatomical and physiological structure. But although this structure is objectively the same as what is understood by the purely theoretical sciences of anatomy and physiology, it is not understood in an abstract or theoretical manner, but rather in a concrete or practical manner, as an end to be achieved by operation.

Thus the calculative knowledge of the skillful surgeon is distinct from the knowledge of the theoretical anatomist. *To know what you are aiming at* is an ambiguous phrase, meaning either to know it abstractly as it is in itself or to know it in relation to operation as its end. The former is presupposed by the latter, but the latter is not presupposed by the former. Practice is specified or determined by theory, but it is wider in scope, including something else besides. In addition to a general knowledge of what he is aiming at (in *both* senses), the doctor must *know how* to judge and calculate concerning the particular patient before him and the particular means of achieving the end *here and now*. This calculative habit can be gained only from experience with particular things in acting upon them.

The arts belong primarily to two major divisions: first, *those which acquire something already in existence,* like mining, diving, fishing, and hunting; and second, *those which give existence to something which otherwise would not exist.*[3] This second group is further subdivided into *the arts of making* or manufacture, like shoemaking, which produce something useful in its own right; *the mimetic arts* (the so-called *fine arts*), which bring images into existence; and finally *the various arts of therapy,* like medicine (the therapy of the human body) and education (the therapy of the human soul), which help to bestow a more perfect existence upon things which already exist.[4] We must postpone a more detailed discussion of these arts and their hierarchical order until a later section.[5] At this point, we must be content with the broad assertion that all these calculative habits concern themselves with the external implements and tools of life. No art is an end in itself. Each one serves either a higher art or some vital operation of life itself. The whole hierarchy of the arts, which we indicate by the term *civilization* or *culture,* exists for the sake of something else—the immanent action of living itself.[6]

The rational control of our own individual acts and passions or interests involves a mode of calculation quite distinct from that of art (the rational control of non-human things). We commonly refer to this as *prudence* or *sagacity*. As we have seen,[7] it is essentially *the habit of deliberation*. This habit involves, first of all, a correct apprehension of the end and the necessary means to achieve this end. What we call the *means* of a practical end, correspond to the middle terms of a theoretical demonstration. But since we deliberate only about what it is possible for us in particular to do, the ultimate means will often consist of many different, contingent alternatives. The sagacious man who knows how to plan and de-

[3] Cf. Plato, *Sophist* 219C–D.
[4] Cf. Plato, *Sophist* 219A–B.
[5] Cf. ch. 12, § 3.
[6] Cf. Aristotle, *Nic. Eth.* 1140B 6–7.
[7] Cf. ch. 3, § 1C.

liberate well will know how to select, among these alternatives, not merely *any* means that are capable of leading him to the goal, but the means that are *best* and *right*.

It is most important to be able to distinguish this virtue from mere *cleverness*, the ability to conjure up effective schemes for realizing any end whether good or bad, and from mere opinion, a finished, theoretical judgment which may be true or false, but is neither right nor wrong, because it has no direct connection with actual aspiration. Prudence is the ability to work out effective plans for the realization of *proper* ends, which are never asserted in a finished form as mere opinion, but are always on the way to a further completion in action. Closely associated with moral sagacity is the virtue of *equity*,[8] which enables us quickly to discern and appreciate the particular difficulties and circumstances surrounding the operations of other men, and that of *moral judgment,* which enables us to enter with understanding into the moral problems of others, to give them sound advice, and to judge their acts correctly. Such judgment, whether applied to others or to ourselves, has two divisions: first, a correct grasp of the basic principles of the natural law, sometimes called *synderesis;* and second, a correct judgment of the application of these principles to our own particular circumstances—commonly called *conscience.*

Political prudence, or social sagacity, must be distinguished from individual prudence. It is a habit which enables us, not only to deliberate properly about means to the individual good, but about means to the common good of which this is a part.[9] Social judgment involves two aspects, analogous to *synderesis* and *conscience* in the individual, which are clearly visible in the structure of any soundly organized society. First, there is the legislative function, involving a clear grasp of the fundamental principles of natural law and the universal means leading to it in a particular society; and second, the judicial function, which involves the application of these to particular cases and circumstances.

In our own country the actual, deliberative planning of concrete means to the common good here and now is performed by what we call the executive branch of the government. Social prudence, or

[8] Cf. ch. 8, § 4.
[9] Cf. ch. 9, § 3.

political wisdom, thus involves three distinct factors: legislative apprehension of the natural law and its positive determination where necessary; executive deliberation and choice of the correct means to achieve the common good here and now; and finally judicial application of the law to individual situations and cases. Is political wisdom then supreme among all the virtues? If not, what is the order of the virtues?

c. THE ORDER OF THE VIRTUES. First of all, it is clear that the arts are all subordinate to the moral virtues which enable us to live happily. But here there is a question. Do the moral virtues depend upon prudence or does prudence depend upon the moral virtues? The answer is that each depends upon the other. In each of the natural parts of our life there is a naturally prescribed virtue by which we tend to the natural end of happiness—in our internal pleasures and pains, by temperance; in our arduous endeavors, by courage; in our dealings with possessions, by generosity; in our social relations, by friendliness; and in our public acts on others, by justice. Without such habits of aspiration we cannot deliberate correctly. But without effective deliberation and judgment (prudence) in the particular situation before us we can never actually attain our end, and moral virtue will die. Thus, although we may possess the *natural disposition* to one virtue without that to another, we cannot possess one *actual virtue* without another. These natural virtues re-enforce one another like the buttresses of a cathedral, and without any one, the whole single structure must collapse.

But what is the relation between individual virtue and social virtue? Which is supreme over the other? There is, of course, no question but that in the imperfectly organized societies known to us, conflicts between individual and society occur, in which each claims to have justice on its side. With reference to a defective social arrangement, the good man will be forced into opposition, and in spite of being a bad citizen he will have justice on his side. But with reference to a rational social arrangement, if the individual falls into conflict with this, society will have justice on its side, and will be enjoined by the law of nature to exercise punishment.

In a properly ordered society there can be no legitimate conflict between the individual good and the common good, which includes the individual good as a part. The whole cannot be perfect without the utmost perfection of its parts, and the part cannot be perfect without the utmost perfection of the whole. But since the whole is greater than the part, the law of nature enjoins that in case of danger the individual good is to be sacrificed rather than the common good of the whole, just as the law of nature enjoins us by instinct to raise an arm to ward off a blow against the head which might destroy us entirely.

It is sometimes right that many should give up a lower good in order that some higher good may be achieved by an individual. Thus it is right that many citizens should pay in tax money to support statesmen and public servants. This is indeed for the common good. But with respect to the *same* good, it is always better that it should be commonly possessed than only by some individual or small group. Thus it is better that *all* the citizens should be adequately housed and fed than that only a few should be, that *all* should be protected and educated rather than some, and that *all* should be virtuous rather than only a few. In the light of this natural supremacy of the *common good* we must admit that political prudence is supreme among all the practical virtues. But we have yet to discuss its relation to the theoretical virtues. Since it is clear that wisdom (*sophia*) is supreme among them, this reduces to a consideration of the relation between wisdom and political judgment.[10]

It belongs to political prudence to appreciate the value of theoretical speculation and that understanding of the laws of nature which can be only thus attained. It also belongs to political prudence to provide the leisure and physical opportunities for the exercise of theoretical reason. We can also see, in the case of the individual, that the will has a certain control over all the other faculties, including even the rational faculty, in that it can decide either to think or not to think. But we must not be led by a recognition of this *efficient* supremacy to fall into voluntarism. The will is the efficient, *extrinsic* cause of the exercise of reason, but reason is the *intrinsic,* formal or specifying cause of will.[11]

Hence political prudence, in its very exercise, must be specified by that understanding of the basic structure of things which belongs to

[10] Aristotle, *Nic. Eth.,* Book VI, chs. 12 and 13, 1145A 7–12.
[11] Cf. ch. 20, § 4.

us by nature, as well as by that more precise and determinate understanding which can be given only by the continuous exercise of
reason in the attainment of wisdom. Without wisdom both the individual will and common aspiration to the common good must become confused and fall into disorder, mistaking some apparent good
for the real good and preferring a greater evil to a less. Hence we
must conclude with the ancient saying: *sapientiae est ordinare*—
it is for wisdom ultimately to ordain. But at the same time we must
not forget that such ordaining requires practical sagacity for its
achievement and even for its maintenance.

   Wisdom and sagacity support and sustain each other, but wisdom
sustains sagacity extrinsically and from above, whereas sagacity sustains wisdom as a part which it includes within itself. One can be
wise without being sagacious, at least for a short time, but one cannot be sagacious at all without the guidance of wisdom. Wisdom
specifies political prudence with respect to an end that is really
good and the order of necessary means to this end. Political prudence then establishes such an order of natural and positive law in
the community as a whole, subordinating the cultural order of the
arts to one another and to the common good. The individual intellect, properly nurtured and trained in virtuous habits, will then be
able to specify the individual end by wisdom and to strengthen
natural inclination to this end by the acquisition and establishment
of moral virtue. By effective deliberation the individual will be able
to moderate his passions and actions by a mean, in accordance with
a right reason which operates freely within himself, and thus to
achieve happiness. Such is the order of the virtues, in which each
acts to sustain and strengthen the others by performing its own
proper function.

   We must now turn to the *moral* virtues, those habits of choice by
which our *appetites* are brought to their proper perfection. The
human appetites are divided into two major kinds: the sensory and
the rational (will).[12] Postponing our discussion of the virtue of rational appetite (justice) to Chapter 8, we shall now consider the
virtues of sensory appetition, or passion (*pathos*), as it has been
called. First of all, we must review the general nature of passion
(§ 3a), how the passions are classified (§ 3b), and how they are

------

[12] Cf. ch. 20.

moderated by rational choice, or virtue (§ 3c). Then we shall examine in detail the distinct virtues which moderate them (Chapters 6 and 7).

3. THE NATURE OF PASSIONAL VIRTUE

a. WHAT ARE THE PASSIONS? At first glance we are apt to oppose the active and the passive in a rigidly exclusive manner, as though any human change must be either completely active or completely passive. This has led to important misconceptions of the human interests or sensory appetites. Influenced by the evident fact that these appetites involve physiological changes in certain organs and that external, physical things are in some sense the cause of these disturbances, some have held that they are purely passive changes necessarily produced in the organism, as the physical impression is necessarily produced in the wax by external pressure. But this fails to explain two further sets of facts. First, why is it that certain individuals are not susceptible to certain stimuli which call forth marked responses in others? Second, why is it that so many of our appetitive responses concern objects that are not physically present? Influenced by *these* facts, others have held that the appetites are purely subjective activities, arising from within the organism, and not passive at all.

This should enable us to see that neither of these extreme views is correct. The passions or appetites are neither *purely* passive nor *purely* active. They are *in part* passive, *in part* active, but rather passive than active. First of all, our nature makes us susceptible to certain external influences, so that we are attracted by agreeable food, for example, and repelled by *noxious* heat. This action of a particular, external object on a passive faculty calls forth the appetite, not anything intrinsic to us. Hence such an appetite is passive rather than active, and is properly called a passion or *pathos*. In the case of man and the other animals, however, this action of the external object is not merely the production of a physical change, but the *noetically mediated* production of a psycho-physical change.[13] Animal appetite, even in man, is no mere reflex to a physical stimulus. We cannot desire what we do not sense or imagine. Without such cognitive mediation the object cannot call forth or elicit sen-

[13] Cf. ch. 20, § 1.

sory appetite. In this subordinate sense our appetites are active.

When repeated experiences have established a firm image in the imagination, this alone may call forth a long train of seeking or avoiding responses in the complete, physical absence of the object itself. This is why so many have been led to suppose that sensory interest is a purely *subjective,* or active tendency within the organism alone. But we must not forget that such an image-guided tendency could never have arisen in the first place without the active influence of particular objects on sense, for all images are derived from particular sensations impressed by such objects. So we must conclude that the structure of desire is complex, including both active and passive factors, but rather passive than active. With this in mind we may define passion, or interest, as the psycho-physical change of an appetitive capacity, which is elicited by the sensing or imagining of what seems naturally perfective of this capacity.

b. HOW THE PASSIONS ARE CLASSIFIED. The structure of sensory appetite involves both a mode of active response in the organism and the action of some object on our seeking faculty through the mediation of sensory apprehension. Hence these appetites may be classified both subjectively according to the mode of response elicited in the organism, and objectively according to the eliciting object, and the way in which it perfects our nature. Let us begin with the former and ask ourselves what are the different ways in which we may respond to particular sensory objects.

(1) *The Subjective Classification.* When regarded subjectively in this way the passions fall into two main types: the concupiscent and the irascible, depending upon whether their objects can be easily achieved or only with effort and difficulty.[14] This distinction, which goes back to Plato, can be discerned even in animals. It is true that the mother bear, defending her cubs against attack, has a positive appetite to preserve them. But it is not true that she has a positive appetite for bloody struggle and possible death. Hence irascible striving and struggling involve an additional element and are rightly distinguished from mere appetite. These two genera are subdivided into eleven major types of passion.

Love for agreeable objects and hate for disagreeable objects are the fundamental passions. Each of these takes on two distinct forms,

[14] Cf. ch. 20, §§ 1 and 2.

depending on whether its object is present or absent. Thus love becomes joy or desire, and hate becomes grief or aversion. These are the six forms of sensory appetite.

If the object cannot be achieved without arduous struggling, it is both loved as a good and hated as something arduous. Hence each of the five irascible passions involves a contrariety of hope and despair. This subjective contrariety endures as long as the struggle lasts. It culminates either in defeat and the passion of grief or in victory and the passion of joy. When the object to be overcome is absent but imminently threatening, the irascible passion becomes a mixture of fear and daring. When this object is actually present, it becomes anger and indignation. These are the five forms of irascible appetite.

The following points are worthy of note. Love and hate are the basic passions which underlie all the rest, as the natural tending of our nature towards sensory objects which agree with it (love) and away from objects which disagree with it (hate). When the object is absent it must be apprehended by the imagination; when it is present, by sense. Since the mode of apprehension is essential to the passion, this difference in apprehension determines two different types: *desire* for an absent object and joy or delight in a present one. In this connection it is important to recognize that love does not cease with the attainment of the object, as we so often suppose, but reaches its climax and fulfillment when it is, not least but most fully, actual, in possession of its object.

We must also notice that in the case of struggling there are contrary passions concerning one and the same object (hope and despair, daring and fear), which are not present in the case of the appetites (desire and aversion). This is because of a further complexity in the structure of the former. An *arduous* good is both loved *qua* good and hated *qua* arduous. It therefore always elicits both tendencies together and becomes determined as hope or despair, daring or fear, in so far as the one or the other finally preponderates. Indignation has no contrary passion, because the presence of any good, whatever it may be, is not arduous, and because the failure to struggle against a present evil is merely to acquiesce in it, and not to strive, i.e., the concupiscent passion of grief or sorrow.

Any particular object apprehended by the senses which strikes our estimative faculty as agreeable or disagreeable will call forth love or hate, desire or aversion, joy or sorrow, hope or despair, daring or fear, or indignation, in various degrees and combinations. These subjective modes of appetite are constantly arising and subsiding within us, and we are easily made aware of them. Now we must turn to the *objects* of these passions in order to see the major divisions into which they fall. These are less easy to focus.

(2) *The Objective Classification.* First of all, we must ask ourselves what kind of object in general calls forth our sensory appetite. The answer is any good thing that is perfective of our nature and that is capable of being sensed. Things of this sort fall into three major groups: (1) our own subjective perfections, so far as they can be sensed by pleasure, (2) non-human things external to ourselves, so far as they can be sensed, and finally (3) other human beings external to ourselves, so far as they can be sensed. If we examine this threefold list more closely we can see that it is exhaustive, for there are no other natural objects besides these that we can strive for. Whatever we sense falls into one of these three divisions. Therefore whatever excites our appetite must be either some pleasant, subjective state of our own; some non-human, external thing; or some external human being or collection of men. Let us now examine these three groups one by one in order to grasp their major subdivisions.

1. We cannot sense the most important parts of ourselves, the rational faculties of intellect and will, or any of the immaterial things which perfect them, except by accident or in so far as we can sense certain other things with which they are materially associated. Indeed, we cannot sense the essential nature of any material thing which perfects us or the essential nature of our own perfection. All we can sense is some particular material object and (by the common sense) the particular pleasure which it yields. Good can become apparent to sense only as pleasure. Hence we have an inveterate natural appetite to maintain our own pleasures and to attain all those particular objects which have given us pleasure in the past. On the other hand, we have an equally powerful natural appetite to avoid pain and all those particular objects which have given us pain in the past. Our own felt pleasures and pains, there-

fore, constitute the objects of two distinct modes of internal appetite, which we shall examine in Chapter 6.

2. We cannot sense the essential nature of external, non-human things as such. We cannot sense honor, for example, *qua* honor or food *qua* food. But we can sense particular men who are honoring us, and particular edible objects. Therefore we desire such external sensible things, for we have a natural need for them. We cannot exist without the approval and respect of other men and without external possessions. Hence our appetites for external, non-human things fall into two subdivisions: first, those elicited by honor and human approval; second, those elicited by material, subhuman possessions.[15]

3. We cannot sense the essential nature of man as such, but we *can* sense the particular individuals around us with whom we exist in the world, and certain special phases of their existence, which call forth certain appetites. We tend to feel pleased when they are pleased, and pained when they are pained. We sense their interference with our own activity and desire to eliminate this. On the basis of these feelings we estimate their utility to us and strive to please them. We sense their demand for communication and for items of interest which will please them. So we develop an attempt to communicate, and to communicate in a way which will be well received. Five types of social appetite are elicited by this general type of object, which we shall examine in greater detail later on in Chapter 7, § 3.

Our human nature necessarily subjects us to the influence of these nine subdivisions of the three primary kinds of object which elicit sensory appetite—our own feelings of pleasure and pain, external things, and other men and their behavior towards us.[16] These appetites cannot be eliminated without at the same time eliminating our human nature, for they belong to us essentially.

On the other hand, without rational guidance (moral virtue), they are brought forth in a random and arbitrary manner, owing either to mere accident or to the external manipulation of unscrupulous lords and masters. This rational control, as we have seen, can be given neither by a remote, theoretical reason that

[15] We shall consider these further in ch. 7, §§ 1 and 2.
[16] Cf. Aristotle, *Nic. Eth.*, Book II, ch. 7.

dwells in isolation nor by a slavish reason that merely devises means for the satisfaction of the passions, but leaves the passions them- selves untouched. It can be given only by a *practical reason* which joins itself by deliberation to a passional habit, properly qualifying its end, choosing appropriate means, guiding it at every step through the concrete nexus of action, and thus establishing it as an essen- tially qualified habit, or virtue, in a rational or natural system of life.

Before we examine these virtues one by one, we must consider the general nature of this rational guidance of appetite—the classical doctrine of *the mean.*

c. PASSIONAL VIRTUE AS A MEAN. As we have seen, the passions include a passive as well as an active element. Since our very nature makes us susceptible to such influence, we can never completely eliminate this passive factor. But the process of rationalizing the passions means activating them and reducing their passivity or irre- sponsibility so far as possible. This can be done only by properly specifying their end and developing a strong habitual tendency of aiming at this end, the living of a complete life in accordance with human nature. This involves much more than the realization of passional tendencies (*purely* voluntary action, for example, which arises from ourselves alone) and the exercise of theoretical reason, which is only impeded by the influence of external stimuli.

This *inclusive* end cannot be attained without toning down or moderating the passions. On the one hand, if our passional appetites receive no satisfaction at all, human life becomes impossible. On the other hand, if some *one* appetite, or even all the passions taken together, are excessively pursued, the more important, *active* phases of human life are frustrated, and the end remains equally beyond our grasp. The attainment of this *integral,* natural end of man necessarily demands a *rational moderation of passion,* an attainment of the golden mean.

We must not mistakenly think of the mean, however, as a com- promise between end and passion in which each is toned down to something less than its perfection requires. This is a complete mis- understanding. The end of man is the most extreme, intense, and inclusive activity of which we are capable. It is by virtue that each thing achieves that highest degree of perfection of which it is capable. So the virtuous life as a whole, from the standpoint of the man who is acting virtuously, lies at an extreme. It is the most intensely lived and richest life. Such a life (as a whole) demands that each of its subordinate parts, as the passional part, must be toned down and moderated to fit in with the whole by the rational principle of the mean. Thus, *speaking formally*, or abstractly, passional virtue is *in itself* a mean, avoiding both excess and defect. But *speaking concretely*, from the standpoint of the virtuous man, this mean is a constitutive part of a whole life which achieves the maximum extreme of activity. Let us now consider this mean as it is expressed in each of the particular, passional virtues (Chapters 7 and 8).

REFERENCES

Recommended Reading

Plato, *Republic,* Book IV, 427C–434D, and 441C–445B.

Aquinas, *Summa Theologica,* Prima Secundae, Qu. 61.

Aristotle, *Nicomachean Ethics,* Book I, chap. 13; Book II, chaps. 5–9; and Book VI.

Suggested Reading

1. Plato, *Republic,* Book IV, 427C–434D, and 441C–445B; Aquinas, *Summa Theologica,* Prima Secundae, Qu. 61. Very little is to be found in recent ethical literature on the distinction between the intellectual and the moral virtues, or on any of the virtues. Cf. Perry, R. B., *The Moral Economy,* New York, Scribners, 1909, pp. 73 ff.

2. Aristotle, *Nicomachean Ethics,* Book VI; Aquinas, *Summa Theologica,* Prima Secundae, Qu. 57–8.

3. Aristotle, *Nicomachean Ethics,* Book II, chaps. 5–9; Aquinas, *Summa Theologica,* Prima Secundae, Qu. 22–5, 59–60, cf. Spinoza, *Ethic,* Part III.

Chapter 6

THE RATIONAL GUIDANCE OF IN-
TERNAL APPETITE (COURAGE
AND TEMPERANCE)

HAVING now discussed the general nature of sensory appetite, or passion, and the natural need for its moderation, we must now consider the different passional virtues one by one, in as detailed a manner as possible. The aim of moral philosophy is to clarify the nature of happiness and to strengthen the natural urge of all men to attain it. Happiness is made up of virtuous action; hence the task of presenting a concrete description of the virtues lies at the very heart of ethical theory. It has been strangely neglected or suppressed in modern times, but its central importance is clearly evident in the great moral classics of our culture.

Most of the early and middle dialogues of Plato are concerned primarily with the virtues. The central theme of the *Laches*, for example, is courage, and that of the *Charmides* is temperance. Four whole books of Aristotle's *Nicomachean Ethics* (III, IV, V, and VI) are given over to a detailed account of the virtues. These classical descriptions are filled with many incidental features which now strike us as archaic and irrelevant to modern life. For this reason many modern critics have dismissed them as outmoded expressions of a dead culture, ignoring the core of essential truth which is embodied within them. What we shall try to do is to recapture this essential core of truth, freeing it from antiquarian detail, and substituting illustrative matter more familiar to modern experience.

As we have seen (Chapter 5, § 3b) there are three major kinds of passion: (1) that concerned with our internal states, (2) that concerned with external, non-human things, and (3) that concerned with external, human things. We shall take up the virtues which guide these passions in this order, beginning with (1). We sense our subjective perfections by pleasure, and our subjective frustrations by pain. These apprehensions elicit two natural appetites which are shared by all men. The first is the love of pleasure and all that seems likely to give us pleasure. The second is the hatred of pain and all that seems likely to give us pain.

Owing to the imperfections of sensory apprehension,[1] these passions, if left without rational guidance in their raw state, are bound to lead us into an unnatural subjectivism. All that is sensed as pleasant and good is not *really* good, and all that is sensed as painful and evil is not *really* evil. Hence these appetites naturally require rational guidance. The rational guidance of the former is provided by the virtue of temperance, that of the latter, by the virtue of courage. Since the task of courage is more difficult than that of temperance we shall begin with the former.

1. COURAGE

Every human individual experiences certain things which obstruct and frustrate his activity. When similar objects loom on the horizon his irascible appetite responds with fear or audacity or a mixture of the two, leading ultimately either to indignation and combat or to despair and retreat. Courage is the rational moderation of such irascible appetites. It is a habit of choice, enabling us to guide our passions in such a way as to hope and to struggle for what is truly hopeful, and to fear what is truly fearful. Such a habit must be concerned with a distinctive, external object as well as a distinctive, internal response. Hence we shall divide our discussion into three parts: (a) the external object or matter of courage, (b) the internal response, and (c) the general nature of courage.

a. THE MATTER OF COURAGE. As we have already seen (Chapter 5, § 1), there is a *general* sense of courage in which it belongs to the definition of virtue and hence to all the particular virtues. This is the sense in which every virtue is always a *permanent* tendency to act—a habit which must *maintain* itself against opposing obstacles. Any such habit will involve a fear of such obstacles and a tenacious clinging to its own mode of action in spite of them. Thus in spite of his fear of social pressure the socially minded man will cling to his deliberate course of controlled sympathy, not sympathizing with anyone in any respect, but with the right person, in

[1] Cf. chs. 18, § 5 and 20, § 1.

the right respect, to the right degree. In spite of his fear of poverty the generous man will continue in his generous course. Such unwavering fidelity to its rational ends is common to all virtue and is similar to that specific mode of fidelity which distinguishes the particular virtue of courage.

In addition to all those objects, which are fearful in that they are capable of leading us from the path of reason, there are *certain* objects which are especially fearful to us as men because they threaten us with disease and death. Courage is concerned with such truly terrible objects in so far as they are marked by two characteristics. In the first place, they must be truly dangerous and capable of overwhelming us with destruction. No one would think of courage in connection with a minor peril such as that of a cold in the head. The peril to be faced must be truly terrible, and death is for us the most terrible of things. Courage is always required to face it, as all men must always face it, throughout the whole of their lives. Without courage we cannot under any circumstances die a good death. But the circumstances also make a difference. This is the second characteristic of the object of courage. So far as death simply comes upon us in the inevitable course of events, our courage is less. But so far as we have to some extent brought the danger upon ourselves in pursuing a truly natural end, our courage is greater in facing it well.

A man may show courage in bravely facing a hurricane or an accident at sea or the progress of a slow disease which has simply fallen upon him. But the doctor who *voluntarily* risks death by submitting to a disease inoculation, or by practising his art in the midst of an epidemic, may show even greater courage. This is the second mark. The matter of courage, therefore, as a specific virtue, consists of situations in which we are faced with a definite risk of destruction, and especially in those situations (like non-aggressive warfare) where we ourselves have been partly responsible for the development of the situation in freely pursuing a legitimate and natural end.

b. THE ACTIVITY OF COURAGE. When such a dangerous situation looms upon the horizon we cannot respond to it merely by a sensuous response of desire or aversion. In the first place, no one simply desires such an object. But in the second place, since its power extends beyond our capacities, we cannot simply avoid it. It therefore calls for a complex response from our estimative, irascible nature. So far as we are threatened with the danger of death, it calls forth a response of fear and terror. But so far as we instinctively seek for survival, it calls forth also a response of daring and opposition, which is governed by the hope of somehow overcoming the threat. We *hope* for a future good, which may be beyond our power to achieve, and which we therefore fear to lose. We *fear* for a future evil, which may be beyond our power to avoid, but which we hope to overcome if there be any grounds for hope, and we also hope for these. Thus hope and fear are interdependent. Even the most fearless hope is a conquest over fear, and even the most hopeless despair is a conquest over hope.

Courage is the habit which enables us to achieve the rational mean in this composite response, avoiding an excess of fear as well as an excess of daring. It is a most serious mistake to think of the courageous man as one lacking in fear. As a matter of fact, he is only a man, and therefore necessarily fearful of the perils of death. But, having a clear conception of the end of man and the greatness of the human soul,[2] he is even more fearful of tawdry and vulgar action. Thus in a sense, he is even more fearful than the cowardly man—but he fears those dangerous objects as they are truly fearful, in the proper order and in the proper degree. Similarly, he does not dare nor shrink from everything dangerous, but finds the rational mean. If there is no rational ground for hope in a dangerous course of action or if such a course is not demanded to sustain the greatness of the human soul, he will not dare it. But if there is ground for the hope that such a course may succeed in overcoming the opposing obstacles, and if it is demanded to sustain the greatness of the human soul, he will boldly risk it and patiently persist in it to the end.

The courageous act thus consists in two parts: first, a certain daring and boldness of action which makes a man *ready* to undergo dangers; and second, a certain ability to endure the danger once it is risked. The first part is summarily expressed by the ancient concept of *magnanimity*, or greatness of soul, as well as the modern concept of *personal dignity*, or self-respect. This is an essential

[2] Cf. ch. 7, § 2.

part of courage, for it alone enables us to fear external perils in the proper perspective, fearing injury to the soul and its habits *more than* any injury to external possessions or to the body. Thus it seeks greatness of the soul itself rather than external possessions, in accordance with the real nature of things. The second part requires two qualities of the irascible passion, once it is properly aroused by magnanimity. The first is a quality which we sometimes call *strength of character* but which the ancients called *patience (patientia)*. This prevents the soul from being broken by the anticipation of coming dangers, so as to give up its purpose. The second is the related quality of *perseverance,* which enables us to follow through any great and well considered purpose to the very bitter end, come what may.

The most important thing to see about the nature of courage is its essential dependence upon hope. Unless we are filled with well-founded hopes for our greatest purposes, we will not dare to risk courageous action nor will we hold on to the bitter end. The basic battle between courage and cowardice is being fought out constantly in the imagination and intellect between two modes of understanding: one, which gives us ground for hoping in great purposes; and another, to which we are all too prone, which gives ground for hope only in the satisfaction of minor appetites, and leads us to despair. If the imagination and the intellect can win this battle and produce real conviction in a point of view that calls attention to the real greatness of the human soul and gives us ground for hoping that its great purposes may be achieved, then we may fear and risk the right things in the right order and may be truly courageous, holding to the right mean in both fears and risks. This mean is opposed by two extremes: that in which we fear too little and risk too much, and that in which we fear too much and risk too little.

The first of these is the lesser danger. There may be some who are congenitally deficient in fear, but such insensitive people are very rare. Also this lack of fear is not necessarily attended by any excess of daring or, indeed, by any daring at all. One may lack fear of pettiness and tawdriness of soul, and will then see no point in risking anything at all for anything. Such wormlike personalities are cut off from all possibility of courageous action. On the other hand, there are those who seem to be rash and foolhardy, and therefore seem to be characterized by a tendency to excessive daring. But perhaps this is a far rarer phenomenon than we suppose. Those to whom we refer in this way are usually excessively daring only in minor matters, rather than in those requiring years of devotion to soul-enriching ends. Their daring, even when it concerns such ends, is apt to arise more from passion than from deliberation. Hence it wears off quickly as the passion dies.

The patience and perseverance which attend true courage, on the other hand, are always cool and deliberate. It must be admitted, however, that men sometimes conceive of vast purposes, far transcending their capacities, without adequate fear of their own weaknesses and limitations. In this way they miss the mean in fear and daring, and fail to arrive at their end. But unless the end to which they devote themselves is wholly beyond our nature, and therefore fantastic, if they show true patience and perseverance, they will achieve something worth while and their efforts will not be wasted. This extreme is very rarely actualized, and even when present, it is not nearly so dangerous as the other.

One who fears too many things too much is sure to be deficient in requisite daring. He is the truly cowardly man. In the first place, his imagination and intellect are unable to justify any view of the world and of man which finds any place for the greatness of the human soul in the natural order of things. Thinking of himself and imagining himself to be only an animal or a bundle of animal appetites, any *great* purpose requiring sacrificial discipline and devotion will strike him as a fearsome task far beyond his limited capacities. He will never question established habits or customs. Who is he to do such a thing as this! He will never question the thought of his superiors or even the prevailing opinions of those about him. He is too humble (i.e., wormlike) in his views of himself.

Having cut himself off from all the higher, stable powers in the universe, which he dismisses as primitive superstitions, he will be left to confront the shifting flux of material objects and his own approaching material end. This will fill him with a further array of fears and terrors, for his appetites feed only on such material things, which are threatened by a thousand dangers. He can escape from them only by not thinking at all or as little as possible. This is his final fear—the fear of philosophy as an endless morass of insoluble problems far beyond his feeble power.

Fearful of taking any intellectual stand, he is even afraid of exercising his mind. Fearful of making any choices, he is even afraid of taking over the responsibility for his own life, eagerly sloughing this off on any tyrant or dictator who will make decisions for him, together with alluring promises of an endless satisfaction of his animal appetites. Such is the cowardly man. We are all too familiar with him and his breed today, and with the disaster that follows in his train.

C. THE GENERAL NATURE OF COURAGE.   We must remember that courage is a virtue, or rational habit of choice. As such, to be truly actual, the act of courage must be *chosen for its own sake* in situations that are truly threatening, and *from rational deliberation* rather than from mere passion. Bearing these essential phases of the courageous act in mind, we shall be able to detect the subtle respects in which many acts, seemingly courageous, really depart from genuine virtue. In the case of five types of act, each departing more and more widely from true courage in the order of his presentation, Aristotle points out that it is peculiarly important to make this distinction.[3]

First of all, there is a whole class of acts which approach true courage very closely, but depart from it in that the motive of action is not love of courageous action *for its own sake*. For example, a courageous act may be performed from a love of self-respect and social honor rather than from any love of courage for its own sake. Since self-respect and honor follow upon courage and since the seeking of them is certainly not vicious, such acts are very close to true courage. Nevertheless they are distinct from it and should be classified rather as zealous or ambitious.

If the motive is that of escaping dishonor and the pangs of a guilty conscience, the act is somewhat further removed from true courage, for the avoidance of vice is not true virtue, but only a necessary accident of it. True virtue is always more than the mere escaping from its opposite. Nevertheless very courageous acts can be performed from such a motive. They are similar to the courageous acts performed by desperate men, as we say, *with their backs to the*

[3] *Nic. Eth.,* Book III, ch. 8.

wall, but the latter are even less courageously performed, since true courage contains a minimum of necessity and is not *forced* upon us. It must rather be caused by an accurate understanding of the risk and a free choice to embrace it for the sake of virtue and the dignity of man.

In the second place, it is very easy to confuse certain acts performed with great technical knowledge, or "knowing how," with genuine courage. Thus well-trained and experienced soldiers often *seem* to perform acts of great daring. Such acts *would* be genuinely courageous if performed by untrained and inexperienced men, but in these veterans it may be rather the result of training than of courage. In virtue of their greater skill, what would be a great danger to an unskilled person is no danger at all. But courage is not the same as skillful action. It is daring in the face of what is really dangerous. Hence trained soldiers, when the situation gets out of their control, often run away before citizen soldiers who may be less skillful but braver in their readiness to face the actual danger of death.

Third, we must distinguish true courage from acts performed in fits of wrath and fury *without deliberation and choice.* Such acts are not freely performed under the immanent regulation of reason; hence they are not virtuously performed. Nevertheless acts performed in this way may be genuinely virtuous and they may be performed in a way which is close to virtue itself, for anger is a part (though not the whole) of a courageous act. Righteous indignation certainly plays an essential role in resisting evil men, our most terrible natural enemies. Of all the passions, we can say that wrath is most akin to true virtue. What is needed to transform it into a true virtue, is a preceding understanding of the nature of the evil against which it is directed, a deliberate choice of combative action, and a rational regulation of the act, keeping it within bounds and preventing it from overstepping its end.

Fourth, we come to acts based upon misunderstanding, and farthest from true courage. Thus a people, having conquered many times before, may fall into a blind overconfidence, trusting an illusory strength, without any accurate self-analysis in relation to the danger now confronting it. This optimistic confidence may result in acts of great daring as long as the self-confidence lasts. But since this irascible passion of confidence is based on soothing images rather than on true insight, it will crumble as soon as the facts become apparent. These men are like drunkards: they stand fast as long as their liquor lasts, but when aroused from their delusions they flee. Such courageous acts, while they last, are based on an ungrounded hope in apparent strength.

Finally, in the fifth place, there is that most serious ignorance which underestimates the danger itself, and thus produces the least enduring, and therefore least courageous, approximations to true courage. Those whose courage is founded in false hope and over-confidence in themselves have at least *something* to withstand the peril in themselves, namely, their false hope. They will therefore stand as long as this drug lasts. But those who misapprehend the danger itself have nothing at all in themselves to enable them to stand. Their "courage" is based wholly on a misapprehension of the *object;* hence they run immediately, as soon as the truth is revealed, like the Argives fighting the Spartans, disguised in Sicyonian shields.

As is true of all virtue, the most essential phase of courage is knowledge. First of all, the courageous man must have an accurate insight into the hierarchy of goods. He must know that the human body is better than external possessions, that the human soul is more valuable than the human body, that the perfection of the soul is the most valuable of individual possessions, and finally that the common good is better than the perfection of a single soul. Then he must have an accurate understanding of the various dangers which threaten these goods and must be able to judge them as they appear individually in the concrete flux of circumstance.

When confronted by such dangers he must be ready to choose deliberately to stand up against them and to struggle with them in accordance with his knowledge. This means sacrificing external possessions to bodily well-being, this to the well-being of his soul, and finally yielding his individual life to the common good, if this be necessary. His understanding of the greatness of the human soul he bears and the responsibility this entails, must lead him willingly to choose such mortal combat when there is no other possible alternative save that of a cringing appeasement which is inconsistent with the dignity of man.

He will thus risk pain and agony in the future, patiently endure them in the present, and willingly persist in them to the bitter end. To endure pain in this way is harder than to refrain from pleasure. So courage is a higher virtue than temperance, though both are hard and onerous. We speak of the end as "bitter," but this is only a way of speech. It is not the end that is bitter, but the way leading up to the end. At the end itself there is joy—the joy of saving a greater good. In dying for a just cause the soldier knows that if victory is won, a greater good (the common good) has been saved at the cost of a good, which, though great, is a lesser good. If victory is not won, he still knows that in struggling courageously against evil, a greater good (the greatness of the human soul) has still been preserved at the cost of a good, which, though great, is a lesser good.

An understanding of the peculiar nature of the human soul as possessing the rational faculties, and therefore as the highest being in nature, lies at the very core of all true courage. It is difficult to see how a materialist or a sensationalist can find any *consistent* justification for courageous action, since such a philosophy must think of physical death as the greatest of all evils. Such men no doubt may perform courageous acts, but when they do, these acts contradict their animalistic philosophy. Their deeds speak better than their words.

2. Temperance

As we have already seen, there is a general sense of temperance in which it belongs to the very definition of virtue, and hence to every special virtue. Taken in this universal, Platonic sense, temperance is the subordination of the naturally lower, sensitive phases of our nature to the naturally higher, rational phases. Virtue is precisely the fitting of all our acts and impulses into the order prescribed by nature, and clearly apprehended only by our practical reason. Thus if our appetites have fallen completely under the control of external chance or tyrannical manipulation, they will not allow us time or energy to think at all. Even though reason clearly apprehends the proper end and elicits a voluntary aspiration towards it, the imagination and sensitive appetites must be ready to submit to this aspiration here and now or the will here and now will be moved rather by passion and swept into an incontinent pursuit of the lesser and apparent good.

Material goods can always be sensed and imagined. Hence every virtuous act aiming at some universal good, in the concrete, must be associated with a host of sensuous inclinations and aversions. Unless these are habitually ready to be subordinated to the will, no virtuous act can ever be performed in the concrete. Temperance, as the general willingness of sense to be subordinated to reason, is an essential phase of all virtue.

But there is another more restricted sense in which we speak of temperance as a *special* virtue and of intemperance as a *special* vice. Let us now attempt to analyze the structure of this virtue, considering: (a) its matter, (b) its immanent act, and (c) its general nature, and relation to the other virtues.

a. THE MATTER OF TEMPERANCE. Temperance is a habit which holds our appetite in a mean state with respect to *certain* pleasures. It keeps us from falling into anguish when deprived of these pleasures, and from feeling too much delight when they are present. But the consummation of any activity gives us delight. What kind of delight is the *special* concern of temperance as a *special* virtue? Let us attempt to distinguish the various kinds of delight.

First, there are the pleasures of the soul, which can be consummated by an internal apprehension alone, without any major physical alteration. Temperance in the *special* sense does not concern such pleasures. Thus he who takes too much pleasure in the sympathetic feelings of others is garrulous and extroverted or too pliable and lacking in stamina, not intemperate. He who takes too much pleasure in self-approbation is proud, not intemperate. Hence we must conclude that temperance is concerned with *corporeal* pleasures rather than with pleasures of the soul.

But if we define corporeal pleasures as those which are derived from the physical objects of the senses, we must make a further distinction. If our interest in such an object is the purely aesthetic interest to see it or hear it, then intemperance is not involved. Those with an overdeveloped interest of this sort we call *curious* or *lazy*, not intemperate. If, on the other hand, our interest in such objects is not merely to sense them, but in some way physically to possess them, then temperance is involved. Thus the *gourmand* who takes an intemperate delight in savory smells is not interested in the smell as such or the taste as such, but in the actual eating with which they are incidentally associated.

Since touch is the only sense remaining, we can see that the tactual pleasures, which consummate our instinctive appetites for self-preservation and preservation of the species, are the *special* objects of temperance and intemperance. These are the pleasures which we have in common with the animals. Hence too great a concern with them is regarded as brutish and destructive of the peculiar dignity of man.

b. THE ACTIVITIES OF TEMPERANCE AND INTEMPERANCE. As we have seen in our discussion of courage, the irascible passions or appetites of our nature need to be stirred up and strengthened. Hence the mean of courage is closer to rashness than to the opposite extreme of timidity. But the passional aspect of our nature which makes us susceptible to appetites for tangible objects, such as food, warmth, and other comforts, is in no such need of strengthening: there is little danger that it may lapse into a condition of insensitiveness. It needs rather to be subordinated and even suppressed. Hence the mean of temperance is closer to insensitiveness than to the opposite extreme of self-indulgence.

Genuine temperance has its origin in the disciplined imagination, which has been freed from any tendency to indulge in pleasing pictures of tangible satiation. When deprived of such objects, the temperate man does not yearn for them and is not unduly pained at their absence. He is distinguished by a certain indifference to such things, which is quite shocking to the pampered glutton or roué. But this indifference is quite distinct from the complete insensibility which is advocated by the Stoics. The temperate man does not regard all sensual pleasure with Kantian suspicion as a sacrilege and sin. He is not plunged into Puritan gloom at the thought that necessary sensitive appetites must be satisfied for his own preservation and that of the race.

The constant concern of his imagination and will is with his *ergon*—the work that he has to do. He desires those necessary pleasures which further the health of his body, and all those which support him in the active performance of his work. But he does not desire them at random: he desires them always in accordance with a rational rule, determining *when* they are desirable and to what degree. If such pleasures are not necessary for health and good habit he will desire them only under the twofold condition that they do not endanger health and are not intrinsically evil.

We have inherited from the Puritans the idea that temperance is to be identified with complete abstinence and prohibition. It cannot be too strongly emphasized that this is a terrible mistake, definitely opposed both to sound philosophical and sound Christian teaching. St. Augustine sharply opposes the idea that sensuous impulses are intrinsically evil, and with respect to drinking, St. Thomas makes the statement that it is proper to indulge this convivial impulse *usque ad hilaritatem*. Utter indifference to such pleasures is an unnatural and subhuman state, in fact a vice which it is stupid to cultivate. On the other hand, it must be recognized that this vice is actually very rare and even more rarely achieved by deliberate effort. Thus the Puritan, in all probability, very seldom achieves this anaesthetic state. What he does achieve, is merely an unstable repression of overt manifestations of these impulses. But the impulses, together with their guiding images, still remain within him, causing the notorious Puritan gloom.

As Aristotle points out,[4] this internal anguish at absent pleasures is precisely the originating source of intemperance. Such a man is not in a temperate state; hence, as we know, his forcibly repressed tendencies are ever ready to burst forth in an orgy of indulgence. It seems paradoxical that pleasure should be the cause of pain and that Puritan gloom should be a deceptive mask for intemperance, but such is the case. A negative cause often produces a positive effect. These gloomy people are sorrowing because of the absence of pleasure, as a ship may be wrecked because of the absence of a pilot or war may occur because of the absence of world government. In their imagination and appetites, the basic sources of action, they are intemperate and too much concerned with pleasure, even though these basic roots are never allowed to flower into overt action.

The self-indulgent man is a hedonist, failing to distinguish between the manifold kinds of pleasure, but seeking *all* pleasure as such, and especially that which is especially pleasing. Hence no one is quite so unhappy as the hedonist, since no matter what particular

[4] *Nic. Eth.*, Book III, 1118B–1119A 5.

pleasure he may be experiencing there are infinite, further pleasures of which he is deprived. Not only this, but he is guided rather by mere concupiscence of what has been pleasing to him before. Since what has been pleasing to him is not necessarily what is really good and really useful, and therefore *really* pleasing, his constant seeking for the apparent pleasures promised him by the alluring images of his warped imagination, fails in the long run to perfect his nature, and therefore in the long run, to yield him pleasure. So he is permanently plunged in gloom and agony of soul.

c. THE RELATION OF TEMPERANCE TO COURAGE AND OTHER VIRTUES. Good things are always pleasant, but pleasant things are by no means always good. The good man, who has formed good habits and therefore takes pleasure in good things, can afford to be a hedonist. But most of us, who are still in the process of habit-formation, cannot safely follow our pleasures. As Dostoievsky has said, man is a creature who can get used to anything, and anything we have got used to is pleasant to us, no matter how vicious or distorted it may be. Hence in order to achieve a stable happiness we must gain a certain indifference to pleasure, especially to the tactual pleasures which affect us most constantly and most violently.

Just as we need the virtue of courage, which enables us to withstand the pain and suffering involved in attaining our rational end, so we need the virtue of temperance, which enables us to withstand the pleasures luring us away from our rational course. We cannot maintain an active life if we shrink away from every real or threatening pain, or if we rush after every entrancing pleasure.

If we are to train ourselves in the virtue of courage, we must exercise our imaginations to conjure up concrete images of painful and dangerous situations, and force ourselves against inclination to withstand such evils whenever they occur. If we are to gain the virtue of temperance, on the other hand, we must delete from our imaginations, so far as possible, the concrete pleasures in which we especially delight, and substitute for them more general pictures and concepts of orderly activity. Both are absolutely essential for happiness. But now we must ask a question concerning the *order* of the virtues. Which of them is harder to achieve and therefore more praiseworthy?

There are three reasons which justify Aristotle in asserting that courage is the harder and more praiseworthy of the two. First, the intemperate pursuit of alluring pleasures is more voluntary and spontaneous than the timid shrinking from pain. You learn a great deal about a person if you learn what he is especially afraid of, but you learn even more if you know what especially pleases him, for this constitutes the reason for the former. It is because he likes *A* that he shrinks from Non-*A*. He seeks the pleasure spontaneously of himself, but he flees from the evil, not wholly because of himself and what *he* is, but partly because of the evil and what *it* is. Hence he is more responsible for intemperance than for timidity, and the former is a greater vice.

In the second place, intemperance is more voluntary for another reason. Pain and sorrow are the effects of what injures and corrupts our nature, which is primarily cognitive. Hence we all know that great sorrow or pain stupefies us, so that our cognitive faculties are impeded. What we do in ignorance is not as voluntary as what we do in full knowledge of what we do. But pleasure does not impede our awareness, and therefore does not detract from the voluntary character of an act.

Finally, intemperance is more worthy of blame because it is more easy to avoid than timidity. There are two reasons for this. First, food and drink and other delectable objects occur constantly. Hence the opportunity for training in temperance is ever present, and we are more to blame if we do not take advantage of it. Second, such training involves no danger to ourselves whatsoever. But training in courage, even though it may not involve any *extreme* danger, nevertheless does involve a certain amount of pain and suffering.

So we must conclude with Aristotle [5] that intemperance is a worse vice than timidity and that courage is a more praiseworthy virtue than temperance, requiring a more arduous and difficult process of habit-formation, and a greater effort of the will and the irascible faculties cooperating with the will. Nevertheless these virtues are both of the highest importance, for they or their opposite vices rule the whole of our interior life, which is constantly affected by the impact of pleasures and pains. If we do not first learn to withstand the appeal of pleasures, we shall never get on the right path at all. If we do not then learn to withstand the pain

[5] *Nic. Eth.*, Book III, ch. 12.

and suffering we meet on this path, we shall not remain long upon it.

These two virtues of courage and temperance underlie all the other moral virtues, for there is no object of any passion which is not sensuously cognized as either pleasant or painful. Hence if we do not get our pleasures and pains under rational control, we cannot get any of our passions under control. As Aristotle says,[6] virtue and vice are concerned primarily with our pleasures and pains. Nevertheless they are not exclusively concerned with these, as the hedonist falsely supposes. Pleasure and pain are only the subjective aspect of our passions, which also have objects, i.e., external things outside of ourselves which excite our appetites. Let us now consider the virtues by which we may guide these external appetites.

REFERENCES

Recommended Reading
Aristotle, *Nicomachean Ethics,* Book III, chaps. 6–12

Suggested Reading
1. Plato, *Laches;* and Aristotle, *Nicomachean Ethics,* Book III, chaps. 6–9.
2. Plato, *Charmides;* and Aristotle, *Nicomachean Ethics,* Book III, chaps. 9–12. For a modern treatment of temperance, cf. Hume, *Treatise of Human Nature,* Book III, Part II, Sec. 12.

[6] *Op. cit.,* Book II, ch. 3.

Chapter 7

THE RATIONAL GUIDANCE OF EXTER-
NAL APPETITE (GENEROSITY, GREAT-
NESS OF SOUL, AND THE VIRTUES
OF FRIENDLINESS)

COURAGE and temperance are concerned with our internal pleasures and pains, and with those objects of biological appetite which are required for the preservation of the individual and the species, and which are therefore the most constant sources of pleasure and pain. But besides the tendency to maintain our internal subjective life in a pleasurable state, we have other appetites for external objects entirely outside ourselves. These appetites, of course, when they attain their objects, yield us pleasure, and when frustrated, yield us pain. This fact still leads many of us to believe that we desire such external objects merely because of the subjective pleasure they yield us rather than for themselves. But this view is false even in the case of the fundamental, biological passions.

A human being senses things external to him [1] which elicit real appetites. Thus when hungry he desires the real steak, not merely the pleasure he will receive from it. As a cognitive being, man is not solipsistically restricted to his own physical organism and what physically alters it. [2] He can also apprehend what is altogether external. Such external entities, as thus apprehended, may excite certain appetites, which require rational moderation if they are not to interfere with maximal activity, or happiness. Such entities are either impersonal things or persons like ourselves. The former are divided into two groups: material objects gained by money and power, and honor or respect gained, not by money, but by virtue. Let us now consider these external appetites and the virtues governing them in this order.

[1] Cf. ch. 18.
[2] Cf. ch. 17, §4.

1. GENEROSITY

Since man has a material, animal nature, he requires many material things such as food, clothing, and shelter as *instruments* for the living of human life. When properly understood, according to the law of nature, such objects have no intrinsic value in themselves but only a subordinate value as instruments for the living of life itself, which does have an intrinsic value. Nevertheless the appetite for these things endures even with no clear understanding of their natural function. Then, instead of being properly and freely moderated by rational deliberation and choice, it may be elicited by mere accidental circumstance or by clever external manipulation into absurd and irrational channels.

Children are led to think, for example, that wealth is the key to happiness and that without great stores of material possessions life is not worth living at all. At an older age they are informed that so great is man's need of such things that greed for them is the only permanent motive for human action; that the insatiable lust for more and more possessions is the cause of all true progress, and that without it men would cease to have any motive for action and would simply collapse and do nothing at all, as though nothing else were of any intrinsic value.

Brought up under this fantastic mythology, countless lives have been wrecked and many human cultures warped and distorted in modern times, because far from being the only intrinsic value, material possessions, as a matter of fact, possess no intrinsic value whatsoever, and are valuable only as a necessary means for the exercise of the intellectual and moral virtues. Money has even less inherent value than these things, for it is only a convenient medium of exchange. Hence to pursue money as something intrinsically valuable is to commit a fallacy even more fantastically mistaken than that of the materialist who pursues external possessions as though they were valuable in themselves. The magnified power of molding material artifacts which has been bestowed on modern man by poietic science, is a genuine instrumental value when used for the common interest to produce those things which are actually needed by individuals in the living of life. But when sought for its own sake, as though it possessed intrinsic value, it has become a curse.

a. THE VIRTUE OF GENEROSITY. We cannot love the virtues too much, for they are an immanent part of human activity, or happiness. But the things which we control by physical power and buy with money are only instruments for human activity. Hence our natural appetite for such things needs to be toned down by the virtue of generosity, or liberality, which consists essentially in a certain detachment with respect to them. This rational moderation of appetite will strike the materialist as an extreme asceticism, the ascetic as extreme materialism, for all virtue is a mean between extremes, and from the standpoint of either extreme, the mean looks like the opposite extreme. The generous man will value material possessions as necessary instruments for the exercise of the virtues. Indeed, without such things life is impossible. But he will value them only as means to their proper use, never as valuable in themselves.

From the common stock he will desire to take only such things as he really needs to carry on his life and work. This he will regard, in accordance with distributive justice, as only his proper due, as it is the proper due of every man. Any more than this he will regard as an unnecessary and obnoxious burden. If he is endowed with such a burden by a system which he is powerless to change, he will use what he does not need to support worthy causes for the common good and to benefit his friends. Indeed, he will do this to the limit of his powers even if he has no more than he needs, depriving himself of his own stores in order to be generous to his friends. Nevertheless he will not give according to impulse or on any occasion to the maximum degree. This would soon interfere with his own work and would soon deprive him of all power to help anyone in this way. He will give only as reason requires, *after* deliberation, on the right occasion, to the right person who will truly benefit, and to the right degree.

b. THE VICES OF PRODIGALITY AND STINGINESS. It is quite clear that the stingy man takes too much and gives too little. Therefore it might seem that the prodigal man is to be defined as one who takes too little and gives too much, but this is not the case. Following unreflective sympathy and impulse, the prodigal man certainly gives too much in the wrong way, at the wrong time, to the wrong people. But then, in order to sustain himself in his wasteful course or even simply to sustain himself, he is forced to take, not merely from his own supplies, but to take too much from the supplies of others, often bringing them into dire want for the sake of his "generosity." Thus the prodigal person may resemble the stingy in an irrational excess of taking from others. The essential difference between them lies in the giving, which is the more active, and therefore the more essential, phase of the true virtue. It is more noble and blessed to give than to receive, for to receive is merely to be acted upon, whereas to give is to act upon another.

But there is nothing noble about giving too much in the wrong way to someone not really benefited by our giving. This is the error of the prodigal person and more characteristic of the young than of the old. As Aristotle remarks,[3] it is not nearly as serious a fault as penuriousness. In the first place, true generosity is certainly farther removed from the latter than from the former. Hence, in the second place, there is much more hope of training the prodigal to true generosity, especially if he is young, for he is not essentially mistaken in his subordination of material possessions to further ends. All he needs to learn is to subordinate them to the right ends, in the right way, and to the right degree. The hope that he may do this in the course of time may not be without justification.

But for the penurious penny pincher, especially if he is mature, there is usually very little hope. He exceeds the rational mean in taking and in clinging to his possessions, and is deficient in giving. He has staked his life on the erroneous judgment that the material instruments of life are more valuable than life. He confuses greed with a virtue, and thinks of lust for possessions as the basic human motive and the sole condition for all genuine progress. He is apt to judge other men in terms of their bank account. He thinks of himself as a practical man and a hard-headed realist, whereas he is actually a soft-headed fool with an idealistic conception of the value of the things money can buy which is entirely out of line with the facts. Money will not buy understanding. It will not buy courage and temperance or any other virtue. It will not buy honor or even security against a common foe. Most of all, it will not buy true friendship. But habits, once established, are the most stable and ineradicable elements of our nature. Hence the greedy materialist

[3] *Nic. Eth.,* Book IV, 1121B 11 ff.

is not apt to wake up to these basic facts of life until it is too late.

c. THE RELATION OF GENEROSITY TO THE OTHER VIRTUES. Penuriousness is often confused with self-indulgence but is really quite distinct. The miserly man, governed by an inordinate passion for
material things, may be quite temperate in his use of them. What he
wants is the mere possession of the instruments, whereas the glutton
cares nothing for the possession but merely for the pleasure he gets
from food and drink. So one may be a miser without being either
self-indulgent or even cowardly. But on the other hand, there is a
strong tendency for the self-indulgent and timid to fall into penuriousness, since material possessions may provide them with the instruments for the satisfactions they seek. An inordinate love for material
things may cause almost all the other moral vices. Thus it produces
meanness of soul and a disregard for the dignity of human nature,
for the materialist is utterly oblivious to the rational nature of
man, thinking of human persons as mere producers of material
goods, or at best as mere consumers. The man who lives according
to this shoddy doctrine is incapable of friendliness and the friendly
virtues.

But the closest effect of all is that of injustice. We cannot be too
greedy for the immaterial goods of understanding and virtue. In
acquiring these, we do not deprive anyone else of his share. It is
impossible to love these things too much. We err only by loving
them too little. But in the case of material things, the situation is
very different. We cannot acquire these things without *depriving*
someone else. Hence if we come to desire them too much, we inevitably deprive others of their proper share and necessarily cause
injustice. One may be unjust without being greedy or penurious.
But one cannot be miserly without being unjust. Hence a society
which prizes material goods above human welfare, is bound to be
characterized by social injustice.

2. GREATNESS OF SOUL

Amongst the external, impersonal things which can be bestowed
upon us, there is one which is immaterial in character and far out-
ranks all the rest in value. This is what we call *respect,* or *honor.*
It is immaterial because it is a judgment of reason passed upon
ourselves. It is external and impersonal because the judgments of

reason are universal and not materially attached to any man. Reason alone is capable of truly defining the human end. Hence reason alone is capable of judging truly in the case of a given individual whether or not he is actually attaining his proper end. An affirmative judgment of this sort is far more valuable than any amount of external, good things. This is verified in human experience, for if a man has self-respect he can withstand the greatest misfortunes, but without it, what value would lie in the possession of the whole world if this were purchased at the cost of real dishonor and disrespect?

With regard to a man's private life and actions, the approval of reason is more adequately bestowed by his own intellect as self-respect, since he alone is in a position to know the circumstances of his action. But with regard to social life, this approval is more adequately bestowed by all the members of the group as honor, since the circumstances of public action are known to all. Aristotle therefore divides the virtue which enables us to seek after honor in the proper way into two: *greatness of soul and ambition.*[4]

a. THE VIRTUE OF GREATNESS OF SOUL (MEGALOPSYCHIA). There is probably no point at which Aristotle's ethics is apparently more opposed to modern moral prejudices, supposedly developed under the influence of Christianity. Many moderns speak as if any form of self-respect were a vice. Hence in the Oxford translation of Aristotle's Ethics we find the Greek word *megalopsychia* translated as *pride.*[5] Thus what was regarded by Plato and Aristotle as a supreme virtue and, indeed, the crown of all the virtues, is apparently regarded by many of us as the supreme Christian vice of *pride.*

That this is a fundamental misconception is indicated by the fact that Aquinas, the greatest of the Christian commentators on Aristotle, saw nothing unchristian in Aristotle's treatment of this subject. A careful reading of the text in connection with *Republic,* Book VI, 485 ff., where Plato describes the same virtue under the same name, must certainly verify this view. A man may possess greatness of soul without committing the Christian sin of pride.

[4] *Nicomachean Ethics,* Book IV, chs. 3–4.
[5] This is found at 1123A 33 and throughout ch. 3 of Book IV, in spite of the fact that previously at 1100B 32, the very same word (*megalopsychia*) is translated without any pejorative overtones as *greatness of soul.*

Neither Christianity nor indeed humanity itself demands that a human being should regard himself or herself as a worm. Indeed, it is impossible for anyone with such a view of himself to become either a Christian or a man. What then is meant by greatness of soul?

Aristotle says that he is truly great in soul "who thinks himself worthy of great things, being really worthy of them" (*Nic. Eth.* 1123B 1). He who thinks himself worthy of great things, not being worthy of them or of greater things than those of which he is really worthy, is a fool (1123B 2) and commits the sin of vanity or pride (1125A 18). But he who thinks that he is unworthy of *anything* great or of less worth than he really is, commits an even more serious form of the sin of pride, for which, interestingly enough, *we* seem to have no clearly developed concept. First of all, then, greatness of soul is the rational mean between thinking too much of yourself and thinking too little.

Is it then possible for a human being to think too little of himself? Here we must remind ourselves of the conclusions of natural philosophy, for realistic ethics must be based upon the real nature of man and his position in the cosmos.[6] What then is the place of man in the world of nature? According to the evolutionary philosophy of Aristotle, man is the highest of all the beings of nature. Endowed with the immaterial faculty of reason, he is able to identify himself with being itself, and thus to assimilate the whole cosmic order as a microcosmos within himself. Knowing the material things below him, he is able to control them and to utilize them for his own purposes by the technical operations of art. Knowing himself and the immaterial things above him, he is able to govern his own acts in such a way as to bring himself to his final end.

He alone of all the entities in nature is rational and therefore free in the sense that he, not only like them, performs a necessary, natural function, but does so *knowingly* and *freely* of his own volition. Is it possible, then, that an individual, human being, endowed with such a nature, should not have respect and regard for himself as well as for all those who ever have been, are, or will be endowed with such a nature? Understanding himself and his nature, he must claim great things and expect great things for himself.

---

[6] Cf. ch. 17, pp. 392–394 and § 4; and ch. 20, § 5.

For physical things such as money, power, pedigree, and even for the vast expanse of physical space, he will have a certain disdain, recognizing that all such things are very little compared with the immaterial greatness of the human soul. As the contemplative spectator of all time and of all existence, he will have no time for petty quarrels and gossip. Cultivating within himself the intellectual virtues, which make man self-sufficient so far as this is possible, he will be incapable of rushing hastily after lesser things (Cf. Plato, *Republic* 485) , of making his whole life revolve around something material, as a flatterer or sycophant, or around anything less than the similar soul of a friend (1125A 1) . Possessing an accurate understanding of his own nature and of the world as a whole, he will certainly apply this understanding to his own acts, cultivating all the rational virtues so far as he can, since this is the only way of living a life in accordance with reason.

Having little concern for worldly advantage, he will speak the truth openly, caring little whether this may be pleasing or displeasing to those about him (1124B 27) . He will seek to confer benefits rather than to receive them (1124B 9 ff.) . Apprehending these virtues within him, he will honor himself, not respecting the virtues for the sake of himself, but respecting himself because of the virtues realized within him, and the dignity of human nature, which they enable him to actualize in some degree. Hence he will not waste his time and energy upon a multitude of little things, but rather reserve his strength and energy for a few of those greater tasks for which his nature makes him worthy (1124B 24) .

Thus it is *impossible* for a man without the virtues to be great in soul, for reason alone is the source of all genuine human greatness (1124A 25 ff.) . Without this we are mere animals and worthy of no more respect than a chimpanzee or some peculiar species of gorilla. But with any of the virtues, self-respect, or a sense of the greatness of the human soul, must supervene upon them as their crown (1124A 1) , not only giving rest and satisfaction to the will, but bringing to it a sense of the tremendous responsibility involved in possessing such a nature, and girding it on to the further task of actualizing its super-animal capacities or of restoring them where they are weakened and distorted.

b. THE VICE OF OPEN PRIDE. It is, of course, a great vice to think too highly of one's nature and especially of one's attainments. This vice is primarily a matter of ignorance and is soon corrected by the acquisition of knowledge. Hence we recognize such people as foolish and ridiculous in their vain pretensions, rather than malicious and morally corrupt. Unless they possess great power, which is rarely the case, their open pride or vanity can do little harm to others. Their vanity soon becomes manifest to others and is more than likely to become suspected by themselves.

Being ignorant of the true source of human dignity, as Aristotle remarks, they are apt to "adorn themselves with clothing and outward show and such things, and wish their strokes of good fortune to be made public, and speak about them as if they would be honored for them." [7] But this only makes them more conspicuously ridiculous and increases the probability that they will themselves eventually discover the falsity of their claims. They are at least right in striving for *some* sort of greatness, though mistaken in their conception of what greatness really is. Nevertheless they are not as completely mistaken or as incorrigible as those afflicted with the *hidden pride* of smallness of soul *(micropsychia)*.

C. THE VICE OF HIDDEN PRIDE *(micropsychia)*. These people, as Aristotle points out, are much more common, though much less manifest, and therefore much more dangerous both to themselves and to others. They are apt to mask their hidden pride under a deceptive cloak of abject humility or utter unworthiness. Religious consecration and devotion are far beyond their limited capacities. They are too *humble* to confuse their modest opinions with such lofty accomplishments as metaphysics and philosophic wisdom or even to seek after such grand things. *Absolute truth* lies far above them, so they must be content with their own poor opinions. Great saints and heroes, no doubt, concerned themselves with those noble virtues of which the philosophers speak, but who are they to delude themselves with such pretensions? *They* must be content with the lesser things in life. This is the mock humility of the microsoul.

Indeed, as one listens to the sham modesty pouring from the lips of these philosophical Uriah Heeps, one gets the feeling that human life itself is beyond them and that they are actually too humble to bear the responsibilities of the rational nature with

---

[7] 1125A 30 ff., Ross translation.

which they have been endowed. But is such humility genuine? This is the question we must ask. Those who *really* think they are unworthy of the human life that has been granted them do not actually stay alive. In moral matters *actions* speak louder than words. The man who *really* feels he is unequal to the tasks of life will not waste time talking about how humble he is. Such men find ways of ridding themselves, as they think, of this intolerable burden.

But, as Aristotle remarks (1125A 33–34), the microsoul is a constantly recurring moral phenomenon. It is easy to see, if we seriously analyze his condition, that such skepticism concerning truth is a mere excuse for intellectual lethargy and a slothful dallying with pleasing opinion. Such "humility" with respect to the moral virtues is a mere excuse for moral lethargy and a swinish contentment with the ever-present surge of passion and animal interest. Even though reason and virtue are almost dead within a man, his shifting opinions and animal nature remain. Watch carefully this diminutive soullet! Is he *more* skeptical of the chance opinions that fill his slothful intellect than he is of the truth? Is he really *as* humble about the passions and desires that bustle him about as he is about his capacity for attaining the virtues? If not, then ask yourself, is he *really* humble?

The nature with which he is endowed includes a higher, immaterial portion much harder to perfect, and a lower, material portion much easier to satisfy.[8] If he is truly humble he must be humble about the *whole* of himself, not merely the highest part. Such an *incomplete* humility concerning the *highest* things alone, is merely the cloak for a *hidden* pride in animalism. This pride "humbly" rejects the more specifically human part of man in order to revel without compunction in the more animal part, which necessarily remains.

Such mock humility is encouraged and strengthened by that type of epistemological skepticism which denies any non-analytic, universal knowledge of the real world, holding probable opinion to be the best we can obtain, and that type of ethical cynicism which denies any distinct, rational faculty of choice or will, holding all aspiration to be merely animal appetite or "interest." The moral effect of such theories is to strengthen the more incidental, material

[8] Cf. ch. 17.

phase of our nature at the expense of the more essential, rational phase. Unless we are to distrust our *whole* nature in its entirety we must give the leadership to one or to the other. The mock humility of the microsoul, too small to be human, is merely materialism and animalism in a respectable disguise.

Aristotle did not present the preceding analysis, but he certainly suggested it by his conclusion that this vice of microspirituality is more opposed to greatness of soul than the opposite vice of vanity (1125A 32).

In the first place, it not only involves an ignorance concerning the real nature of man and his capacities, but an ignorance that exercises a far more corrupting influence over the will. The vain man still goes on striving for an apparent good beyond him, but the microsoul gives up all aspiration for any good beyond, deeming himself unworthy and thus resting content with his animal nature and the paltry, material appetites that happen to rule over it.

In the second place, the vain man is more corrigible, since his absurd claims are made openly and are thus more apt to become manifest not only to others but also to himself. The microman never embarks upon any great enterprise: he withdraws from all noble activity as above his powers and *seems* to make no claims for himself at all. Hence his *hidden* pride in those petty concerns with which he tries to satisfy himself is harder to detect and much harder to correct.

Finally, in the third place, this vice is more common, for it is easier for men to think too little of the mysterious, rational nature with which they are endowed than to think too much of it.

Hence we should constantly gird ourselves to think more highly of this nature and of ourselves as possessing it—to love ourselves *more* rather than *less*. In another place,[9] Aristotle gives a most penetrating analysis of the notion of *self-love*, which we so commonly regard as a vice. If the self we love is only a microself, consisting of petty passions and lusts, then in truth this is a vice. But the trouble with such people is not really that they love themselves too much, but rather that they love themselves too little, for if they had loved themselves more they would certainly have taken the trouble to find out more about themselves and the many good

[9] *Nic. Eth.,* Book IX, ch. 8.

things of which they were really worthy, and would then have striven with all their power to achieve them. To understand the *real* nature of the human soul must result in loving it, and this must result in an intensive aspiration to acquire and to strengthen all the virtues.

d. THE RELATION OF GREATNESS OF SOUL TO THE OTHER VIRTUES. As Aristotle says, this fundamental virtue both causes and confirms all the other virtues, and follows after them as a crown (1124A 1–2). Greatness of soul cannot fail to call forth a more intense aspiration for the theoretical virtues, since reason is certainly the highest and most remarkable of all the human faculties, and the ultimate source of human greatness. Courage, as we have already seen, is impossible without greatness of soul,[10] for a man must have a very high regard for the immaterial part of his nature and must esteem its health and perfection far more than that of the body, if he is bravely to face terrible dangers, and especially the perils of death.

As Aristotle also remarks (1123B 5–6), the microsoul may fall into a temperate state in which he no longer possesses any great desire even for corporeal delights and pleasures. But this is apt to be either an unstable condition of temporary repression or a gradual shrinking of the soul into inhuman insensibility, complete lassitude, and finally death. Those who are great in soul will tend toward temperance for a very different and positive reason. Their love of knowledge and other good things which perfect the soul will be so intense that they will have little time or energy to spare for corporeal enjoyment, beyond that which is necessary for the maintenance of life and health. In the same way they will tend towards generosity, not merely because their aspiration is so repressed and shrivelled as to care little for material possessions and power, but because they are so intensively devoted to more important things as to have little interest in the hoarding of corruptible goods.[11]

Respecting and admiring greatness of soul in themselves, they will respect and admire this in others and will tend to cultivate habits of friendliness, loving virtue wherever they find it and seek-

[10] Cf. ch. 6, § 1b.
[11] *Nic. Eth.* 1124A 16–B6; cf. Plato, *Republic* 485.

ing to communicate with it and strengthen it for its own sake. As
to justice, why should he seek to escape his fair share of the burdens
of common life whose primary concern is with the integrity of
life and the health of its moving principle?

Thus, greatness of soul fosters all the other virtues and confirms
them. Loving the soul for its own sake and whatever actually perfects it, this primary aspiration of reason will not rest until it has
achieved some virtue in itself. Then, apprehending this by the cool,
impartial judgment of reason, it will perfect this achievement by
the crown of human dignity and self-respect, not as the end of all
further endeavor—this would be pride—but as a goad to further
activity.

Far from being a sign of weakness and moral selfishness, the
delight in virtue is an essential part of its full attainment, for a
man cannot continue to love that which remains painful and op-
pressive to him. It is really selfish to be indifferent to what is finest
in ourselves and to feel pain and anguish at all that is immaterial
and best in life. In the Middle Ages this lethargy, or lassitude, of
the soul was called *acedia*. In modern times the Puritans confused
it with a virtue.

But the ancients gave it the more expressive name of *smallness of
soul* and unerringly recognized it as a fundamental corruption of
life, a shrinking and withering of the vital human principle. Human nature is a great and admirable thing, placing upon everyone
who possesses it a grave and arduous responsibility. Whatever leads
us to love this nature more and to devote ourselves more whole-
heartedly towards perfecting it in any respect, is a virtue. One of
the greatest of these is that rationally directed love of self which
Plato and Aristotle called greatness of soul—*megalopsychia*.

3. THE VIRTUES OF FRIENDLINESS

We have now considered the rational moderation of the appetitive tendencies elicited, first, by our own internal pains and
pleasures (courage and temperance), and second, by external and
impersonal possessions and honors (generosity and respect). Now
we must turn to those tendencies which are elicited by the external
persons with whom we exist. Man is necessarily a social animal who
cannot perfect himself alone and whose very aloneness is a pri-

vative mode of being *with* others whom he misses and needs. By his very nature he exists *with* them, responding to their passions and acts by passions and acts of his own, and communicating his own thoughts and feelings to them.

But these natural dispositions require rational control and moderation if the common good, which includes the individual good, is to be achieved. We must not only share the life of others, but share this common life in the right way as commanded by practical reason. The *individualism* of modern thought has led to a general neglect of these virtues of the common life which dispose us to friendship. Aristotle, however, with a keener sense of the social nature of man, allotted to them an important place in the list of the passional, moral virtues.

Following his classification in the main, but attempting to clarify and interpret it where it is obscure, we may distinguish five such virtues of social life, to which we shall now turn our attention. These are: (a) that which enables us properly to *sympathize* with the passions and fortunes of others, (b) that which enables us to *respond* properly to their acts towards us, (c) that which enables us to *behave* in a correct or friendly manner towards them, (d) that which enables us to *communicate* truthfully our passions, attitudes, and abilities to others, and finally (e) that which disposes us *to do so in a pleasing and tactful way.* (a) and (b) concern our feelings towards others, (c) our behavior towards others, and (d) and (e) our communications with others.

a. THE VIRTUE OF FRIENDLY SYMPATHY. Since we are rational beings, we can understand and share the successes and failures of our neighbors. When those about us are pleased, we tend to be pleased; when they are pained, we tend to be pained. Such attitudes are notoriously infectious and spread like lightning from one part of a community to another. This tendency to *feel* with one another is a necessary aspect of our nature without which the common life would be impossible. But without the deliberate guidance of reason, it may merely weaken our resistance to forms of mass hysteria brought forth by irrational propaganda, and may lead whole communities to corruption and disaster. Hence we must carefully watch over our raw sympathies and antipathies, subjecting them to rational choice, so that we sympathize with the *right* people at the *right* time to the *right* degree in accordance with the law of nature.

We must be on guard against two opposite, unmoderated extremes. First, there is the *overly sympathetic* person who vibrates in unison with any passional influence from any source, whether it be good or bad. When those about him rejoice, no matter what the cause may be, he is also filled with joy. When those about him are despondent he is plunged in gloom, even though they may deserve such misfortune. This undisciplined sympathy may lead him to agree and then to disagree with the very same thing or to agree with very opposite things when surrounded by different sets of people.

On the other hand, there is the *antipathetic* person who falls into the other extreme and always reacts in an opposite way. The good fortune of his neighbors plunges him into grief, and their bad fortune calls forth a secret joy. This is because of an envious, or grudging, spirit which cares nothing about the universal good for its own sake wherever found, but only its possession of the good, as the microsoul cares little for what is intrinsically good, but only for its limited, material existence and the animal appetites attached to it. Such a soul easily falls into the grudging spirit of envy, for it has cut itself off from those immaterial goods which are increased rather than decreased by sharing. Conceiving of itself as a mere animal, concerned only with material goods which are decreased rather than increased by sharing, it grudges any good in another, viewing this as a deprivation of itself. This *grudging* spirit easily turns into *jealousy,* the desire to possess for one's self what belongs to another, and finally into unlimited *hate* of other men.

Our raw feelings can easily be led into one or the other of these dangerous and irrational extremes. We can avoid them only by watching carefully over our sympathies and antipathies, deliberating over their objects, judging which are really deserving of sympathy or antipathy, choosing *where* to agree and *where* to disagree, and finally establishing permanent habits of feeling in accordance with such rational choice. Aristotle calls this virtue of proper sympathy and antipathy, the habit of *nemesis*.[12] By it, we are prevented from accepting *any* communicated passion, like the glutton, to whom *anything* edible is satisfactory, and are led to feel pleasure only at

[12] *Nic. Eth.,* Book II, 1108A 35 ff.

deserved bad or good fortune and to feel pain only at *undeserved* bad or good fortune. Moderated by this important virtue, our social feelings no longer spring up wildly and at random, but in an orderly way, agreeing with reason and justice.

b. THE VIRTUE OF GENTLENESS. Since we live in a social world with others, we are constantly affected, not only by their passions and feelings, but by their *acts* as well. When the acts of those with whom we live seem to oppose and frustrate our own activity, our irascible faculties are naturally disposed to feel anger and resentment, and to seek after revenge. But unless this raw tendency is subjected to the control of rational judgment and deliberation, it will fall either into a state of quiescence, which may lead us into passive servility, or into a state of overirascibility, which may cut us off from all cooperative action and friendship. It is easy, for example, to confuse the frank advice or chastisement of a friend with enmity and malicious frustration of our activity. Even when someone else interferes with us it is often very hard to make a proper allowance for all the circumstances of his act.

Was it really intentional? If so, then anger is legitimate. Or was it a mere accident? If so, then anger is illegitimate. Was the interference due to deliberate, malicious scheming? Was it produced by sudden passion, for which we also were partly responsible? Or was it due to invincible ignorance on the part of the agent? If caused in either of the last two ways, only *mitigated* anger is in place. But firm habits of judgment and deliberation are required if we are to determine these complex points in each given case with any degree of accuracy and train our anger to follow the results of such deliberation.

In particular we must learn to become sensitive, not only to injuries done to us, but to those done to others as well. Otherwise our raw, irascible nature will lead us into a vicious, moral subjectivism. We have many words for referring to the virtue by which we are enabled to become angry with the *right* people, in the *right* way, to the *right* degree, for the *right* length of time, such as *gentleness* and *good temper*. But *even temper* is perhaps the word that best conveys their essential meaning.

This virtue is opposed by two extremes of excess and deficiency. On the one hand, there are the "soft" people, who do not get angry enough and endure insults to themselves and to their friends. Such people are apt to be trampled over without defending themselves, and thus to be reduced to quietism and inefficacy. The best of them may have been influenced by the Stoic notion that all anger is to be avoided. But this notion is a mistake. As a raw tendency anger is neither good nor bad. It all depends upon *how* it is governed and used. There are certain human situations which definitely call for anger and resentment.

On the other hand, there are many situations resembling these externally, which do not call for anger at all or at least only a mitigated anger. Those who never make allowances but fall at once into passion on the slightest pretext, are *bad tempered* or *hot tempered* and *hard to live with.* Those who are *quick in temper* retaliate openly and at once, and then their anger ceases. But those we call "sulky" or "morose" repress their rage, nursing their grievances within themselves for long periods of time. As Aristotle remarks, such people "are most troublesome to themselves, and to their friends." [13]

But even this vice is not as dangerous as that of envy, which begrudges the good of a neighbor *as good,* not merely opposing him *in a certain respect* as having injured us. The *hate* which grows out of such envy can be turned against *anyone,* whether he has done us an injury or not. Such hatred cares nothing as to whether its victim knows why he is punished, and has no limit of satisfaction. But anger and vindictiveness are aimed only at those who seem to have injured us unjustly in a certain respect. They want their victim to know the source and reason for punishment. Hence they have a limit, which can be satisfied.

c. THE VIRTUE OF FRIENDLINESS.   If we learn to respond rationally to the passions and acts of our neighbors, we shall be disposed to the virtue of friendliness, which enables us to *act* in a manner which is congenial to those about us. It will be difficult for an unfriendly man to make real friends. Nevertheless a friendly disposition is not the same as the having of a friend, for as Aristotle points out and as we shall see later (Chapter 11), the latter involves a real love or affection for the friend which friendliness may lack. A friendly disposition is a *condition* for true friendship, not its *cause.*

[13] *Nic. Eth.* 1126A 26.

We call such people pleasant or agreeable, meaning that they tend to behave in such a way as to give pleasure rather than pain to their neighbors and associates. Nevertheless they will not acquiesce in everything nor will they seek to give pleasure under any circumstances. For example, they will not agree with the schemes and attitudes of one who is bent on a ruinous or dishonorable course of action: in such cases they will prefer to give pain rather than pleasure. Thus the friendly person will purify and moderate his friendly tendencies by rational choice, so as to be friendly with the *right* people, in the *right* degree, and at the *right* time.

This virtue is opposed first of all by the extreme of contentiousness and churlishness which tends to oppose any attitude originating from another source and which makes cooperative action very difficult or impossible. Such people, as we say, always seem to have a chip on their shoulder and seem to enjoy contention for its own sake. On the other hand, there is the opposite extreme, which seeks merely to please with no regard for the nature of that which it is supporting. We recognize these people as *obsequious,* when they seek merely to give pleasure with no ulterior object, distinguishing them from *the flatterers* who have some object in view, such as gain, rather than the common good. Of these, of course, the flatterers are the more dangerous, for they have subordinated the common good to their own advantage, whereas the obsequious men have not necessarily done so.

d. THE VIRTUE OF TRUTHFULNESS. The habit of correctly apprehending the truth and of expressing this truth in words, is an intellectual virtue wholly disconnected from any sensitive appetite: hence it has no mean. We cannot apprehend too much of the truth or express what we have apprehended too accurately. But we do possess as a part of our social nature a tendency to impress others with the importance of our own purposes, claims, and achievements. This tendency requires rational direction, for sometimes it is much better for us to be impressed by others than to impress them. On the other hand, if one has really done something and if he has legitimate claims, it is sometimes his duty to communicate them to others, without understatement, for the common good.

Truthfulness is the virtue which enables us to communicate our own attitudes, claims, and deeds as they really are, to the *right* people, in the *right* degree, without boastfulness or exaggeration on the one hand, and without too much deceptive irony or understate-ment on the other. The actual carrying out of verbal agreements and promises is a part of justice, but truthfulness has a wider range, tending towards a literal correspondence of word and deed even in minor matters where nothing important is at stake. A man who is truthful in these lesser things will certainly tell the truth about more important matters where justice is at stake. Hence this virtue disposes us towards justice.

It is opposed, on the one hand, by the extreme to which we give such names as *extroversion, self-conceit,* and *boastfulness.* Such persons have an exaggerated sense of the importance of their feel-ings and attitudes. Hence they tend to magnify their passions and especially their deeds into something much greater than they really are. They talk too much and listen far too little, assuming that their own opinions and desires are of the utmost significance and interest to almost everyone. On the other hand, there is the far less dangerous extreme of understatement and uncommunicativeness. It is certainly possible to carry what we call *modesty* to such an ex-treme that we fail to communicate what is to the common interest and shrink from making claims on the attention of others which really should be made. Sometimes it may be a form of ostentation, a sly or hidden boastfulness.

But, as Aristotle points out, the virtue of truthfulness is far nearer this extreme than the other. It is far better to flavor any account of our own doings and claims with a tinge of detachment and irony rather than to abandon our reason wholly to the servile task of recapitulating them and impressing them upon others for the sake of making an effect.

e. THE VIRTUE OF TACT. Truthfulness enables us to communicate to others who and what we really are without undue embellishment or reservation. But in order to do this effectively we need the addi-tional virtue of *tact.* We must know what is fit for truthful com-munication and what is not fit in the case of a given person, what will offend him and what will not. This ability to feel out the sen-sitiveness of another person must be highly developed and trained if we are to communicate anything more than the rudimentary facts. Among other things it will help us to know when to speak and when to keep silence, one of the greatest of assets for all social intercourse.

But it must be crowned by the further gift of ready wit, a quickness in emphasis, expression, and change of style. This enables us to change our words to meet new communicative exigencies ferreted out by the communicative sense which we call tact. Unless we can express ourselves in such a way as is pleasing to our audience we shall not succeed in communicating the subtle shades and overtones of our practical thoughts and desires.

If we are unable to communicate these thoughts and feelings to others in a witty and agreeable manner we cannot expect them to treat us in a just and friendly way, for they will know nothing of our more intimate needs and purposes. Similarly, if we know nothing of what they really want we cannot hope to treat them in a just and friendly manner. Hence ready wit and tact are crucially important factors in the perfection of our human nature, for men cannot be perfected one by one, but only together in striving cooperatively for the common good of all. This virtue is opposed, on the one hand, by that glum boorishness which, in its attempts to communicate, arouses not interest but rather distaste and nausea, and on the other, by that exaggerated buffoonery which, in attempting to make a joke out of everything, produces the same effect.

Such are the virtues of friendliness which rationally moderate our natural responses to persons around us. We can live effectively with others only by first learning to share their passions and desires by a purified sympathy, by responding to their acts without either aggressive irascibility or servile quietism, by behaving towards them in a manner which is neither obsequious nor quarrelsome, by communicating our claims and desires, without either exaggerating them or concealing them, and finally by communicating in a way which is neither tedious and boring nor frivolous and indecent. Thus each member of this group of virtues involves the attainment of a rational mean in certain raw tendencies of our nature.

We have now completed our survey of the *moral*, passional virtues which are concerned with the purification of those appetites to which our nature makes us subject. As we have seen, these belong to three major groups: (1) appetites called forth by the pleasures and pains of our own inner life, (2) those called forth by

non-human things of a material or immaterial sort, and finally
(3) those called forth by the human persons with whom we live.

Our tendency to withstand and to endure necessary pains needs
to be stirred up and strengthened by the virtue of courage, whereas
our tendency to pursue what happens to give us pleasure needs to
be toned down and resisted by the virtue of temperance. Our ambition for the immaterial goods of honor and self-respect needs to
be magnified and confirmed by greatness of soul, whereas our appetite for external, material possessions needs to be reduced and
weakened by the virtue of generosity. Finally, our tendencies to
communicate with others and to share in their hopes and activities
all need to be purified by a rational mean. No one of these raw
tendencies is bad in itself. But without the moderation and guidance provided by deliberation and rational choice, they will all
become evil and burdensome. With such moderation and guidance,
they will play their proper subordinate role in the perfection of our
nature and will dispose us to that final, moral virtue of *action*,
called justice, to which we must now turn.

References

Recommended Reading

Aristotle, *Nicomachean Ethics*, Book IV, chap. 1, and chaps. 3–8.

Suggested Reading

1. Aristotle, *Nicomachean Ethics*, Book IV, chap. 1; Aquinas, *Summa Theologica*, Secunda Secundae, 117–119.

2. Plato, *Republic*, 485; Aristotle, *Nicomachean Ethics*, Book IV, chaps. 3
and 4. Many modern commentators, and writers on ethics hold that
greatness of soul is egotistical and inconsistent with Christian humility.
Cf. Ross, W. D., *Aristotle*, London, Methuen, 1923, p. 208. For an opposite point of view, cf. Aquinas, *Summa Theologica*, Secunda Secundae,
Qu. 129–133.

3. Aristotle, *Nicomachean Ethics*, Book IV, chaps. 5–8. The importance of
sympathy as a raw, psychological fact of human nature has been widely
noted in modern times. Cf. Hume, *Treatise of Human Nature*, Book III,
Part III, Sec. II. Benevolent impulses have also been recognized. Cf.
Hume, *Enquiries*, Selby-Bigge, Oxford, 1902, pp. 247–255. But the moral
importance of a rational control over these raw passions has not been
widely recognized. Very little is to be found in modern ethical treatises

on the virtues of friendliness or, indeed, on friendship itself. Many modern moralists, influenced by the Puritan tradition, have extolled individual profit-seeking and saving as virtues. Cf. Tawney, R. H., *Religion and the Rise of Capitalism,* Harcourt Brace, New York, 1926, chap. 4, especially pp. 227 ff.

Chapter 8

THE RATIONAL GUIDANCE OF ACTION (JUSTICE) AND THE HAPPY LIFE

UP to this point, we have considered human nature so far as it is psychophysical and subject to the influence of particular, external things and persons. But now we must remember that man is endowed with a rational faculty which is able to assimilate immaterially the essential natures of all existent things, including himself. Hence he responds, not only to a sensory apprehension of particular things outside him, but to a universal understanding of these things which elicits another mode of striving, known as *will*.

The activity of our sensitive appetites becomes free and voluntary, so far as it is taken over by reason, and fitted into a rational plan of life by deliberation and choice. But in addition to moderating our subjective passions by the moral virtues there is another phase of our life in which we are not acted upon at all, but simply act upon the things and persons making up our environment according to rational choice. Here we leave the subjective realm of private impulses and step out into the public realm to affect things outside ourselves in the pursuit of active purposes we have chosen. The general virtue by which such acts are ordered to human happiness is justice.

1. THE STRUCTURE OF JUSTICE AND ITS THREE MAJOR KINDS

The natural passions are the raw material of human action and as such are neither good nor evil. They are simply presented to us as the stuff out of which our life is to be made by ordering them into some rational plan. It is silly to ignore them or to try to eliminate them. We must first accept them, then modify and qualify them by choice. But with respect to our external acts, we are not necessarily restricted in this way. Once having gained control of our passions we can act without reference to passion at all. Of course we must act as men, not as brutes or as angelic beings. But within the limits prescribed by human nature we are always free within a certain area to direct our human energies simply as we choose. This sphere of purely voluntary activity is the sphere of justice. Of this, there are three kinds.

First of all, there is justice in the broad sense, which includes even the voluntary moderation of the passions and therefore the whole of virtue. Justice will then mean the rational guidance of all human life towards its ultimate end. Since the ultimate end of man is the common good of all men, which can be achieved only by cooperative habits and acts, this all-inclusive justice will be social in character. Men exist individually, one by one, but they can be perfected only together by a common perfection. *Social justice* therefore will include both the definition of the common good and the determination of those means, both necessary and contingent, by which this end is to be achieved. These means will include both the intellectual virtues and the moral virtues, which can be realized in each individual only by his immanent action.[1]

We shall postpone our consideration of social justice to a later section (Chapters 9–12) and shall turn now to a consideration of a more limited kind of justice, which is also included within the scope of justice in its broadest social sense. We have this last sense in mind when we criticize certain modes of social organization and certain social institutions as unreasonable or unjust. But sometimes we speak of certain individual acts as selfish or unfair. Here we have something more limited in mind. If a man timidly fails to resist oppression for the sake of avaricious gain, he has committed timid acts, but strictly speaking he is not guilty of the vice of cowardice. He is guilty of another different vice which is not all-inclusive: this is the special vice which we call avarice. The avaricious man tends to want too much of the common things of life for himself and too little of the common evils. The corresponding virtue is justice in a special and restricted sense. It has two forms: the first and more fundamental is *distributive justice;* the second and less important is *the justice of exchange.*

[1] Cf. ch. 9, § 3.

2. Distributive Justice

This virtue is concerned with the fair distribution of common goods, such as honor, the material necessities of life, and leisure; and common burdens, such as responsibility, labor, and sacrifice for the common good. If an individual tends to demand too much of the good things and too little of the bad for himself, he is unjust or unfair. Hence this kind of justice involves at least two persons and two sets of external things. If A has more than he deserves and B less or B more than he deserves and A less, then injustice prevails.

From this we can see that distributive justice is not a mean between two vices, like the passional moral virtues, because it is purely active and social in character rather than passive and individual. There can be no extreme of just *action,* no such thing as too much justice, but only too little of it. Even this defect of justice (injustice) is not a failure to act on my part, but a positive act of somebody else on me. If I get more than my neighbor, then I *act* unjustly on him. If he gets too much, then he *acts* unjustly on me. In the first case I *commit* an injustice on him; in the second case I do not fail to act on my own part, but *suffer* an injustice from him. Justice is not a mean of passion within a single individual between too much desire and too little. It is rather a mean between the *acts* of two or more individuals—a common activity on common objects in which all act justly and no one suffers injustice from any other.

Such action always has the nature either of equality or of an equal proportion. If one worker has worked twice as long as another, it will be unfair to pay them equally: they must be paid in proportion to their deserts—in this case, one twice as much as the other. If one general has done more for his country than another, it will be unfair to pay them equal respect: each should be granted honor in proportion to his deserts. If A and B are persons, and C and D are, respectively, A's and B's share of external goods, then as the merit of A is to the merit of B, so should the quantity of C be to the quantity of D. The same should hold good of the demerits and penalties involved in distributive justice. Here again there should be a proportional equality, not a punishment of all alike. As A's demerit is to that of B, so should A's punishment be to that of B. Such is the nature of distributive justice.

As we shall see, distributive justice is the primary concern of governmental agencies in properly defining the rights and duties of the members, in seeing that they are all fulfilled, and in properly correcting them when not fulfilled.[2] But this kind of justice is not merely the concern of the political community. Even the smallest and most informal groups have an analogous function to perform. Hence justice must be a constant concern of every individual, for every one of his overt acts affects others, and the way that he plans such acts affects others either justly or unjustly. Thought precedes action as lightning thunder. Hence unjust habits of thought will lead to unjust modes of action. The tendency to treat equals unequally is always unjust.

For example, little children have not had time to develop any great inequalities in capacity and moral worth. They all have the potency of becoming mature human beings. Their basic needs are equal. Hence it is unjust to discriminate against certain ones or in favor of others. They ought to be treated as equals, each being given the material support and care which is required for his development. Anything less than this is injustice. Also, each child should be given the educational and material means of developing any special natural talents he may have. The *moral* worth of each child does not become clear until he shows how he has used these natural capacities and talents, and this takes a long time.

When this does become clear, certainly those who have made the best use of their natural capacities for the common good deserve some reward. This reward should not be paid in the form of money and possessions beyond what they really need, for this is a burdensome superfluity. Neither should it be paid in the form of power, for if power is rightly used, it also is a burden rather than a reward. It can be paid rightly only in the form of additional honor and respect. This distribution of honor is a matter of grave importance in which every man has a part.

If a society honors the wrong people, for instance those who are the most greedy and rapacious, rather than those who work for the common good, then having committed injustice in its thought, it must reap a harvest of overt injustice in fact. If a man lives in such a society he should not passively acquiesce in the injustice but should do all that is in his power to dispute its legitimacy and to

[2] Cf. ch. 10, § 3b.

correct it. Otherwise, in acquiescing, he becomes an accessory to the injustice. At the present time distributive justice is far too little emphasized and thought about in our society. We have thought very little about the virtues and have failed to recognize them as the primary source of merit. This is already to commit an injustice in thought and to prepare the way for overt injustice in life.

Such materialism may lead to admiration of the greedy profiteer rather than the real benefactor of society, and to think of that money and power, which the profiteer wants, as a higher reward than honor. This is to prepare for further injustice. In heaping great power and material possessions on the most unscrupulous members of society, many are deprived of their natural rights to health and power over their mode of life. Such a society may show great inequalities in the possession of wealth and power, but a general uniformity in the possession of honor, which is not distributed with any great care but is allowed, on the whole, to limp along after power and wealth as a sort of rubber stamp for what is called "social success."

This mode of distribution is irrational and against the nature of things, since legitimate human needs for material possessions and power are, on the whole, naturally equal. Hence their merits in this respect are equal or at any rate not vastly diverse, and a just order will distribute to all a fairly equal share. But with respect to virtue, their merits are very diverse. In this regard they deserve very different rewards of honor, which should be given without any reference whatsoever to the material instruments of virtue. These matters deserve the most careful consideration of every just man, who should seriously confront himself with such questions as these.

What are the legitimate, natural needs of those living in the community? Are these needs being fairly satisfied? If not, are intelligent plans being made for their satisfaction? What sort of man really deserves the most honor and respect? Are such men being honored and admired in the community? Do I myself honor those around me as they really deserve or just as others tend to honor them? Do I respect myself as I really deserve? Do I claim my *fair* share of the good things of life or a little more? When others claim and acquire more than their fair share, do I resist their claim or do I passively acquiesce and thus become an accessory to the injustice they commit? Do I assume my fair share of the necessary, common burdens of life, or a little less?

If justice is really to be achieved in any society or any minor group, these questions must be habitually raised by the members. If distributive justice were achieved to a higher degree, the less important, more purely *individual* type of justice—that of exchange —would occupy far less attention than it now does. At present it is often regarded as an adequate substitute for distributive justice, but an examination of its nature must show that this opinion is incorrect.

3.   THE JUSTICE OF INDIVIDUAL EXCHANGE

Since individual men are rational and therefore free, they are able to exchange the powers and goods that have been distributed to them with each other, one by one. The exchange may be carried on justly or unjustly. But this is a different kind of justice. Distributive justice involves the assignment of *different* duties to be performed for the sake of the common good, and the bestowal of *different* goods upon different persons in accordance with *different* needs and merits. Such justice therefore consists of a *proportional* equality. As the function and merit of the person, so are the common goods distributed to him.

If this has been adequately or justly achieved, which is apt to be assumed even when far from true, then any further exchange made by two individuals, should be on a basis of strict or arithmetical equality, not merely a proportional equality. Otherwise the original, distributive justice will be overturned. Hence, as we say, all individuals are equal before the law. One individual may be entitled to more than another in performing some special function for the common good. But no single individual has the right to take any such good from another after it has been fairly distributed to him for his use, though he may gain it through an exchange with the other's consent. In all such exchange, *absolute, arithmetical equality* should prevail.

This is clear, as Aristotle points out,[3] from the corrective procedure adopted when injustice has taken place. In this case the judge attempts to return to the injured party what he has lost, so

[3] *Nic. Eth.*, Book V, ch. 4.

that the original, distributive equality, so far as possible, may be restored. Since the ability to act rationally or voluntarily is a natural right which must be guaranteed to every individual by any just distribution, it is always wrong and unjust for one individual to act on another against that individual's will. Such an act is an unjust injury for which some recompense is owed. Hence any unilateral breaking of an agreement or contract by one party alone is unjust. What if both parties agree to perform such an act? Then neither one is doing wrong to the other, though both may be doing wrong to society. But in this case there is no longer any question of commutative justice.

This kind of commutative justice is now relatively well understood and occupies a most prominent role in our social thinking. In fact, as we have indicated, it occupies far too prominent a role, for many people tend to identify it with the whole of justice and to ignore the far more fundamental modes of social and distributive justice which underline it. Thus if the original plan of social institutions (social justice) and the distribution of functions and common goods are not just, then a rigid adherence to the justice of exchange will only irritate and aggravate these original injustices.

If, for example, certain persons in a community are denied their original, fair share of nurture and educational opportunity, it is no good telling them that they are treated with perfect arithmetical equality from this point on. We cannot too much emphasize the fact that commutative justice rests upon a foundation of natural and distributive justice. Without such a foundation it is meaningless. Indeed the relation of distributive justice to the justice of exchange is analogous to the relation between natural law and positive law.

Natural law lays down the basic principles of which positive law is a further determination. Similarly, distributive justice makes the original distribution of common goods which the individual recipients may then exchange freely with one another. Natural law prescribes positive law in *general* but not in particular. In the same way distributive justice demands that rational individuals should have the general freedom of exchanging their goods and powers with one another: it does not lay down what they should exchange in particular. Finally, natural law prescribes that no positive law should violate the fundamental principles of natural law. Similarly, distributive justice demands that no individual exchange should interfere with its own original distribution made in accordance with the demands of nature. Hence the principle of arithmetical equality in exchange. Modern thought has tended to ignore these basic principles of social and distributive justice, just as it has ignored the basic principles of natural law. Hence it has tried to substitute positive law for natural law, and commutative justice for distributive justice, with disastrous effects in both cases.

In the field of international politics the ignoring of natural law has brought forth the concept of the particular sovereign state, each regarding its own positive law as a supreme authority and unable to resolve its conflicts with other positive decrees of other states except by brute force. In the field of economic life the ignoring of natural, distributive justice has brought forth the concept of the individual, sovereign competitor, each regarding his own interests as a supreme authority and competing with other individuals for economic power.

In the last century it was held that such unregulated competition in all fields must somehow inevitably lead to the common good. Now we have seen that it leads rather to barbarism and death. If we are to avoid this peril nations must recognize the universal authority of natural law and subordinate their separate interests to the common good which it prescribes. Similarly, individuals in their economic activity must recognize the universal authority of distributive justice and subordinate their so-called "freedom" to the fair distribution of common goods which it prescribes.

This, of course, will not lead to the elimination of all free enterprise and exchange, as is often fallaciously supposed. In fact the opposite is true. It is precisely uncontrolled and untrammeled competition that not only leads to a general frustration of common need but to the strangulation of free exchange through the formation of monopoly. Free exchange is possible only within the structure of a justly distributed permanent *status* which assures to each individual that he will always have something to exchange. Otherwise the system of untrammeled competition must lead to that paradoxical position in which most of the people have nothing left to exchange, and those who possess everything have nobody to exchange it with. This, of course, is the state of slavery.

We can avoid it only by first remodeling our institutions in accordance with the law of nature and the basic demands of social justice, making a fair, or democratic, distribution of all common goods and opportunities to every citizen, and then by seeing to it that this distribution is guaranteed to everyone and strictly maintained. Within this framework of permanent *status,* free exchange with its law of strict equality may be allowed free scope.

4. EQUITY

All law, whether it be natural or positive, is universal. Hence the laws of justice, which govern the interaction of men, are universal. But the men to be governed by those rules are individual men who have to act concretely in particular. The important characteristics of such contingent situations can be foreseen by the lawgiver as *likely* to happen or to hold *for the most part,* but not absolutely, because of the infinite indeterminacy of matter, which is always open to the influence of independent causes and which may produce novel and unforeseen contingencies. It often happens in such peculiar cases that if the positive law were strictly followed, natural law would be violated. Hence a certain adjustment of positive law to meet the individual case is always required: this is called *equity.* An individual must have a strongly developed tendency to make such adjustments if he is to avoid injustice.

This is obviously true if the fundamental, distributive justice of the community in which he lives is imperfect. If so, by following literally the prescriptions of commutative justice he will commit great injustice. In such a situation it is the duty of those more fortunately situated to give more than they receive in exchange. Such gifts are *not* works of generosity or charity: they are demanded by justice itself. Also in a tyrannical state, oppressively organized against the law of nature, it is the duty of every citizen to disobey its positive laws and to work for a revolution. To acquiesce is to become an accomplice in terrible acts of injustice.

But even in a naturally ordered community equity is always required in applying the universal prescriptions of positive justice to individual situations. Thus *in general,* it is just to return what has been left in one's keeping to its rightful owner. But when the object is a weapon and the owner is in a mad fit of rage, equity may require that an exception be made. Otherwise one may become an accessory to some crime against the law of nature.

We are apt to become so impressed by these exceptions as to hold that equity is opposed to justice and that we must choose between one or the other—either the letter of the law or equity. But this is a great mistake. Equity is sometimes opposed to one kind of law (positive law), and in such cases is to be preferred to *this* kind of law. But it is not opposed to law in general. It is never equitable to act contrary to natural law and natural justice, which are always and everywhere right.

Indeed, it is never the intention of just lawgivers to lay down positive laws which will give rise to injustice in any given case. If they themselves were present they would make the necessary, equitable adjustment to meet such an exceptional case. But since they cannot foresee all the infinitely possible peculiar cases which may arise, they necessarily rely on each rational individual to apply the law equitably to his individual circumstances, and appoint judges to apply the public law equitably to exceptional cases.

We must conclude, therefore, that equity is not a habit opposed to, or distinct from, that of legal justice, but a necessary portion of it, required by the basic facts of material nature to adjust the universal law which is just *for the most part*, to the unpredictable individual case. No individual can be just who lacks this habit of equity. Justice itself demands that we be constantly ready to make suitable adjustments to the peculiar exigencies of the particular situations confronting us.

5. Who Is Just and Who Is Unjust?

We are so entirely dependent upon the rational or just behavior of others towards us, and they are so entirely dependent upon our just behavior towards them, that it is peculiarly important to have a clear conception of the different levels or grades of justice and injustice in the concrete. In order to do this we must briefly recapitulate what we have already said about responsibility, but now with special reference to justice. An *unjust act* need not imply, either in our own case, or in the case of another person, that the act has been *unjustly performed by an unjust man*. Also, a *just act* need not imply that it has been *justly performed by a just man*. What then constitutes the justice or injustice of *the man*?

First, we must remember that responsibility involves two factors:

primarily knowledge, which guides the voluntary act, and second-arily the free motive power of the will itself, emanating from the man, and not from some *other* source.[4] If either of these factors is impeded, then the act is not wholly voluntary, and the man is not wholly responsible. If a just act is to be justly performed, a knowl-edge of the end and of the various circumstances surrounding the concrete act, must be present in the agent. In this case the end is justice. Can a person plead ignorance of its general nature, and thus excuse an unjust act?

This would hardly seem possible for anyone endowed with a rational faculty. Any failure to exercise his reason to this extent or to pay any serious attention to its conclusions, must be due to a master obsession with some passion or to an extreme laziness which would probably make the person indifferent to justice, even though he knew its general nature. Such ignorance of the end may make the act *non-voluntary,* in the sense that it was not specifically willed *as injustice,* but it cannot excuse the man, for there are certain fundamental things of this sort that anyone with a rational faculty is under an obligation to know.

But how about the concrete circumstances of the act? Here cer-tain forms of ignorance may operate as an excuse, for these circum-stances are infinitely variable and subject to accidental coincidences which cannot always be foreseen, even by the most conscientious person. Thus it would be wrong to accuse a man of patricide if in a battle he killed his father, believing him to be an enemy, or of murder, if he gave poison to the sick, believing it to be medicine. These circumstances may be connected with *what* he does, *to whom* he does it, *by what,* and *for what end.* If he took *reasonable* precau-tions to guard against misunderstanding these, then such ignorance may mitigate his responsibility for the unjust act. But in this case it will be against his own real intention, and he will repent of the act.

The worst degree of injustice is achieved by one who freely and without compulsion chooses simply to commit an unjust act and performs it with pleasure and satisfaction. This is perfect injustice for which the agent is thoroughly responsible, since he has chosen it for its own sake. If a man chooses to commit injustice not for its

[4] Cf. ch. 4.

own sake but rather for the sake of profit, or of preserving his life, he is guilty of some vice, but of injustice only incidentally. His *real* sin is that of illiberality or cowardice, which causes injustice as a by-product. But he is, of course, responsible for the injustice he commits.

Those who commit unjust acts because of momentary passion are *less* to blame. They choose justice *in general,* but in a *particular* situation they are overcome by some passion, perhaps that of rage, and voluntarily do something they would not choose to do in a cooler moment. In this case he who externally caused the passion is perhaps primarily responsible, say for starting the quarrel, but a man is always responsible for his passions. They come out of him even though brought forth by something external, and he is responsible for controlling them or for letting them get out of control.

Still, such a man is unjust through *weakness* rather than through deliberate malice, and if he repents, is capable of reformation. His practical reason at least is not yet wholly corrupted, as is that of the man who commits injustice deliberately and delights in it. Finally, he who is actually forced by overwhelming, external power to commit injustice is not responsible, and therefore not guilty at all.

Men fall into injustice, therefore, by allowing their understanding to be distorted by false opinions and false practical judgments, and by allowing their passions to conquer their better judgment in individual instances. In this way they commit unjust acts without really meaning to commit them. But if this process is not checked by a clarification of reason and imagination and by a ruthless suppression of passion, they will gain a permanent habit of injustice. This will finally lead them to seek injustice deliberately for its own sake, and to delight in unjust acts. It is by a similar process that children must be gradually trained in the formation of habits of justice.[5]

First of all, they must be led to understand the nature of equality and justice, and the necessary means of attaining them. Then they must be trained to judge carefully of all the circumstances of their acts. At the same time they must be wheedled and cajoled into per-

[5] Cf. ch. 3, § 2.

forming just acts by external rewards and punishments, controlling their passions for some such extrinsic reason. They will then perform just acts, but not in a just manner as the just man performs them, from a love of justice for its own sake. But by the repeated performance of such acts they may acquire a permanent disposition to justice and may come to love it for its own sake, until finally they may delight in it.

Sometimes certain passions, like that of sympathy, may aid in the formation of the habit of justice. But the performance of a just act from sympathy is just only *by accident,* and not *essentially* just. Similarly, the performance of a just act simply because such action is the accepted tradition of a certain society is only incidentally just, for if the society were to change its tradition, the agent also would become unjust. The just act, if it is to be justly performed, must be known to be just by the agent, must be chosen freely by him of his own accord without external pressure, and must be performed with pleasure and joy. The man who can achieve just acts *in this way* is a truly just man. This is the goal we must set before ourselves in order to judge ourselves and others with accuracy and understanding.

Justice, or equitable action on all those with whom we live, requires a clear understanding of the nature of man, and his legitimate needs. Hence it rests upon the intellectual virtues. It also requires courage in struggling against the myriad manifestations of injustice, and also a temperate control of our own appetites for pleasure, which if unchecked will invariably lead us to commit injustice upon those around us. It requires generosity, for unless our desires for material possessions are rationally moderated, they will lead us to take more than our share of the common goods of life. It requires greatness of soul, for it cannot be understood by one who fails to contemplate the whole state of man and the natural order of human life, and cannot be achieved by one who does not feel himself to be worthy of striving to achieve such a goal within the limits of his finite capacities. Finally, it requires the virtues of friendliness, for no one can be just who takes no interest in his fellow men and is content to lock himself up in the private world of his own material passions.

So justice is built upon the other virtues, and requires them as a firm foundation before it can manifest itself in freely-chosen, rational action. Here the human being emerges into the public world and shows himself as he really is for good or for ill, either acting justly upon his neighbors and leading them towards their natural end in accordance with the insights of reason, or doing them injustice and leading them, together with himself, into misery, in accordance with his irrational, subjective impulses.

Justice always involves at least two persons. Hence, as Aristotle points out,[6] no one can do an injustice to himself. If he acquiesces in what *we call* an unjust act upon himself, he becomes an accessory to an unnatural act, which violates the law of nature and injures the society in which he lives. Even if he commits suicide he does no injustice to himself, for the same man cannot both act and suffer anything all at once. But he does commit an injustice. Against whom? Against the community, which he has deprived of a citizen and which shows its disapproval by criticism and disgrace.

No one willingly suffers injustice. This is always painful, against the will of him who suffers it, and therefore evil. As Plato argued, however, it is not *as evil* as to commit injustice, for *this* attacks our highest faculties of intellect and will, contaminating us in our principal parts with disorder and misery, whereas the suffering of injustice attacks only our bodies and the sensible faculties attached to them. *By accident,* however, suffering injustice may be the greater evil, in so far as it may lead us to commit a great injustice in our turn. In the same way, *incidentally* a foot sore may be worse than pleurisy in so far as it leads us to stumble and thus to fall into the hands of a barbaric enemy. But no one would say that a foot sore *per se* is worse than pleurisy. In the same way, as Plato argued in the *Gorgias* and elsewhere, doing injustice is far worse than suffering injustice, for the latter leaves our higher faculties untouched by disease and disgrace.[7]

6. The Happy Life

We have now completed our study of the moral virtues. Unless we understand them, love them for their own sake, and seek to act according to them, we cannot attain that perfection of our nature

---

[6] *Nic. Eth.*, Book V, ch. 2.

[7] For Aristotle's confirmation of this, see *Nic. Eth.*, Book V, 1138A 28–1138B 4.

which we all call happiness. But, as we have noted, although these virtues are a part of happiness, they are certainly not the whole of it. A man may tend to all the virtues in the right way but if he is deprived of the opportunity of acting according to them, we do not call him happy. The final perfection of our nature is not merely *a tendency to act* but *an actual activity in the concrete.* In order to perform such particular acts we must not only seek virtuous action for its own sake: we must also possess that technical understanding which enables us to control the external things of nature so that we can act, and that practical, intellectual virtue of moral insight which enables us in each case to choose the correct means leading us to a virtuous end.

If we merely love courage but lack any understanding of how to perform a courageous act in actual life, we shall never be truly courageous. If we merely love friendliness but are so maladroit that we offend those about us in our awkward attempts at kindliness, we shall never be truly friendly. All virtuous acts of this sort require external instruments, and therefore a technical mastery over nature. What is the use of admiring distributive justice, if we have nothing to distribute? To act virtuously, therefore, we must possess both prudence and art as well as the moral virtues. Having these all together, we can rationally moderate our sensuous appetites: those for pleasures and pain, those for external things, and those for the sharing of life with those around us. Finally, we can manifest that rational aspiration, which is the mainspring of our human nature, by overt acts that are fair and just.

Such an active life will certainly realize a large part of our nature, and therefore bring us an essential part of happiness. But there is something more, a still higher perfection that our nature needs, before it can perfect itself to the maximum degree. Let us now examine the active part of our nature more critically, remembering that *perfect* happiness must leave nothing further to be desired, and thus attempting to gain a clearer conception of what the *active* life still lacks.

In the first place, we must notice that such a life does not include what would seem to be the highest and most distinctive part of our nature, which most radically sets us apart from the brutes, for the other animals possess something at least analogous to these moral virtues. The bees in a beehive cooperate together, each performing a different function which leads to a common good. They thus possess something analogous to *justice*. The mother wolf fights "bravely" for her young, and thus possesses something analogous to *courage*. The same would seem to be true of the other *moral* virtues. Is there not something still higher than this, which distinguishes us far more radically from the brutes and which requires a distinctive perfection of its own?

In the second place, we can see that the operations of these moral virtues require external instruments and the use of such instruments by movements of our own bodies. Hence they fatigue us and wear us out, so that we require rest and relaxation from them. This is not only true of the very arduous process of acquiring them, which is tiring in the extreme. It is also true of the actual exercise of them. Courage, for example, is hard and wearisome to carry out, so that it is utterly impossible for the most courageous man to be courageous all the time or even for a considerable portion of the short time at his human disposal. The same is true of all the moral virtues. They cannot be *continuously* exercised, but only in fits and starts. Are we to conclude that such interrupted action constitutes the most perfect human felicity? Are we not capable of some mode of activity which can proceed more continuously without requiring so many intervals of quiescence? If so, this must constitute a still higher part of happiness, for human happiness is activity rather than rest. All of us must waste a great deal of time in rest and sleep. But few of us would think of these periods as the best and happiest intervals of our lives.

In the third place, we must note what seems to be an imperfection in the acts and pleasures of the active, moral virtues. These involve the whole of our composite nature, body as well as soul. Hence they are concerned with material things, like our own psychophysical pains and pleasures and the psychophysical pains and pleasures of those around us. Are we not capable of acts and pleasures which are unmixed with such passing things, and therefore more pure in character? These things all pass away; hence the active life is inescapably mingled with sadness. The material opportunities for the exercise of the moral virtues pass away; hence their pleasures also fade and die. Are we not capable of more lasting joys? The animals, which possess both an animating *psyche* and a body, have pleasures like these—so we call them friendly and courageous. But no one thinks of calling them really happy or of congratulating them on their felicity. Is there not then some higher activity which is needed to perfect our human happiness?

In the fourth place, we can see that each of the moral virtues requires many other things beyond itself to operate. The active life is very far from being self-sufficient. The courageous man needs external obstacles to overcome and many instruments with which to overcome them. The just man needs other men, on whom he can act justly, with whom he can do justice, and external things to distribute and exchange with them. But human happiness is surely self-sufficient in the highest degree, for it is that state of activity in which we least of all need anything beyond. But in order to exercise the moral virtues we are always in need of something beyond. Is there not then something more which our nature needs to make it maximally self-sufficient, or complete in itself?

In the fifth place, we observe that whereas virtuous action is desirable for its own sake, it is not desirable for its own sake *alone*. We do not seek temperance just for the sake of temperance, but also for the sake of something more. We do not respect the dignity of the human soul merely for its own sake, but so that it can go on performing not only this but other operations worthy of its dignity. This is true of all the moral virtues taken together. We perform these operations as integral *parts* of human happiness which we desire for their own sake, but not as *exhausting* the whole of human happiness. We perform all of them, hoping that in addition to themselves they may bring us something more, complete in itself, which is not only desirable for its own sake but desirable for its own sake *alone*.

Finally, in the sixth place, we recognize that the most perfect happiness is a kind of rest or leisure (*scholé*) in which we may find a final peace, with nothing more to be looked for ahead of us. But no one of the moral virtues, nor all taken together, are capable of giving us this final peace. We may see this if we closely examine the highest of all the acts of moral virtue, which involve all the rest, the individual soldier, courageously dying for the good of the whole community, and the individual statesman, devoting his life to political justice. These excel all the rest in moral grandeur, because they concern not merely the *private* good but also the *common* good. Such men, however, do not fight merely for the sake of fighting: they look for a final peace beyond. In the same way they do not pursue the political life as their final end, for the true aim of all politics is the attainment of peace and order in which some further and more ultimate rest can be found. What kind of rest is this?

We are very apt to confuse it with the rest of what we call a *vacation*, which gives us relief from strenuous toil and enables us to come back to our work with renewed energy. But clearly this is not the *final* rest with which we are now concerned. Surely the whole of life is not for the sake of *idle* relaxation and amusement! We do not act in order to gain relief from acting, or it would be better to be dead. Amusement and what we call *vacation* have their legitimate place as necessary means for *greater* activity. But the moral activity we have been considering is itself a means to some further end, some final *vacation*, in which we can achieve an ultimate rest, not in idleness but in activity that is perfect and self-complete. Of all the manifold acts of which we are capable, is there any one which can give us a hint of what such final rest-in-activity might be? There is such a mode of activity.

At first, its nature is apt to surprise us, for we do not often think of it in this connection. Indeed, we do not often think of it at all with any care. It is too familiar and apparently commonplace to attract our serious attention. It is also too easy for us to pretend to ourselves that we are engaging in it, when we are not *really* engaging in it at all but only making a few feeble gestures in its direction. Nevertheless, we are all vaguely aware of it as a real capacity within us which now and then, every once in a while, casts a gleam of light upon the dusky scene confronting us and beckons us on to its strange and mysterious mode of activity. This is the activity of pure, theoretical thought, or contemplation. Let us now contrast it point for point with the moral activities we have been examining.

First of all, contemplation is the activity of the highest and most distinctive part of our nature, which marks us off most radically from the other animals, which are certainly incapable of meditation and contemplation.

In the second place, this is the least fatiguing of all human operations, which least of all requires periods of rest and relaxation. This is because it is essentially immaterial in character and includes only a minimum of physical change, namely, that involved in the formation of images in the imagination.

In the third place, it is not the activity of our whole, composite nature, but of the immaterial part alone. Hence it provides us with the *purest* of pleasure in the immaterial natures it apprehends, and the *most enduring and lasting* of pleasures, since these objects are changeless and eternal. It is this that the evanescent pleasures of the animals always lack.

In the fourth place, this activity of contemplation requires the very minimum of external necessities for its support. One cannot think, it is true, without those necessities of life which are also required for the exercise of the moral virtues. But beyond these nothing more is needed. In order to understand the truth and to contemplate it we need no external instruments whatever. Such external things only act as distractions from the absolute concentration needed for the exercise of thought. Indeed, we do not even need other men to carry on this activity, once it has started within us, though we do need others to help us in bringing it to the highest stage of perfection. It stands, however, as that mode of action in which we, as individuals, are most nearly self-sufficient within ourselves, and the least in need of external support.

In the fifth place, this activity has no other result than the activity of understanding itself. It makes no change in anything else. It leaves everything as it was. It results in nothing save the truth itself, which is ultimately desirable for its own sake alone.

Finally, in the sixth place, being desired for its own sake alone, it can bring our aspiration to a final peace and rest, not a rest in mere idleness, which prepares us for something further, but a rest in the most vital and intense activity of which we are capable.

This, then, is that final mode of human activity, wisdom, prayer, and contemplation, which we need beyond the moral virtues to complete the perfection of our human nature. It involves not only the process of discovering the truth but that of contemplating the truth once discovered. It cannot be accomplished by apprehending only the subordinate causes of the events around us. The first cause of all things must also be apprehended.[8] The human mind, making its way through the labyrinths of philosophy, finally comes upon this ultimate object. Here it finds itself at rest, for it knows that it need look no further for an explanation of things. And yet this object is in itself inexhaustibly rich and unfathomable in its depths. Even to hold it before our minds requires the most intense concentration, and the exploration of its unfathomable depths demands all our powers of concentration to eternity.

This object ends the philosophic quest. At this point philosophic contemplation merges with religious prayer and meditation, for as Aristotle says, "it is not in so far as we are men that we will live so, but in so far as something divine is present within us." [9] This is the highest and most perfect part of our human happiness, for *in it,* that which is most divine *in us* contemplates that which is truly divine. Without it our happiness can only be transitory and imperfect, and thus unworthy of the mysterious nature with which we have been endowed.

7. THE INDIVIDUAL AND SOCIAL JUSTICE

Nevertheless, though this is the highest part, it certainly is not the whole of human happiness. Although we have a divine and immaterial portion, after all, we are only finite, material beings, born as helpless, utterly ignorant infants into the world we inhabit. During the whole protracted period of this helpless infancy we are in need of the most elaborate and painstaking nurture even to live—to say nothing of living well. For this we also need intellectual teaching and discipline in the moral virtues. In order to attain the truth of contemplation we need the kindly help of friends and the peace of social justice, which alone can make such contemplation possible. Hence the more a man has really tasted of the fruits of wisdom, the more he will recognize his obligation to climb back into the Cave, using the words of Plato's incomparable analogy, and to do all that is in his power to help others achieve that perfection whose exact nature and means of attainment he alone is in a position to know.

Such a man, as Plato says (*Republic* 496), will understand that to help save his own soul is a matter of no small importance, but

[8] Cf. ch. 16.
[9] *Nic. Eth.* 1177B 26 ff.

that to help save the souls of a whole community is something much nobler and greater still. He will recognize that it is only by chance or by divine destiny that some individual here or there may achieve any small degree of perfection without the assistance of a sound social order. He will recognize that without social justice, the chances for individual virtue and justice are very slim. He will understand that human beings can be effectively perfected only *all together* in a justly ordered, cooperative community. He alone is capable of understanding the whole of virtue and the whole order of social justice which this demands. Hence he will recognize his obligation to do all in his power to clarify the multifarious aspects of this difficult concept, to awaken the thought of it in the minds of those about him, and to urge both himself and them to do all in their combined power to achieve it so far as is possible in the concrete actualities of life.

If he lives in a just community he will do all that he can to strengthen and maintain it in existence, seeking himself to be a good citizen of such a community. If he lives in an unjust community, which is more likely, he will strive then to be rather a good man himself than a good citizen of a bad society, willingly accepting the conflict with prevailing vices and corruptions which must result. All genuine social improvement must have its inception in the individual intellect and will. The human person is the first source and origin of the good society, for the intellect resides only in the human person, and he alone therefore is able to apprehend the social end and to inaugurate the process of its realization.

So, having completed a survey of the moral and intellectual virtues which perfect the human individual, let us now turn to the survey of that more complex *social order* which perfects the whole community and contains the individual as one of its substantial parts.

REFERENCES

Recommended Reading

Aristotle, *Nicomachean Ethics,* Books V and X, chaps. 6–9.

Suggested Reading

1. Plato, *Republic,* Book IV, 432 ff., and 441C–445B; Aristotle, *Nicomachean Ethics,* Book V, chaps. 1, 2, and 4 to 1132A; Aquinas, *Summa*

Theologica, Secunda Secundae, Qu. 58–61. Cf. Mill, J. S., *Utilitarianism,* chap. 5, for a utilitarian interpretation of justice.

2. Aristotle, *Nicomachean Ethics,* Book V, chaps. 3 and 7.

3. Aristotle, *Nicomachean Ethics,* Book V, chaps. 4 and 5.

4. Aristotle, *Nicomachean Ethics,* Book V, chap. 10; Aquinas, *Summa Theologica,* Secunda Secundae, Qu. 120.

5. Plato, *Gorgias,* pp. 469–481; Aristotle, *Nicomachean Ethics,* Book V, chaps. 6–9.

6. Plato, *Republic,* VII, 540; Aristotle, *Nicomachean Ethics,* Book X, chaps. 6–8; Aquinas, *Summa Theologica,* Prima Secundae, Qu. 3–5.

NATURAL LAW AND THE STRUCTURE
OF SOCIAL LIFE

THE neglect of classical philosophy and its replacement by sub-jectivistic modes of thought in modern times, have undermined the ancient belief in the natural basis of society and social organization. In place of it, the view of the fifth-century Sophists, that social organization is merely a human contrivance or convention, has been revived and widely promulgated. Like their ancient predecessors the modern sophists and their followers, with various degrees of emphasis, deny the Aristotelian dictum that man is by nature a social or political animal. According to them, the state of nature is a state of war waged by independent, predatory individuals. Justice and social order arise from an arbitrary compact, which varies from place to place according to the whim of the human inventors of society. Man, not nature, founds the human community. Two sets of facts, however, are in conclusive conflict with this conception.

First, there are the facts of history and anthropology, which fail to offer any evidence for the antisocial state of nature which is here supposed. No matter how far back into the dusky obscurities of pre-history we press our investigations, nowhere do we find any traces of those antisocial, feral men. There is plenty of evidence for governmental contracts and social agreements all through history, but these invariably developed out of a preceding social condition. Nowhere do we find any evidence for men with no government at all.

Second, there are the basic facts of human nature itself. It is enough to think only momentarily of the inescapable, prolonged state of human infancy to realize the absurdity of this image, which asks us to think of separated individuals, each shifting entirely for himself with no fellowship and cooperation. How is a helpless infant to shift for itself in the jungles of prehistoric nature? We need not dwell on the picture: one glimpse is enough to dispel this illusion. Man cannot exist without cooperation and division of labor. He cannot cooperate without some agreement as to a common plan of life to achieve the common good. He is by nature a social animal. But we cannot leave the theory of the social contract without examining briefly two of the more persuasive arguments which have led to its popularity in modern times.

1. MODERN OBJECTIONS TO THE THEORY OF NATURAL LAW

The first of these is the argument first exploited by the Greek Sophists, but easily presented as something very modern because of new evidence concerning the striking variation of human customs and traditions with which it has been recently elaborated. Surely, it is argued, if nature prescribes a certain pattern of social organization for man, this same pattern should be manifested over and over again in every primitive tribe and advanced human culture, as every falling body moves exactly according to the law of falling bodies. But no such strict uniformity is observed. What is just for the South Sea Islanders is unjust for the Eskimos, and each deviates in the most glaring manner from the ideas of the modern European. So we must dispense with the conception of a uniform law of nature governing social organization. This is not supported by the facts. These complex facts can be explained only by the divergent, conventional agreements of different tribes and civilizations, depending upon the inventive genius of their individual founders.

We have already commented upon this and other fundamental objections to the conception of natural law as the foundation on which all human perfective action or morality is based.[1] Here we need only point out that every act of a material being, even the acts of falling bodies, are concrete, and therefore materially diversified according to their individual accidents and circumstances. Thus no falling body ever falls *exactly* as another, even though our measuring instruments may not be able to detect the difference. Hence it is not surprising that material, human beings should use their distinctive faculty of intelligence to meet the social prescriptions of nature in diverse ways, in accordance with their varying, material accidents and circumstances. Far from being an argument against the natural

[1] Cf. ch. 2, § 2.

basis for communal life, this universal variation is precisely what the material nature of man prescribes, and is therefore a further example of natural law.

Since matter cannot exist without some form,[2] variation cannot exist without something uniform that is varying. This is manifest in the facts of anthropology. Though the human community, wherever it concretely occurs, is always full of distinctive accidents and peculiarities not found elsewhere, nevertheless it is always unmistakably a *human* community which *is* unmistakably found elsewhere. The positive code of justice in the South Sea Islands is doubtless materially diverse from that of the Eskimos, and each is no doubt defective in comparison with that of a more fully developed community. But the fact remains that some code of justice, no matter how distorted or deficient it may be, is found in each case. Otherwise they would not be comparable.

No doubt, in the history of every concrete community, the primordial, general pattern of just or rational organization, in which each individual plays the role for which he is best fit and receives some proportional recompense, has been further specified and adjusted by numberless socially approved contracts. But each contract must have been based on natural principles already recognized, or the contract itself would be an uncaused mutation with no explanation, and history would lose all continuity. Why, indeed, should men enter into specific or rational contracts with one another unless their rational nature prescribed this for them as a natural necessity? When properly understood, the facts of social variation do not constitute an objection to the concept of natural law.

The second objection is closely connected with the "liberal" social and political movements of modern times. These movements took their origin from mathematical science and the new power over nature which it placed in the hands of modern men. This made it possible, and indeed practical, for the first time to think of freeing great masses of men from the crushing burdens of toil which were previously required of them, in order to provide that leisure without which higher cultural endeavors are impossible, and civilization languishes. Hence before the advent of modern science and the industrial revolution, this division of labor, resting heavily on

[2] Cf. ch. 13, §4.

the masses, had been defended as justifiable on the basis of natural law, which prescribes the cultivation and use of reason, the highest human faculty, and the leisure required for this use, at least on the part of those best qualified.

But it was easy for reactionary forces, working simply for the preservation of their power and the perpetuation of slavery, to use this argument in the new situation to which it was really no longer applicable. Natural law thus became associated in the modern mind with a reactionary clinging to ancient modes of life, and class oppressions no longer justified. This was the nature of things—the way they actually were—and it was no use trying to change them. Nature lost its original formal or prescriptive meaning and sank to the level of a purely descriptive term, applicable to the unanalyzed, material situation as given—the accidental together with the essential. The natural state no longer signified the universal way things ought to be but merely the material way they happened to be. Thus for the modern mind, natural law was allowed to become associated with a reactionary defense of class oppression and resistance to progress.

German idealism broke completely with the classical conception of the law of nature. It saw in the state, not the realization of a natural prescription, but rather the supreme achievement of human constructive, or even creative, power. The expression of this human idealism in German politics has certainly not been such as to justify the willingness of modern liberals to rest their whole platform on the shifting sands of human interest and unlimited, human, constructive power. It is most instructive that in spite of the vogue of idealism, the great democratic movements of modern times, the American and French Revolutions, appeal rather to the ancient principles of natural law and natural justice. These facts should make us examine very carefully the charge that natural law is a principle leading necessarily to social reaction and immobility.

As a matter of fact, as we have already seen, the precise opposite is the case. By *nature* is meant the essence alone apart from all that is extraneous and incidental. As Plato clearly saw, the appeal to nature can never be used legitimately to justify any given situation in all its factual detail. Such a material state of affairs, as he pointed out (*Republic* 471C–474B), can never do more than approximate the truly natural state. Hence the prescriptive appeal to nature is always revolutionary or reformist in its effect. It offers us no hope of rest in any prevailing social state but rather a fixed and immutable goal, spurring us ever forward to further endeavors. Even the most perfect, prevailing state must be ceaselessly maintained against material corruption and purged of irrelevant and imperfect accidents.

The Platonic principle, repeated by Augustine and his great mediaeval successors, that *an unjust law is no law,* is the guiding principle of all true revolutions. Men will not actually risk their lives for the sake of exercising constructive ingenuity. They will not actually die merely because a number of people do not like something. They will actually run such risks only if they are convinced that the whole nature of things is being flouted and denied.

We must conclude that this second charge also is mistaken, like the first, and rests on a misunderstanding. Man has not made or constructed his nature. This nature has been presented to him by the causes of the natural world as a whole, of which he is a part. He has not invented the social groups and communities in which alone his nature is perfected. These groups are necessarily prescribed by the nature which has been presented to him. What he must do is to carry out these prescriptions as best he can, amid the confused, material circumstances in which he finds himself. But granted that social life is prescribed by nature, what mode of being does it have? What is its relation to the being of the human individual? What is a human group? Let us now attempt to gain some light on these difficult questions. Only by so doing may we then hope to gain further light on the various kinds of human groups, and finally on the great controversial issues in which these groups are involving us in our own time.

2. THE NATURE OF THE HUMAN GROUP

As the very term "group" implies, it is in some sense a single entity and in some sense a plurality of individuals. This structural complexity calls forth two fundamental misunderstandings which must be avoided if any sound insight is to be achieved. On the one hand, there are the organic social theorists who think that the group is a single substantial entity and that the individuals making it up are only incidental or instrumental parts, as certain parts of the living organism are dispensable and naturally subordinate to the substantial whole. On the other hand, there are the opposed social individualists, or pluralists, who think that the group is a mere number of individuals and that its unity is incidental and instrumental, as a business partnership may be terminated at the desire of either partner and may be continued solely for the sake of what each may get out of it. Our attempt to gain an accurate understanding of social life will be greatly aided by a preliminary criticism of these two views which are widely current at the present time.

The organic social theorists can point to several indisputable facts which seem to verify their position. Any corporate entity, like a nation, a college, or a business corporation, certainly possesses some kind of unity, which is not explained by the physical individuals making it up, for these individuals are physically quite separate from one another. But the group is in some sense one. We can identify each single group and distinguish it from others. It is distinct from any one of its individual parts or members, for it often outlasts many generations of such members. Furthermore, the group is a whole which includes these members in something transcending any section of them. The common good of the group includes the good of the individual member, and is therefore more valuable. Hence when a choice is forced upon us, we say it is reasonable that the individual good must be sacrificed rather than the common good.

From these authentic facts the organic theorists conclude that we must, therefore, assume a corporate, substantial entity which possesses an existence of its own apart from that of its human members. But what kind of an entity? What kind of existence? Here our thinking tends to become vague and confused, and we fall back upon analogies. In the 17th and 18th centuries mechanical analogies were popular. So the group was conceived as a great machine, made up of individual rods and wheels, but operating according to distinct laws of its own. In the 19th century organic analogies were used. The group was conceived as a great, living organism, made up of tiny, individual cells, but living a distinct life of its own apart from them.

Whatever analogies are used, the theory is that the group is a substantial entity distinct from the individuals making it up, and that it uses them for peculiar operations which follow laws of its own. At the present time this theory is very widespread. It generally attempts to defend itself by the widely held view that any kind of a whole is something more than its parts. Thus it is held that there is nothing extraordinary in the fact that a number of individuals coming together should constitute a new entity over and above themselves. Do not the colorless gases, hydrogen and oxygen, come together to form a new compound, water, which is more than its parts? Do not non-living substances come together to form life? In the same way human individuals combine together to form the new, emergent structures of social life.

But in spite of this metaphysical argument and the interesting analogies used to bolster it up, there is no actual evidence whatsoever to verify the assumption of a separate group substance. Wherever we search for such a corporate entity we find only individual substances. This is true at every level. If we look for a corporate body we find only the bodies of individual, human beings. If we look for acts we find only individual acts. If the state is to execute a criminal, it must call upon an individual hangman. If we look for group thoughts we find only some individual thinking them. But if there is a separate, group substance which is thinking and acting, we cannot hold the individual instruments responsible any more than we can blame a cell in the hangman's finger for the execution.

Who then is responsible for corporate acts? Certainly no *one* can be blamed, and the corporate entity cannot be found. Hence there is a widespread confusion about such questions at the present time, a general failure to hold anyone responsible for group activities, and a resulting demoralization of corporate activity. One of the basic causes of this demoralization is the prevalence of the group-substance idea. How can *I* be blamed for what the group substance does?

As to the metaphysical argument which is generally used to bolster up this idea, a close examination will show that it is based upon a fallacy. A whole is greater than any *one* of its parts. It is greater than any number of parts, short of all. But it is not greater than *all* its parts. Hydrogen and oxygen are not the actual parts of water:

they are only the potential parts, which may become actual parts if they are acted upon and transformed in certain ways. The matter of hydrogen and oxygen may become the matter of water by gaining another order and formal structure. An analysis of water will reveal these relational and formal parts as well as the material parts. If we find a whole which is evidently more than all the parts revealed by a certain analysis, this is not due to the mystical emergence of a novel entity of wholeness that is distinct from the parts. It is due rather to a faulty analysis. We have not as yet grasped all the parts distinctly. The whole is simply all the parts grasped indistinctly and implicitly. All the parts are simply the whole made distinct and explicit.[3]

In the case of the human group we find that it is something more than all the separate, physical bodies of its individual members. These are many. The group is one. But we need not jump hastily to the conclusion that a new entity has mystically emerged which is distinct from all the parts. We need to look for *other* parts which may have escaped our attention. We need to make a more adequate analysis. We may understand this need more clearly if we first examine the theory of the sociological individualists, who make no new analysis.

They are perfectly content with the analysis of the human group into physical individuals, numerically distinct from one another. These thinkers pride themselves on their "empiricism." Physical organisms alone are evident to sense; hence these alone exist. The human individual is the only substantial entity: the group therefore is merely a number of such individuals, physically juxtaposed and physically acting on one another. The Supreme Court is merely nine old men around a table. Just as the group-substance view appeals to idealists and extreme realists, so this view tends to appeal to nominalists and materialists.[4]

But this view absolutely fails to account for the evident sense in which the group is a single entity having some kind of existence. The Supreme Court is in some sense one entity, not nine. It came into existence at a certain time and has had a certain history, which no doubt will end at a certain time. On the individualistic view,

[3] Cf. ch. 13, § 6, pp. 294 ff. for a further discussion of this question.
[4] Cf. ch. 19, § 3.

the court will become something entirely different every time a member leaves it to be replaced by another, for "it" is simply the name given to nine material entities which are physically juxtaposed at a certain time. Nine *other* entities are certainly not the same. Hence this nominalistic theory does not account for the unity we recognize in nations, civilizations, and other corporate institutions which in some sense remain the same, and endure through centuries and millennia, while their component individual members come and go.

Since there is no group entity of any sort, there is no common good of the group as a whole, but only a sum of separate, individual goods. Hence this view cannot explain why it is sometimes reasonable for the individual to sacrifice his good to the common good. It must simply explain this obligation away as a delusion. Neither can it give any account of corporate responsibility. Since there is no corporate entity, obviously no one is responsible for it. Each individual is responsible only for his own acts. Who, then, is responsible for the acts of the U. S. Army, or the General Motors Corporation? There are no such entities and no such acts —only a sum of individual operations, as though the military campaign were no more than the acts of this soldier, plus the acts of that soldier, and so on. No one is responsible for non-existent corporate acts.

Unfortunately, however, we are all very definitely aware of such corporate acts. A business corporation, for example, as we all know, may own property, pay wages, produce artifacts, sell them, expand, and contract. Furthermore, it is capable of making mistakes and committing injustices. Who then is to blame? The individualistic theory cannot help us here. By refusing to take account of such facts it joins with its opposite, the group-substance view, in fostering that irresponsibility and demoralization of social life which is such a characteristic feature of the modern age. These theories are based upon an inadequate, materialistic analysis of man. What then is a better analysis? Let us attempt to deal with this crucial question first of all by stating the problem as sharply as possible.

The facts are these. The only human substance is the individual man. There are many of these in each human group. But the group is something more than a mere sum of such entities. It has a unity and existence of its own over and above the physical existence of these members. They are many. It is one. They come and go. It remains. Yet if only these individuals exist and there is no evidence for any supersubstance, the group entity must inhere in the individual substance as an accident.[5] But how can a single physical individual be one with other individuals who are physically distinct from himself? What kind of an accident is this? How can something in one individual include not only this individual but many others as well? Can such questions as this be answered? They can be answered, but not in a way which can be harmonized with the widespread materialistic predilections of our time.

The empirical facts of human group life can be explained only by first clearly recognizing the rational nature of man. The human individual is a physical being, separated from all other physical entities by his quantitative dimensions. But he also possesses noetic faculties, which can overcome this physical isolation.[6]

Two human individuals who are physically quite separate can nevertheless share the same thoughts. They can communicate and agree upon the same common goal to be achieved, not by additive, but by ordered, cooperative action. This, in fact, is the only way in which human life can be really lived. The other animals have been given hereditary instincts which act automatically for the common good. But man has been supplied with no such congenital instincts. Instead of this he has been endowed with the immaterial faculties of intellect and will.

By exercising his reason he may understand the need for human cooperation in the attainment of a common end. By rational communication he may agree with his fellows on the nature of this common end—the human perfection of all.[7] Then by free choice he may voluntarily pursue this common end, performing his share of the common duties and receiving his share of the common fruits. Group life is thus made possible by the immaterial, rational nature of man. The group is unified by a single, immaterial idea shared by many minds. It is realized and sustained in being by the immaterial aspiration of many wills striving to a single, shared idea. *The*

[5] Cf. ch. 15, § 2.
[6] Cf. chs. 14, § 6, and 17, § 4.
[7] Cf. ch. 19, § 1.

human group is a set of diverse, individual activities made one by their common reference to a single end, rationally held in mind by the different members. It is a shared purpose in process of realization. In terms of this definition we may work out an intelligible answer to the questions concerning corporate action and responsibility.

The group is not a material substance like a machine or a living animal. Its structure is very different. It is not basically material at all. The group is an immaterial, moral entity. Its unity is the unity of a single idea. It exists in the same way that a purpose exists in the mind of an individual agent before it is actually realized. Such a purpose can be shared by many minds. Furthermore, this purpose may include, not only a conception of the agent and his good, but a conception of many others and their goods—all integrated together in an ordered whole.

Physically each individual is subjectively restricted to himself, but noetically he is able to assimilate things which are quite distinct, indeed all things. The knowledge that an individual carries about with himself is always a self-transcending attribute. The human group is a self-transcending, noetic accident of this kind. It is the idea of a common good, known and loved by many minds. Ideas, of course, are not material. They have no size, no weight, nor shape; hence they cannot be sensed. But this does not mean that they do not exist.[8] Every great group structure, even though it be misguided and perverted, is a demonstration of their existence. Each group is an infectious idea in process of realization or frustration. Each group is a human purpose. The groups to which you belong show the purposes that really guide your life.

This analysis enables us to avoid the pitfalls of the group-substance theory, as well as those of pluralism. With the pluralists we agree that there is no group substance, that only human individuals exist. But we utterly disagree with the materialistic analysis of human nature that underlies this view. In addition to being a physical organism the human individual is also a mind with ideas.[9] Many individuals can conceive and love the very same idea of a common good to be achieved and shared by all. The human group is a set

[8] Cf. ch. 19, § 1.
[9] Cf. ch. 17, pp. 392 ff.

of ordered activities in different individuals, unified by a single end. Thus we may agree with the antipluralists that the group is an entity with a certain peculiar unity and existence of its own. But the unity is not physical: it is rather ideal or noetic. The existence is not subjective nor quantitative, like that possessed by a machine or an animal: it is rather a noetic, intentional existence before many minds and wills, which then strive to give it a further material reality.

This ideal, noetic being of the group is not possessed by any superhuman substance or entity. It is possessed precisely by the material individuals making up the group, for they have immaterial minds and wills. They literally *are* the group, for they are their ideas and their choices. And the group is its members, for it exists as a single pattern of aspiration in their habits of thought and action. In the light of this analysis we can answer the embarrassing question concerning group responsibility. The group is its members, and you are in a vital part of your being the various groups to which you belong. Hence you and every other member of a group, are responsible for the actions of the group.

No doubt some are more responsible and some less, depending upon the division of responsibilities in a given group. But unless certain members of a group are reduced to the condition of utter slavery with no choice but to perform their functions at the point of a bayonet, they must share a certain minimum responsibility. As we have seen, responsibility means knowledge of what is being done and the power to do otherwise.[10] All adult members of any group have a knowledge of what the group is doing, for the group is a noetic entity. Without such knowledge there would be no human group but merely an animal herd or hive, or a mass of slaves. Unless the functions are imposed tyrannically by brute force there are alternatives. Even slaves have the choices of death and revolution. But with knowledge and alternative courses of action there is responsibility.

So we can answer without confusion, that every adult member of a group is morally responsible for what the group does. No matter how vast and powerful the group may be, it rests upon a structure of ideas. If this structure is erroneous and misconceived in

[10] Cf. ch. 4.

violation of the law of nature, it is your duty to clarify and correct it. If the structure is correct and in accordance with nature, but is not being carried out, then it is your duty to protest and revolt. You are in part the groups to which you belong. Hence you are responsible for what they do, as you are responsible for all your ideas and purposes.

This discussion may enable us to understand the complex structure of the human group, which is not a physical, substantial entity, but rather a purposive, accidental entity. The *material* causes of any human group are the rational individuals making it up. The *final* cause is the universal, common good which is the object of their aspiration and which must be rationally or intentionally present in their minds. The *formal* cause is the union of the group in certain duties and offices required for the common good. The *efficient* cause is the aspiration of the will towards the common good and the obligation resulting from a knowledge of the sanctions punishing unnatural action.

Any social group, once constituted, must give rise to some form of *authority* as a necessary accident or property. Authority is the means by which the group operates, the moral power of commanding what different individuals in different situations should do for the common good, and how the common good should be distributed. Unless the group itself is established in accordance with social justice and unless the group authority is exercised with distributive and remedial justice, it cannot exist in a sound condition. Justice is the peculiar *virtue* of social life, an intermediate end or part of its perfection. Lacking this virtue, the group becomes an evil and malignant power but still remains essentially a group.

The four causes, however, and the peculiar *property* of authority, are to be found in any group, though with striking variations in different groups. The rational individuals constituting the material cause of social life are a constant factor, requiring no special comment. Before turning to an examination of the different major types of group, let us now turn to a brief consideration of the other four factors in turn, attempting first of all to reveal their essential and invariable nature, and then to consider the most fundamental general principles of all group life, which necessarily arise from them.

3. THE COMMON GOOD (FINAL CAUSE)

This is the primary, invisible source of all group life from which everything else follows. Every social group of whatever sort exists for the sake of some common good that can be achieved only by cooperative action. Each human group *is* a human purpose, and the way groups are subordinated to one another shows the way in which purposes are subordinated to one another in a society. This final cause exists *subjectively* in all the members as an effect of group action, so far as it is realized and shared. But before it is realized it exists *objectively* or intentionally in the intellects and wills of the members.[11] This common *purpose* is what binds them together as one group, for in spite of their substantial diversity, this end is one and the same in all, so far as it is understood and loved. But here again we must guard against misunderstandings.

First of all, the common good is in no way opposed to the individual good of any individual member. It includes *his* individual good, as it includes the goods of the other members. So far as it is achieved, the common good is participated by *each* member of the group. If *his* good is attained then the common is at least partially achieved. If the common good is achieved then *his* good is also achieved. There can be no *natural* conflict between the two. Any conflict which arises is due to a misconception either of the common good, of the individual good, or of both. If one or the other must be sacrificed, then it is preferable to sacrifice the individual good, since *by nature,* the whole is more important than the part. But in so far as an individual good is lost, the common good, *to this degree,* is damaged and diluted. The army is weakened by the loss of a single soldier, though this is less evil than the loss of the whole army.

Secondly, we must not think of the common good simply as a summation of the various individual goods, its last material effect. This effect is produced only by an ordered system of efficient causes, which in turn can be determined or ordered together only

[11] Cf. ch. 19, § 2.

by a *single, final cause.* This is the common good, which must be grasped in its single, integral totality by reason before it can be materially achieved. This common good is something *sui generis.* The symphony is not *the sum* of the sounds of the harp, *plus* those of the violin, *plus* those of the wind instruments, and so on, though these may be its material results. The victory for which a whole people struggles is not the victory of this man *plus* the victory of that, and so on, though the former will produce the latter. To confuse the two is to confuse cause with effect. Given the cause, the effect must follow. To know the cause is to know the effect, but to know the effect is *not* to know the cause. The conductor who strove simply for single effects of single instruments one by one, would soon become confused and lose the symphony. The general who became obsessed with the single victories of each of his single units, would lose sight of the whole campaign and would surely lose the victory.

Even less is the common good, the good of *all,* to be confused with the good of a *majority* of the members. The symphony will not be played well merely by an adequate performance of a *majority* of the members of the orchestra, though we may be sure that if it is played well as a whole, a majority will have performed adequately. One bad note may ruin it. The whole campaign will not necessarily be won merely by the victories of the *majority* of soldiers. One failure of a minor unit may lead to total defeat. What is good for the country as a whole is not to be achieved merely by making a *majority* of its members happy. The unhappiness of a clearheaded minority or even of a single member may be a far more significant indication of the true state of affairs than the happiness of a muddleheaded majority. Understanding of the common good can never be achieved merely by the simple expedient of counting heads.

Thus the common good is neither an alien good, *opposed* to the individual good, nor is it *materially* identified with the latter. It is not the good of any majority or the good of *all,* understood as a mere *particular* collection, for this is only another "larger," material good. The common good is based on a true universal, the good of *all,* that which is essentially good for man as such, abstracting from what is accidental and contingent. It is this universal good as attainable here and now by a particular human group. It is a whole, not of common *substantial* being, but of common perfection of being. It is something which cannot be touched or seen or pointed at or counted. It is something which must be *understood.*

This understanding can be literally shared by many minds. Hence it can bind different individuals together into a single group, which is physically many but morally and intentionally one. When this rational apprehension of the common good becomes confused, the common purpose disintegrates into myriad individual purposes, and social life is atomized. The only alternative to chaos is then the rule of force and arbitrary decree, which can no longer achieve the true common good but only the supposed good of this particular party or even of this particular man.

4. Love of the Common Good (Efficient Cause)

If we ask what brings the group into existence and what permanently sustains it in being, we must answer *love of the common good* on the part of its potential members and that obligation to pursue this good which arises from an understanding of the natural sanctions called forth by lethargy and neglect. Thus failure to pursue the common good must be followed by a loss of the individual good and by many other evils. The country that refuses to fight against aggression is naturally punished by falling into ways of appeasement, and ultimately by common slavery or destruction. In this case no individual can achieve his natural good. Such *negative* sanctions call forth a sense of obligation which is based upon *primary* understanding and love of the common good. These two factors reenforce each other in calling forth that cooperative aspiration which is the primary, efficient cause of all group life.

When this love, to which we are susceptible by nature, is weakened or diluted, the group itself is weakened and confronted with dissolution. The usual cause of this is a confusion of the common good with the particular good of some individual, some majority, or the collective good of the whole society, *materially* conceived, and therefore hypostatized into a particular entity distinct from the individual substances making it up. These ways of thought lead either to collectivism, which thinks of the group and the group

values as something quite alien to the individuals, or to individualism, which thinks of the individuals alone as real, and of the whole
group as an artificial or useful construction.

Such tendencies can be prevented only by cultivating and
strengthening the pure, immaterial insights of reason. Before men
will aspire to the common good they must first apprehend it, and
sense alone is helpless in this respect. Such understanding can be
greatly aided and fostered by those sensory images of the fine arts
which, if skilfully constructed, provide the intellect with fitting
representations of the common good, from which the concept itself
may be easily abstracted. Hence it is that flags, symbols, signs,
memorials, and other material insignia play such an important role
in all group life. Standing like the Acropolis in conspicuous places
where they can be sensed by all the citizens, these images in color,
marble, sound, and human action itself, lead the individual reason
to think of that colorless, soundless, motionless good which is the
first cause of all their endeavors and which alone binds them together into a cooperative moral entity.

5. THE PATTERN OF DUTIES AND RIGHTS (FORMAL CAUSE)

The common good is a whole of perfecting activity. In order to
be actually achieved, it requires that certain acts (duties) be performed by every member. These group offices or functions are universal or formal in character. It does not matter who in particular
does them. But they must be done. Hence they are the most essential portion of the formal cause of the group, that which makes it
what it is. But once achieved by these offices the common good must
be distributed to all the individual members in particular, each being given the share that is his due. The law of nature prescribes
this share to each individual member as his right.

In view of particular circumstances such natural rights must be
further defined and determined by the group authority, in which
case they become positive or legal rights. But ultimately all legal
rights are founded on natural rights. Rights make up the less essential portion of the formal cause of the group. Taken together, duties
and rights constitute that universal, formal union of giving and
receiving the common good which the group actually *is*. In this
union the giving and providing is *more* essential and prior to the

rights of receiving, for unless the offices are first performed, the rights are never actualized at all. Nevertheless the rights are also essential, for unless the common good is properly distributed, the offices themselves are only partially performed.

The various offices must be universally defined and prescribed in the original conception or constitution of the group in accordance with the law of nature and social justice, which defines the most general institutional requirements of this law. But the different offices themselves must be determined exclusively in the light of the demands of the common good. So far as possible provision must be made for the selection of those with higher capacity for the more difficult and more arduous offices, and for the removal and punishment of those who fail in the performance of their duties. The rights of all members must also be universally defined and prescribed in the original conception. Here, *distributive* justice must be the guide, shares being distributed in proportion to the offices and functions performed.[12] But *corrective* justice must also provide so far as possible for the redress of injury both positive and negative. Once the general pattern of offices and duties has been laid down and accepted, the group actually exists, for it is now a number of individual substances morally united in the pursuit of a common good. But the group will not be completed until some authority is established to administer the plan in concrete action.

6. THE GROUP AUTHORITY (NECESSARY ACCIDENT)

The common good and the pattern of duties and rights which follow from it, are universally definable. But the common good must be achieved and shared by different, *concrete,* individual substances, who must act and share *in particular.* Hence in order to function in the concrete, the form of the group must establish some *authority* to bring the acts and rights of individual members into accordance with the universal plan. But, it may be asked, if every individual understands the common good and agrees with the plan, may it not be left to each individual to modify his acts in the concrete?

The answer is that the *common* good can be achieved only by action which is genuinely *common.* Hence all the individual modifi-

12 Cf. ch. 8, § 2.

cations must have a *common* character. If it were left to each individual to adjust his acts to the concrete situation, without reference to the corresponding adjustments of others, chaos would soon
ensue. These myriad adjustments to varying circumstance can be
given a *common* character only by a *common* authority with the
power to decide and act quickly, and thus to keep all the concrete
acts, in their continuous adaptation to shifting conditions, congruent with the common plan. Authority therefore is a necessary
property of the group as such.

This authority performs three important functions, analogous
to deliberation, judgment, and choice in individual practical reason.[13] First of all, the group authority must preserve an understanding of the basic natural law from which the group structure is
derived. It must maintain the positive laws introduced into the
original constitution and lay down new positive laws when the
situation so requires. In the second place, it must exercise a judicial
function, applying this body of law equitably to varying individual
cases in accordance with distributive and corrective justice. In the
third place, it must choose and decide between alternative courses
of concrete action and carry them out in practice. Since the common
good, which is the object of social endeavor, possesses a higher
degree of universality than the particular good, which is the object
of individual endeavor, this executive function in the case of the
group is more clearly subordinate to the other two functions of
deliberation and judgment.

The individual is more immersed in contingent accidents, and
therefore less able to adhere continuously to a universal pattern
leading necessarily to the end. Group life, on the other hand, is
more stable and continuous. Hence it is more important for a society to possess an absolutely clear understanding of the common
good and the universal, necessary means required for its attainment. Once this understanding is achieved it is far more possible
for the group to maintain a stable, undeviating policy on this
course, making only temporary and minor adjustments to altering
circumstance, which for an individual might involve a revolutionary
free decision.

Such decisions are required in group life far more rarely when

[13] Cf. ch. 5, § 2b and c; and ch. 20, § 4.

the group is confronted with situations of extraordinary novelty or when the whole structure of group life has become critically diseased or inverted. At such times, when great changes and transformations are required, the executive branch of group authority may legitimately take things into its own hands and temporarily subordinate the other two. But this may be justified only as a temporary expedient in the face of abnormal emergencies. The lasting ascendency of executive authority over legislative is always a sign of social decay and corruption.

7. SEVEN FUNDAMENTAL PRINCIPALS OF GROUP LIFE

In the light of this classical analysis of the causal structure of the human group, the following principles may be recognized as applying to all group life.

1. The human group is not a substantial but a *moral* entity. It is not subjectively determined but is rationally elicited, and is therefore distinct from any hive or herd or animal association. Every human group has a visible, material aspect. It is made up of material, human individuals. It may use buildings, machines, and other paraphernalia as social instruments. But the final, efficient, and formal causes of social life are all primarily immaterial in character, for they are an integrated system of universal relations in the intellect, and the aspiration elicited by this system in the will.

This essential rationality radically distinguishes the human group from an animal association or cluster which by instinct may achieve the particular good of this collection. The members of such an animal group do not purposefully *know* the common good or the means by which it is achieved, even though they are determined to use such means.

2. Although a group may be materially annihilated by the destruction of its members, this very rarely happens of *natural* groups, for the survival of one rational member is enough to preserve the group. Groups are weakened and destroyed rather by immaterial, rational causes, than by force and external agencies which are helpless against the immaterial purposes of the will.[14]

The formal union of the group may be weakened by four such causes. (1) The requisite *offices and duties* may not be compre-

[14] Cf. Toynbee, A. J., *A Study of History*, New York, Oxford, 1947, chs. 13–16.

hensively or correctly understood, so that the common good is not actually achieved. (2) Even though understood, they may not be chosen and performed by concrete individuals. (3) The universal *rights* of the members may not be correctly or comprehensively understood, so that the common good is not fully achieved. (4) Even though understood, these rights may not be actually realized, owing to external difficulties, lack of power, or individual immorality and injustice.

The group authority may fail in any one or in all of its three functions. First, it may fail to achieve or to maintain an accurate and comprehensive understanding of the natural and positive law directing the group. Second, it may fail in equitably applying this law to individual cases and situations. Finally, the executive branch of the group authority may get out of hand, either failing to make the proper common adjustments to changing situations or jealously clinging to its power without sufficient regard for law and justice. But in themselves these are minor defects which may be corrected if the common good is really understood and loved by the members. If really serious, these difficulties have their roots in some defect of this understanding and the love which it elicits. Two *basic* diseases of group life attack this final and efficient cause.

First, there is the materialistic error of collectivism which misconceives the group as a different entity, *alien* to the individuals making it up. The common good is then opposed to the individual good, the group to its own members. This confronts aspiration with an impossible alternative which must weaken it, and lead finally to disintegration. Either it must love the group itself, conceived as another, distinct entity, *the state*, the nation as an organic whole, and so forth, or it must love the individual members. It cannot love both. The result is that it loves neither.

Next, there is the chaotic atomism of individualism to which the first error is likely to lead. One error easily breeds its opposite. Seeing that the group is not a substantial entity, existing in itself, the mind is apt to conclude that it is no entity at all, that only the material individuals are real. The common good then is pursued, not for its own sake *because it is good*, but only because it is helpful in attaining a purely individual or personal good. This good, however, is unfit to become the *primary* object of aspiration.

Entirely apart from what it *ought* to be, taken merely materially as it *happens* to be, this is confused with irrelevant and conflicting accidents. Furthermore, it is by nature only a part not a whole, and the part without the whole to which it naturally belongs, cannot help but be imperfect. Such aspiration for the individual self alone as the highest end is warped and weakened. It is in fact a rebellion against order and subordination, which must lead to chaos, for each individual self is different, and hence pitted against the rest. One will prefer *A* to *B*; another will prefer *B* to *A*. Without any invariable universal standard to determine the *natural* order of subordination, the whole order of culture must become inverted, means being confused with end, and end with means. As Plato pointed out, such anarchy must lead ultimately to tyranny and despotism, the final corruption of group life.

When a single individual or mass of individuals manages to subordinate the whole group structure to its own private ends, then all the distortions we have described become rampant. The common good is confused with the material good of *this* man, *this* party, or *this* majority. All other purposes are subordinated to its particular purposes which, having no stable basis in any rational principle, wobble back and forth in an unstable opportunism. Voluntary aspiration degenerates into externally determined, material interest. The group is formally disunited, *duties* degenerating into enforced services to a tyranny, and *rights* into the capricious bestowal of unearned rewards. Authority is replaced by mere force, law and equity by mere executive power.

Such a group no longer performs a *natural* function in subordination to its *natural* end, but rebelling against all order and subordination, attempts to exist for itself alone, blindly struggling, like a spreading infection, to enslave all humanity to itself. Such diseased or inverted group life is more horrible than a psychically diseased or inverted individual, for group life is more perfect than individual life, and *corruptio melioris pejor* (the better the thing, the worse is its corruption) . Human degeneration can go no further.

3. The group is *of* the members of the group, being materially supported by them and formally constituted by their duties and rights. The group is not an alien entity that exists apart from the members. They are the matter out of which it is composed. Their

accidents are its form, the pattern of their own perfection. Hence
the group essentially inheres in, and belongs to, its members.

4. *The group is for the sake of the members.* The group exists
for the sake of the *common* good, which is the perfection of *all*. This
good is not good because they happen to desire it or because they
think it is good for them. It is good because it is really and essentially their own proper perfection. In this sense the group is theirs
and belongs to them, because it exists *in toto* for the sake of an
end which is theirs.

5. *The group is sustained by the members.* The whole group is
efficiently caused and sustained by the members. Therefore the
supreme authority, which establishes any *de facto*, secondary authority, lies with the members. This is a supremely important principle
which applies to *every* group. It is derived ultimately from the
unequivocal domination of the end over the means. The means
exist exclusively for the end, and are essentially and really relative
to this end. Hence the means must naturally be ordered by whatever it is that possesses the end, or, as Aquinas states it, "the
ordering of the means to the end always belongs to that which
possesses the end." [15]

Since the common good belongs to all the members of any group
as their proper perfection, the ordering of the means to the end,
including the establishment of an administrative authority and the
correction of such an authority, also belongs to them. It is crucially
important to recognize that the group is not brought into existence
by the group authority. Since that which brings anything into existence and that which sustains it belong to one agency (the total,
efficient cause), all the members *by nature* possess the right to
criticize and correct the administrative authority. The whole group
structure is sustained by all the members.

6. Since this group structure is primarily rational in character,
the group cannot be properly sustained unless all the members are
given a comprehensive understanding of the nature of the group,
the broad principles of social justice on which it is founded, and
unless they are granted the greatest possible freedom in discussing
possible alterations in line with these principles. A sound system
of universal education and freedom of expression, both vocal and

[15] *Summa Theologica,* Prima Secundae, Qu. 90, Art. 13.

written, are absolutely essential for the maintenance of healthy group life.

7. *An unjust law is no law* (Plato, Augustine, and Aquinas). Hence the *right of revolution* against the unjust administration of authority is granted to the members of any group by the law of nature. The right of criticism does not end with the employment of speech and writing. The function of sustaining the group belongs to *all* the members. Therefore, against the unjust decrees of a ruling authority the members possess, not only the right of passive resistance, but also the right to use forceful means to correct the abuse, provided that the advantage to be gained is not clearly outweighed by the disadvantages always attached to the use of force.

Bearing these fundamental principles in mind, which apply invariably to all groups of whatever sort, we must now turn to the vast network of groups existing everywhere around us, with a view towards distinguishing their major kinds, and how they are naturally related to one another. Only after we have arrived at some sound classification of these distinct types of groups can we profitably turn to an examination of the great group problems of our time.

REFERENCES

Recommended Reading

Aquinas, *Summa Theologica,* Prima Secundae, Qu. 90–97.

Suggested Reading

1. The concept of natural law, though not always referred to by these words, underlies the whole moral philosophy of Plato and Aristotle. Cf. especially Plato, *Republic,* Book II, 368–9; IV, 443–4; *Laws* VII, 793A ff.; Aristotle, *Nicomachean Ethics,* Book V, chap. 7. For an exact statement of the theory of natural law and positive law, cf. Aquinas, *Summa Theologica,* Prima Secundae, Qu. 90, 94, 96–97. For modern objections to the theory, cf. Sabine, G. H., *A History of Political Theory,* New York, Henry Holt, 1944, pp. 595–596 and 601–606; *Anarchical Fallacies,* in *Select Extracts from the Works of Jeremy Bentham,* Edinburgh, 1843, pp. 67 ff.; Ritchie, D. G., *Natural Rights,* New York, Macmillan, 1895.
2. Aquinas, *Summa Theologica,* Prima Secundae, Qu. 90. For the common good as the supreme object of human aspiration, cf. Plato, *Republic* VI,

497A 1–4 (Adam) ; Aristotle, *Nicomachean Ethics,* Book I, chap. 2. For the denial of any opposition between the common good and the individual good, when each is properly conceived, cf. Plato, *Republic* IV, 419–420, and the final answer to Adeimantus' question, V, 465–466. For the idealistic theory of the group as an organism, cf. Bradley, F. H., *Ethical Studies,* London, King, 1876, *My Station and its Duties,* pp. 145 ff., and Bosanquet, B., *The Philosophical Theory of the State,* second ed. London, 1910. For the individualistic theory of human social life, cf. Sabine, G. H., *A History of Political Theory,* pp. 432–433, 587–588, and 667; Laski, H. J., *Studies in the Problem of Sovereignty,* Yale University Press, New Haven, 1917, chap. 1. For evidence confirming the view that civilization rests primarily upon ideas and the mimesis of rational thoughts and acts, cf. Toynbee, A. J., *A Study of History,* Oxford, 1947, Part IV.

3. For Principles (1) and (2), cf. Aquinas, *Summa Theologica,* Prima Secundae, Qu. 90, Art. 1, and Qu. 91, Art. 2. For Principle (3), cf. Aristotle, *Politics,* Book III, chap. 1 to 1275A. For Principle (4), Prima Secundae, Qu. 90, Art. 2, especially answer to objection 2. For Principle (5), Prima Secundae, Qu. 90, Art. 3. For Principle (6), Qu. 90, Art. 4. For Principle (7), Qu. 96, Art. 4; cf. Augustine, *De Libero Arbitrio,* Book I, chap. 5.

Chapter 10

BASIC NATURAL GROUPS

TRADITIONAL social philosophy has concentrated its attention so exclusively upon two of the basic natural groups (the family and the state) that it has tended to neglect the rich variety of human associations which exists in any mature society. At present, for example, we know that in addition to the family and the state there are also labor unions, industrial associations, governing bodies, and colleges and universities, to mention only a few. As we have seen, every human group is the manifestation of a common end which can be understood and desired. There will be as many groups in a given society, therefore, as there are purposes which are taken seriously by its members. To understand is always to classify. Our first task must be to attempt a classification of this bewildering array of group purposes. What are the different ends that men can hold in common? What are the major kinds of human groups?

1. THE GENERAL CLASSIFICATION OF HUMAN GROUPS

The most fundamental division of human groups is that which distinguishes what we may call *final* groups from *instrumental* groups. A final group is one (1) whose final cause includes all those activities which are necessary for life, (2) which can exist either alone or together with some other final group it has included, and (3) to which the whole substantial being of each member contributes something. An instrumental group is one (1) whose final cause includes only some subordinate phase of life, (2) which cannot exist alone but only in some final group, and (3) to which only a single phase of the activity of its members contributes something. In brief, a final group is one which can carry on all the functions necessary to sustain life. An instrumental group is incapable of this and always exists as a subgroup within some final group.

Final groups are always devoted to the positive end of life itself.

But instrumental groups may be devoted either to the achievement of some positive end, such as the making of some kind of artifact, or to some negative end, the elimination of some evil. Both the positive and the corrective instrumental groups fall into three subdivisions: (1) noetic, (2) politic, and (3) poietic. We shall examine these more carefully in Chapter 11. First, we must examine the more fundamental, final groups.

Final groups are divided into those which are life-sustaining and those which are life-completing. All final, life-sustaining groups are natural in the sense that they are required by human nature itself for its perfection. Life-completing, final groups fall into two divisions.

First, there are friendship groups, not demanded by nature but rather by *the second nature* of virtuous habits developed in each individual through his free rational choices. The strengthening, purifying bonds of friendship may penetrate into any natural association of men: this is in accordance with nature but not demanded by nature. Sometimes a smaller natural group, like the family, may be included by a friendship group.

Second, there is the religious group, which is founded neither on nature nor on second nature but rather on some special gift from a supernatural source.[1] Such a group, when it actually exists and is maintained in a sound condition, can clarify and confirm the purposes of other final groups, including them all, without absorbing them or interfering in any way with their autonomy.

One group *A includes* another group *B* when the final cause of *B* is seen to be contained in the final cause of *A* and when all the legitimate functions of *B* are integrally performed within *A*. Thus one group can *include* another without destroying it. All instrumental groups are included within life-sustaining groups. This must be sharply distinguished from that process of *absorption* or assimilation by which one group destroys another opposed group.

One group *absorbs* another *B* when the final cause and operations of *A* are substituted for those of *B*. This rarely happens by physical conquest alone but rather by ideational propaganda taking advantage of intellectual confusion and apathy in the weaker group. Ideas are more important weapons for social war than armies.

[1] Cf. ch. 12, §§ 1 and 2.

A group with soundly articulated ideas, clearly grasped and loved by its members, has little to fear from alien groups. As Toynbee has shown, civilizations are rarely destroyed by the *physical* force of external enemies. They rather commit suicide by intellectual anarchy and deadening of aspiration for a sound, overarching purpose.[2]

Let us now turn to the basic natural groups.

2. LIFE-SUSTAINING GROUPS

Final, natural groups are all life-sustaining, or at least almost life-sustaining (as the family). They are prescribed by nature for the perfection of man, and fall into three distinct divisions: the family (tribe and nation), the constitutional community, and the world community, now in an inchoate stage of development. Nature demands that they be included in the order indicated. Though the family and the tribe possess a degree of finality, the constitutional community is more perfect and more final, whereas the world community, should it ever be actualized, possesses an even higher degree of finality. It alone would be capable of carrying on all the functions necessary to sustain life with maximal efficiency. It alone would be capable of existing in complete independence and autarchy. Finally, it alone could command the unqualified, complete, and rational allegiance of every member.

Hence this world community is prescribed by nature itself as the most adequate mode of sustaining human life on this planet, and our neglect of this prescription is punished by the imposition of natural sanctions,[3] such as national competition, aggression, and war. The less perfect forms of group life are also demanded by nature and cannot be eliminated by the more perfect form under which they should be subsumed. Thus the family still exists in the constitutional community, and the local community with certain autonomous rights must still exist in the world community, if this is ever established.

In the material order of generation, the more perfect is preceded by the less perfect. Hence the first family and tribal organizations emerged as a result of sensitive and estimative apprehensions and

---

[2] Cf. Toynbee, A. J., *A Study of History*, pp. 260 ff.
[3] Cf. ch. 2, § 2b.

appetites, with only a minimum apprehension of the common good and the necessary means of achieving it. The common good was apprehended merely as a particular cluster of interests of particular members of the group, without any sharp distinction between pure appetite and genuine, natural *need*. The group authority, not being rationally established, simply grew into accidental, despotic forms, arbitrarily laying down customs and traditions with very little real relation to any clear understanding of the nature of man and his necessary needs. Education and the higher rational arts were not developed.

Hence these primitive groups: the tribe, the people, and the nation, unified only by the accidents of blood, soil, and tradition, have attempted, as in many places they are still attempting, to perfect the complex nature of man with an extremely inadequate and imperfect equipment. What is really amazing is that we can still recognize those living under such ineffective administrations as still *essentially* human.

The transition from this primitive and undeveloped stage of group organization to that of the constitutional community, which has required the whole era of recorded history in the more favorable temperate zones of the earth, is still far from complete. This transition involves the development of rational understanding and self-consciousness in the community as a whole, the most arduous and laborious of all human tasks. But here and there it has been partially achieved by the acquisition of some insight into the nature of the common good and the essential rights and duties it requires. Then, either by a lengthy and gradual process, as in England, or by a sudden revolution, as in France, the people have overturned despotic and archaic forms of tribal government. In constitutional charters and agreements based on the law of nature, they have established modes of government really responsive to the natural needs of the community as a whole.

But these new forms of natural government have not eliminated the family and the tribe altogether. They have subsumed these less perfect groups, allotting to them only those functions which nature prescribes, and taking from them those functions which can be better performed by the community. Similarly, if a world community is ever established we need not suppose that it will attempt to eliminate the local constitutional community. It will allot to such subordinate communities many governmental rights which they are alone fitted to perform, and will take away from them only that absolute sovereignty and final authority which they are certainly not fitted to possess. Let us now briefly examine the main structural features of these three *natural*, final groups.

a. THE FAMILY AND THE TRIBE. The family is an imperfect, *final* group prescribed by natural law. It is made up of one man, one woman, and their offspring. The final cause of the family is the procreation of children, the completion of this process by nurture and education, the satisfaction of a natural inclination, and finally, the opportunity for a peculiar and unique mode of friendship. Its efficient cause is threefold: first, the natural procreative impulse; second, a rational understanding of this impulse and its natural ends, together with a voluntary aspiration to achieve them; and third, a free contract between the two parties (marriage). The formal cause is a union of rights and duties, many of which are directly decreed by nature. The positive determinations of these and the deliberate direction of married life may be left to friendly consultation without the setting up of any special group authority, as in larger natural groups.

Nature has certainly allotted to the female a greater share in the burden of nurturing and educating the children in the earlier stages of their development, and to the male (in virtue of his greater strength) a larger share in bearing other burdens. But beyond this, it is impossible to go. Both partners have been endowed with rational faculties as human beings. Both are capable of deliberation, judgment, and choice. Hence a single, directing authority is unnecessary for the family. Nature has left it to the *second nature* of friendship to take over this directing function. The family is an original and basic form of group. It can never be legitimately eliminated or superseded in its proper sphere by any more perfect sustaining group, such as the community.

Intermediate between the family and the community is that vague amalgam of families descended from a common stock which we call the tribe, the race, and the nation. This is an inchoate or incipient community with certain critical defects which must be first corrected before it can attain the full status of community life,

First of all, its members are not simply human beings, but rather human beings *qua* possessing certain physical accidents such as shape and stature, skin color, a common dwelling place, common ancestors, and so on, essentially irrelevant to membership in a constitutional community. In this respect the tribe or nation is a sort of enlarged family devoted rather to the aim of perpetuating certain accidents of birth and place than to that of achieving the common good of its members. Such associations are too large to be guided by friendly discussion and deliberation, hence some group authority must be set up.

Since the efficient cause sustaining the group is a common, *sensuous* inclination to particular, *incidental* ends rather than to any clearly envisaged *common good,* this authority tends to be established in response to sensuously felt necessity without any explicit pact or constitution defining the natural purposes and limitations of this authority. Hence the authority tends to become despotic, confusing its own positive decrees with natural law, and arbitrarily defining rights, duties, and patterns of conduct with little regard for *natural* order. Those who are weak or who fail to meet some arbitrary standard of race or historic origin, are oppressed and enslaved, whereas those who possess mere power or incidental advantages of origin, are admired and elevated to positions of rank, irrespective of their genuine human virtue. Such tribal structures often fearfully distort and obstruct nature by fantastic overgrowths of functionless complexity. Such overgrowths must be carefully weeded out and corrected before a genuine community can be formed.

b. THE CONSTITUTIONAL COMMUNITY. The family, though prescribed by nature, is not completely self-sufficient. By itself it is unable to perform *all* the functions necessary to supply the complex wants of human nature. Furthermore, unless the diverse families are subsumed together under some larger group structure, they will respond differently to the different situations confronting them. If this process is not checked by rational criticism, they will develop entirely different traditions and habits, and thus become alien and inimical to one another. Man, when he becomes alien and inimical, is the most terrible enemy of man, for his gift of intelligence, when turned to destructive uses, is the most powerful and terrible of all natural weapons. So the family is destined by nature not to be a whole but a part of a larger and more perfect whole, the human society or community.

The *final cause* of the community is the common good of all its members, irrespective of their race, blood, or accidental attributes. This common good consists primarily in the free activity of each member in accordance with individual virtue.[4] To make this possible, three kinds of good must be supplied to every member, in accordance with his natural rights. These are: (1) material property over which he has a natural right of ownership, (2) immaterial goods for his rational faculties, and (3) a free and orderly performance of the duties required for the realization of these universal and inalienable rights.

The *efficient cause* of the human community is twofold: the common love of the common good by the common man, and an implicit or explicit contract to which this has led. This contract specifies three essential aspects of the formal structure of the community: (1) the natural law on which it is based, (2) the natural rights and duties prescribed by this law, and (3) the group authority which is required to direct the community in the flux of events by further positive law.

The *formal cause* is the union of rights and duties in the way of life thus defined. The *virtue,* or well-functioning of the community, will depend on the degree to which the various rights and duties (1) have been *wisely* defined in the constitution, (2) have been exactly and *justly* carried out by the common action of the whole community, (3) have been *courageously* sustained in spite of all difficulties and obstacles, and (4) have *temperately* subordinated all other tendencies to common action for this common end. If the form of the community has been accurately conceived and adequately perfected by such action, the four social virtues of wisdom, justice, stability, and order will consummate the life of the group. Otherwise it must sink into confusion, injustice, instability, and revolution.[5]

As we have seen, an authority capable of directing common action in the flux of events is a necessary accident of any human

[4] Cf. chs. 9, § 3, and 2 § 1.
[5] Cf. ch. 5, § 1.

group. In the community this authority may be either despotic or democratic. A despotic authority confuses its own interest with the common good, and its own positive decrees with the order of natural law. It admits no inalienable, natural rights in its subjects, and no limitation of its own sovereignty. Any decree is regarded as legitimate, provided there is power to enforce it, no matter how malignant or unnatural it may be. Law is replaced by arbitrary decree, authority by force.

Despotic rule is either unpopular (without the consent of a majority of the people) or popular (with the consent of a majority). Each of these is an illegitimate and unnatural form of rule, but the second is far more dangerous than the first. There are two reasons for this. An unpopular tyranny is still limited by sound habits and modes of action still prevailing in the community. Furthermore, it can be easily removed by eliminating a relatively small number of individuals. But once a tyranny gains the consent of the people as a whole it can enforce its unnatural decrees under the disguise of democratic procedure, as though it were actually working for the common good. Such a mass tyranny of the people, having lost all sense of the distinction between natural and positive law, is internally unlimited and can be revoked only by revolution or by some greater, external force.

Democratic authority recognizes its subordination to natural law and to the *unsurrendered,* natural rights of the members of the community. It exercises its authority for the common good. Such authority takes two distinct forms, either paternalistic or representative. A paternalistic authority works for the common good but without the knowledge and consent of the people. It is justifiable only in communities where the people have been previously enslaved, lack all political habits, and are generally uneducated, as a transition to representative democracy. In the latter, any adult member is allowed the right to criticise and oppose the *positive* decrees and rules of its government. No one is permitted to advocate the overthrow of *natural* laws, rights, and duties, of which these are only specific determinations.

Democratic authority is *essentially* undermined by two causes: (1) a failure of educational agencies to teach the people the basic principles of natural law and social order and (2) a failure on the part of the people to act in accordance with these principles. These causes may lead imperceptibly to paternalism and tyranny. It is *accidentally* rendered imperfect by two further cases. First, even though a majority of persons are in possession of their natural, political rights (education, criticism, and representation), certain depressed groups may be deprived of such rights and reduced to political slavery. Second, even though all persons are in possession of their natural, political rights, certain depressed groups may be deprived of other natural rights, such as the right to have enough material property for the proper sustaining of life or the right to a democratic administration of minor groups to which they belong. Any one of these causes, unless corrected, may lead to instability, revolution, and incidentally to tyranny, a necessary consequence of chaos.

c. THE WORLD COMMUNITY. We have already seen that the family is unable to stand alone as a natural, sustaining group. The very same arguments which lead to this conclusion in the case of the family group apply also to the geographically limited community. The present-day national state is unable to achieve the ends decreed by nature to the maximum degree of efficiency without the aid and cooperation of other national states. Knowledge and science, for example, are extremely hard to achieve and extremely precious, since all human activity depends upon them. Hence each local society is in desperate need, not only of the knowledge which has been discovered and preserved by its own scientists and philosophers, but also of all that has been discovered and preserved in other communities. The satisfaction of the natural *immaterial* needs of man require global organization. This is also true of the natural *material* needs of man.

Different raw materials of common value are found only in certain restricted areas. Different productive techniques are better developed in certain countries and certain climates. These cannot be used to the best advantage of all without global organization. Finally, unless they are guided by common principles and laws the different national communities will respond differently to the situations confronting them and develop different habits and traditions. As a result, they will become alien and inimical to one another. Without a world community social anarchy and war must arise.

Far from being the natural state, as Hobbes supposed, such a state is acutely unnatural and ultimately incompatible, not only with the attainment of any high degree of human happiness, but even with the very existence of man as man.

By attaching two or three billion human beings to a single small planet, nature has prescribed a single planetary society. Whether we ever achieve it or not, this is clearly nature's decree. Without it this creature cannot be adequately perfected or even exist. The present-day nation-state is very defective and far from being nature's goal. But as in the analogous case of the family, we need not suppose that it must be entirely superseded and eliminated by a less imperfect world society, including it.

Nature has not only placed two or three billion men on a single planet, but has also divided the habitable portions of the planet from one another, giving them very different climates, physiographies, and geographic characteristics. There can be no doubt that the societies inhabiting these different areas must be allowed free scope to determine those different positive laws and institutions by which they can most effectively meet the different conditions surrounding them.

3. NATURAL INSTRUMENTAL GROUPS

In addition to the fundamental life-sustaining groups, there is, in any highly developed society, a vast array of instrumental groups, such as labor unions, governmental agencies, and learned societies, each of which performs some definite subordinate function. No one can belong to such a technical or professional group without also belonging to a life-sustaining group. The clear-cut organization of instrumental groups is a late stage of social development. This is one reason why until recently instrumental groups have been neglected by social theory.

We have already noted the process by which life-sustaining groups develop from the vague, instinctive level of the tribe or nation to the more highly conscious and articulated level of the constitutional community.[6] Instrumental groups follow a similar course of evolution. They begin with individuals performing similar functions in a sustaining community. We refer to such individuals as

6 Cf. this chapter, § 2.

classes. Thus we speak of *the farmers, the teachers,* and *the working class.* Such classes are not yet human groups but only the matter from which genuine groups can be formed. A class does not become a group until the individuals become conscious of their similar situation, agree upon a common end, and take common measures to achieve this end. Until this occurs they are only a quasi group in process of formation. When a clear class consciousness is awakened in the individual minds of a class, the group is ready to be formed. When a common end and common means for the attainment of this end are determined and agreed upon, we have an instrumental group.

The activity one performs as the member of such a group is labor, work, or professional activity of some kind. The activity one performs as the member of a sustaining group is the living of life itself. Every laborer or professional worker is also a citizen, endowed with the natural right to a share of the fruits of all the instrumental groups. To deny this and to identify a man's human status with his technical status in some subordinate functional group, results in slavery. Here, however, we must note a significant difference between three major types of functional group.

Man's nature contains three major parts: reason, which simply apprehends the truth; will, which knows how to attain the natural end; and the physical part and its material instruments, which must be used as means for attaining the end. The individual cannot perfect himself unless he knows something of his end, knows how to attain it, and possesses the material means. The sustaining group cannot attain the common good unless this good is apprehended, loved, deliberately desired, and sought with the necessary material instruments. Hence all men possess a natural right to knowledge, practical knowledge, and the instruments required for action. Without the cultivation of these three goods men cannot act. Hence there are three basic types of instrumental group supported by any sustaining group: (a) noetic groups, specially concerned with knowledge, (b) politic groups, concerned with deliberation and planning for action, and (c) poietic groups concerned with supplying the material instruments of action. Let us now consider these natural instrumental groups one by one.

a. NOETIC GROUPS. Each human being is endowed with rational

faculties which give him a right to a rational education so that he can apprehend the truth and enjoy it as apprehended. Hence there are three subordinate rational groups which attempt to satisfy a natural immaterial human need: educational groups, trying to train the rational faculties; scientific groups, trying to apprehend further truth and to preserve what has been apprehended; and aesthetic groups, trying to make material objects in which being may be intuitively apprehended and enjoyed.

The arts practiced by these groups must to some extent be practiced by any human being, and the immaterial goods they achieve (discipline of the noetic faculties, truth, and beauty, which perfect these faculties) belong to human perfection intrinsically, and are therefore essential parts of the common good. Hence those who professionally practice them are not devoting themselves to what is merely instrumental for the living of life, but to a most important part of life itself. The distinction can still be made between the man *qua* man and the man *qua* philosopher or artist, but the distinction is *inadequate* (like that between a man and his body), for the one is really a part of the other. Philosophy, for example, is not a mere means but an intermediate end of life. Hence these groups have less distinct boundaries, and especially in cultivated communities, merge with the sustaining group. No matter how intensively a man cultivates these arts he cannot become enslaved thereby. He cannot make truth for another without also philosophizing for himself. The attainment of truth and beauty are highly important perfections of life, and no man becomes a slave by perfecting himself. We may see this more clearly if we analyze the causal structure of these arts and that of the groups practicing them.

The end of such an art is the establishment of an utterly invisible and immaterial habit of apprehension or appreciation. Its efficient causes, in the case of the noetic arts (science and philosophy), are immanent acts of knowing and enjoying, which only the individual can carry out. In the aesthetic arts and the educational arts material images are also constructed to aid in the eliciting of such acts. But these material transformations are only incidental to the major purposes of the rational arts. Their primary aim is not to make a material thing but rather to actualize an immaterial capacity either in the individual himself (the noetic arts) or in some one else (the fine arts and education). They aim not so much to make something not in existence before as to assimilate something already in existence. Hence they are mimetic in character.

The trained mind learns how to imitate the reality he knows, the trained student to imitate the mind of the teacher. Hence these arts are purely active and are ruined by passivity at any point. The mind cannot assimilate the structure of nature without intense activity. The student cannot be taught unless both teacher and student are actively understanding. The aesthetic audience must be actively assimilating and enjoying. In all such techniques there must be an indirect, inciting, suggesting factor, which does not so much impose action on another as call forth an action of his own. These arts are a mode of therapy rather than one of making or generation. They are engaged not so much in helping nature as in enabling nature to help herself.

The group of individuals practicing such an art must be moved by a love of the common good, of which the practice of their art is an integral part. The efficient cause of their activity must be a love of the art for its own sake, since there is no good greater than this, save the entire living of human life, which must include precisely what they are doing. The activity itself must be an immanent action, with only a very subordinate phase of transitive action on imperfect matter. The pattern of rights and duties, which constitutes the formal union of the group, involves very little division of labor, for each of these arts can be practiced only by a free and autonomous individual.

He must understand and enjoy to the very limit of his apprehensive capacities and then communicate what he has grasped so far as possible to others. No external power or authority has the right of exercising any control over him. In fact, no external power as such has the power to do so. What force is there that can make an individual intellect see what it cannot see or enjoy what it cannot enjoy? The apprehensive faculties, being immaterial, are by nature free from any subjection to external force. They are absolutely and exclusively under the control of their external, formal objects and can only apprehend them as they are.

But surely, it may be said, some sort of authority must be found, as in all groups, to direct the common action of the noetic group, to maintain continuity with the efforts and discoveries of the past, and to bring forth concerted effort in applying past knowledge to new problems of the present. This is certainly true. Groups devoting themselves to immaterial, invisible ends necessarily produce such an authority of themselves and out of themselves, just as other groups necessarily produce authorities armed with power to enforce their positive decrees. But in this case physical power is powerless, and the threat of physical power without avail. What kind of authority can this be, and armed with what? The authority of truth and beauty themselves, armed with the power of inspiring shame if they are ignored and tossed aside!

Such authority can be embodied in an intellectual tradition which may play the same role in noetic groups that is played by governmental power in other human associations. When truth, for example, has once been discovered and embodied in some classic text, supported by sound tradition, it may continue to exercise a valuable mimetic power over those who are devoting themselves to the truth. Such classics may not only serve to maintain the truth that has already been discovered. They may also foster the discovery of further truth, since one insight, clearly understood, leads on to others. A genuine classic produces further discoveries, clarifications, and corrections of itself. No intellectual tradition is sound unless it is in a process of constantly clarifying, criticizing, and extending the truth that is already possessed. This spirit of the sound, self-critical tradition was pungently expressed by Aristotle in speaking of his revered teacher and master, Plato, "He is a dear friend, but the truth is even dearer." [7]

When the "classics" are rather slavishly admired and repeated than really grasped and understood, they may become a terrible obstacle to free enquiry. An intellectual group may then be chained by its own tradition and its dead deposit of half-grasped words and formulas. Such a diseased "tradition" must be overthrown and cast aside, though there is always a danger of throwing away nuggets of truth with the rubbish. When this happens the group is left without guidance, and a new start must be made. This chaotic condition is dangerous and unhealthy. But it is not so dangerous

[7] *Nicomachean Ethics* 1096A 11 ff. Cf. Plato, *Republic* 595C.

and unhealthy as that state of being firmly chained to falsehood, which is so apt to follow in its train.

It is the essential duty of any noetic, educational, or aesthetic group to establish a sound tradition, embodied in classic works, and then to keep this tradition from freezing into a slavish immobility by constant criticism, correction, and advance. It is very bad for a noetic group to lose all truth and tradition. But there is something even worse than this—to be dominated by a false and defective tradition. As in the case of all governing power, chaos is the mother of tyranny. So the first evil leads to the second. It can be overcome only by carefully keeping the truth that has been discovered alive in the minds of successive generations, and by constantly attempting to refine it and extend it further.

b. POLITIC GROUPS. Noetic groups are composed of single autonomous individuals, each performing the same rational functions and unified by an immanent tradition. Poietic groups, as we shall see (section c, below), are composed of dependent individuals and machines, each performing a different function in some transitive act on matter, which must be integrated and ordered by external authority. Politic, or governmental, groups carry on an ordering function, which is both noetic and operational in character. Hence they show a composite structure. At the upper noetic levels they are highly individualized, whereas at the lower executive levels they are socio-technical.

In more simple primitive societies the deliberative and judicial functions of the community are often turned over to a few individuals who choose and plan for integrated action and apply these decisions to the concrete case. They may be enforced by small armed groups or sometimes by the mere threat of force by the whole community. In highly developed modern communities, deliberation is exercised by large law-making bodies, judgment by a complex structure of courts, and the executive branch of government is carried on by a vast array of choice-making, planning, and enforcement agencies, ending in huge police and military forces.

Confronted by this vast and intricate organization, we must not lose the forest for the trees. All governmental functions fall into three main groups: (1) those which deliberate general, contingent laws and policies to meet changing, concrete situations, (2) those which apply these to concrete cases and judge of infractions of the law, and (3) those which make the ultimate decisions and choices of action, and carry out the laws in the concrete. All special governmental groups are either deliberative, judicial, or executive. At present we are apt to think that this is all there is to government. What is it, after all, besides these special instrumental agencies, having little or no connection with noetic groups and with the rest of the community? But this is a great mistake, as we may see, if we ask ourselves the following questions: What is the art of government? For what does it exist? Who set it up in the first place?

The *final cause* is the common good of all the members of the community. This cannot be achieved without division of labor and common action in the performance of natural duties for the satisfaction of natural rights. In a shifting world, ever developing into a new kaleidoscopic array of accidents, such common action cannot be sustained without some common authority, which can act quickly to meet new cases and situations. This is the reason for governmental authority, which, as we have seen,[8] is a necessary accident of any sustaining group and of any instrumental group within the province of its instrumental action. Man's reason is universal. He himself is a material animal, who has to act in a fleeting, particular situation. Authority is the way in which the former enters into the latter. But who sets up the authority, and what are its limits?

Here we must refer to a preceding discussion.[9] The common good belongs to the people as a whole. Authority exists for the sake of achieving this end in the concrete. It is a necessary instrumental means to this end. Hence in accordance with the fundamental principle that the means exist purely for the sake of the end, and that he who possesses the end should order the means, we must conclude that the people *as a whole* establish the governmental authority and maintain its power as an ultimate, efficient cause.

Why do they set it up in the first place? Because of the law of nature, which demands that they live in accordance with the universal dictates of their rational faculty and that they govern their common action in the concrete by such universal dictates.

[8] Cf. ch. 9, § 6.
[9] Cf. ch. 9, § 7, principle (5).

All governmental agencies therefore are subject to the law of nature. They exist only within the framework of this law, which defines the fundamental rights and duties of natural, human life. Their authority in no sense abrogates or supersedes that of natural law, as Hobbes and other social-contract theorists have supposed. Governmental authority is based on the ultimate authority of the law of nature. Its function is not to set up some higher law, but only to give certain contingent determinations the framework of the universal natural law, in order to make concrete action possible. It follows, therefore, that Payne was quite correct in maintaining against Hobbes and others that no natural rights were surrendered in the setting up of any government, for government is established for the single purpose of achieving these rights in the concrete.

If there are no natural rights, then there are no governmental rights. Hence, as long as the government continues to function all the citizens have the right of criticizing its structure and action in accordance with the rational traditions by which their understanding of nature is sustained. Furthermore, they have the right of changing and improving their form of government in the light of the truths contained in these growing traditions. Beyond this, when their instrumental governmental groups fail to achieve their natural ends of distributive and corrective justice, the people have the right of revolution against this unnatural government. It is, in fact, their duty to overthrow it and replace it by a governmental structure less unable to satisfy their natural needs.[10]

But what if the people in a time of desperation hand over all their authority, in some Hobbesian contract, to an absolute dictator? Has he then the right to claim unlimited authority and to make decrees in violation of the law of nature? Not so long as men remain men! As long as they remain men they are subject to the law of nature, and they cannot unmake themselves by *any* act, no matter how far-fetched or fantastic it may be. All governmental authority goes back to some explicit or implicit, bilateral contract between the people and a representative authority, involving certain rights and duties on both sides. But the people set up the authority. The authority never sets up the people.

[10] Cf. chs. 9, § 7, 6 and 7.

What law demanded the contract? Certainly not that of any preceding *contract,* for there was none. The *law of nature* demanded that the people as a whole set up such a contract to establish such an authority. *They* sustain it as long as it exists. In case there are any defects in it, they have the right of correcting them in accordance with the law of nature. In case it proves incorrigible they have the natural right of revolution.

The responsiveness of governmental agencies to sound traditions widely understood by the community as a whole is essential to democracy. In small communities the force of discussion and the threat of disapproval and ridicule are often enough to achieve such responsiveness. Plato, in his *Republic,* imagined a community well enough educated and guardians (not rulers) wise enough to achieve practical harmony without any voting procedures at all. Such a system is no doubt impractical for the large communities of our present world. On the other hand, we cannot agree with those who go to the other extreme, insisting that voting procedures as we now have them are of the essence of democracy. The elaborate voting techniques used to buttress fascist governments have taught us that this is a mistake. There is no point in making government responsive to the wishes of a deluded electorate which it has misinformed.

Democracy certainly requires a responsiveness of ruling agencies to the practical opinions of an intelligent and well-informed electorate. To achieve this, we need first of all more effective systems of public education and more reliable news services. In order to bring about a greater responsiveness of government to such an electorate, the present cumbersome and slow-moving voting procedures must be improved. The new technique of public-opinion sampling offers many suggestions in this respect. By democracy we mean wise government for the common good, which is understood by the people and imposed by the popular will. Such government cannot endure without a well-informed public opinion, which can quickly and constantly influence public policy.

We must conclude that the basis of all government is an understanding of the common good on the part of the people as a whole. Its first efficient cause is the will of the people, defining their government, the natural rights it is to satisfy, and the natural duties it is to order and direct. The proximate efficient cause is the contract itself, which prescribes the exact functions of the government authority in achieving concerted common action. As we have seen, these functions belong to three groups, which correspond to the three distinct phases of practical action in the free individual.

One branch of government must be *deliberative*. On the basis of a broad, traditional understanding of the common good and the necessary means for achieving it, this branch must lay down those further *positive* laws which it judges to be most effective in achieving this aim in particular. It must lay down the positive laws of the community, and change them from time to time in response to changed conditions and situations as they develop. But this positive law must always be laid down in accordance with the general framework of natural law, as maintained in the guiding traditions of the community. This law must aim primarily at distributive justice, providing for a fair allotment of natural duties and a fair satisfaction of natural rights in the concrete.

The second branch of government is *executive*. It must carry out this distributive justice in the concrete. First, it must plan for concrete action, then decide when and how to act, and then carry out the action with the threat or use of force, if necessary. Against external enemies it has the instrument of military power (corresponding to the irascible faculty of the individual). Against internal rebellion it uses the instrument of police power (corresponding to shame in the individual). In an effectively governed community the threat of police power is usually sufficient to ensure order, and in better communities even the existence of such power would probably become unnecessary. These power *instruments* of government are highly elaborated, socio-technical agencies, with much machinery and a high degree of division of labor.

The *major* functions of executive government in achieving distributive justice are three. First of all, the whole community must be protected against enslavement by foreign predatory enemies. Second, the lower, socio-technical arts must be ordered to one another and to the common good by a proper subordination of duties. Finally, the natural rights of all members of the community must be satisfied to avoid the enslavement of one class by another. Government must see to it that rewards and emoluments are bestowed upon those performing the more valuable services, and that the lower duties are properly subordinated to the higher in accordance with the *natural* order of the arts.[11]

It must provide for the natural right of every citizen to as much education as he can assimilate. It must also make sure that each citizen is granted the material instruments which he needs to live and do his work, and that his absolute individual right to ownership over such property is safeguarded. It should itself order and administer the instruments of production, turning them over to the various material arts for proper use and exploitation in the interest of the common good. Only in this way can distributive justice be achieved.

The first two branches of government are concerned with the common action of the whole community, the just distribution of universal rights and duties. They do not concern the concrete individual human being. They regard him simply as a member of the community, possessing certain universal rights and duties. But each human being is also an *individual* human being, existing in a concrete matter permeated with indefinite material accidents.[12] Common, distributive justice may break down here, and require correction by the third branch of government, the judicial, in two respects. First, the general rule may fail to take into account certain peculiarities of an individual case: here an equitable correction must be made or in the exceptional instance, common law may lead to a violation of natural law. Secondly, the individual may *break* some positive or natural law and commit injustice: here a twofold correction must be made.

The law must be reasserted and vindicated by punishment, for a law with no sanctions is no law but a mere wish. Why is a violation of natural law, such as murder, punished by the state? Because the state and its positive laws are based upon natural law. The state is itself a natural expression of natural law. Hence the state is the implement used by nature in advanced societies, not only to punish violations of positive law, but violations of natural law as well. It is only in states which are badly and unnaturally organized that individual men have to take natural justice into their own hands,

---

[11] Cf. ch. 12, § 3.
[12] Cf. ch. 13, §§ 4–6.

punishing the natural criminal by their own personal vengeance. The other correction is remedial in character. First, it must attempt to remedy the condition of the criminal who has committed the crime, either subjecting him to a process of retraining or insulating him in such a way that he can do no further harm. Then it must attempt to remedy the injustice which has been done, so far as this is possible, by fines, reimbursements, and the like.

Such is the general structure of the art of government, which corresponds to the distinct faculty of will in the human individual.[13] It is the art of common rational action for the common good. Its final cause is the common good of the whole community. Its *ultimate,* efficient cause is an understanding and love of this common good in the people, and the necessary, natural means to this end. Its *proximate,* efficient cause is an explicit or implicit contract, setting up a governing authority and its necessary branches. Government itself is the efficient action carried on by these branches in the concrete.

This action involves *deliberation* of contingent means, or positive laws; *execution* of these in the concrete; and *application* of them to individual cases. It cannot be carried on by a single entity or the single faculty of a single entity, for there is no such physical group spirit or soul. Different individuals and groups must carry out these actions for the people as a whole. This whole is not a physical or hylomorphic whole but a moral or purposive whole, *one* in the common pursuit of a common end. It is perverted and destroyed when the understanding of this end grows dim either in the people themselves or in their officials, and when common aspiration flags and falters.

c. POIETIC GROUPS. The third kind of natural instrumental group is that which makes some material instrument required for human action by a material transformation of nature. The body is an essential part of human nature. Without the body no human being can act. This body cannot be maintained in a sound and healthy condition without a constant supply of material artifacts such as food, clothing, and the like, which it needs in order to operate. In primitive communities these needs together with the intellectual needs (section 1), are partially satisfied by the whole community

[13] Cf. ch. 20, § 3.

without any highly developed division of labor or the formation of distinct instrumental groups. But in more advanced cultures such a division of labor does occur, and with it a much greater efficiency in the production of material instruments of action by the different making arts.

These arts fall into four major subdivisions: (1) those giving us that basic power over nature without which we cannot trans-form it in any useful manner, such as the art of transportation, providing us with power over space and places in the natural world; and arts like mining, diving, fishing, and hunting, procuring the raw materials of nature, (2) those which transform these raw ma-terials into useful artifacts, such as food, clothing, shelter, warmth, and the like, required for the living of life, (3) those which dis-tribute and exchange these things in such a way as to satisfy legiti-mate need, and (4) those arts of hygiene and medicine which exer-cise therapy over the living human body, first determining what are the legitimate material needs of man, and planning how these needs can be satisfied, then preventing accidents, and finally, so far as possible, curing disease when it arises in spite of all precautions. It is clear that nature has allotted to hygiene the controlling posi-tion over all the rest of these arts. Each is, in fact, naturally subordi-nate to the rest in the order named.

It is a natural duty for every individual to practice the imma-terial arts. But the material arts do not have to be practiced by every human being in order to live a human life. It is not a natural duty for *every* individual, but only for certain ones, to practice these material arts, though every individual has a natural right to the artifacts produced by them. Hence the laborers who carry on these arts run the risk of falling into either the *unmitigated* slavery of ancient times or the *mitigated* slavery of medieval and modern times. The former involved the exercise of these instrumental func-tions for the sake of a sustaining community of which they were not even regarded as members. The latter involves the exercise of these functions by certain members of the sustaining community who are prevented from receiving their fair share of the common fruits of culture. This also is slavery, for a slave is one who is forced to work for the welfare of some other person or group in which he has no fair share, or for something other than the common good in which *all* have a fair share.

Let us now attempt to analyze the causal structure of these arts and that of the groups which exercise them. The *end* of such an art is the bringing into existence, not of a pure form, but of some embodied form, capable of satisfying some need, i.e., a material form in relation to something else. This can be known without having any exact knowledge of the pure form as such. The efficient causes are transitive acts, passing out of the agent into instruments, and through the instruments, into some passive matter capable of transformation. This transitive action must be guided by an efficient or *poietic* knowledge (part of the efficient cause), which is not so much knowing as a *knowing how*.[14] Such knowledge does not need to know what the thing being acted on really is in itself, but only how it responds to efficient action applied by the agent to produce a certain result. The formal cause impressed on the matter is only an accidental material form, merged with other material accidents, in relation to some interest or need which it meets. The material cause of the art is some passive matter, supplied either by nature or by some lower art.

These material arts therefore are constructive in character. They do not so much involve immanent acts, remaining in the human agent, as transitive acts, passing out of the human agent to perfect something external by the imposition of some accidental form. These arts involve a certain kind of *poietic* or pragmatic knowledge, which is quite distinct from pure theoretical science. Much of what we now call "science" consists of such a *poietic* knowing how to do something to something, without knowing precisely what either of these *somethings* are. Such knowledge differs from pure science in two ways. First, it knows the object *materially* rather than formally. Second, it knows the object only accidentally as it responds first to our action and then to our need, rather than essentially as the object is in itself. Such technical knowledge is perfected and clarified only by reference to pure theoretical science, for a thing always acts and responds as its nature prescribes. But it can exist and be endlessly proliferated without such reference.

The group of individuals practicing such an art must be moved ultimately by the common good, which is the final cause of their action. They cannot love what they are doing for its own sake alone. It is not a *part* of the common good but only an extraneous instru-

[14] Cf. ch. 3, § 1b.

ment for achieving it. So they are moved to this activity, not by a love of the activity itself, but because it is a means to something else. The activity is not an immanent action remaining within the agent to perfect him. It is a transitive expenditure of energy, passing out of the agent to perfect something external. Hence it may be aided and expedited by external instruments. Indeed, the worker himself is acting as an instrument of the sustaining group to carry out an instrumental rather than a final function. So he acts as an instrument, together with a vast array of other non-human and non-living instruments, which may be endlessly varied and proliferated. The great variety of functions to be performed requires a high degree of division of labor for the attainment of an instrumental end.

None of these functions is performed for its own sake alone, but only as a means to such immanent activity. Hence anyone performing such a function has a natural right to receive compensation for the service he has rendered in proportion to its importance. Since this service consists in supplying material instruments of life to the community at large, it is naturally appropriate that it should be recompensed by such material instruments, rather than by honor, which should be reserved for those who have made extraordinary contributions to life itself and its immanent parts. Nevertheless, no one should be paid more than he can use in satisfying legitimate needs in providing himself and his family with adequate opportunities for enjoying the fruits of the higher immaterial arts.

Such groups must be governed by some authority exercising three essential functions. First of all, they are acting on a variable, contingent matter with variable, material instruments. Hence their transitive action must be varied constantly to meet changes in the shifting material situation. Such common adjustment of the common action to shifting situations can only be achieved by a supreme managing authority. Thus the ship must have a captain to keep her on her course and to bring forth common responses in the crew to meet sudden changes.

Secondly, the vast array of diverse instruments and instrumental functions, all serving a common end, requires a central management to plan them and to keep them correlated with one another, so as to achieve the end with a minimum waste of energy and time.

Thus the builders of the building require a contractor and architect.

Finally, since these functions are carried on for the sake of the
common good, there must be some ultimate authority to decide
which of these functions are more important and which are less so,
to plan for the just distribution of duties and rewards, and to see
that all of them are carried on for the common end in an orderly
and effective manner.

The first two functions are integral to the arts themselves. But the
last clearly extends beyond the province of any of the material arts.
Justice is certainly not the special concern of any one of them. Hygiene concerns itself with bodily health, which is an intrinsic part
of the common good. Hence it exercises a natural control over all
the material products of the material arts which serve this end. But
they also serve other higher ends. Health is only one part of the
common good and in certain exigencies such as war, it must be sacrificed for other higher parts. Hence we must ask what is the ultimate governing authority prescribed by nature for the general integration and ordering of all the material arts for the integral common
good?

At the present time great confusion reigns concerning this question. This is chiefly because we have confused two kinds of instrument: *property,* the instrument of life; and *capital,* the instrument
of production. As a result we have also confused the *owner* of
property with the *manager* of capital. These confusions have caused
a splitting of productive, distributive, and even hygienic functions
into separate competitive enterprises with no natural justification
whatsoever. Disintegration of material functions has now proceeded
to a point at which these arts are threatened with chaos. Goods are
no longer produced in response to natural need or according to
any integrated plan for the common good, but merely in response
to the private decree of those who have been allowed to gain complete possession, not of that property over which they have a natural right of ownership, but over the apparatus and instruments by
which such property is produced.

Thus sometimes so much is produced that it cannot be profitably
disposed of, and there is a feverish search for external markets for
things that never should have been produced. When such markets

cannot be found by imperialist methods, the useless goods are sometimes eliminated and thrown away, even though a desperate need
for them may have meanwhile arisen. Then for long periods of
time insufficient goods are produced and people live in want, though
there is adequate productive power to satisfy their needs. This fantastic situation has arisen primarily, as we have indicated, because
of the failure to maintain a basic distinction of classical social
thought (Aristotle, *Politics* I, chapter 4) between instruments for
life and instruments for production.

Material things are not *parts* of life. They are *instruments* for
the living of life. But there are *two* kinds of instrument: (1) those
like the food that we eat, the clothes that we wear, and the house
we live in—*for the living of life itself,* and (2) instruments like
machines, factories, power houses, dams, and so on, *for production
of the former.* Now there is no question that the individual person,
endowed with intellect and will, has a natural right of complete
possession and ownership over the *first* kind of instruments, which
he requires for the living of life. He has a natural right to be supplied with such property as he really needs. Once supplied with it
he has a natural right to consume it, wear it out, use it as he wills,
provided that he does not unnecessarily waste it. The subordination of man to non-human entities is a complete perversion and
distortion of nature which is easy to discern, for man is clearly the
superior being. Food is only performing its natural function in
being eaten and sustaining human life. Hence the individual has
an indefeasible right of ownership over those material instruments
he really needs in the living of his human life.

But how about the other kind of instrument—farmlands used to
produce food, sunshine, river and ocean shore used to produce fish,
factories used to produce clothing, and so on? The individual does
not use these things as instruments for the living of life. They are
used rather as instruments for the production of the former kind of
instruments. For whom are the great factories and machines of mass
production utilized and activated? For one man, for two, for any
group of men? This is absurd. They are utilized in order to provide *all* the people with the necessary instruments of life. Who then
has the right to dispose of them and order them to the common
good?

There can be only one answer to this, in accordance with the ancient principle: "he to whom the end belongs should order the means to the end." (*Ordinare in finem est eius cuius est proprius ille finis.*) [15]

The end of my dinner is in me. Hence by nature it belongs to me (the individual) to own the food I actually use and to control the process of preparing, cooking, and eating this *food*. It is against nature to yield control of the means of eating to anyone else. But what is the end of the packing plant where matter is made into food? The end of this food is not in any individual but in the people as a whole. It is made into food, not for any one man, but for all. Who, then, has the natural right to control this process? By nature the people have it. They can exercise this right only through that controlling art of government by which their will is deliberated, chosen, and expressed.

To surrender this natural right of ordering the instruments of production (not the instruments of life) to single individuals is a violation of the law of nature. As such it is punished by natural sanctions, as we are discovering. By nature only the people as a whole, for whose sake they are utilized, have any right to control the instruments of production. Here there is no *natural* place for an individual *owner*. There is a natural place for the individual manager, *managing* these instruments for the production of instruments in the common interest under authoritative control for the common good. To agree with the later, decadent scholastics that any individual has an indefeasible right of ownership over all the material property he can manage to occupy before anyone else, is to abandon the law of nature for the law of the jungle. It is to abandon right for might or happy accident.

REFERENCES

Recommended Reading

Plato, *Republic* 414–444; Aristotle, *Politics,* Book I, chaps. 1 and 2.

Suggested Reading

1. For the basic structure of the life-sustaining group and a treatment of the family and the constitutional community (§ 2) , cf. Aristotle, *Politics,*

[15] Aquinas, *Summa Theol.,* Prima Secundae, Qu. 90, Art. 3.

Book I, chaps, 1 and 2. For the world community, cf. Carr, E. H., *Nationalism and After,* New York, Macmillan, 1945; and Kelsen, Hans, *Peace through Law,* University of N. Carolina Press, Chapel Hill, 1944. For a report on the International Bill of Human Rights now in process of formulation as the proposed legal basis for a world community, cf. United Nations, Economic and Social Council, *Report of the Drafting Committee to the Commission on Human Rights,* July 1, 1947.

2. For the three-fold division of instrumental groups into noetic, politic, and poietic (§ 3), cf. Plato, *Republic* 414–444. For a corresponding division of the sciences into those which are purely theoretical, those which understand how to command, and those which are purely practical, cf. *Statesman,* 258–260. For the distinction between instruments of life and instruments for the production of instruments, cf. Aristotle, *Politics,* Book I, chap. 4. For a clear statement of the principle that all just law and social procedure should be subordinated to the common good, cf. Aquinas, *Summa Theologica,* Prima Secundae, Qu. 90.

Chapter 11

CORRECTIVE GROUPS AND
FRIENDSHIP

THERE is a clear distinction between instrumental groups which are guided by a positive purpose, the attainment of some commonly envisaged good, and corrective groups which are guided by a negative purpose, the elimination of some evil. Thus governing agencies are instrumental groups engaged primarily in the attainment of justice, a positive good. But parties of reform and revolution are corrective groups engaged primarily in the elimination of injustice, a negative evil.

Since we cannot actually achieve the common good without avoiding common evils, these two purposes really belong together. The instrumental group, if it is adequately performing its function, will correct abuses as they come up, and there will be no original justification in nature for the formation of separate corrective groups. Nevertheless once the evil exists, it is in accordance with nature to establish such corrective groups. Friendship between concrete human persons is also not demanded by the universal nature of man. Nevertheless it is in accordance with nature and completes our human life in most important ways. Hence we shall deal with these corrective groups and human friendship in this chapter.

1. THE NATURE AND ORIGIN OF CORRECTIVE GROUPS

The existence of factional, negative groups means one of two things. Either the instrumental group is not adequately performing its function or if it is, the members are not being properly educated. So in either case the existence of a rival group is an indication of social disorder, for the very existence of a human group depends upon a sound understanding of its structure and functions on the part of its members. We can discern three phases in the disintegration of an instrumental group, and through this, of its sustaining group.

The natural condition is that in which differences can be settled by argument and persuasion, evils being avoided by the group as a whole. Here, there is no separate corrective group. The first step of disintegration is that in which permanent *factions* within the group are developed, like the rival parties in our community, which in spite of their differences can sustain a common mode of group life, each tolerating the rule of the other. The second is that in which the difference of the factions with respect to the *means* becomes so acute that they are forced to divide into two separate groups, like our religious sects, each operating under separate authorities and separate laws for the attainment of a common end. When the end itself is differently conceived, there is incipient warfare in which the one group becomes entirely inimical to the other. Such a relation now exists between atheistic bodies and religious societies, and between a governing body and a revolutionary party. In our society at the present time it is easy to find opposition groups of the first, second, and third degrees, at every level of social action. It would be fatuous to regard this as anything but an indication of grave social misinformation, maloperation, and disintegration.

The normal condition in which the group carries on all necessary corrective functions without subdividing into permanent corrective factions is no doubt an ideal hardly ever realized in important natural groups. Nevertheless it is often realized in small instrumental groups, like schools and business associations, which succeed in attaining their limited ends over long periods of time without factional strife, and sometimes even in smaller sustaining groups, like the family. As long as a group is in this condition there is no essential disagreement concerning the final end, the *necessary* means to achieve this final end, and the authority for common action. Disagreement is restricted to subordinate *contingent* means, always a variable factor, and such disagreement is settled by conference and persuasion.

In the first stage of social disorder disagreement is still restricted to contingent matters, but is hardened into fixed partisan attitudes that no longer are capable of complete practical adjustment. This situation does not become dangerous as long as the common end and the *necessary* means are understood and sustained by all parties. The common authority will be obeyed by all, no matter which party happens to be in control, as is true of the major political parties of the United States. But when one faction no longer accepts the essential structure of the common end and the necessary means (stage two), it will not accept the rule of the other. Then it seeks either to set up a new authority of its own (as in the case of dissenting Churches) or if this is not possible, to inaugurate a revolution.

The opening of such a rift is the most crucial phase of social disintegration. Heroic statesmanship and abnegation are then required from both sides if conflict is to be avoided. On the one hand, the commanding authority should at such times allow the widest latitude in the expression of opposing points of view as long as its authority is obeyed in fundamental matters of action. Free discussion may elicit a wider and deeper understanding of the essential common purpose. Concessions in contingent matters may preserve a common mode of action. On the other hand, the incipient revolutionary faction should do everything in its power to remain as a *faction* within the group, trying to correct abuses by the power of persuasion and by the winning of concessions which leave the final end and the *necessary* means still intact.

For those who are genuinely attempting to correct group abuses and malformations, this is the hardest and the most agonizing course, far harder than that of making a complete break and establishing a new and independent group (stage two). Those who remain inside a diseased and inverted social structure, attempting to fight abuses at their very source, become subject to a deadly cross fire from those within as well as those without the group. As members of the group they are attacked by those outside as representatives of the very abuses they are fighting to correct. But as rebels and dissidents they are also attacked by those within.

This dangerous and difficult path (stage one) is the only way in which group life can be effectively maintained and relieved of disease and inversion, once they have crept in. The *easier* path (stages two and three) of running away from the malformation of the parent body is often confused with genuine reform. But it is subject to two inescapable defects. First, it leaves the original malformation still rampant and uncorrected. Second, it sacrifices such essential value as still remains in the parent body. It must be granted, of course, that group structures sometimes become so dis-eased and malformed that no essential goodness remains. In this case revolution is the only justifiable course. But we must note that no group would ever have sunk into such a condition if hardy re-formers *within the group* had been courageous enough to fight against the original malformations.

Social life cannot be maintained in a sound condition without the sacrificial endeavor of individual members to exercise their critical faculties. Abuses must be detected at their earliest origin and freely denounced. Corrections must be attempted by individual persuasion and example. Then if these fail, but only then, resort to revolution may be justified. A meticulous preservation of the right of individual and factional criticism, and in times of tension, a prudent readiness to compromise on all contingent matters, are both required for the successful administration of group authority. These are the only means by which differences of dangerous depth and intensity, once they become manifest, can be overcome with-out destruction of the common order.

Since any human group, in so far as it actually achieves a legiti-mate common end, must also avoid evils and correct abuses, the very existence of purely factional groups with a purely corrective function is an indication of cultural disease or inversion. If the corrective group is justified, then some positive, instrumental group either does not exist at all or is not adequately achieving its natural function. If the function is being adequately achieved, then the corrective group has been brought forth by misinformation and educational failure. So in any case, the existence of corrective groups, working solely to correct real or imagined abuses, is a symptom of cultural disease. This disorder of culture may proceed to the point where almost every cultural group, instead of subordinating itself to its proper function within the whole sustaining it, pursues some special end of its own in chaotic opposition to other cultural groups. Such anarchy cannot proceed far without giving rise to the inevi-table consequence of tyranny.

Certain large portions of our common western culture reached this stage of cultural anarchy in the 19th and early 20th centuries, and passed over into tyranny. Whether our own culture at present is near or far from such anarchy we need not judge. But it is clear that it is characterized by a vast array of factional, corrective pressure groups at every level of group activity. Many of these are guided by no clear apprehension of a natural end. They merely exert a random pressure for purely incidental or unnatural ends, and must therefore be considered as illegitimate. Such groups are the by-product of ignorance, and quixotic rebellion against all discipline. Their number is indefinite. There is no point in trying to classify them.

But there are other corrective pressure groups which are guided by a clear understanding of the natural order and which are directing their efforts against genuine abuses. They fall into three major classes: (1) those attempting to correct sophistic abuses in the higher, immaterial, noetic arts, (2) those attempting to correct disorders in the basic natural structure of political life, and (3) those attempting to correct abuses in the poietic arts. A brief consideration of them should provide us with an instructive introduction to that natural order of instrumental functions which is required for the preservation of a sustaining group, and which we shall attempt to examine more carefully in Chapter 12, § 3.

a. THE CORRECTION OF NOETIC GROUPS. There are certain human agencies whose function lies, not in producing any material change or artifact, but in exercising therapy over the human intellect and will, the highest, immaterial faculties of human nature. Thus through a communion with powers and agencies above the level of man, religion seeks to clarify reason and strengthen the human will, so that life may be saved and lifted to a higher degree of perfection. Philosophy and theoretical science attempt to maintain the most fundamental insights into the nature of reality which have been achieved, and so far as possible, to extend the range of these insights. The mimetic arts, or fine arts, as we call them, attempt to construct beautiful images of these, by which they may be readily grasped and enjoyed. The manifold techniques of education exercise therapy over the human soul from its entrance into the world to the time of its departure, disciplining it so that it can make the best use of its higher faculties in receiving the truth, and loving the proper ends which the truth reveals.

Unless these higher arts are effectively sustained life cannot be lived well, but it can be lived. They are subject to a peculiar perversion which Plato called *sophistry*. This disease attacks the art at its very roots, leading it to confuse an apparent effect with a real effect. Since the real effect in this case (understanding and virtue) is invisible, it is extremely difficult to distinguish this from the apparent effect. Knowledge is easily confused with opinion, and virtue with success. When this happens, these higher arts, though apparently in a flourishing condition, may actually be lost.

To correct such an inversion of the higher immaterial arts, a peculiarly drastic procedure is necessary. It is not enough to extend the range of the arts or to reorder them, for they are not actually in existence. What is required is the actual exercise of an art that is no longer *actually* practiced, though it may be *apparently* practiced by a host of *apparent* practitioners. There is no deeper chasm than that which yawns between the real and the apparent, and no more difficult task than that of recovering the former in the midst of the latter. Nevertheless such corrective endeavors are now proceeding in the higher arts.

In the case of religion this means, first of all, a recapturing of the essential idea of religion as distinct from the nominal religiosity of the sham article; secondly, an actual practise of religion itself; and third, an ironic attack on the apparent forms which *seem* so much more real and attractive than the genuine article. In the case of Christianity this task of revival will be a most difficult one, owing to the subjective misconstructions of it so widely popularized by modern thought, both within and without the Churches. As a result of this, many moderns think of Christianity, so far as they think of it at all, as a subjectively soothing and pleasing pathway of extrication from the troubles and difficulties of actual life.

As a matter of fact, its central doctrine, that of the Incarnation, is certainly directed towards this world of matter rather than away from it. Genuine Christianity, as a matter of fact, has much more in common with authentic materialistic thought, which at least concedes the existence of the material world in which we live, than with that extremely widespread spiritualism, which claims to be certain only of its own subjective states and tries to deny matter and other basic facts of life. How surprised most of our contemporaries would be if they could discover the fact that Christianity, far from being a despairing escape from the evils of this world to some other world, is actually a hardheaded campaign for the conquest of ourselves and the world we inhabit, inspired by courageous hope, and requiring a discipline in those really entering into the struggle, which is anything but soothing!

If such truths as these could be again recaptured, our whole cultural situation would be greatly altered, for nothing is of more decisive importance for a people and its civilization than its religion, and how this is understood.[1] But the process of questioning widely held dogmas and of attempting to correct widespread mistakes in a field where it is held that no mistakes are really possible (one is as good or as bad as another), is not apt to seem congenial to the modern mind.

In the case of philosophy also, corrective movements cannot take the form of any *novel* or *progressive* development which is apt to attract much sympathy and support. Such *progressive* developments, in fact, have already plunged this necessary and vital art into sophistry and confusion. What then needs to be done if this ancient and utterly inescapable human discipline is to be revived?

First of all, the whole community must achieve a radical skepticism concerning personal opinion and apparent philosophic truth. The peculiar difficulties attaching to the enterprise of philosophy must be more widely understood. Men cannot hope to learn anything about philosophy until they develop healthy doubts about the likelihood of an untrained individual's gaining any reliable insights simply by sitting down and speculating by himself. Would this work in any other scientific enterprise? Then, the most stable insights achieved by the disciplines of realistic philosophy throughout the ages must be recovered by serious and protracted study. Finally, these insights must be extended so far as possible, applied to modern problems, and defended against the spurious products of seemingly more sound and attractive versions of the art.

If democracy is to be actually achieved the common truths must be brought to the common man, at least at the level of right opinion. This cannot be done unless a revived respect for the great tradition of philosophy can be recaptured in the community as a whole. This cannot be accomplished without a complete break with the prevalent view of academic philosophy as a Babel of conflict-

[1] Cf. ch. 12, §§ 1 and 2.

ing "original" systems in which it is the duty of each philosopher to make up his own thoughts and to disagree with everybody else so far as possible, especially the great classics. As long as ignorance is thus confused with human freedom, philosophy cannot be revived. What would happen to mathematics or to any other scientific discipline if all of a sudden it began to ignore everything that had been hitherto discovered, insisting that from this moment, every scientist was to go his own way, oblivious of the rest? How long would it remain a science?

Until philosophy once again is respected *as a science,* it cannot come to life. It must die before the positivistic and pragmatic criticism inevitably called forth by the confused array of edifying speculations and constructive systems which the "new philosophy" has produced in the last 300 years, and is still producing. Over against all this, the positivistic critique is well taken. The positivist is correct at least in pointing out that *this* is certainly not a science. If the growing sense of need for a philosophical science can be partly satisfied by nourishment on the sound insights of traditional realistic philosophy, and led into truly constructive channels, there is some hope that philosophy may be revived. This will not happen all at once, however. If it happens at all, it will be the result of a long and difficult process—not to be achieved by impatient careerists.

As to necessary corrections in the imitative arts, we may be more brief, for they are essentially dependent upon the noetic disciplines, already discussed, for a knowledge of their archetypes. In every mimetic art there are two essential factors: the archetype which is imitated, and the sensible *ikon,* or image, which imitates this. The great artist must have some sound understanding of what it is he is imitating—patriotism, friendship, social justice, whatever it is, and a technical mastery over his sensible medium which will enable him to produce a sound image, or *ikon.* Of these, the former is more important than the latter. What our imitative arts at present need most of all is not technical dexterity and virtuosity. We have enough of this. What they need primarily is a sound understanding of important realities worth imitating. They are unlikely to gain this without a revival of the basic theology and philosophy on which our democratic way of life is founded. This is apt to strike us as a way of going backward.

Similarly, true progress in education can only be made by what seems to be going backward, back of many "progressive" inversions which have really brought forth disorder and even chaos. Such corrective movements are peculiarly difficult to carry out, for they involve the deepest sort of break with prevailing tendencies. Almost no point of common agreement is possible, and issues must arise at every part of the way. The corrective movement must meet the charge of being reactionary and completely out of step with all that is going on. It will be difficult for it to deck itself out in attractive colors or to win admiring adherents, for the genuine practice of an immaterial art is arduous and wearing in the extreme. Such corrective movements, however, are actually proceeding in our culture at the present time.

b. THE CORRECTION OF POLITICAL GROUPS. The second class of corrective politic tendencies is concerned with disorders in the basic governmental structure of community life. If in a given community this structure has become wholly inverted into irrational tyranny, revolution is the only recourse. Such a condition, of course, arises only from the failure of corrective political movements to eliminate incipient disorders in the past. In our world two legitimate corrective movements are now at work.

The first works within the framework of the present nation-state, attempting to eliminate prevalent injustice in the apportionment of rights and duties. This corrective task has two phases. On the one hand, there is a primary intellectual and rhetorical phase in which insight is sought concerning the common good, the necessary means by which it is to be achieved, and the just apportionment of rights and duties required for its attainment. On the other hand, there is the culminating phase in which corrective information is circulated, concrete plans are made for social improvement, and group movements are inaugurated either within the framework of existing parties, or in the formation of new parties, for the rectification of injustices and abuses.

The greatest of these abuses at the present time is that of slavery, the assignment of arduous duties to certain members of the community without allowing them a fair share of the common fruits of culture, both material and immaterial. In ancient and medieval times, without the extraordinary power of mass production, such an arrangement was perhaps necessary, and therefore not unjust, for it could be argued that unless most of the members of the human community gave up the major portion of their energy in the performance of necessary menial tasks, there could be no leisure for the performance of the higher immaterial arts, on which the general welfare of the human community ultimately depends.

But now the whole picture has been changed by the vast power over physical nature which modern mathematical techniques have put into our hands. It is no longer necessary for vast hordes of men to labor ceaselessly in the production of barely enough to sustain life and to provide a small modicum of leisure for the pursuit of the immaterial arts. We are now in a position to substitute machines for serfs, thus shortening the working hours and making it possible for the first time to plan for a living community in which all the members can realize their natural right to share in the religious, philosophical, esthetic, and educational fruits of culture. Such plans have already been conceived and planted in the minds of the masses. But their realization will require great alterations in the archaic organization of the present nation-state, based on the rigid class divisions of a prescientific economy of scarcity.

Corrective movements are already proceeding, and a great deal will depend upon whether they can achieve their goal within the general framework of our political life. If so, great concessions must be made by those in privileged positions, and great restraint and willingness to compromise must be exercised by those seeking to realize their natural rights. If the political structure of national communities has become too rigid for these corrections to take place within the existing framework, by persuasion and gradual compromise, then revolutionary conflict will take place.

The second movement of political correction extends beyond the archaic framework of the present nation-state, with its outmoded structure of absolute sovereignty. Of the three final forms of community which are required by nature, we have as yet achieved only two: the family, and the local community. The third, and most important of all, the world community, is still in the process of formation. The corrective movement to eliminate the terrible anarchy of sovereign nation-states is opposed by many obstacles.

The most dangerous of these is the antirationalism of modern philosophy, centered in Germany, which has undermined the realistic conception of an independent, natural world, with prescriptive natural laws, entirely independent of human opinion or desire. Without the law of nature the positive law, which is arbitrarily decreed by a sovereign state, becomes the supreme authority for action from which there is no appeal. Each nation becomes a law unto itself, subject to no higher law, and anarchy is the inevitable result.

Instead of being regarded as a moral entity, bound into moral unity by a common understanding of a common good (the perfection of all the individual members), the national community tends to be materialistically regarded as a substantial entity, quite distinct from the individual members, who are looked upon as tiny cells or drops in the superorganism of the state. From this totalitarian standpoint, the state is no longer viewed as an immaterial unity of understanding and will but rather as a supposed fantastic unity of superindividual blood, and race, and soil. Cooperative social action is no longer for the sake of the common good but only for the sake of this leviathan, conceived to possess a good of its own, opposed to that of the individuals making it up, whose tiny ephemeral goods are thought to be a legitimate sacrifice on the altars of this bloodthirsty superanimal.

Since without the guidance of clear understanding, all power tends simply to expand with no further purpose than its mere expansion, each sovereign state, following the ever-present urge of material desire, tends constantly to increase its power until it runs headlong into some other expanding leviathan, and the two engage in total war. Western culture certainly cannot survive unless the whole world can join together in the formation of a genuine world community.

This must aim, not at the good of this nation or of that, but at the common good of all human individuals in the world, not as prescribed by tyrannical decree, but by the law of nature herself, which has placed all of us here together as interdependent members of a single world community. Any corrective movement devoted to the actual attainment of this end must begin by attempting to revive an understanding of the law of nature. Without this crucially important concept any plan to set up a world order will only result, if achieved, in the generation of a superleviathan, dictatorially suppressing everything else to its own tyrannical decrees. At the present time only a bare prophetic start has been made in reviving the ancient realistic concept of the law of nature, and the allied concepts of the common good, natural rights, and natural offices or duties. But a start has certainly been made. Insights have been achieved and plans have been begun.

In most countries political pressure groups have actually started to work in this direction. Their task is easier than that of those devoting themselves to the correction of the purely immaterial arts, for though the root causes of national anarchy and war are intellectual, and therefore invisible, their effects are visible and tangible. Hence there is less difficulty in stirring up interest and gaining recruits for the struggle.

Also a world community has never before existed. Hence the effort to build such a community may be presented as a wholly novel and progressive measure, sharply contrasted with the prevailing anarchy of national sovereignty. It is easier to push on toward a new goal where the direction is clear than to rediscover an old one whose direction has been lost. But many difficulties lie in the way. Nationalism has many disguises. The great leviathan nation-state will not be killed without a struggle.

c. THE CORRECTION OF POIETIC GROUPS. The third class of corrective movements concerns the lower, *material* arts of hygiene, distribution, production, and acquisition of material goods. Here the task lies not so much in recapturing a lost art or in further perfecting and extending the range of an already existent art, as in ordering and subordinating different arts, each of which by itself is now functioning in a very effective manner. Thus the arts of production and acquisition, under the guidance of modern mathematical science, have reached extraordinary levels of productive efficiency. The trouble with them is that they are not subordinated in peacetime to any sound overarching plan for the satisfaction of natural needs in the community as a whole.

Correction here must take the form of devising plans and planning agencies capable of guiding and controlling them, so that they will produce the right things, in the right amount, at the right time, to be justly distributed. Also the arts of business exchange and distribution are, if anything, overdeveloped. They need to be simplified and subordinated to hygienic planning. Instead of attempting the fantastic and infinite task of distributing anything whatsoever to anybody who has the money to buy, wherever he may be, they should be guided rather by the rational aim of distributing according to natural priority, first necessary things, and then luxuries, in the order of their importance. Only in the case of hygiene, the ruling member of this bracket of techniques, do we find an art which is intrinsically defective.

At present the more sensational, corrective phase of the art (healing or medicine) is enormously developed, whereas the more important supervisory and preventive phases are seriously neglected. Movements in the direction of large-scale hygienic planning and public-health precautions are already under way. Necessary natural needs must be distinguished from incidental demands for luxuries, and priorities established. Productive and distributional planning for the satisfaction of real needs in their natural order must be worked out in cooperation with governmental agencies and the higher arts.

There is some hope that these corrective measures may achieve some success in the near future if the higher immaterial arts can be revived to the point where they can cooperatively stir the community to an intensive pursuit of a sound, overarching plan of life. This is the crux of all present-day corrective endeavors. Without such a plan economic slavery will not be mitigated, rational government will further degenerate to the familiar game of power politics, and the uncontrolled oscillations of the material arts, guided solely by the urge to individual profit, will produce both overproduction, unemployment, and blind imperialism.

Such are the major corrective tendencies now at work in our sadly disordered culture. Unless they achieve some measure of success our democratic western civilization cannot live.

2. FRIENDSHIP

The final cause of the natural group is the common good, the common perfection of every member of the group. The efficient cause is a natural love for the common good, or a general good will towards any individual participating in it, which is reinforced and implemented by the group authority. Such good will is no longer a mere instinctive benevolence towards fellow members of a tribe, possessing common accidents, but a friendly impulse elicited by a rational understanding of the common good. The formal cause is a just union of rights and duties achieved in such a way that each receives a share of the common good in proportion to his contribution. Such a natural group, whether sustaining or instrumental, is not made up of human persons so far as they are concrete individuals, but so far as they possess human nature. They are abstract in the sense that anyone may participate in them by the common nature he possesses. We must now turn to the consideration of another higher mode of human association which is concrete and personal in character.

a. THE GENERAL NATURE OF FRIENDSHIP. Friendship like the individual virtues is founded on nature. Injustice being against nature, ruins it and makes it impossible. It can exist only in a justly ordered natural group. But it confers a further perfection on all such modes of natural organization. This perfection is derived from the freely chosen, moral and intellectual virtues of the concrete human person. It can enter into any mode of natural human association, binding it together into a new and more intimate mode of human union. Without this additional union of *second nature,* nature itself is imperfect and undeveloped. What is friendship and what are these additional perfections which it is able to bestow?

The members of society have in common their aspiration for the common good and the necessary means of achieving it. They must share the same universal truth and similar material artifacts, i.e., those which can satisfy their necessary material appetites. But it is not necessary that they think the very same thoughts together or use the very same material artifacts. Friends have these in common. Hence the ancient saying: friends have *all* things in common, not merely *universal* things.

The members of society must feel something more than mere tribal benevolence towards one another. They must have good will towards anyone striving to the common good and performing the just acts necessary for attaining it. But the love of one friend for another is something more than this. We may be well disposed, or have good will, towards those we have never seen, like the Greeks who fought at Thermopylae, or towards whole societies, like the Chinese people, or whole subordinate groups, like the labor-union movement, which we may never hope to know concretely. But we cannot be friends with them. Friendship presupposes good will. But in addition it requires long and intimate association, the sharing of common feelings in the concrete, and agreement with respect to individual choices of contingent acts not required by the common good of a whole society.

Society binds individuals together only *qua* men. Friendship binds them together not only *qua* men but *qua* complete, integral persons, with all their concrete virtues and accidents. This is why the family and those more intimate subordinate groups which require the common, individual exercise of the intellectual and imaginative faculties, are the most fertile ground for the development of friendship. But any natural mode of association, whether it be sustaining or instrumental, where individuals are permanently brought together, can provide the basis for friendship. Indeed, it may be said that nature intends such intimate associations and herself provides the necessary basis for them. But to actualize them, free, individual choice, and the development of long-range habits of individual association, are also required. Hence as we have said, society is strictly the work of *nature*, friendship the work of *second nature*.

Justice, not equality, is the rule of natural association. But as we have seen,[2] justice, being a similarity of proportion, is a sort of equality. Justice is in fact a necessary condition for the stricter equality of friendship. Nevertheless the two are different, and as Aristotle says,[3] even the just are in need of friends. Justice may rule in a family, where the functions of parent and child are very unequal, or in a classroom, where the functions of teacher and student are very unequal, if each function is treated in accordance with its natural merit. Friendship can spring up on a basis of this sort after a long period of time, when the greatest inequalities of the initial stages have been overcome. But where the inequalities are too great, friendship is impossible. Thus a king can have few friends, and no one can be the friend of God *qua* God. He is too far above us. Also a freeman cannot be the friend of a slave, *qua* slave, for there is too great a difference between a self-ruling person

[2] Cf. ch. 8, §§ 2 and 3.
[3] *Nic. Eth.*, Book VIII, 1155A 26.

and a mere animate instrument. Rigid class divisions place great obstacles in the path of this perfection. Friendship is impossible between men and the other animals or non-living things, though these can be loved and admired.

Any injustice at once destroys friendship, for it introduces a gulf of inequality. As Plato remarks,[4] the tyrant has no friends, for he has enslaved all who might be capable of this in his immediate surroundings. Hence the more just and democratic a society, the more fertile a ground it becomes for the development of friendship.[5] To my fellow workers and fellow citizens I give what is proportional to their natural rights and their achievements, expecting to receive from them what is proportional to mine. Here the rule of justice prevails, to each according to his merit. But to my friend I give exactly what I expect him to give me. Here the golden rule prevails, do to others as *you* would be done by.

Natural sustaining groups and subordinate instrumental groups are made up of individuals *qua* possessing the universal nature of man and the capacity to act according to this nature. Friendships are made up of individuals not only *qua* man but *qua* free persons, exercising contingent choice through the concrete flux of circumstance. My friend is not merely a man but an integral *person* placed near me in the material course of events. We enter into friendship, not only with our common humanity, but with all our concrete feelings, passions, and virtues as well. The entire integral man is my friend, and I am his friend with the entirety of my essential and contingent being.

b. THE DEFICIENT MODES OF FRIENDSHIP. As Aristotle pointed out, there are three different modes of friendship: (1) that based upon utility, (2) that based upon pleasure, and (3) true friendship based upon virtue. None of these can be reduced to good will, for they all involve long habits of mutual association, whereas good will may arise all of a sudden. Hence they possess a certain minimum similarity to one another, which leads us to call them all by the same name. A careful examination, however, must show that only the third really deserves to be called by this name. The best that can be said of the other two is that they bear a certain analogy

---

[4] *Republic*, Book IX.
[5] Cf. Aristotle, *Nic. Eth.*, Book VIII, 1161B 8–10.

to true friendship. The least friendly of all modes of friendship is that based merely upon utility.

This mode of friendship never reaches the status of an intrinsic good but is merely useful as a means to further ends. Each possesses something useful for the other. Hence the friendship is a sort of bargain by which each supplies the other with something which he needs, such as money, security, social recognition, flattery, and so on. The relation is based upon a dissimilarity between the two parties, for if they were alike in all these respects there would be no utility in an interchange. In fulfilling the terms of the bargain the underlying motive is unimportant. What is important is simply that the desired article should be given and a proportional return be made. The friend of this sort is not interested in us as integral human persons, but merely in some accidental aspect of our personality which can be useful to him. Men of wealth and power can usually gain such friends with ease by trading their wealth or security for flattery and adulation.

This mode of friendship is really little more than a sort of concrete justice by which an equal bargain is achieved that is satisfactory to both parties. In societies distinguished by a high degree of social justice the tendency to form such low-degree friendships is diminished, because no one is in dire need of money or security. It is not entirely eliminated, however, because people will always have different skills, charms, and personal advantages useful for others, and therefore subject to trade. These friendships are deficient in value because they do not offer us that activity in which human happiness consists, but at best only some instrument, making action possible.

Since both the personal accidents which are traded and the incidental needs which solicit them, are subject to constant change, such friendships are unstable and unable to survive any great strain such as that of slander or disgrace. We are friendly, not to the man himself, but only to some contingent aspect of the man or to something he possesses. But clearly the man himself is more valuable than any contingent aspect of the man. Hence this mode of friendship binds us to an inferior object by an inferior bond. We can be friends in this way with animals, who perform a useful service for us. In the true sense of friendship we can be friendly only with the most valuable of all natural objects, namely, with the human person himself.

The second mode of friendship, based upon pleasure, is not quite so far removed from true friendship, since physical appearance, rhetorical charm, sympathy, and ease in the communication of sympathy are not so far removed from the central core of personality as external possessions and power. Young people's friendships are apt to be of this type, since they have had no time to develop either the deep-seated vices of avarice and love of power for its own sake or the deep-seated habits of moral virtue. They are creatures of sense and of sensitive appetite. What impresses them in other persons is a pleasing appearance and a pleasing manner. What attracts them is a facile sympathy and a communicative re-echoing of their own passions.

Though less removed from true friendship such friends are still deficient in the same respects as those of the utility type. They are unstable and unable to withstand any great strain such as physical misfortune or public disgrace. They are interested, not in the permanent person of their friend, the central core of decisions and choices by which he acts to perfect himself throughout his entire life, but only in certain peripheral accidents of appetite and manner. They are not interested in the way in which the gift is given them but merely in the giving of the gift, their subjective reception of something pleasing to them. The motive does not matter. Hence their conversation and interest skim the surface of appearance, never penetrating to the fundamental depths. They are bound to something less valuable than the human person himself. They love something less than the integral being of a man or woman. Hence their love is lukewarm, unstable, and deficient.

c. HUMAN FRIENDSHIP. True friendship is based upon personal virtue.[6] It is conditioned by the proportional equality of justice (there can be no friendship between a freeman and one who is deprived of political rights) and by such an absolute equality of age and status as will offer equal opportunity for the development of the individual virtues. Thus it is difficult for those who are older to develop any deep friendship for the young. It is also con-

[6] Cf. chs. 6 and 7.

ditioned by the individual virtues of friendliness in the actual communication and sharing of passions.[7]

We cannot be friends with one who never communicates his passions and attitudes, and whom we therefore never know, or with one who, even though he does communicate his thoughts and feelings, elicits no sympathy from us. But friendship is more than mere friendliness. It is also conditioned by theoretical understanding and agreement. We cannot be friends with one whose ideas we cannot understand or whose whole philosophy is radically different from our own. But friendship is more than intellectual understanding.

Friendship includes all these but something more as well, a practical understanding of a person's habits of choice and action, and a practical agreement with them in the concrete flux of circumstance and passion. Such agreement can be attained only by the virtuous, whose passions and acts are moderated by rational choice. Raw passions or interests controlled by mere accident or external decree will agree only temporarily or by accident. Eventually they will shift and alter, and the agreement disappear. Even though a permanent attachment should happen to remain, it would remain only as a passional tendency, not reaching the level of friendship, which requires an act of choice.

We may sympathize with those around us and even care for them, but we *choose* our friends. Our love for our acquaintances must be taken over by deliberation and choice before we can become friends. Such friends are friends to the very death and even beyond, surviving every accident, even slander and public disgrace. Such a friend is an *alter ego,* and we are related to him as we are related to ourselves. In so far as he has any virtue in him, a man is friendly to himself; in so far as he is vicious, inimical to himself. It is instructive to follow Aristotle's contrast of the two attitudes point for point.[8]

It has become fashionable in modern times to hold that a good man should have no regard or love for himself. But if a man has no respect and regard for the human nature he bears, for its great

[7] Cf. ch. 7, § 3.
[8] *Nic. Eth.,* Book IX, ch. 4.

capacities for good, and even for the good that has been realized in him, how can he be expected to have any respect and regard for the good in others? How can such a man ever be devoted to another as a friend? But if he respects the good in others, how can he fail to respect it in himself? If what we mean by self-love is merely a preoccupation with greedy passions and personal foibles, then this is a dangerous vice. But as Aristotle reminds us,[9] the trouble with such a man is not that he loves himself too much, but that he loves himself far too little.

If he really loved himself, he would take the trouble to find out who he really is. Then he would certainly respect the admirable nature, the highest of all material natures, with which he is endowed, and the perfection of this nature, so far as it is realized in him, as well as in those surrounding him.[10] As a matter of fact, the idea that a man can live without any concern for himself is a fantastic delusion. All men are concerned with their own well being. They are therefore friends of themselves and wish themselves well, unless their lives have become grievously distorted and ruined by passion and vice. Such men indeed may hate themselves, but they do not remain on the scene to advocate a hypocritical self-hate and a supposedly Christian "humility."[11] They eliminate themselves and disappear. As long as a man can see any good in himself, he will love himself as he loves his friend.

In the second place, he will love himself and his friend because of the good that is in them, not as instruments for the attainment of further good, but as intrinsically good in themselves. He will wish his friend, as he will wish himself, to exist and to live for his own sake, and will seek to be with him and to enjoy his presence as something inherently good. Indeed there is nothing in the whole range of nature more valuable than the being of a friend. On the other hand, those who are evil get tired of their friends, as they get sick of themselves, seeking constant relief in external distractions. They cannot bear to be alone with the selves they despise, and keep shrinking away until they may seek a final, delusive relief in suicide.

[9] *Nic. Eth.,* Book IX, 1168B 28 ff.
[10] Cf. ch. 7, § 2.
[11] *Ibid.*

Finally, in the third place, the virtuous man, in so far as he has achieved some virtue, lives in practical agreement with himself as with his friend. His appetites follow the decisions of practical reason, performing their acts as reason decrees and enjoying this activity, as friends enjoy their common activity. The whole soul under the guidance of reason, grieves and rejoices together, as two friends grieve and rejoice at the very same things. But the vicious man is at war with himself. When his incontinent passions rebel against the authority of reason, the better part of himself is full of repentance and remorse, but rational delight brings forth sullen bitterness in his passions. Thus vicious and irrational men, not understanding or loving the same things, must eventually fall into enmity with one another, each grieving at the other's delight and delighting at the other's grief.

As a good man is to himself, so is a good man to his friend. He loves his friend as he loves himself, for the good that is in him. He seeks his company and does good to him for his own sake. Finally, he shares the same tastes and grieves and rejoices with him. But why, we may ask, does a good man need other friends than himself? Why should not a good man be content to dwell alone with himself and his justice? Why is it not true that a man is his own best friend? As Aristotle says,[12] even the happy need friends. But why is this so? What can a man get from his friend that he cannot get from himself, if he possesses the virtues? There are three things that he can get. Let us consider them in the order of their increasing importance.

First of all, he can act more constantly and more intensely with his friend than he can by himself. The highest acts of intellect and will are *immanent* acts, which must be finally achieved by the individual. But these acts do not occur in a vacuum. They may be enormously strengthened and confirmed by the conjoint activity of a friend. It is harder to act alone than with another—thinking, choosing, suffering, and enjoying in common with a friend, who sees more clearly what we do not so clearly see, who re-enforces our hesitant choices, shares our sorrows, and heightens our joys.

In the second place, we can intuitively apprehend and contemplate in our friend a concrete embodiment of the activity we love

[12] *Nic. Eth.*, Book IX, 1169B 21.

and seek, and which it is difficult to contemplate in ourselves. When we ourselves are thinking the thoughts and making the choices, we are wholly taken up with these acts, and there is little of us left over to contemplate what we are doing. But in the case of a friend we can *intuitively* behold this highest activity of material nature spread out physically before us. We can apprehend it in its integral entirety and then enjoy it to the full.

But finally and most important of all, the good is always diffusive of itself. It is good to receive. It is better to gain something by ourselves. But it is best of all to give all the good we have to another. As Aristotle says,[13] it is nobler to be active than to be passive, better to give than to receive. In the case of material things we lose that which we give to another, but we gain the activity of giving. In the case of immaterial things we lose nothing in the giving, but gain the activity of giving. This is pure gain. Hence to give both kinds of thing is activity, and therefore an added happiness.

It often happens that the greatest gift we can give our friend is to provide him with an opportunity to give to us. In this case it often seems as though we were only passively receiving, but this is not true, for his active giving is itself an active gift of our own to him. The more perfect the friendship, the more perfect is this co-operative sharing of activity in which each actively gives to the other without passivity on either side. This is the final, natural perfection of human happiness or activity.

Such friendship is therefore necessary to perfect and strengthen the universal bonds of justice throughout the whole of society. Binding concrete persons together into a mutual activity of the highest degree of intensity, one does to another as he himself is done by, and friendship cements the whole social fabric at every level into the closest possible, concrete, personal unity. This is the highest and strongest unity of which our nature is capable.

It can be surpassed only by that supernatural power which perhaps can elicit a divine love with no hope or even expectation of any friendly return. The rule of friendship is the golden rule— do as you would be done by! The rule of *caritas* is the divine command to love your neighbor as yourself, irrespective of what he may be or do.

[13] *Nic. Eth.*, Book IX, 1169B 11 ff.

REFERENCES

Recommended Reading

Plato, *Gorgias* 481–520; *Republic,* Book VIII Aristotle, *Nicomachean Ethics,* Books VIII and IX.

1. For a general account of sophistic character and the forces molding it, cf. Plato, *Republic* VI, 489–495. For a display of sophistic argument, cf. *Theaetetus* 151E–187. For a penetrating diagnosis of the ultimate root of sophistry (subjectivism), cf. *Sophist* 233B–236D. For a portrayal of the clash between sophistry and philosophy, cf. *Gorgias* 481–520. Cf. Wild, J., *Plato's Theory of Man,* Harvard University Press, Cambridge, 1946, chap. 8.
2. For an account of political inversion and its various stages, cf. Plato, *Republic,* Book VIII; and Wild, J., *Plato's Theory of Man,* chap. 3 for a modern commentary.
3. For a description of the anarchic disease which attacks the productive arts when they lack hygienic control, cf. Plato, *Republic,* Book II, 372A–374C, and *Gorgias* 514–520.
4. On friendship, cf. Aristotle, *Nicomachean Ethics,* Books VIII and IX. There is little to be found on this topic in modern philosophical literature.

Chapter 12

RELIGION AND THE NATURAL ORDER
OF HUMAN CULTURE

WE have now studied the basic structure of the human group; the various kinds of group, both sustaining and instrumental, which are demanded by nature; and friendship, in which human nature attains its highest, social perfection. This completes our survey of the modes of human activity which nature can produce without the intervention of higher powers. But our survey is not yet complete. No study of human social life can be complete without a consideration of that culminating cultural activity which we know as religion. This takes us beyond the finite entities of nature to its first source and end. Religion is not only a universal cultural phenomenon, but the most critical and decisive of human operations, on the basis of which alone it is possible to gain an inclusive understanding of that vast array of interwoven activities which make up human culture. Hence we shall try to win a vantage point in this chapter from which we can view the structure of human culture as a whole (§ 3) .

We shall divide our discussion into three parts: first, the relation of religion to the other activities and groups we have been considering; second, the problem of evil, to which religion alone provides us with an intelligible and practicable answer; and third, the natural order of human culture.

1. Religion and Culture

There is a widespread tendency at the present time to separate religion from the rest of human culture on the ground that it is concerned with another world, divorced from the natural world which we inhabit. But this is a great mistake. As was clearly recognized by the great pagan philosophers, Plato and Aristotle, religion is deeply rooted in human nature. The best way of gaining an understanding of this essential fact is to think of the goods which are provided by the other cultural activities of man. No one of these alone is capable, nor are all of them together capable, of ultimately satisfying the aspiration of the human will.

Material artifacts provided by the constructive activities of poietic groups are good things. But we are not purely material entities. Hence without something more we remain restless and unsatisfied. Man cannot live on bread alone. The realization of the natural rights to nurture, education, and freedom of expression, provided by the political activities of politic groups, are good things. They give to each individual the opportunity of living. They do not give him life itself. Man cannot live on government alone. Rational insight and the enjoyment of truth are cultivated and sustained by noetic groups. These are perhaps the most precious of all, for they give us the purest and most lasting pleasures and satisfy the highest and most distinctive part of our nature.[1] So far as they go, they are very good, but they do not go far enough.

Philosophy can tell us that there is an eternal, first cause of nature, but it can tell us very little of the intrinsic nature of this cause. Philosophy can tell us that human nature contains a deathless immaterial part, but it cannot tell us what our destiny is to be after separation from the body. These and many other things we need to know. Even after it has assimilated the deepest truths which are naturally accessible to it, the human mind is still unsatisfied and endorses the famous words of Socrates in the *Apology* that human knowledge alone is of little worth. *More* is needed.

Perhaps this *more* is to be achieved in the integral life of sustaining groups, where all these instrumental goods are to be found merged together in the concrete life of the family, the community, and the temporal world. But temporal happiness alone still fails to quiet the restless urge of the human will. This is because human reason is able to apprehend the existence of a perfect and eternal good. It is this apprehension which elicits in the human will a natural appetite for an unchanging good and frees it from any necessary, animal obsession with the particular, finite goods of temporal life. This does not mean that we are not necessarily attached to such finite goods as are naturally required. It does mean that we are not necessarily attached to any one of them or to all of them

[1] Cf. ch. 8, § 6.

together, as to our *ultimate* end. The *ultimate* end lies beyond these goods.

Family life is a great human good which is certainly demanded by nature. But it is not the final human good, at least in the form of our present experience, for the family passes away. Hence it cannot offer final satisfaction to that immaterial, deathless part of each of its members which seeks another and more lasting home. The life of the human community is enriched with a vast array of good things, but this community must pass away. No human state or empire is eternal. Those of the past have already vanished. Those now in existence will have their day and die. Even though a world community were formed at last to inaugurate a natural order of world peace, this could not be the lasting peace we seek, for the whole temporal world must eventually pass away, together with all that is in it. Even human friendship, the best of all these finite goods, is tinged with this same pathos, for it too is transient and must pass away unless it is taken up into some higher mode of association.

Here we must return to our starting point, the basic insight of Heraclitus, which underlies every sound philosophy of nature. We ourselves and all the other things with which we are in sensory contact are in flux.[2] All is passing (*panta rei*). This is an indubitable fact. Think of this fact and dwell upon it, for there is no more fundamental fact. If you do, you will see that it is responsible for the underlying sadness which attaches to human existence on the earth. Then think of *this* fact! Why should this be sad unless we are by nature destined to some more lasting end?

Sadness is always an indication of frustration. How then could we feel this sadness unless we were actually seeking some deathless goal from which we seem to be hopelessly separated by the sensory fact of change? There is no other explanation. All men feel this sadness. Hence all men, whether they clearly understand it or not, are seeking something eternal in which alone they can rest content. This *amor aeternitatis* is indeed a most basic fact of human nature, lying at the root of many phases of human experience which at first sight seem to have no connection with it.

At its vaguest and least articulate level, it is evident in the sadness all men feel at the transiency of themselves and their accom-

[2] Cf. ch. 13, § 1.

plishments, as well as all the things they see and touch. In the same indirect way it is evident in the *ennui* and boredom which even the worst men feel when they have set their hearts upon some material end, and then attain their heart's desire, only to find it as dust and ashes. Men have tried to satiate themselves with riches, power, fame, and sensuous delight, only to discover the infinite capacity of the human soul to be *bored* with such things. Even though they never escaped from their boredom, they illustrate the truth of that famous prayer which opens the *Confessions* of Augustine: *Inqueatum est cor nostrum donec requiescat in te* (the human heart is restless until it finds rest in Thee) .

This love of the eternal is less unclearly manifest in virtuous action and in the admiration which all men feel before such action, even though they themselves are incapable of it. Why should we respect the courageous soldier dying for a just cause? If our nature seeks only the transient enjoyment of material things, then he is a fool, and fools are not respected. Every virtue demands a certain indifference to these transient things,[3] and an aspiration to something higher which alone is worthy of the dignity of man.[4] This natural love of an invisible, eternal end is more or less clearly reflected in the great classics of secular literature. But we need dwell no longer on these indirect manifestations.

It is clearly and *directly* manifested in a certain distinctive mode of group activity. All men have at least a vague understanding of the first cause beyond themselves which brought the transient world of nature into being.[5] They also have an understanding of their own weakness and of their need for the assistance of powers higher than any they have at their command, not only in bringing them to their final end, but in bringing them to the intermediate ends for which they struggle day by day. They are dimly aware of the obligation they are under of entertaining right feelings concerning these powers and of performing overt acts which may be pleasing and propitious to them.

Hence it is not surprising that in every human culture of which we have record, with few exceptions, certain groups have been set

[3] Cf. ch. 6, § 2b–c.
[4] Cf. ch. 7, § 2.
[5] Cf. ch. 16.

aside to maintain and to strengthen any *link* which may exist between living men and these ruling powers. The name given to this
binding link is *religion,* and such natural groups are *religious* groups.
Their function is to receive such revelation as may be made from
higher authority concerning matters of importance which are in-
accessible to the limited, rational faculties of man, and then to
attempt so far as possible to act in accordance with them.

This is not a treatise on theology. Hence it is not our function to
describe the content of any revelation which may have been made
either as the basic core of Christianity or any other religion. We
are engaged in the enterprise of philosophy, and are therefore making no appeal to any authority but that of the unaided faculty of
reason. Nevertheless, as we have tried to show, the realm of nature
does lie within the province of philosophy. We can gain certain
sound insights concerning the changing world, and the nature of
man, its highest manifestation. Religion rests on the claim that a
certain aid (Grace) has been given to the natural faculties of man
from a higher, supernatural source. The study of this is theology.
Certain questions concerning the relation of nature to Grace, however, lie within the province of philosophy. Hence we may appro-
priately try to make a few relevant comments on this relation.

The greatest thinkers of the West, both ancient and modern,
have held that philosophy is able to demonstrate the existence of
a first, eternal cause,[6] capable of granting special aid to our human
faculties. This does not show that any revelation has occurred. But
it does show that revelation is possible. Nothing we know about
the world of nature in general or the nature of man in particular
is inconsistent with it. Human aspiration is naturally directed to
an eternal end. An eternal first cause brought this aspiration into
existence and still sustains it. Why, then, should it not grant further
aid in enabling it to reach its end? Philosophy can go this far and
even further.

From what it knows of the nature of man it can infer something
about the general nature of such aid, if it be granted. Such knowledge may be of use in distinguishing between genuine Grace and
spurious imitations, for if any supposed revelation fails to meet
these specifications it cannot really aid us in attaining the natural

[6] Cf. ch. 16, §§ 3–5.

end, and we may therefore safely conclude that it is spurious. What we know of human nature may be summarized under three heads.

First, man is a natural or material being, emerging by a continuous process of evolution from the subhuman things of the changing world, and dependent upon them in myriad ways for his existence.[7] From this we may infer that any genuine aid granted him from a higher source must take the form of enabling him to master the material world in which he lives, and his own material nature. Any supposed aid which ignores this material nature or which pretends to extricate him from it, is contrary to demonstrable facts, and therefore clearly false.

Second, the highest and most distinctive part of human nature is the *immaterial intellect* and the voluntary aspiration it elicits. From this we may infer that any genuine aid granted him must take the form of further enlightening his understanding and of quickening his will. Any supposed Grace which denies this dignity of human nature and pretends to offer help by asking him to abandon reason or the freedom of his will, must lead him rather towards destruction than salvation. It is also contrary to demonstrable facts, and therefore clearly illegitimate.

Third, man is by nature a *social* creature who can be perfected only by cooperative action with his fellow creatures in attaining a common good. From this we may infer that any real aid granted him must take the form of a society in which different individuals are united even more closely than in those natural forms we have been studying, by a more adequate vision of their common good, and a more vital, sacrificial aspiration towards this good. Any supposed Grace which would deny this social nature, pretending to save each individual alone, by turning him away from his neighbors into the subjective, "spiritual" realm of his own private feelings, is opposed to the nature of man, and therefore clearly spurious.

Grace must *perfect* nature, not destroy it. Hence authentic religion always befriends nature, enlightens reason, and aims at the final perfection of man in a unique form of social order. These three characteristics belong to all authentic religion, including Christianity. Such religion is always a *social ferment,* aiming to penetrate into every phase of human activity—everywhere strength-

[7] Cf. ch. 17, to § 2.

ening, ordering, and purifying by the aid of Grace, until it has brought good out of evil and regenerated the fallen nature of man. This leads us to another problem on the borderline between philosophy and theology.

So far we have considered only the *natural* reasons which have led men towards religion and the formation of religious groups. But there are other reasons as well. These are connected with the terrible fact of human evil and guilt. At first sight this fact would seem to constitute a powerful argument against religion. How is it possible, we tend to ask, for the world to be so full of warfare, murder, misery and vice if it is under the governance of a beneficent first cause?[8] But this is because we have not asked some further questions. Let us think a little more about the mysterious fact of evil and its origin. Whence did the first evil arise *in any world at all*, with or without a beneficent governor?

Once we raise the question in this more radical form, as St. Augustine raised it, we see that we are by no means immediately confronted with a clear-cut answer as soon as we have disregarded God. If anything, the origin of evil becomes even *more* mysterious than before. In fact, if we think about it at all seriously, it becomes altogether unintelligible. Are we then to deny the existence of evil? This would be too fatuously unrealistic. Evil now is most certainly a fact. Hence it must have originated. Did it always exist, embedded in the very nature of things? No, because then it would not be evil, which is always a frustration or privation of nature. Whence, then, did evil *first* arise in what was originally good? How could it have arisen except in a nature not self-sufficient, but related to something beyond its finite understanding? Thus our question has taken on another form.

Furthermore, now that evil has come into existence, as who can deny in this day and age, what real hope is there of our ever overcoming it? This is a practical question. There was a time, not so long passed, when men could soothe themselves with the thought of an inevitable, automatic progress carrying them along, day by day, towards an earthly millennium. We now know that this "progress" was really a regress, carrying the diseased culture of our immediate forebears, not to the millennium, but in precisely the op-

[8] Cf. ch. 16, § 5, pp. 365 ff.

posite direction, towards social frustration, anarchy, and the final desolation of war. Compared to the great modern delusion that man can easily save himself, if left to his own devices, the view that man cannot now save himself unless he humbly accepts the assistance of forces much stronger than any at his disposal, seems like a sound and sober realism.[9]

Do you believe that man can save himself by his own efforts alone? Do the facts of modern history bear out this view? Perhaps if you will ponder these questions you will begin to see them taking a slightly different form. At any rate these philosophical questions and the reflections growing out of them, have constituted one of the most powerful arguments leading men to see the fundamental reasonableness of sound religion. So let us now attempt to clarify them a little further.

2. THE PROBLEM OF EVIL

As we have suggested, this problem has two distinct aspects. First, there is the *theoretical* problem of how to account for the *origin* of evil. Then there is the *practical* problem of how to overcome evil in its deepest manifestations. We shall now consider these two problems in this order.

a. THE ORIGIN OF EVIL. Individual weakness and corruption, social disorder and chaos, are at present ubiquitous and evident facts of life. All through the ages men have sought from human philosophy alone an explanation of these hard facts. But they have looked in vain. It is not too difficult to understand the reason why. By nature man is either good or he is evil. But whichever we assume we cannot give an intelligible account of the evil which is now so clearly a fact. Once evil has come into existence we can see how it tends to increase and leads to further evil. This is not the question. How did *the very first evil originally* come into existence? This is the problem of *original evil*, or sin, which defies a purely philosophical solution.

Let us start with the pessimistic alternative. Why not suppose that human nature was simply evil from the very beginning? Then we shall not have to *explain* any "origin" of evil. We simply *accept* it as a primordial fact. But what was responsible for this fact? Man did not bring himself into existence. He cannot sustain himself. He

[9] Cf. Toynbee, A. J., *A Study of History*, Oxford, 1947, chs. 19, § 10, and 20, § 5.

owes his existence to manifold causes outside himself, which work together to sustain what we call the order of nature. Hence if human nature *as such* is evil, then the whole order of nature which produced it is evil, together with its first cause. We have then committed ourselves to the assertion that everything whatsoever, *being itself*, is evil. But what meaning can be given to this assertion?

Evil means privation—the lack of some being in a thing required for its perfection, as blindness (privation of sight) is an evil in man. To say that being itself is evil, therefore, is to say that being is deprived (of being) —what is, is not. But this is contradictory and unintelligible. Unless *something* were good in the first place, nothing could be frustrated or deprived, and evil would be impossible. Being itself cannot be evil. The alternative of a radical pessimism is inconceivable. We must assume that human nature is good to begin with. How then are we to explain the origin of that human evil which is now most certainly a fact? Once again we are in difficulty.

We cannot explain this original evil by any natural appetite to disobey reason, for example, because this *natural* appetite is good. Hence by nature it is capable of obeying rational guidance. We cannot explain the *original* evil by any failure of appetite. Can we explain it by a failure of reason to apprehend its own proper objects, and thus to provide adequate guidance for appetite? Not if we are consistent, because then we would be supposing that our nature was defective or evil in its most distinctive part. But we are now arguing on the assumption that human nature is basically good. Otherwise the whole of nature would be evil and self-contradictory.

We seem to have fallen into an inescapable dilemma. On the one hand, if human nature as such is radically evil, we cannot explain good, or evil, which requires something to frustrate, as a parasite requires a host. On the other hand, if human nature is good, we seem to be unable to explain the origin of evil. Is there any way out of this dilemma? There is one way, which involves a recognition of the religious fact that human beings are linked with a higher being who transcends their nature and all their human faculties. How does this explain the difficulty? The explanation briefly is this.

Human nature is good, but it is also finite, or limited. Finiteness is not evil. A mouse is not in an *evil* state because it lacks the proper perfections of a lion. A lion is not in an *evil* state because it lacks the proper perfections of a man. Human nature lacks many perfections, but it does not become evil unless it is deprived of some *proper perfection* required by its nature. These proper perfections, however, fall into *two* groups, not merely one, as we mistakenly tend to suppose. First, there are certain perfections which human nature can provide for itself, once it has been brought into existence. The first, or original, evil could not have involved any such perfection as this, for human nature, being good, would certainly have supplied it. We cannot explain the original evil unless we recognize the existence of *a second class of proper perfections*. This is the crucial step of the argument.

There must be certain perfections required by our nature which it cannot provide of itself alone, but only with the aid of some higher being beyond it, to whose commands it must first freely and humbly submit. A human being could act in accordance with his uncorrupted but finite nature and still disobey such a command *whose nature he could not fully understand*. This offers us an intelligible explanation of original evil, the only one which has as yet been offered—perhaps the only one which can be offered.

The fact of moral evil is to some degree evident to all men. This fact cannot be intelligibly explained without recourse to some being higher than man. Such reflections as these on the mysterious and unnatural fact of evil, add further weight to the other *natural* motives which have led men throughout the ages to cultivate religion. Most men are at least vaguely aware of the fact that the cosmos is no work of theirs, that it is the work of some cause, and that this cause transcends their faculties. Their recognition of the moral law [10] reveals a link between themselves and this being. This leads naturally to religious worship. Their sense of guilt shows them that the link has been broken—that it needs to be restored. In any right-minded man this must strengthen his natural urge to religious devotion.

Weighed down by the evil he finds in himself and in the cultural life around him, such an individual will rightly join with his fellows in trying to link himself with something higher and better that is capable, not only of directing his own scattered interests and impulses, but of guiding the whole vast array of confused social activities toward their natural end. Without such a link the

[10] Cf. chs. 2, § 2, and 9, § 1.

people perish, and human culture sinks into mass pride and barbarism.

b. SOCIAL DISORDER OR CULTURAL INVERSION.   We have already considered the nature of individual vice,[11] and have seen that it is in itself nothing positive but rather a lack of conformity with natural law which deprives our individual acts of rational order. In the same way social evil is not a positive entity, as we are so apt to think of it, but rather a lack of conformity with natural law, which deprives our group activities of rational order. We have already considered certain special phases of social disorder in Chapter 11. We must now attempt to grasp this disorder in its integral entirety, for we are now certainly aware of the fact that it is possible for a culture to become diseased or inverted *as a whole*. Such a diseased culture is commonly referred to as barbaric. Let us now try to analyze more exactly the meaning of this term.

We are apt to use the term *barbarism* in referring both to primitive peoples who have an undeveloped culture and little scientific knowledge, and to "civilized" states possessing science and technique, but in a disordered form. This leads us to slur over the importance of the latter phenomenon and to be less critical of ourselves, for we tend to take the easy view that if the arts and sciences are cultivated in a given community, we have no right to call it uncultured or barbaric. The Greeks, who first used the term *barbaric,* applied it unhesitatingly to the Persians and to other "civilized" peoples who were certainly very far from being savage tribes. Such civilized barbarism is clearly possible, for in addition to the separate instrumental arts taken one by one (civilization) , there is the order in which they are cultivated (culture). A nation like modern Germany, for example, may possess all the arts and crafts developed to a high degree of efficiency, and yet be a highly inverted or barbaric state.

Such disorder does not necessarily express itself in chaos; in fact, when most acute, it expresses itself in a rigid kind of order that is very difficult to distinguish in its incipient stages from the incipient states of culture. It must be remembered that related things can be mutually subordinated in two ways: the higher to the lower or the lower to the higher. The miser's actions are not chaotic or disorderly in any apparent sense; he would be better off if they were. He has

[11] Cf. ch. 3, § 3.

subordinated the end to the means in a perfectly orderly way, but in the wrong way.

This sort of *anatropism*, or inversion, is far more possible in a great human culture (sustaining group), where the different arts and techniques are not held together within the nature of a single, substantial being, and have a certain natural autonomy of their own. In such a community it is possible for all the arts to be cultivated, as well as to be ordered with respect to one another, but in an order which is partially, even completely, upside down.

Let us see if we can grasp the theoretical limit of barbarism, which these inversions of culture approach. If so, we shall have a standard by which to grade differing degrees of barbarism and barbaric tendencies.

Art is the rational guidance of power. Art becomes *anatropic*, or barbaric, to the extent that this guidance is undermined, even though subordinate technique and power remain. A single art or function becomes inverted when, instead of forming and controlling its natural subject matter, it merely pretends to exercise this function, but really allows the subject matter to go its own way. Such a false or inverted technician in medicine we call a *quack*. With a great display of technical virtuosity, especially in vocabulary, the quack pretends to direct and to treat the patient decisively. In reality he fawns over his charge, feeling for what the patient thinks is wrong rather than giving an objective diagnosis. Finally, for a fee he administers something temporarily soothing.

In the lower arts, which deal with visible material things or situations, such deception is relatively rare. It is difficult for a shoemaker to sell us shoes that are not shoes at all or for a navigator merely to pretend to get us across the sea. Here the lack of any material result is easily detected. But inversion may easily occur *between* the different arts. Thus, instead of really ordering and regulating the agencies and interests of the community, the politician may merely evade difficult decisions, yield to strong interests, and let things take their course. Instead of eliminating wasteful and unnecessary demands, and regulating distribution in such a way that legitimate and necessary demands are satisfied, the hygienic arts may treat all demands as though they were equally legitimate, and without attempting actual control, passively accept any chance mode of distribution.

As disorder increases, the instrumental arts become disconnected from their natural sustaining groups, but continue to be elaborated with no clear reference to the natural needs they fulfill, as though they lived a life of their own in competition with the life they now serve only haphazardly. A remedy for overproduction is sought in the scramble for more markets in undeveloped countries rather than in the imposition of order and discipline. A remedy for underproduction is sought in a feverish expansion of productive apparatus and in a restless search for the raw materials of unexploited countries to feed them.

The result of both is the gradual surge of imperialism, from which, as Plato long ago pointed out (*Republic,* Book II, 372A–374E), arise war and the chief evils of mankind. This inversion among the material arts and government is the first degree of cultural barbarism. As Plato also points out in his *Gorgias,* such an inversion occurred in the progressive era of fifth-century Athens, so similar to our own 19th century. Both periods ended in a great "world war."

Such a general inversion of the arts could not occur, of course, if the higher, rational phases of culture were adequately maintained. It is here that cultural disease takes its inception, since it is here that culture as a whole is first conceived and directed. The higher arts are peculiarly adapted to quackery. The ancients had a name for it, sophistry; they clearly recognized its drastic threat to the whole cultural enterprise. We have no accepted name for it now. The word *sophistry* no longer means what it meant to Plato, but has been trivialized to mean "captious quibbling," which is no serious threat to anyone or anything.

This has blinded us to the terrible peril of quackery in the arts of the highest instrumental groups.[12] It flourishes most readily in these all-important arts because of the intellectual, hence invisible, character of their essential work. To all external appearances the quack teacher, who instructs pupils in "original" ideas of his own, seems to be just as good as the genuine teacher, who has spent long years in ferreting out a few grains of truth. In reality, between seeming to know and really knowing there is a sinister chasm fraught with the most serious consequences.

---

[12] Cf. ch. 11, § 1a.

Men have suddenly awakened to the discovery that everything they thought good was really bad and what they thought bad was really good. For an individual there can be no more horrible experience than this. There can be no more horrible experience for a great sustaining group. The only way of guarding against it is to cherish the higher rational arts and the individual intellect, which it is their duty to nurture and support. The untrained mind is notoriously unable to distinguish the real from the apparent, the true from the false. Yet the ultimate fate of every culture depends upon the maintenance of this distinction, especially in those broad philosophical issues where it is most difficult to maintain.

When the higher arts are inverted by what the ancients called sophistry, culture rots. True religion is confused with a comfortable sham. True philosophy is confused with appealing constructions. True art and true education are confused with quackeries, which pander to the ingrained habits and instincts of those whom it is their duty to instruct. Not only is each art individually inverted, but the whole order of the higher arts is turned topsy-turvy. Religion, instead of providing needed guidance to philosophy, mixes itself with the subordinate discipline, achieving a bastard product which is neither religion nor philosophy.

Philosophy, in turn, unable to order or interpret the sciences, passively accepts their results, piecing them together in a mere encyclopedia, or yields to the dictates of some fashionable science, which thinks its special methodology is capable of unlocking all the secrets of being. Left without firm guidance from philosophy and science, the educational arts fall into a chaos of separate disciplines, and finally, without any broad and stable pattern of knowledge, gradually fall under the dominion of politics or of some group which has usurped political power.

As in the case of the socio-technical arts, this disorder is attended by an artificial separation of the higher arts from the sustaining groups which they normally serve and preserve. They come to be looked upon as lovely, cultural constructions rather than as human necessities, and become the exclusive concern of certain groups rather than of the people as a whole. Religion is regarded as providing a peculiar kind of comfort to those of a certain temperament. Philosophy falls prey to antiquarians and other supertechnicians

who are no longer interested in truth. Finally, education is regarded as an ornament that is essential, not to life itself, but rather
to social success.

Reason and will, thus left without clear and decisive guidance,
achieve truth and integrity only by coincidence. The intellect, presented with no coherent body of universal truth capable of inspiring certainty, falls into skepticism and relativism. The undisciplined will, provided with no clear conception of its natural end,
yields to shifting impulse. This inversion of the higher arts is the
second, and more serious, degree of cultural anatropism. It is a
familiar phenomenon in history.

At the end of the disastrous 19th century most of the great nations of the world, including our own, had achieved both the first
and the second degrees of cultural anatropism. The arts and sciences were severally intact, even the higher intellectual arts, the
great heritage of the western past; but they were pursued in an
anatropic mode. In countries like our own where political tradition had received a strong impress from western religion and philosophy, individual rights were still respected, but with little understanding of the imperative duties and functions on which they
were based and with the vague assumption that all that they meant
was doing as you pleased. Such governments were saved from complete capitulation to subpolitical interests, though all were on the
verge of internal anarchy and revolution. At such a time politics
is of supreme importance, for it remains the center of fluid power
in the state and the only possible source of order. Everything depends on how this power is utilized. Chaos cannot long endure.
What sort of order is politics to establish? What is the natural
order of social arts and activities?

3.   THE NATURAL ORDER OF HUMAN CULTURE

Fortunately for us, we are not the first who have raised this question and attempted to answer it. Plato, Aristotle, and the greatest
philosophers of the Middle Ages laid the foundations for an answer,
on which we have already leaned heavily. It is time for us now to
summarize it in brief. This answer is still to be read, not only in ancient books on the library shelves, but in the actual structure of our
living democratic institutions.

At the very basis of this structure there are what we may call the acquisitive arts, by which man's feeble power to gain access to the materials needed by all the other arts is multiplied many times over. He has some power, of course, to move himself from place to place to begin with. But by the arts of transportation, navigation, and now of flying, this power of gaining access to physical places is enormously enhanced. The human voice is able to transmit communications over restricted distances. By telephone, telegraph, and radio, this power is multiplied many times over. Human memory is able to preserve a certain limited record of things which have already happened. By the various arts of writing and recording, this power is greatly extended, so that vast ranges of past events are made accessible throughout great stretches of time.

These fundamental arts of *access* are utilized by all the other natural arts and faculties. But we must not forget the further acquisitive arts of exploration, mining, digging, diving, hunting, and fishing, each of which enables us to gain possession of some type of material thing in the environment—of the land itself, of the sea, and of non-living and living things in the land and the sea. But we do not seek to possess such things as an end in itself. These necessary techniques are naturally subordinated to others, which utilize what they provide for further purposes.

First of all, they are utilized by the various manufacturing or making arts. Of all the myriad arts and crafts these are the most sensational in their effect, for they bring into existence some visible object not in existence before. This leads us to look upon all the arts as though they belonged to this group. If we think for a moment, however, we may see that this is not the case. Every manufactured article, such as a steamship, a hammer, a knife, and so on, is only an instrument that is used by some vital human faculty or the art which enhances its power. The steamship is used by the art of transportation; the hammer by a kind of making art, that of building; the surgeon's knife by the art of medicine. The making arts are not final. They are all subordinate to further arts. What is the master art?

Associated with each making art there is a branch which does not make the thing, but gives it care or therapy, preserving it in a sound condition and prolonging its existence. There is no use in making anything if it is going to break down immediately. Hence the art of shipbuilding includes the technique of overhauling ships; and in general, every making art includes a technique of repair. Acquired natural things are not repaired, but rather purified and preserved. Thus we have arts like agronomy, metallurgy, oil-refining, and the like, which purify and preserve certain inorganic things; those like forestry and horticulture, which look after plants; and finally those like veterinary medicine, herding, and animal husbandry in general, which look after animals. The results of all these technical agencies is an enormous collection of material things necessary for the maintenance of life and the exercise of the higher human faculties. But since society is a collection of individuals, these goods cannot be utilized until they have been distributed in some way.

This essential task is achieved by exchange—everything we now include under the blanket term *business*. This intricate process has been greatly facilitated from early times by the use of money, an easily transported and convenient instrument by which different goods and services can be measured against one another, and thus exchanged with the least expenditure of energy and the greatest accuracy. We have no time to study this in detail or the distortions to which it is subject. At present we are interested in a bird's-eye view, and need only point to the obvious but essential fact that distribution, together with all the agencies of banking, measurement, storage, wholesale, and retail exchange which accompany it, is not an end in itself, but *for* a further end. This is the actual use of what is fairly exchanged by members of the community in satisfying the physical demands of life. We have thus climbed to a higher level in the hierarchy. Goods are produced to be distributed; they are distributed to be used for the satisfaction of *legitimate* demand.

At the present time we tend to regard "demands" as ultimate, as though the satisfaction of *any* human demand were equally legitimate. This widespread error shows the need of trying to gain a broader perspective on human culture *as a whole*. During emergencies we are forced to distinguish very sharply between *necessary* and *unnecessary* demands. Although this distinction is peculiarly evident in times of stress, it can never be neglected except at the cost of disorder and confusion. Every housekeeper and every community must learn to discriminate between needs and luxuries, giving priority to the former and subordinating the latter. Unless men possessed the natural ability to make this distinction they would not have long survived. It is rendered more precise and more effective by a whole array of techniques which we may call the arts of health, which care for the material needs of man.

First of all, they clarify our understanding of the complex nature of health, thus enabling us to decide which demands are necessary and by what means they may be adequately satisfied. Second, they provide us with the information, and often with the means, necessary for the *prevention* of many accidents and diseases. Finally, in a third, *corrective* branch, which we are apt to identify with the whole of hygiene because of its more sensational results, they enable us to correct certain accidents and diseases after they have been allowed to occur. Corrective hygiene, or medicine, is not, therefore, the most fundamental branch, since, as the first two are perfected, it becomes increasingly unnecessary. The Chinese have a sounder view of this. They pay doctors only so long as they are not sick.

But even though his body is in a healthy condition the *man* may be miserable. He may become enslaved to a foreign despot or be oppressed by domestic lords. As long as he is healthy he can live, but he cannot live *well* unless further needs, aroused by his imagination and intellect, are also satisfied. These cannot be satisfied by material things alone. Men seek friendship, for example, and honor and education for their children. The whole array of tendencies, movements, and institutions established by these aspirations and by material needs must be justly organized and governed by some supreme power, protected against internal rebellion, and defended against external attack. We have not yet reached the highest art.

There are reasons for believing that this is the art of government and the natural governing power of man. We must certainly place this above hygiene, for government may justly demand a man to give up his health and his life for his country. Government *practically* regulates all the activities of the state, even those of education. As long as the community endures, the greatest mass of fluid power is at its disposal. This power is divided into police power and military power. By the actual use of the former or by its threatened use, every agency and activity in the state is efficiently controlled and internal faction and rebellion overcome, so far as possible, in their incipient stages. If not, the government is overthrown and is succeeded either by anarchy or some other government. By the actual use of the latter or by its threatened use, external aggression and invasion are warded off. Otherwise the state will be overthrown and succeeded either by slavery or destruction.

Individual power is unable to satisfy any of the needs so far discussed. They must all be met by instrumental groups, requiring the combined powers of many men. This is certainly true of the ruling power of government, which is enforced by the power of every active citizen who is not actually fomenting rebellion. By carrying on his technical function, whatever it may be, he adds to the resources of the community, over which the government has final *efficient* control. No human force can withstand this physical force of government. Have we then reached the master art? Must we agree with the totalitarian theorists who claim that the state is the ultimate arbiter of human destinies? We must agree if physical force is the ultimate kind of cause.

But it is not the ultimate kind of cause.[13] Power and force must be exercised in a certain way, according to some plan. This is no mere idealistic theory but a hard fact, observable in the actual exercise of every technical power of man. It must be directed by some stable pattern of thought. Otherwise it loses its force and becomes a set of chaotic eruptions. In the case of government we call this controlling plan, which in itself is not physical though it has the most gigantic, physical effects, the constitution, or the way of life which really governs the government. There is one thing in the community more powerful than the most powerful government. This is the non-physical power of the intellect, which resides in the individual man, whose *physical* power is insignificant.

This alone can formulate and understand the plan. This alone can govern the government. So governing is not the ruling power in human nature nor is the art of government the highest art. This is why it is a natural function of government, clearly recognized in

[13] Cf. ch. 14, §§ 1 and 2.

our democratic constitution, not only to provide wealth and order in the community as a whole, but also to guarantee individual liberties for the performance of those rational functions which only the individual can perform, and for those arts of therapy which sustain him in this performance.

The first of these is education. Strictly speaking, government *cannot* control education. This is another cold fact. All the force on earth cannot produce a single truth, and truth alone can educate. Force *can* place obstacles in the path. It can make genuine education impossible and substitute something else in its place. It must be remembered that in a relatively short period of time all the older citizens who know anything pass off the scene. They are replaced by a number of potential human beings, born in utter ignorance of themselves, of the world in which they live, and of the society surrounding them. Unless these individual infants are first of all taught to respect and to seek for the truth and then trained to exercise their apprehensive faculties, all the intricate, technical agencies of culture, including those of government, will be left without guidance, to sink into aimless routine and confusion.

That is why those democratic nations in which western culture is still alive, maintain a universal system of education, where the effort at least is made in the case of each child to remove ignorance and prejudice which obstruct the free exercise of intellect. In schools of this sort the teachers are free, not to teach anything they please, but to teach the unadulterated truth which has been discovered and to seek after that which has not yet been found. This is enough to show us that we have not yet reached the master art. The teacher does not make up what he teaches, or we could not distinguish between a school and a propaganda bureau. He must teach what has already been learned in some existent body of knowledge or science. Education is made possible by the power of government, but it is essentially governed by the theoretical sciences.

These sciences make no implements. They do not consist of physical things at all or of motions or of any array of power and efficient force. They consist of universal insights into the nature of some kind of being. It is by such immaterial insights that all the technical motions and powers of men must be directed if they are to work effectively. Thus the operations of the navigating art, in piloting a physical vessel across the sea, must be guided by the pure theoretical insights of mathematics and astronomy; and those of the surgeon, in removing an appendix, must be guided by the pure theoretical insights of anatomy and physiology.

This is true even of the stupendous operations of government in ruling a people. These operations must be governed by insights into the nature of man, his major faculties and functions, his end, and the means of achieving this end. Such knowledge, of course, includes economics, sociology, the science of government—all the sciences of man. It also includes something more, for man's reason, unlike animal instinct, is not restricted to any special range of entities but extends universally to all being. Hence man cannot be understood unless being is also understood. Man is a rational or philosophical animal, and the governing of man therefore is a philosophical art. Being is understood, so far as this is possible, by the pure theoretical sciences and philosophy. This understanding is intuitively enjoyed by an appreciation of the fine arts and their artifacts. Have we not then reached the highest arts?

If man's reason were without limitation and if man himself were the highest being in the universe, this would certainly be true. But whereas the light of human reason extends to the whole range of being, the light itself is certainly flickering and faint; and altogether aside from the weighty evidence which points to the contrary, it would seem a bit provincial for man to hold that there is no higher being anywhere than he. Unless his reason is aided by further light, it leaves many crucial questions unanswered, and his aspiration weakens and falters. The record of history has shown that without the support of religion the finest achievements of sacrificial endeavor are hardly possible and that human culture drifts into confusion and barbarism.

Since religion, so far as it really exists, apart from human pretence, is derived from a more-than-human source, it cannot be called an art or technique except in an analogous sense. Overarching the whole of culture and the whole of life, it sharpens the individual's intellect, sustains and guards his highest aspirations. Certainly no other science, technique, or discipline can justifiably claim to be the master art.

Can these higher arts be revived from confusion and lethargy?

Can they be infused with new life? Will a natural order of culture be established? In view of the anarchy now prevailing in the higher arts and the many inversions and disorders now confronting us, it is not easy to answer these questions with a confident affirmation. The correction of these disorders will surely require sacrificial endeavor and arduous struggle on the part of individuals from whom the impetus must come. If human powers alone were the only ground for hope, it would be difficult to face this situation in the light of history without falling into despair. But possibly there are other grounds for hope. The higher arts, though exerting little cultural influence, are still alive. In spite of many inversions of order, all the arts are being practiced. What is needed is to bring them into a sound, natural order of subordination. The main prerequisite for this is rational insight and understanding. There never was a time when it was more important for us to clarify our concepts of life and civilization, and to think them through to their ultimate foundations.

We have now finished our survey of the field of realistic ethics, individual and social. This way of life has been recommended and pursued by many of the great personalities of our western culture. It has been analyzed and described in some of the great ethical classics of western thought. But it does not stand alone. A moral philosophy rests upon a theory of the nature of man and the whole natural world. It is to these problems of the philosophy of nature that we must now turn in Part II.

REFERENCES

Recommended Reading

St. Augustine, *Confessions,* ed. Pilkington, New York, Liveright, 1927, Book I, chaps. 1–5, IV, VII, VIII, and X; Plato, *Republic,* Book IV; and Toynbee, A. J., *A Study of History,* New York, Oxford, 1947, chap. 19, §§ 10–11, and chap. 20, § 5.

Suggested Reading

1. On religion as an essential phase of human culture, cf. Plato, *Theaetetus* 176B, *Laws* 716 and 884–888; Aristotle, *Politics,* Book VII, chap. 8, 1328B 13–14; and especially Augustine, *Confessions,* Book I, chaps. 1–5, and Books IV and X.

2. For a gripping statement of the problem of evil and a religious solution, cf. Augustine, *Confessions*, Books V, VII, and VIII.

3. Aristotle refers to the natural order of the arts in Book I, chap. 1 of the *Nicomachean Ethics*. In the *Physics*, Book II, chap. 2, 194A 33–194B 8, he points out that the art which knows the form naturally directs the art which prepares the matter (cf. Plato, *Republic*, X, 600–601). The natural order of human life and the arts is the major theme of the *Republic* as a whole. Its general outline is given in Book IV. For an attempt to follow these suggestions in working out a theory of the cultural order in greater detail, cf. Wild, J., *Plato's Theory of Man*, chap. 2.

PART II
The Philosophy of Nature

CHANGE

PHILOSOPHY is the name given to a peculiarly human enterprise in which every human being participates, whoever or wherever he or she may be. It is the attempt to understand being and its causes. The mode of being which we know best is that *natural being* which is possessed both by ourselves; and the other evolving, changing things we feel and sense around us. Since human nature is the highest mode of natural existence we know and since this mode of existence is of peculiar interest to us because of the fact that we are human beings, we shall divide this study of the changing world into two parts. First we shall consider the structure of natural being in general.[1] Then in the second section, we shall study human nature in particular, starting with an examination of its essential characteristics and faculties.[2]

The first *general* fact which we observe in the external world around us is the basic fact of change. Indeed it is so general that it is easy for us to pass it by or take it for granted. If we think for a moment, however, we may see for ourselves that everything with which we have any sensuous contact at all, including ourselves, is in flux or process. The stars are moving; the sun is moving; the planets are moving around the sun; the earth is moving; the chemical elements on the earth are combining and separating; plants are growing; animals are hunting their prey in the jungles; and man himself is constantly undergoing the complex process we call human history.

We ourselves come into existence and pass away like all these other things, and as long as we exist we are changing in various ways. Everything with which we are directly acquainted is in change. Hence it is not surprising to discover that we divide or classify

[1] Part II, chs. 13–16.
[2] Part II, chs. 17–20.

natural things according to the different ways in which they change. Plants, or as the Greeks called them, growing things, grow; animals sense and move from place to place; and we not only change in these ways but also think and act.

But there are also technical artifacts which change in a different way. The clock is ticking away the time; the food is being cooled in the icebox; and the water flowing over the dam is generating power. What is the difference between such technical change and natural change? If we can clearly grasp it we may come to see more sharply what we mean when we refer to the *natural world,* or simply, to *nature.*

1. ART AND NATURE

The ticking of the clock, the cooling of the food, and the hydro-electric generation of power are all processes, but they are technical rather than natural. The clock, the icebox, and the power plant are artifacts, not natural things. Let us see if we can state the essential difference briefly and sharply. The clock, the icebox, and the power plant did not grow or produce themselves without the intervention of human purpose, an independent agency not bound up with the clockwork mechanism nor with the structure of the power plant. These artifacts cannot generate themselves: clocks do not come out of clockwork. Neither can they run themselves, once they are brought into existence. The clock has to be set and rewound; the icebox has to be turned on and off and supplied with matter to cool; and the power plant has to be regulated and repaired.

Natural things, on the other hand, are generated by other natural things of the same kind and run of themselves. Hence, as Aristotle says, nature is that which has a source of change or rest in itself. If the clock factory could start and stop itself, it would be a natural system, like our sun and planets which move of themselves, not through the intervention of an extraneous human cause. If the clock, once produced, could set and wind itself, it would be a natural substance like a tree or an animal. But the clock cannot do this. The elements out of which it is made are natural. But the sources of its motion and behavior *as a clock* are inherent neither in it nor in the clock factory. They arise from the extraneous nature of man, which is neither a clock nor a clock factory. Hence the clock is not a natural but a technical product, and it moves not naturally, according to an inherent nature, but *artificially* according to an extraneous, human source.

On the other hand, the planets move according to nature, because the source of their motion lies in the sun and the whole galactic system to which they belong. Nothing external can make a seed grow into an oak tree unless the seed has the nature of an acorn. It is this nature, inherent in the acorn, which makes it grow into an oak, rather than into a sycamore tree. Hence we see that this process is natural or internally caused.

Every process is out of some matter (such as the seed) into some form (such as the structure of the full-grown oak). Hence nature must possess two inseparable parts: the matter *out of which* the structure emerges and the form *into which* the matter emerges. Sometimes we use the word *nature* for the matter alone, as when we speak of the bodily *nature* of man or when, like the ancient Ionian philosophers, we ask what is the ultimate *nature* of things, meaning the first matter out of which the changing world has evolved. More commonly we use the word *nature* rather in referring to that peculiar form or structure of a thing which differentiates it from other entities, as when we ask, what is the distinctive nature of man (a different question from the other) or in general when we inquire concerning the peculiar *nature* of anything. Here we mean the actual form distinguishing this thing from others of a different kind.

In any natural or changing thing there must be a material nature out of which it has developed (as the wood of the wooden table) and a formal nature which distinguishes it when fully developed (as the pattern of the actual wooden table). These two, form and matter, constitute one entity, not two. Thus if the wood is separated from its pattern the table is destroyed. In other words, form and matter constitute one, single, natural, or changing thing. In this table before me, the matter requires the form and the form cannot exist without its matter. Each needs the other, though the form, which makes the thing actually *what it is,* is more important than the matter, and therefore it may more properly be said to be the thing's nature rather than the matter, which by itself is only *able* to be the thing.

What is ultimately responsible for these formal natures in things? What is the ultimate efficient cause of the natural world? What put these moving natures into the world and why? In the case of artificial entities, like tables, we can answer such questions, for we ourselves are the ultimate external causes of these things. Hence we refer to such processes in terms of their ultimate efficient causes, which gave them the artificial nature they have and by which they were made. We know *why* a watch exists in the first place. Hence we speak of its motions as the keeping of time. We know *why* the processes of medicine have been set in motion—for the sake of health. Hence we refer to these in terms of the efficient and final causes, as the processes of healing.

But in the case of natural processes we have no such prior knowledge of the efficient and final causes producing the development. We can achieve here only *some* knowledge of the form which terminates the process of evolution, without at first knowing anything of the causes or reasons which brought it forth out of matter, as the human carpenter brought forth a table out of the wood. Since the efficient causes of nature are for the most part hidden from us, we are forced to fall back on the formal cause which terminates a natural process of change or evolution. Thus we speak of the evolution of *life,* the process of *digestion,* the fall of the Roman Empire, as though the process were simply the pathway into the nature (the terminating form), with no external cause or final reason. As we shall see, this mode of speech is due to an ignorance concerning the efficient causes of nature, which may be at least partially remedied by the study of natural change.[3]

The Latin word *natura* is related to *nascor* (come into being), and *nativitas* (birth). *Natura* (*gnatura*) and its related words are ultimately derived from the same root as the Greek *gignomai* (become). The world of nature, which the Greeks called *physis,* (growth), means the realm of material, changing things, which either contains sources of motion within the whole system, as is the case with the non-living things of nature, or within each single being, as is the case with living things. Man himself is such a living, evolving, material being, though he possesses certain peculiar fac-

[3] Cf. ch. 16.

ulties which distinguish him sharply from the rest of nature, as we
shall see.[4]

Let us now turn to this ever-moving, natural world with a view
towards gaining a more exact understanding of the basic fact of
change which it presents to us. We cannot do this without asking
certain questions and dealing with them in succession. First of all,
what is a process or an event; what are the sources from which it
springs? (Discussed in this chapter.) Second, what are its causes?
(Chapter 14.) Third, what are the basic kinds of natural being?
(Chapter 15.) Finally, we must ask if this vast, flowing world of
nature provides us with any clues concerning its ultimate cause
(Chapter 16).

2.   OBJECTIONS TO NATURAL PHILOSOPHY

Before turning to these questions we must first deal with certain
objections to such a study which come from contemporary philosophical tendencies noted in the first chapter—scientism, pragmatism, and positivism. Those influenced by scientism are apt to
ask if there is any legitimate place for natural philosophy. Has not
modern science disproved the ancient theories of nature? Must we
not rely on its experimental techniques to give us all the reliable
knowledge we may hope to gain concerning the actual facts?

In answer to this question we grant, of course, that the ancients
were wrong on many points concerning special phases of the natural world. But this does not mean that they were also completely
wrong in their analysis of the basic structure of this world. Even
though we accept all the results of modern science concerning the
measurable aspects of nature (which of course we do), the more
fundamental questions of natural philosophy remain unanswered.
What is change in general? What are its sources and causes? Such
questions extend beyond the province of any of the special sciences.
Hence in seeking a solution to them, we are not infringing upon the
legitimate objects of these sciences.

The pragmatist is apt to raise another sort of question. Even
though we find such a solution, what good will it be? Modern science has brought forth the industrial revolution and freed men

[4] Part II, *Section* II.

from the curse of slavish labor. Hence it is real knowledge, for real knowledge gives us power. But natural philosophy is merely a maze of words and formulas which gives us no power at all. Why then should we pursue it in our modern scientific age?

This pragmatic argument ignores the distinction between theoretical knowledge and fabricative, or technical, knowledge. It is one thing to control nature, another to understand it. Neither theoretical knowledge alone nor technical knowledge alone is enough to meet the needs of men. We need both. Theoretical insight alone, without technical knowledge, leaves man helpless before hunger, disease, and slavery. But technical knowledge alone, as we moderns now know to our cost, is apt to be misdirected to a wrong end. Then it brings forth an insidious slavery of its own. How can we find out what is the proper end? Surely not by *doing* anything. Man did not contrive his nature or that of the world he inhabits. He cannot *fabricate* his natural end. He can only discover these things by pure, theoretical contemplation, which seeks the truth for its own sake. This is the aim of our study.

From positivism comes still another sort of question. Even though such knowledge might be most desirable, can we ever attain it? Exact knowledge must be checked by direct observation of empirical fact. But this is the business of science. The a priori theories of philosophy, devised without reference to experience, are not subject to empirical verification and are probably meaningless.

In answer to this, we must point out that each science makes direct observations, but from a certain point of view. Take a plant growing in the field. The chemist may observe the composition of its material elements. The botanist may observe its vital structure and its relations with other living forms. The agriculturist may observe its effects upon the soil. Each science observes certain restricted aspects of the plant from a restricted point of view. The natural philosopher also directly observes the plant, but from a less restricted point of view, as an existent, changing entity. What mode of change has given rise to this? What sort of being does it have? These are philosophical questions that must be answered by the formulation of philosophical hypotheses.

Such hypotheses are not necessarily constructed a priori without reference to the facts. They may consist of concepts drawn from experience and may be checked by direct observation. Is not change an empirical fact? Can it not be truly described and analyzed? Is he an empiricist who tells us that this cannot be done without even making a serious attempt? The other sciences have paid no attention to such dogmatic opposition. Let us then make the attempt.

3.   THE DISCONTINUOUS SOURCES OF CHANGE

By a *source* we mean *that from which a thing originates in any sort of way.* Thus the building in which I am working originated from a certain plan, from certain materials, and from the activity of the workers. These are causal sources from which something positive in the existent building is derived. But certain sources are not causal. For example, the building came into existence at a certain time, and thus originated from this moment. Nevertheless this temporal source is not a cause of the building, giving it any positive determination. In Chapter 14 § 3 we shall examine the causes of change. Now we are seeking the sources of change in this broader sense. What are the necessary factors from which change immediately springs?

Locke and his "empiricist" followers have asserted that motion or change is a simple thing, represented by a simple idea.[5] If this were true it would include no structural complexity and would spring from a single source, namely, itself. But it is not difficult to see the error in this view. A thing having no structural complexity at all would not change into anything different. It would simply remain what it is. The sensible changes which are proceeding around us are all *from* something *to* something else. If my watch is going, the hands must be moving *from* one position on the dial *to* another. If the water is freezing, it must be moving *from* a liquid *to* a solid state. If the leaf is turning yellow in the Fall, it must be changing *from* another color, namely, green. This complexity may be verified by the careful examination of any concrete example of change. Hence we must conclude that change springs, not from one source, but from a variety of sources. What are they?

[5] "These I call *original* or *primary* qualities of body, which I think we may observe to produce simple ideas in us, viz., solidity, extension, motion or rest, and number." Locke, Essay 1, Book II, chap. 8, § 9, Fraser ed., vol. 1, p. 170; cf. Berkeley, *Principles of Human Knowledge*, Sec. 7; and Hume, *Treatise of Human Nature*, Book I, Sec. IV, Selby-Bigge ed., pp. 228–229.

It is clear from these examples that change necessarily involves two distinct sources: a *terminus a quo from* which the change begins and a *terminus ad quem to* which it proceeds. Without this discontinuity, there would be no change at all, but a mere persistence in sameness. The hour position on the watch dial is *not* the half-hour position. Solidity is *not* fluidity. Greenness is *not* redness. These two discontinuous sources of change negate each other. But they negate each other in a special way which we shall call privation.

Greenness is not fluidity. These two natures are different. But one is not the privation of the other, because there is no direct mode of change between the two. Up vs. down, however, green vs. red, big vs. little, are privative negations, because there are modes of change connecting them: locomotion, alteration, growth, and decrease. It is evident, then, that all change springs from two necessary sources, one of which is the privation of the other. We shall call these two discontinuous sources the *superstrates* of change. Every transformation is *to* some positive, formal superstrate *from* a negative superstrate which is its privation.

At first sight it would seem that these two principles are sufficient. Indeed their existence is so manifest that many attempts have been made to account for the fact of change without reference to any further source. But these attempts have failed, and it can be shown that they must fail. Change begins with a privative superstrate non-*A*, and ends with a formal superstrate *A*. Without a third source the change must be interpreted as non-*A* becoming *A*. But there are only two ways in which this could happen, one of which is impossible and the other irreconcilable with the empirical evidence.

The first possibility is that non-*A* actually and continuously turns into *A*, that fluidity turns into solidity, greenness into redness. But the same thing cannot become what it is not. This is a contradiction, an impossibility. Those who adopt this mode of oversimplified explanation are led to one of two equally embarrassing conclusions. They may agree with the ancient Greek philosopher, Parmenides, and the modern idealist, Bradley,[6] that change, being contradictory, never really occurs, and is only an illusion. This means dismissing the whole world of nature and human life itself as an illusion, for everything with which we are in any direct contact is changing.

[6] Cf. *Appearance and Reality*, Part I, ch. 5.

Or they may agree with the modern Marxian philosophers and others who have held that although change is contradictory, nevertheless it does actually occur. But how can the same entity (non-*A*) both be non-*A* and also *A*? Even granted that this contradiction might occur, it means that the world of nature must be dismissed as hopelessly unintelligible and closed to the human understanding. We certainly cannot hope to make any sense out of such a contradictory occurrence. Each of these conclusions is contrary to the evidence. Our senses tell us that change does go on. The existence of science tells us that it is not hopelessly unintelligible. So we must dismiss this first hypothesis as unsatisfactory.

The second possibility is that the privative superstrate non-*A* does *not* turn into its contradictory *A*, but that the former simply precedes the latter without itself becoming *A*. This reduces change to a mere succession of diverse entities. First, there is non-*A*. Then this disappears and *A* suddenly appears, without coming from anything. First fluidity, then this is annihilated, and solidity is created *ex nihilo* to take its place. Each entity is just exactly what it is and cannot come out of any other entity. It lasts for a time, then disappears without trace, to be replaced by an utterly new entity, having no connection with the first. This view is not self-contradictory. Nevertheless it violates a vast array of empirical evidence, which clearly indicates that natural change does not proceed in this absolutely discontinuous manner.

For example, man can bring "new" artifacts into existence by many forms of technical change. But experience shows that none of these artifacts is absolutely "new." They are certainly not created *ex nihilo* to replace something else which is annihilated without leaving any trace. They are rather slowly prepared and formed out of a pre-existent stuff which is not annihilated, but which remains within the finished artifact. Thus the original steel remains within the finished airplane, and the original wood within the finished chair.

The evidence furthermore indicates that the same is true of natural processes, which never seem to involve the sudden emergence of something *ex nihilo*, with no antecedent basis. The new luminous star comes, not from nothing, but from an older non-luminous star, and contains its matter within it under a new struc-

tural pattern. The burning wood does not disappear without a
trace, to be replaced by something altogether new. It remains after
the fire in the form of gas in the air and ashes. So unless we are to
disregard this empirical evidence we must conclude that natural
change is not a mere succession of entirely discontinuous entities.
This hypothesis also must be dismissed.

4.   THE CONTINUOUS SUBSTRATE OF CHANGE

The only remaining alternative is to recognize the necessity of a
third source of change, a *substrate,* which underlies the passage from
the privative superstrate to the positive terminus of the change. We
must not forget *the hand of the watch,* which passes from one position on the dial to another; *the water,* which is first liquid then
solid, but which passes through the change without losing its material nature; and *the leaf,* which alters from green to red. These
material substrates underlie the different changes. They exist at the
beginning as well as at the end of the process, and therefore explain
the continuity of the discontinuous change.

If it is asked how one and the same process can be both discontinuous and continuous without falling into contradiction, we may
now give an intelligible answer which accords with empirical fact.
This answer, however, must be stated in terms of three sources, not
two. The change is discontinuous because of its two opposite superstrates. It is continuous because of its material substrate.

Now we must ask more about the nature of this substrate. What
is it? We have identified water, for example, as the material substrate of a certain change from the solid state of ice to vapor. But
now we must note that water itself has a certain determinate nature.
It is the formal superstrate of a more fundamental change from the
elements hydrogen and oxygen, which are its matter. These, in turn,
are the formal superstrates of changes in an even more fundamental
matter, and so on. What is the first or primal matter from which
every actual, determinate being has evolved and which underlies
the whole evolution of nature? If we are radical evolutionists we
must hold that every determinate, natural being has evolved. From
what?

We cannot say from nothing, for this is not evolution but creation. We cannot say from something already formed and actual, for

this is the superstrate of some more basic matter. The *first* matter, therefore, is not nothing. Yet it is not fully actual. It is incomplete, or *potential,* being not yet fully formed but able to be formed in an indefinite variety of ways. Only such a purely potential or dynamic being could underlie all the radical, evolutionary changes of nature, and give them continuity.

Matter is neither living nor inorganic nor chemical nor physical nor qualitative nor quantitative nor does it possess any definite shape or figure. All these are the formal superstrates of changes in a more primal matter. In itself this primal matter is indeterminate, having no determinate form, no quality, no quantity, but a capacity to receive these in a certain order, first the simpler ones, then the more complex ones which are built upon these. But who has ever observed such indeterminate potency floating about by itself? Where is the empirical evidence to support such an extraordinary hypothesis?

There is none. No one has ever seen pure potency all by itself. In fact it cannot exist by itself, but only in combination with some form, which brings it into determinate being as the *terminus ad quem* of some process. Matter is potential, indeterminate, and cannot exist without determinate form, depriving it of other forms. Nevertheless it is present in all the entities of nature. What is the empirical evidence for this assertion? Why is it necessary to assume anything more than the formal characteristics, which we can clearly understand and observe. To this question a clear-cut answer can here be indicated, though it can be completed only in the following chapter. There are three lines of empirical evidence which require the existence of such matter or potency.

First, there are the facts of natural evolution to which we have referred. This evidence indicates, not only that new species have arisen by a continuous process out of preceding forms, but that these species are sometimes radically different from what has preceded them. What then bridges the gap? It cannot be something formally determinate, for then the two forms would not be essentially different. They would have something in common, and the emergent species would not be radically new. But if there is no bridge at all the continuity of evolution is destroyed. This bridge therefore can only be the incomplete potency of matter, which retains its capacity to receive further determinations even when a process is complete, and thus underlies the universal dynamism of nature.

Second, there is the fact of chance and indeterminism in nature. We shall examine this line of evidence in greater detail in Chapter 14 §§ 4 and 5. Here, we need only note the constant occurrence in nature of unpredictable exceptions to the general rule and extraordinary coincidences. These chance events, as we call them, cannot be adequately explained unless, in addition to determinate form, there is something vague and indeterminate in nature, i.e., the substrate, matter.

Finally, there is the omnipresent fact of individuation.[7] The formal nature of anything, say animal or man, does not demand that it be restricted to *this* animal or *this* man. Hence they can be apprehended by the mind as universals. But the empirical evidence shows conclusively that only individual entities are found in nature. This also requires a non-formal factor in nature, which can act as a first substratum for the reception and restriction of forms within an individual.

In the light of this empirical evidence we must conclude that there is a third source of change, the material substrate, which is responsible for the dynamism of nature. This *matter,* as it has been called since the time of Aristotle, is not fully actual but potential. It is capable of being determined in an indefinite variety of ways, but not in itself actually determined. Though everywhere present in nature it cannot exist by itself without some formal determination. Nevertheless, even when it is actualized by such a form it retains its insatiable potency for further change, and thus underlies the processes of nature. It is also responsible for the indeterminism and individuation which are everywhere found in the changing world.

This evidence therefore leads us to conclude that change has three sources: a privative superstrate and a formal superstrate which are responsible for its discontinuity, and a potential substrate (matter) which is responsible for its continuity. This substrate is so important and at the same time so elusive, that we must now consider certain misunderstandings which cause confusion at the present time.

[7] Cf. ch. 14, § 6.

5.   Difficulties Concerning the Concept of Matter

Of all the necessary factors of change matter is by far the most difficult to grasp. It cannot exist alone apart from a form which deprives it of other forms, and is therefore easily confused with each of the other sources of change. These confusions lead to certain widespread misconceptions.

Since matter cannot exist without form, it is easily identified with the formal superstrate of some fundamental mode of change, like extension, shape, and other quantitative determinations. Thus at the present time, when the word "matter" is expressed, most people think of small, atomic bodies with a spherical shape. These small bodies are then supposed to underlie all further modes of change, that have to be interpreted as mere rearrangements of these atoms, which remain essentially unaltered throughout all higher processes. This atomistic view reduces evolution to accidental change [8] and is inconsistent with the emergence of essentially different species, for which, as we now know, there is decisive evidence. Hence we must conclude that although matter exists only together with some form, it nevertheless is distinct from any form whatsoever. Even when realized under a certain determinate structure it remains as an indeterminate potency for further change.

Matter is also easily confused with the privative superstrate. Then change has to be interpreted as the emergence of being from non-being, or, according to the Marxists, as a "dialectical" process of contradiction in which non-A becomes A. As we have already pointed out, this is unintelligible as well as impossible. The confusion of matter with privation or non-being has also led to the view that matter and the whole material world are evil, for non-being is surely not good. The aim of life is then identified with an escape from matter and change instead of the realization of material capacities through change. But although potential being is not fully actualized, it is not nothing. Through its possession of some lower form, matter may be incidentally deprived of a higher form. But as long as it is able to realize this form through change, it is good and not evil.

In addition to these confusions of matter with the other sources of change, many arguments have been formulated by modern ideal-

[8] Cf. this chapter, § 6, and ch. 15, § 2.

istic thought which call its very existence in question. The most important of these are the following. First, it is argued, following Descartes and Bradley, that matter (potential being) is contradictory because it neither is nor is not what it is able to be. But according to the law of excluded middle, a thing must either be or not be what it is. This argument may be answered as follows. As long as matter is only *potentially* some form, it is definitely not that determinate form. While the water is in the process of solidification, up to the very instant when this process is terminated, the water is definitely not solid. There is no instant when the water is both solid and liquid. This is ruled out by the law of contradiction. But neither this law nor that of excluded middle rules out the possibility of a being which is potential in the sense of being incompletely actualized. While not yet definitely solid, the water may be capable of solidification. Every process of change shows us such capacities and potencies being completed. Potential being is not something that neither is nor is not. It is exactly what it is, namely, incompleted being.

Another similar argument proceeds by going through all the determinate objects of sense and understanding, and pointing out that matter cannot be identified with any one of these. Thus Berkeley argues that matter is neither any definite color, sound, shape, smell, or touch. It is neither a quality nor a quantity, which is very true. So he concludes that it is merely nothing, a *merum nihil.*[9] But this conclusion does not follow. Matter is no definite, determinate form. This is granted. But how do we know that the world of nature does not also contain something indefinite and indeterminate? This can only be settled by observation. Such observation shows us the ever-present dynamism of nature which requires an indeterminate, potential substrate, namely, matter.

Finally, it is argued by Berkeley [10] and other idealists that even if matter does exist, it cannot be known, for it cannot be defined by any clear concept. Wood is the matter of a table; marble is the matter of a statue; the acorn is the matter of an oak tree; and the child is the matter of a man. But what does wood have in common with a child, or marble with an acorn? No single concept can cover such

[9] Fraser, *The Works of George Berkeley,* Vol. 1, pp. 302, 437.
[10] Fraser, *op. cit., pp.* 435–436.

a vast diversity of things. Hence matter cannot be defined, and therefore cannot be known. In answer to this, we may grant that wood, marble, acorn, and child, as matter, have nothing in common, and that table, statue, oak tree, and man, as the things formed from them, also have nothing in common. Nevertheless a single concept of all these can still be attained by what is called in realistic philosophy an *analogy*. Matter is not something fixed but something relative. Each matter is a relation to a form. These relations may be similar and may be embraced by a single concept. Thus the wood is to the table *as* the marble to the statue, the acorn to the oak, and the child to the man. Thus the relative structure of potency can be expressed by an analogous concept, and matter can be understood.

Change therefore springs from a minimum of three sources. There must be a potential substrate, or matter, which is susceptible to either of two contrary superstrates. One of these is the *terminus a quo;* the other the *terminus ad quem* of any transformation. Matter, privation, and form are the three necessary sources from which change springs. They are quite distinct from one another. Yet no one of them can exist alone without the rest. Though matter can exist without any given form, it cannot exist without *some* form. Form, on the other hand, although it can exist apart from this or that given matter, nevertheless cannot exist in nature apart from *some* matter, which it deprives of other forms. Privation also requires both form and matter for its existence, since matter is deprived of a given positive form only by the possession of some other positive form. These, then, are the three necessary sources from which change springs.

6. The Hylomorphic Structure of Natural Entities

It is true that one source cannot exist without the other two. We must nevertheless take account of a most important fact concerning the privative source. It adds no positive being to the matter but only something negative—the lack of formal structure. Thus copper and tin, which are the matter of bronze, lack this formal structure. Nevertheless they do not lack all formal structure, since matter cannot exist without some form. They are positively copper and tin, but they lack the form of bronze. In the process of becoming bronze they lose this privation. Each acts upon the other and combines with it to form the new substance. This new entity, once brought into existence, is deprived of other forms. Hence it can act as the substratum for further changes.

But as a positive, actual being it is constituted of a certain matter (copper and tin) united in a formal structure (bronze). Hence if we ask what are the actual components of any natural entity at any level from the lowest to the highest, we must answer matter and form. This view is therefore properly referred to as the *hylomorphic* theory of nature, from the Greek word *hylé,* meaning matter, and the Greek word *morphé,* meaning form. We must now contrast this theory with two opposed views of the nature of evolution—atomism and creationism, each of which has its own peculiar theory of the nature of change and of the resulting entity.

According to the atomist everything in nature is ultimately made up of very small, quantitative units, described in different ways according to the state of science in any given age. But the exact terms used in the scientific description make little difference. Atomism is a *philosophic* theory of nature which can adapt itself to an indefinite number of scientific variations. All it requires is the basic concept of very small units of some kind, spread out in quantitative form. Given these, the atomist then describes change in the following terms.

Every kind of process leaves the atoms ultimately intact. They always remain essentially what they were before the process occurred. They may be moved about and juxtaposed to form new spatial configurations, but they are never radically transformed into really novel entities. As we shall see, all change is interpreted by the atomist as something accidental, which leaves the essential nature of the atomic matter unaltered.

But indubitable empirical facts clearly indicate that evolution has brought forth new entities of a radically different type, obeying new laws of action and response. Thus the two colorless gases, hydrogen and oxygen, can be changed into the liquid substance water, which possesses very different properties and modes of action. It is clearly something more than oxygen added to hydrogen. Similarly, living matter has emerged from non-living matter, and the human animal from the brute.

Hence another theory of change has arisen which is violently opposed to atomism. This theory insists upon the emergence of radical novelty in the process of evolution. It has been defended in recent times by many like Lloyd Morgan, Smuts, Sellars, and others, who use the concept of "emergent evolution," [11] and by Bergson and his followers, who use the concept of "creative evolution."[12] According to this view, certain changes are absolutely discontinuous. They involve the emergence of something radically novel, altogether absent when the change began. The new entity may include material parts which were previously existent, but in addition to these, it also consists of something distinct from them but joined to them—the new entity, or "organic whole." Thus water may include hydrogen and oxygen. But in addition to these, there is a new, emergent whole which, though joined with the parts, cannot be identified with them. Thus, as we have seen, evolution loses all continuity and has to be interpreted as the mere succession of divergent entities.

The *hylomorphic* theory of nature, which we have been explaining, lies between these two extreme views and cannot be identified with either one. As against atomism, it holds that although there are accidental changes of place and position such as the atomist describes, there are also other substantial changes in which certain entities in a fluid state lose an essential nature, which is replaced by a radically different form. In such evolutionary processes the matter itself is transformed, the preceding structure being replaced by a new structure which penetrates down to the basic prime matter or potency which underlies all change. The new entity resulting from such a substantial change cannot be interpreted merely as a new spatial arrangement of the same atoms, for it is a new whole, in no sense the same. The various parts act upon one another in various basic ways, producing a new structure which penetrates to the most ultimate parts of the preceding matter. Hylomorphism agrees with the emergent evolutionists in that the evidence for such radical novelty is to be found in the well-authenticated facts of evolution.

[11] Cf. Morgan, Lloyd, *Life, Mind, and Spirit*, New York, Henry Holt, 1926; Smuts, J. C., *Holism and Evolution*, New York, Macmillan, 1926; and Sellars, R. W., *Evolutionary Naturalism*, Chicago, Open Court, 1922.

[12] Bergson, H., *Creative Evolution*, tr. Mitchell, A., New York, Henry Holt, 1911, especially ch. 1.

But as over against the emergent evolutionists, hylomorphism maintains that even such radical changes involve a factor of continuity. They are not *completely* discontinuous, or we could see no connection with what existed before. But there always is some connection. Water cannot be formed out of iron and nitrogen. Furthermore it can be formed out of hydrogen and oxygen only under certain conditions, as when they have been thrown into a flexible state by an electric spark. A new biological species cannot be formed out of *any* preceding species: it can be formed only out of certain approximating species. Furthermore it cannot be formed out of species which have reached a stable condition of specialized adaptation by natural selection, but only out of species less well adapted and holding themselves in a flexible and dynamic state.[13]

The facts show clearly that even the most radical changes are evolutionary rather than creative, and that they therefore involve a continuous, material potency which must first be prepared and made ready for the change.

Hence hylomorphism rejects the whole concept of a new emergent, or "organic whole," distinct from the material parts but united with it. In fact we can see the falsity of this view by the following argument. Suppose we have two parts, *a* and *b* which unite to form a whole *c*. According to the emergent evolutionist, *c* is something different from *a* and *b* together, but nevertheless united with them. Now let us ask him the question: does this new entity or whole *c* unite with *a* and *b* to form a new entity *d*, or not? If not, then why was it that *a* and *b* united to form a new entity *c?* If so, then *d* will unite with *a, b,* and *c* to form a new entity *e,* and we are in an infinite regress, which will prevent any whole from finally being formed.

We must conclude from this that the attempt to distinguish the whole from its parts is impossible. Such a whole is a fictitious entity made up by the mind with no real foundation. Any real whole is simply *all* the parts in an implicit and unspecified form. *All* the parts are the whole made explicit and distinct. The idea that the whole is a new entity distinct from the parts arises from a tendency to ignore a certain kind of part that enters into the essential composition of any natural entity—its form or structure. The parts that

[13] Cf. ch. 16, § 5, 366 ff.

impress us most obviously are the *integral,* quantitative parts of a thing. These are called integral because each of them is a whole which can exist apart from the rest.

If a physical thing were made up exclusively of parts of this kind it would not be essentially one, but only one by accident, like a heap of rocks piled up together. After we have analyzed a thing in this purely quantitative way we often get a dim sense of the underlying unity which binds these quantitative parts into one entity of a certain kind. We realize that there is something more there than a mere agglomeration of quantitative parts. But this *something more* is not the whole. It is another, more basic kind of *part,* the substantial form, or structure, which determines the matter from which the thing has evolved and spreads out the quantitative parts in a unitary pattern. Matter and form are the essential physical parts of any natural entity.

According to the theory of hylomorphism, these physical parts exist only by reason of one another. Hence they are not integral, quantitative parts, each of which can exist in separation from the rest. The matter of this plant exists only by reason of the plant structure that now determines it, and the plant structure exists only by reason of the matter that has received it, as a substratum. They are not two *things* joined together, but one *thing* consisting of two constitutive principles, each of which plays an essential role in bringing the other, and hence the whole, hylomorphic entity into being. They are not held together by any bond or link distinct from them. They are held together simply by their causal action on each other, that of matter in *sustaining* the form and that of form in *determining* the matter. The effect of this interaction is the existence of the compound hylomorphic entity.

What then is responsible for the union of the matter with the form? This brings us to the next topic with which we must deal, that of causation. Change has three sources from which it proceeds, a privative superstrate, a positive superstrate, and an underlying potential substrate. But what is responsible for this proceeding? What are the causes of change?

REFERENCES

Recommended Reading

Aristotle, *Physics*, Book I, chaps. 5–9, and Book II, chaps. 1–2; *Aristotle: Natural Science, Psychology, Ethics,* edited by Wheelwright, Odyssey Press, New York, 1935, is strongly recommended, though *The Works of Aristotle* (Oxford Edition), Vol. 2, *Physics,* translated by Hardie and Gaye is usable by students.

Suggested Reading

1. For an expression of positivism and scientism, cf. Ayer, A. J., *Language, Truth, and Logic,* Oxford, New York, 1936. On the other hand, for a clear statement of present-day agnosticism concerning the real nature of things, cf. Jeans, *Physics and Philosophy,* Macmillan, 1943, pp. 1–16, especially pp. 15–16. For an exposition of the pragmatic attitude towards philosophy, cf. Dewey, *Reconstruction in Philosophy,* New York, Henry Holt, 1920.

2. For the basic arguments against the existence of matter, cf. Berkeley, *Principles of Human Knowledge,* Part I, Sec. 1–20. Cf. also Bradley, *Appearance and Reality,* Part I, chap. 5.

3. On emergent evolution, cf. Morgan, Lloyd, *Life, Mind and Spirit,* New York, Henry Holt, 1926 (Gifford Lectures), and Bergson, *Creative Evolution,* New York, Henry Holt, 1911. For a summary statement of the hylomorphic theory, Aristotle, *Metaphysics,* New York, Oxford, 1928, Book VII, chaps. 7, 8, and 9.

Chapter 14

THE CAUSES OF CHANGE

WE have observed that change arises from three sources or principles: privation, matter, and form. If any one of these is lacking, there can be no change. If the matter is not deprived but already possesses the form, no change will occur; also if it remains deprived and does not receive the form. Finally, without any matter to act as a permanent substratum we will have first mere negation, then being, which is not change but creation. These are therefore the three necessary sources from which change arises as starting points. We must now ask, what are the causes of change?

A cause gives positive existence to another thing, whereas a source, being only a beginning, need not do so. Thus the starting point of a line is the beginning of the line, not the cause of it. If it were, as soon as the point actually existed we should have the line. But this is not the case. All causes are sources, but not all sources, or beginnings, are causes. Let us now consider the sources of change. Which of these are only sources, and which are not only sources but also positive causes, contributing actual being to the change? This question is not difficult to answer.

It is clear that the privation is annihilated in the process. Hence it contributes no positive being to the change and must be considered only a source not a cause. The matter, on the other hand, underlies the process, enduring to the very end. It contributes the positive receptacle for the change. The form also is present as the *terminus ad quem*. It contributes the positive, determinate being into which the indeterminate matter changes or proceeds. Of the three sources, matter and form are intrinsic causes, giving being to the change and positively effecting the material entity which results from it. Their coming together *in* the matter constitutes the process.

The matter cannot make its contribution (sustaining the form) without the elimination of its privation through change. But the form makes its contribution without changing at all—simply by

uniting *as it is* with the matter, giving it a new form and actuality which it did not before possess. Thus in the process of growth
the plant loses its immaturity and becomes actually formed in root,
stalk, and flower. In the process of learning, the mind loses its indeterminate ignorance and becomes determinately aware of this
or that. The two privations, immaturity and ignorance, are only
beginnings, *not causes* of the processes.

1. THE FOUR SPECIES OF CAUSE

Every process of change and evolution is intrinsically caused by
a matter out of which the new entity emerges and which remains
as its substrate, and some definite pattern or structure which determines and distinguishes this entity. Without the union of these
causes in the process there can be no change. With the union change
must occur as a necessary effect. Hence form and matter are the
two *intrinsic* causes of change, becoming united in the changing
thing and remaining united in the new changed entity which
emerges.

But our explanation is not yet complete. Change is caused by a
union of form and matter *in* some matter. But what is the cause
of this union? The undeveloped seed is not the plant. The matter
is not the form. Of themselves they are not necessarily united. If
so, they would already be united and could not *become* united in
a process of change. What then brings them together? Our explanation of change is not complete until we have found the cause of
this union.

Of course there are certain different things which necessarily
belong together, since one of them formally requires the other.
Thus the nature of a triangle requires that the internal angles be
equal to 180°. These are both *formal* determinations. One form
may demand another form, and thus explain it. But such a purely
formal explanation, typical of mathematical science which abstracts
from matter and change, is of no help to us, for we are investigating
the actual world of nature which is characterized, not only by a
union of forms with other forms, but by a dynamic union of form
with indeterminate matter. If the very nature of matter required
that it be united with form, there would be no natural, evolving
world at all, for the matter would already be necessarily united

with form—the seed would necessarily already be a plant, and change would not exist. But we need only open our eyes to see that everything around us is actually changing. Matter is constantly becoming united to forms with which it is not of itself necessarily connected. The seed *can* become warped or stunted or not grow up at all. Neither matter nor form in themselves require that they come together.

Shall we simply accept this fact as inexplicable? This of course would be to abandon the quest for understanding. To understand means to answer the question *why,* and we can answer this question only by giving the cause or the reason. All scientific investigation is a seeking for causes. In certain cases, you may say, the quest succeeds, but in others there may be no cause. Is science then simply a pursuit of useful human prejudice? Is the search for causes simply grounded in the structure of the human mind or is it rather grounded in the nature of things? Can we say that there must be an extrinsic cause to account for the union of form with matter? This would explain the obstinacy with which we refuse to admit that the forest just burned of itself or that the sickness just came without a cause. But is there any real reason for this, other than the make-up of the human mind? There is such a reason.

The organism is one thing A, the disease another, non-A. If the organism A should become diseased, non-A, of itself without any extrinsic cause, then A by itself would become non-A, and we should be faced with a contradiction. But a contradiction cannot be. This is a basic law of being. The very same thing cannot both be and not be all at once in the same respect. Matter cannot of itself unite with what it is not, viz., form. If this occurred, matter would both be what it is, and what it is not—a contradiction. Hence even though we do not know the cause of some change, as we often do not, we know that there must be some extrinsic cause of the change. This is the reason for that stubborn search for causes which marks every scientific endeavor of man.

Change without a cause is not a fact to be accepted with natural piety, but a downright contradiction. Change without its cause is an incomplete fact. The search for causes is the search for a completion of the facts. The very existence of human art and natural science offers sufficient inductive proof of the existence of causes to justify further search. But the basic proof of the need for such a search lies in the metaphysical principle of contradiction. An uncaused process not only is not, and has not been; it cannot be.

Hence in addition to the intrinsic causes, form and matter, change requires an extrinsic, efficient or moving cause which brings the form to the matter, uniting the two. Fire was brought to the forest by lightning. Disease was brought to the organism by a germ. This moving cause which brings form to the matter is known as the *efficient* cause. If this moving or impelling cause lies outside the whole system to which the process belongs, we have technical change.[1] If the efficient cause lies in the whole system, but not within the single, changing entity, we have natural change or evolution. If the efficient cause lies within the single, changing being, this is a living, natural substance, which grows and moves and acts of itself.

As the great Arabian philosopher, Avicenna, points out, there are four subspecies of efficient cause. First, there is that sort of influence which prepares or disposes the matter, making it ready for the form. Thus the seed has to be prepared by the parent organism before it can become the substratum, or matter, for an independent plant or animal. Second, there is the subordinate influence which aids in introducing the form. Thus the energy of sunlight is *used* by the plant in achieving its growth. In agents which act purposively, like men, there is a third, special type of *aiding* efficient cause which introduces, not so much an active influence, as the form of such action. This is the influence of counsel and technical "know-how" which determines the way in which some aim is to be achieved. Finally, in the fourth place, there is the efficient cause proper, the *perfecting* efficient cause, which actually achieves the forming of a potential matter and brings the process to its *terminus ad quem*. Thus in the case of the plant, this is what we call its growing power, which, using many subordinate instrumental organs, finally brings the seed to its mature form.

In the case of a technical process such as the building of a house, where the efficient causes are better known to us, these four subspecies may be clearly recognized. First, there is the preparation of the wood and bricks until they are finally susceptible to the build-

[1] Cf. ch. 13, § 1.

ing process. Second, there are the saw, the chisel, the hammer, the mason's trowel which instrumentally aid in forming the house. Third, there are the technical skills of the carpenters and masons, which determine the precise way in which this or that subordinate part of the process is to be brought about. Finally, in the fourth place, there are the building movements of the workmen which use the various instruments to achieve the complete building of the house, in which the matter (wood and bricks) loses its disarrangement (privation) and is united to the finished structure of the house. These move the matter by their own physical motion. Hence they are subordinate, efficient causes. But they are themselves moved by the aspiration or striving of the builders. This psychic aspiration is the first, efficient cause which brings all the rest into motion.

But our task is unfinished. We may still ask why this first, efficient cause, the psychic aspiration, acts in such a way as to introduce a certain form into the matter. This question demands an answer. Efficient action *by itself* is indeterminate. It does not tend of itself to any one result rather than to another. Why do the builders act in such a manner as to build a house? The answer is to be found in a changeless, intellectual cause—the plan in the mind of an architect. It is this *final cause* which guides the building operations from beginning to end.

Like the formal cause, it does not change throughout the process. If it did, the efficient cause would lapse into indeterminacy and would cease to act, just as matter would cease to change if it lacked a fixed *terminus ad quem*. Indeed in the world of nature, the formal cause plays the role of the final cause, since the operations of non-rational entities are immediately directed by their natural forms. Thus the growth of an acorn into an oak is directed by the fixed structure which is physically (not rationally) inherent in it. This is of course also true of the inorganic elements. The immediate, final cause of their active tendencies of attraction and repulsion is simply their formal nature.

But in human purposive activity we observe a final cause in the strict sense of this term, which is quite distinct from the physical form. Otherwise human operations would be automatic and constant like those of fire and water. They are flexible and free in so far as they are guided by a directing idea in the mind, the *final cause* in its strict and proper sense. The question as to whether the world of subhuman nature requires such an extrinsic, final cause we shall have to postpone until Chapter 16. Here we shall only note the indubitable evidence which shows that it exists in man, and therefore we list it as a fourth species of cause, which exists as a rational concept in the mind and is capable of guiding efficient action.

The empirical evidence reveals these four causes at work in nature. Matter and form are intrinsic causes, remaining within any natural entity after it has emerged from the course of evolution. The moving cause and the final cause, however, are extrinsic to the process they determine. But all four causes must be at work to produce any real change. There must be a matter out of which it emerges as its *terminus a quo*. There must be a form to which it tends as its *terminus ad quem*. There must be an efficient cause which brings the form to the matter and unites the two. Finally, there must be something fixed which determines the efficient cause to act in one way rather than another. This is the final cause in a broad sense which includes both natural forms and purposive ideas. There must be some such final cause, or no moving cause would ever act in a determinate way to produce a determinate effect.

2.   Current Misconceptions of Causation

This complex structure of causation has neither been clearly understood nor adequately defended by realistic philosophy in modern times. Partly as a result of the attack on final causation at the beginning of the modern period, this notion has fallen into widespread disrepute as an anthropomorphic fiction. It is commonly interpreted as an attempt to read human purposes into subhuman phenomena, as though a magnet, for example, were supposed to make up its mind to attract iron filings. As we have just explained, this rests upon a complete misconception of the doctrine of Aristotle, who clearly asserts that the only final cause in subhuman processes is the natural form.[2] Nevertheless this distorted idea has had a widespread influence on technical thought and even on common sense.

[2] *Physics,* Book II, 7, 198A 24.

Thus when we think of extrinsic causal action we tend to think of blind, efficient power with no final determining cause. This has led many to misconceive individual freedom as a purely indeterminate upsurging of the will, and political freedom as the rampant power of a sovereign state unchecked by any final cause. But the final cause is the cause of the other causes. Hence when its nature is misunderstood or denied, this leads to confusion concerning the other causes and the structure of causation in general.

Perhaps the most important of these is the prevalent idea, supported by Descartes, Locke, Berkeley, Hume, Kant, and Mill, that the cause must precede the effect *in time*.[3] This idea is now extremely widespread, but it rests upon a misconception. The cause is indeed prior to its effect in the sense that it already possesses some mode of being which can be received as an effect. But the action of the cause is not *temporally* prior to the reception of the effect. The cutting of the orange (cause) does not temporally precede the orange's being cut (effect).

But surely, it may be objected, some effects follow after their causes. Does not the motion of the billiard ball (effect) follow after its impact with the cue (cause)? This must be answered by distinguishing between two sets of contemporaneous causes and effects. While the cue is bringing the ball into motion (cause), the ball is being moved (effect). The result (not the effect) is the motion of the ball. But this motion is itself sustained and influenced by the cloth, the air, the table, and other contemporaneous causes of nature. Thus the building of the house (cause) goes on while the house is being built (effect). These are followed by a *result*, the finished house, which is sustained by the ground, the air, and other contemporaneous causes of nature.

The cause produces the result, not by itself, but only through the agency of the stable causes of nature. It is these stable causes of permanent, contemporaneous effects through long periods of time which are responsible for what we call causal sequences, not the vanishing causes of vanishing effects. The actual cause always begins and ends with its actual effect.

But a further objection may be raised against this realistic theory

[3] Cf. Wild, J., The Cartesian Deformation of the Structure of Change and Its Influence on Modern Thought, *Philosophical Review*, January 1941.

of causation. Is there any real difference, we may ask, between the cutting of the orange (cause) and its being cut (effect)? Is this not obviously one and the same process? If so, then the supposed difference between "cause" and "effect" is a purely verbal one. Of course a thing is contemporaneous with itself. This objection must also be answered by making a distinction. In a certain sense the process is one, just as the distance between Boston and New York is one distance. But it can be read in two ways, from Boston to New York or from New York to Boston. These directions are not the same. Similarly there is only one process in the orange. But this process can be read in two ways, as the effect received in the orange or as the action by the knife. These two aspects of the process are going on during the same interval of time, and are really distinct though not separate. The war is one, but Germany's invasion of the Netherlands is not the same as Holland's being invaded by Germany. Cause and effect are not the same. They are distinct aspects of one process.

The four species of cause, cause one another in any given process. Matter provides a restricted substratum for form, and the form actualizes and determines the matter. The efficient cause brings the two together, and the final cause determines the efficient cause. This also leads to difficulty and misunderstanding, especially when the relation of cause to effect is misunderstood as involving temporal priority. How, it is asked, can each of two causes be prior to the other? Is this not a contradiction? It would be if the two causes belonged to the same species and exercised the same sort of causal influence. But this is not the case. Each of the causes provides something distinct in the total effect. In its own specific sphere each cause is prior, in other respects posterior. Thus, as intentionally determining the mode of efficient action, the final cause is prior to the efficient. But as an actual end to be realized by efficient action, it must wait for this action to be achieved, and is posterior. Each cause acts on the rest in a peculiar manner, making its own, distinct contribution to the change. Hence there is no contradiction.

We must now note that within each species of cause there are different modes.

3. The Modes of Causation

a. PRIOR AND POSTERIOR. There are two senses in which one cause can be *prior* to another. In each species the more universal, generic cause is prior to the more specific cause. Thus if man is the formal cause, animal is a prior, formal cause. If sculptor is the efficient cause, artisan is a prior, efficient cause. If iron is the material cause, metal and inorganic prime matter are *prior* causes in this material order.

The second sense of priority is this. Formal, final, or efficient causes may occur in serial order. In this case that subordinate cause which is nearer the *first* cause is prior. Take the following case of demonstration through formal causes: knowledge is universal by nature; what is universal is communicable; what is communicable can be taught; what can be taught can be learned; hence knowledge can be learned. Here is an ordered chain of formal causes. Universality is essential to human knowledge. Communicability, and the other forms, however, follow from this with formal necessity as posterior, formal consequences. As in the case of the other causes, such a chain of formal causes may be the foundation for a demonstrative argument. If x is a case of knowledge, then it can be taught and learned.

In the case of final causation, the first cause is called the *end;* the subordinate causes, *means* or *intermediate ends.* Thus I desire happiness. This requires virtue. Virtue requires virtuous acts. Hence I desire to act virtuously.

In the case of efficient causation, suppose a man on a ship desiring to pull up the anchor. This decision is the first efficient cause. This moves his nerves, which move the muscles of his arm, which moves his hand, which gives an impulse to the end of the rope it touches, which moves a further portion of the rope, which finally lifts the anchor, the last effect of this chain of prior and posterior efficient causes.

b. ACCIDENTAL AND ESSENTIAL. In each species of cause we must distinguish that which is only more or less closely associated with the cause in some way. Very often what we refer to as the cause, is not the cause at all but only something connected with it—an accidental cause. As we shall see, this lies at the root of what we call *chance* (this chapter, §4). For example, that which essentially makes man formally what he is, is his rational, animal nature. Light or dark color is only accidentally connected with this cause. When the accident is identified with the essential cause, so that, for example, man is defined as a blond animal, tragic confusion arises.

The distinction between the essential and the accidental *final* cause is of the greatest importance in judging moral motives. The final cause of a human act is the end which is chosen for its own sake, whatever the circumstances may be. If we judge that the final cause of an act resulting in death was precisely to kill, then we are judging the act to be murder. If on the other hand we see that the final cause was really something else, say self-defense, and that the killing was only accidentally associated with this major purpose, we are judging it not to be murder. Virtue itself is the *essential* final cause of a virtuous act, which must be done for the love of virtue for its own sake. The very same act, however, may be done merely for the sake of reputation or gain. In this case its virtue will be entirely incidental.

The efficient cause is peculiarly subject to this confusion. What made the statue? When we say Polyclitus, we have not given the true efficient cause, which is a set of operations governed by the sculptor's art. Polyclitus involves many other attributes and operations which are only accidentally associated with the essential cause.

The accidental cause may be necessarily connected with the essential cause or it may be merely connected with it. Finally, there may be only an imaginary connection. The same is true of the effect. Instead of the true essential effect we may give only some accident necessarily connected with the effect, or the results, as when we say that Samson brought down the whole roof of the temple, when what he really did was merely to break a pillar. Or we may give some accident merely connected with the effect, as when we say that Samson destroyed some statue that happened to be in the temple. Or we may give some merely imaginary accident not really connected with the effect at all, as when we say that Samson caused the great drought which followed the destruction of the temple.

c. THE ACTUAL VS. THE POTENTIAL CAUSE. In each species of cause, the actual must be distinguished from the potential cause.

Words like *building material* and *builder* refer only to the potential matter and the potential, efficient cause. The failure to make this distinction clearly is one of the reasons why we fail to see that the actual cause and the actual effect are contemporaneous. The builder (potential cause) temporally precedes the actual building of the house and may remain a builder after the house is actually built—even after it is destroyed. On the other hand, the house may often outlast the builder. But the actual building of the house (the actual cause) is necessarily contemporaneous with its being built (the actual effect).

4. Chance and Fortune

The efficient, final, and, of course, the formal cause act in virtue of a definite formal determination. There are many such causes in the world of nature, each of which necessarily produces a definite, formal effect. The idea of an angry act elicits an angry impulse; the compact, molecular structure of igneous quartz makes its matter rocky and harder than glass; the stone smashes the window. Here every cause has its necessary, determinate effect. The more we learn about nature, the more we glimpse such causal action, for to understand anything is to understand its causes. Hence the philosophical conception of determinism has arisen. According to this view, every definite occurrence unfolds with inescapable necessity from its determinate causes.

But we must not forget the elusive, material cause which underlies all change and permeates the whole of nature. This cause is not determinate like the rest, but indeterminate and potential. It is ultimately responsible for certain indeterminate deviations in the course of events which have led others to embrace the opposite view of indeterminism. According to this theory, chance is the lord of nature, and there is no necessary cause of anything.

The argument between these opposed positions has continued through the ages. Each has shown grave weaknesses in the other. Neither has proved its case. Accidents do happen. Nevertheless every event must have some cause. Is there any way of reconciling these seemingly opposed facts? If there is, it may help us to penetrate some of the darkest secrets with which we are confronted by the mysterious world we inhabit. There is such a way. But in order to understand it we must turn once more to the material cause of change and try to analyze one of its most puzzling effects —that which we call chance and fortune.

Mathematics abstracts from individual matter. Hence mathematical laws, which concern form alone, admit of no coincidences or exceptions. It may be that the particular triangle observed by a mathematician is colored white or red. But if so, this is of no interest to him. He abstracts from all such coincidental qualities, paying attention only to the triangular form and its formal effects. If he discovers such a formal effect, as that of the angles equalling 180°, he discovers this as timelessly true and admitting of no exceptions.

Nature, on the other hand, is full of coincidence. The triangle existing in nature is made out of some matter, susceptible to many other determining influences besides the quantitative forms of mathematics. The triangle in nature also reflects light. Hence it is white or blue. Its whiteness neither requires triangularity, nor does this require whiteness. Of course certain definite causes are responsible for the one, and certain definite causes for the other. But if we ask what is responsible for the coincidence of the independent effects of the two independent sets of causes we give an ambiguous answer. We do give an answer—as though there were some cause. Yet we do not give a determinate answer, as though there were a determinate cause. We say: well, it just happened to be so; or by accident (not by any determinate cause) it was the case.

This answer is correct. Each of the two determinate causes produces its determinate effect. The wind blew the seed to the side of the stream; the life of the seed caused it to grow; the spring rains caused the flood. Why did the results of these coincide in the early destruction of this buttercup? By accident, or by reason of that indeterminate matter of the seed which was susceptible to all these influences. Nature is full of coincidence.

We do not notice these ubiquitous coincidences except in certain cases which especially strike our attention. One of these is when one coinciding cause cancels the effect of another. Thus millions of salmon eggs are poured forth in the spawning season. These are not only susceptible to the helpful environmental influences which support vital growth, but also to opposite influences which cause destruction. These contrary causes in thousands of cases cancel the helpful influences. Accordingly we say that in such cases nature acts in vain, or that her work is of no effect.

Another case is that of abnormal growths, or monstrosities, in nature, when the normal cause is not only frustrated by some opposing obstacle, but replaced by some accidental combination of influences which produce a wholly exceptional result—a mistake of nature. But these are only a few of the more sensational coincidences which strike our attention. The ordinary ones are far too numerous to be noted.

Every natural cause coincides with many accidents which by themselves cause no determinate effect, though they are materially associated with the real cause. The germ really causing the epidemic, for example, was contained in milk. In this case milk was not the real cause but only the cause by accident. Every natural effect also coincides with many accidents which are not so much the real effect as the effect by accident. The cessation of a certain vital secretion (the real effect of a disease) is attended by high blood pressure, loss of weight, paleness, inertia, and many other accidental symptoms, more or less remote from the real effect of the real cause of this disease.

A primary task of scientific investigation is to eliminate the more remote accidents from the effect and especially from the cause. Until this cause is known in itself or at least through its necessary accidents, our control over nature rests on a shaky foundation. Milk may precede the disease. By eliminating milk we eliminate the disease. But this does not prove that milk is the cause. Milk may be only a remote accident of the real cause, which may finally return with a new cluster of coincidental accidents.

Of course, on the whole, the efficient and final causes of nature impose their determinate, formal effects on the unlimited capacities of matter without frustration. In consequence the general structure of organic nature is maintained, so that in the case of the salmon, for example, enough survive to preserve the species. In other words, nature proceeds continuously from one step to another and *for the most part* achieves similar results. Such facts show that organized causes are in control.

Nevertheless, once given such a stable order of independent

causes, the infinite capacity of matter, never fully realized, must lead to those indefinite accidents which constitute the individual histories of natural substances. Among these there are bound to be frustrating and distorting coincidences. Without them there could be neither individuality nor change, inasmuch as these accidents all have their root in that same indeterminacy of the material cause which is the source of evolution.

We are living beings containing ends (final causes) and activities (efficient causes) within ourselves. Sometimes our action imposes useful forms on nature, as in the arts and techniques. Sometimes it further perfects our own forms, as in what we call our own behavior. But our lives, together with the whole endeavor of human culture, proceed in the great surrounding matrix of the material, natural world. This world is governed by non-human causes and their inevitable accidents. So far as we learn these general causes we can anticipate their general results and fit them into our purposes, but their individual, indeterminate coincidences can never be predicted. When independent, natural causes coincide with our action in a favorable conjunction which might have been planned by us but which merely happened by accident, we name this fortune, the opposite, misfortune.

In thus furthering or frustrating our purposes, chance, which besets the whole changing world, is brought into a much clearer light. This is because our own purposes (efficient and final causes) are much better known to us than the efficient and final causes of nature as a whole. A party of men go to dig a grave. As a result, *by accident,* they happen upon a treasure. The treasure was buried in a place determined by one set of causes. The grave was dug in a place determined by a wholly independent set of causes. That the place happened to be the same was a fortunate coincidence for the gravediggers.

The mountain side is tilled because the soil is fertile. The volcano erupts when the pressure of gas is sufficiently strong. Each is the result of determinate causes and effects. But that the eruption should sweep away the farm of this individual man X is a misfortune caused by the indeterminate susceptibility of matter to be influenced all at once by independent chains of causes. Fortune is a special kind of chance. Thus we call misfortune also mischance. All fortune is chance. But not all chance is fortune. Fortune is material coincidence as affecting human purpose. Chance is material coincidence as affecting the order of nature. The former is better known to us. Hence its structure sheds light on the latter.

For instance, it is clear that without a settled purposive endeavor there can be no fortune or misfortune. Hence we do not attribute luck or misfortune to infants or animals. Luck presupposes a decisive purpose. When this is furthered by accident, as if by foresight, we call it luck. When it is thwarted by some external accident, as if by foresight, we call it unlucky, and say that we labored in vain. Similarly, chance presuppose a settled order of nature maintained in matter for the most part. When a coincidence furthers this order, as when a horse not acting from instinct, moves to safety, we call it chance. When some coincidence frustrates this order we do not call it a misfortune, for chance is immanent in nature, but we say that nature has acted in vain.

When a man goes to town for bread and happens to meet a friend owing him money and is paid, we say that this fortune was by accident. Had he not gone for bread he could not have been paid, but the coincidence of this with the presence of the friend was the cause, not merely his going for bread. Any number of other reasons might have sufficed as well. He might have gone from boredom or to escape an enemy. The same is true of the immanent chance in nature. The horse may have moved away from the tree struck by lightning from fear of the shadow, but hunger or restlessness would have sufficed. It is not merely the moving away we are trying to explain, but the coincidence of moving away with the independent striking of the tree. Only the insatiable susceptibility of matter can explain this, by accident.

Fortune cannot be known or anticipated. Hence the goddess is pictured as blind. Events of this sort just happen. This is because they are indefinite and indeterminable. We know only what is definite and determinate. Furthermore, they happen all of a sudden with no gradual, causal preparation such as is required for the production of a determinate material effect. This is because each single fortune or misfortune is really the coincidence of two independent results in one matter. Each result requires an antecedent, causal process. But the coincidence of the two results happens all of a sudden with no determinate causal antecedents of its own.

Fortune is unstable and fickle. We do not attribute what necessarily follows upon an act to luck, or even what *tends to happen for the most part*. If a man commits murder and then is caught and punished, we do not look upon it as a frightful piece of bad luck. The same is true of chance in nature. The necessary and the ordinary are not attributed to chance even if we do not know the causes. No one has ever attributed the sequence of day and night to chance or the whiteness of clouds or the downward course of water. Chance is always the exceptional, the rare. It may be defined as a coincidence of the natural results of independent causes which resembles or frustrates a normal natural result.

5. DETERMINISM VS. INDETERMINISM

This explanation offers us a middle way between the two extremes of indeterminism and determinism. When properly interpreted each of these views contains a certain truth. But as ordinarily understood, when pushed to an extreme which denies any truth to the other, each becomes false. Thus there is truth in the indeterminist assertion that there are exceptions to the gradual, determinate, predictable processes of nature. Chance results are achieved all of a sudden by the coincidence of two such processes in one and the same matter. They may not proceed from a single, determinate beginning at all, but from two such beginnings whose results coincide all at once in an exceptional and unpredictable occurrence. There is abundant empirical evidence to show that such sudden, freakish happenings do occur. But when the indeterminist concludes from this that such events spring up spontaneously of themselves with no causes whatsoever, he is in error. Such a view was defended in the 19th century by those who believed that the biological principle of "natural selection" was sufficient to account for the whole process of evolution.

Suppose a number of entities in a fixed environment—so the explanation runs. Then suppose a number of spontaneous, chance variations. Those better adapted to the fixed environment will be selected, and those less well adapted will be weeded out. Thus chance alone will explain the existence of harmonious adaptation.

This "Darwinian" theory contains a certain truth. Natural selection plays a limited role in the evolution of living forms, though it is now agreed that this role is less important than Darwin was led to suppose.[4] It may also play a restricted role in other fields of change, for chance cannot be eliminated from a dynamic universe. But when the theory is expanded into a universal explanatory theory, it faces insurmountable difficulties which may be suggested by the following questions.

Why were there any "entities" in the first place? Did they simply spring into being with no cause? This is impossible, a contradiction. What was responsible for the variations? Did they also emerge of themselves with no cause? This would also be an unintelligible contradiction. Why among the purely chance variations did an adapting variation occur? Millions of retrograde variations were conceivable, to say nothing of many more wholly irrelevant. What caused the "fixed environment"? What maintained it in a "fixed" state through long periods of time? Such stable structures are never attributed to chance. Who would say that the constant heat of the equatorial regions or the constant coldness of the polar regions was due to chance? Such an attitude would soon put an end to the scientific search for causes.

These considerations are sufficient to show that nature never acts by chance alone. In spite of exceptions natural processes on the whole are continuous and gradual, like the growth of a plant. They start from some determinate beginning as the seed. Furthermore, similar effects are constantly reproduced in stable cycles. Day succeeds night; plants continue to send their roots down rather than up; the seasons are repeated in regular sequence. These stable effects require permanent, stable causes. They cannot be explained by chance alone.

Here the indeterminist may raise a question. When, as sometimes happens, a particularly violent fall of rain destroys some plant or cultivated field, we do not attribute this to a malignant cause in nature, but only to chance. Why, then, should we not be consistent and also attribute the generally beneficent effects of rainfall on plants to chance rather than to some stable, natural cause supporting vegetation? The reason is that the two cases are quite different. Therefore we should not be consistent in treating

[4] Cf. Lecomte du Noüy, *Human Destiny*, New York, Longmans, Green, 1947, pp. 55–105, for a lucid statement by a modern biologist of the reasons for this change in emphasis.

them as though they were alike. The destruction of the individual plant or field was an exceptional case, not the general rule. If it were there would be no plants at all. The beneficent effect is what happens *for the most part*. Hence it requires a stable, natural cause.

A similar confusion of chance occurrences with stable, natural tendencies, which maintain a constant effect in spite of exceptions, is found in a certain way of interpreting the recent return of physical science to the realistic concept of natural law as a statement of what holds true *for the most part*. Science, it is said, has now shown that the laws of nature are founded merely on statistical averages. Each electron acts in a completely unpredictable manner. But when millions of electrons are observed, the individual differences are canceled out and their actions may be expressed in a statistical law. But the law does not hold of the individual electron, which is wholly indeterminate.

This conception expresses a reaction against the outmoded, deterministic science of the last century, which ruled out all potency, chance, and indetermination from the world of nature. As such, it contains a certain truth. The deterministic view is false, and modern science is once again approaching the Aristotelian view that physical laws hold good only for the most part (*epi to polu*), and unlike mathematical laws, admit of exceptions in material individuals subject to the influence of independent counteracting causes.[5] If the electrons acted in a "wholly unpredictable manner," however, their actions would be expressed in chaos rather than in any "statistical law." Such a law must express some stable tendency based upon the nature of an electron. If the electron had no such determinate nature it would not be an electron rather than a proton and would not tend to act in any one way rather than in another. Nevertheless the action of individual electrons may show great deviations from the normal, owing to chance coincidence, which is always present in nature. This is the truth in the position of so-called indeterminism.

But there is also a truth in the opposed position of determinism. Every mode of finite being must have some cause, determinate modes requiring determinate causes; indeterminate modes, indeterminate causes. This is certainly true. But when the determinist

[5] Cf. *Metaphysics* 1025A 13 ff.

then goes on to argue that everything in nature must be a determinate fact with a determinate cause he is going too far. There are also indeterminate modes of being with indeterminate causes. The determinist is apt to argue: if certain things happen by chance without any cause, then the law that every effect has a cause is overthrown, and we must give up the attempt to understand nature. But this is a twisted statement.

A chance event is not an event "without any cause." Such an event always has at least two coinciding parts, each of which is the necessary effect of a determinate cause. Without necessary, determinate causes, chance would be impossible. Take the gravediggers who find the treasure by accident. The grave digging is the necessary effect and result of a series of causes. The burial of the treasure was also the necessary effect and result of an independent series of causes. How about the unpredictable coincidence? This also has a cause—the indeterminacy or indefinite susceptibility of matter to causal action. Nothing is uncaused.

We have thus arrived at a mode of explanation that can be identified neither with determinism nor with indeterminism, though it sees a certain truth in each view. Determinism is correct in holding that every aspect of nature must have a necessary cause. It is wrong in holding that every aspect of nature must be determinate and must have a determinate cause. There are also indeterminate, accidental aspects of nature with indeterminate causes. The indeterminist is correct in calling attention to these accidental aspects of nature. They are everywhere present. But he is wrong in holding that these events have no cause whatsoever. At their root lies the indeterminate potency of matter.

In the last chapter we considered the role which this elusive cause plays in the change and dynamism of nature. In this chapter we have considered its role in producing the unpredictable coincidences of chance and fortune. Now we must briefly consider its third role as an indispensable factor in producing an even more ubiquitous fact of nature, the fact of individuation.

6. THE FACT OF INDIVIDUATION

If we examine any determinate form like humanity, quality, or quantity, we find nothing about it which demands that it be restricted to this or that instance. Indeed the facts of experience show that these forms are communicated to a great number of different instances. The nature of man is possessed by a multitude of individuals. The nature of quantity and quality is universally diffused among all the entities of nature. But when we examine one of these entities we find that although it possesses many such communicable forms, it also possesses something incommunicable which belongs to it alone. This trait, whatever it is, came into existence with the entity and will disappear when the entity disappears. It belongs to the entity as long as it endures, and divides it from all other things. It is by virtue of this trait that we call the single entity an individual.

The trait itself may be called individuation. All the material things of nature are individual. Not only is every tree an individual, but all its parts and properties are individual as well. We ourselves are material beings, and therefore individuals. Not only do we possess this trait of incommunicability which cuts us off from the rest of the world, but through our possession of cognitive faculties we are also aware of it, particularly in connection with our fellow men. Sometimes it dawns on one with poignant clarity that his whole material existence, including a large part of his sensations and feelings, are restricted to himself and cannot be shared with any other individual. But this sense of cosmic loneliness is ever latent within us.

It can be overcome only in one area of our experience, the field of rational thought and discourse, which can be communicated without alteration to another human mind. Such communication is made up of concepts which are universal and immaterial, and therefore capable of being shared.[6] But at every other point our experience is private and incommunicable except in so far as it can be conceptualized. Let us now attempt to analyze this cosmic separation. What is this universal fact of individuation, and how is it to be explained?

The word itself clearly means in-division, or un-divided, and a glance at the facts will show that this is an important aspect of its meaning. The different parts and properties of an individual communicate with one another and are undivided from the substance.

[6] Cf. ch. 19, esp. pp. 442–444.

Thus the different branches and leaves of a living tree communicate with one another. Separation means death. Furthermore, this is also true of the properties, like the green color, and the circular shape of the trunk. These also belong to the tree and cannot be separated from it. The individual entity is individual, or undivided from itself. This is the primary aspect of individuation. But it is not the only one. There is another aspect which is even more evident. The individual is divided from all other things. The tree occupies its own quantitative position and is spatially separated from the other entities which lie "outside." These two aspects are accurately expressed by the following definition: *an individual is that which is undivided from itself and spatially divided from all other things.* How then are they to be explained?

Let us take the second aspect first. This is clearly connected with the attribute of quantity which spreads its parts out in such a way that one lies outside of another in a certain order.[7] One individual is divided from another because of the quantitative dimensions which give it a certain position separate from other quantities. This fact is so evident that many have held that quantity alone was sufficient to account for individuation. But a careful examination will show that this is not the case. In addition to quantity a more ultimate source of individuation is required for two reasons.

In the first place, quantity is a definite, formal nature that cannot exist alone by itself. We never find the quantity, *two centimeters,* alone by itself, but two centimeters of steel, wood, or linen. At the root of quantitative spread there must be something which is spread out. This is always some kind of matter.

In the second place, there is the more basic aspect of individuation which we have already noted, the indivision of the individual within itself. Quantity, which spreads out its parts and separates them from one another, cannot be responsible for this. It certainly cannot explain its own individual union with other qualities from which it is radically distinct. What is it that can receive these different qualities and separated, quantitative parts without being destroyed? It must be something lacking any positive determination of its own. This can only be the potency of matter.

Matter is the ultimate source of individuation which receives

[7] Cf. ch. 15, § 4.

and holds together the different formal traits of the individual without becoming actually divided. Once having received quantity, it is then divided from other quantities and separated from other things.

The divisive role of quantity is far more evident; the unifying role of matter more elusive and hidden. Hence doubts are apt to arise as to whether it is really required. Modern idealistic thought has always betrayed a strong tendency to question the existence of matter. Hence it is not surprising to find certain recent theories which attempt to account for individuation in terms of space and time (a special kind of quantity which measures change). Spatial quantity alone, it is granted, cannot cause individuation, for *two centimeters* is a universal property which can be shared by an indefinite number of instances. Even *place* is similarly universal, for an indefinite number of bodies may occupy the same place at different times. Time alone, it is also granted, cannot individuate an entity, for one and the same time may be shared and is actually shared by all the material individuals in the universe. But time and place together, it is argued, can account for individuation, since it is impossible for more than one individual to occupy the same place at the same time.

That this is a consequence of individuation, however, rather than its ultimate root, can be seen from the following consideration. Suppose a single individual moving from one place to another. At every successive instant he occupies a different place and a different time. Hence if these alone were the causes of individuation we should have to say that at each succeeding instant he is a different individual. This conclusion is absurd. Hence the premises must be incorrect. Before an individual can occupy a place, its matter must be spread out quantitatively. As long as its matter retains this quantitative spread, it is the same individual even though it occupies different places, at different times. Matter and quantity together are the ultimate sources of individuation.

REFERENCES

Recommended Reading
Aristotle, *Physics,* Book II, chaps. 3–9. For §§ 1–3 of this chapter, cf. chap. 3 in *Physics;* for §§ 4–5, cf. chaps. 4–6 in *Physics.*

Suggested Reading

1. For an influential criticism of final causation (§ 2 of this chapter), cf. Spinoza, *Ethic,* New York, Oxford Press, 1927, Part I, appendix, pp. 38–46. The classic statement of the view that a cause precedes its effect in time, and the famous example of the moving balls, which is commonly believed to support this assumption, are to be found in Hume's *Treatise of Human Nature,* Book I, Part III, section 2. Cf. also Mill, J. S., *System of Logic,* 10th ed., London, Longmans, Green, 1879, Book III, chap. 5.

2. For a modern statement of the issues between determinism and indeterminism (§ 5 of this chapter), cf. Bergson, *Creative Evolution,* New York, Henry Holt, 1911, pp. 36–66.

3. On the question of individuation (§ 6 of this chapter), cf. Aristotle, *Metaphysics* 1016B 33, 1058A 29, and 1074A 33; and Aquinas, *Summa contra gentiles,* IV, 65.

Chapter 15

CHANGING BEING AND ITS MODES

WE must now once again remind the reader that he is living and changing in a world of change. The planets, and the sun and the other stars have emerged from a process of cosmic evolution. The plants, the animals, and finally the human species have emerged from a process of biological evolution. We ourselves have emerged from the peculiar process of human history. But these processes have not stopped. The sun and stars are radiating their energy. The earth is moving. Plants are growing. We are facing the great historic crises of our time. Everywhere we turn there is movement of some kind. This is the primary fact of our sense experience. The attempt to analyze and explain this fact is the primary task of any realistic philosophy.

So far we have studied the sources of change and its finite causes. Now we must turn to an examination of the different kinds of being which are involved in change. Our common sense, of course, has already worked out a vague system of classification which underlies all intelligible discourse. In this chapter we shall attempt to look critically at this scheme and if possible to make it more exact. If we succeed, it may help us also to classify the primary kinds of change. But before we embark on this task it will be well to examine the nature of change in general. In the light of what we have learned of its sources and causes, how is change to be defined?

1. THE DEFINITION OF CHANGE

Once we know what the beginning of a thing is and what makes it as it is, the nature of the thing should be clear. We might try to work out a formula of our own. But we could hardly improve on the famous definition of Aristotle which, wasting no time in circumlocution, runs as follows: *Change is the actualization of that which is potential, in so far as it is potential.*[1] This definition has

[1] *Physics*, Book III, ch. 1.

been ridiculed in modern times, for example, by both Descartes and Locke (cf. references at end of this chapter), but no better formula has been suggested to take its place. In fact many of the confusions which we have noted in the modern philosophies of change, might have been avoided if this definition had been more closely studied. Let us see if we cannot approach it in the light of what we have already learned and perhaps do better than either Descartes or Locke in grasping its precise meaning.

Change is *the actualization of that which is potential* (the forming of matter). As long as the wood and bricks remain only *potentially* a house there is no process of building. After the house is actualized there is no more process of building, though other processes, of course, may ensue. The capacity of a thing to endure, first by maintaining itself and secondarily by acting on other things, is not change (the actualizing of the potential) but energizing (the actualizing of the actual). Change has an essential duality of potency (matter) and actuality (formal being) in its nature. All change is hylomorphic in character, out of matter (hylé) into form (morphé).

But what is the meaning of the next phrase, *in so far as it is potential?* It sounds at first like the jargon Descartes thought it was. But if we reflect a moment we may see that it makes good sense. We must first remember that matter cannot exist at all without form. What we call matter is never matter alone, *pure potency,* but always matter under some form. The wood is not merely a potential house, but matter with a definite form of its own. Even the energy of an electric field has a definite quantitative and qualitative character. Since the matter out of which change is actualized is not only matter but also form, we may regard this compound either *in so far as* it is matter (*qua* matter) or *in so far as* it is form (*qua* form).

As we shall see, in some types of change (as the building of a house), the form of the matter remains. Thus *qua* its form, the matter does not change at all. In other types of change (as when a new animal is generated) the form of the matter vanishes to be replaced instantaneously by the new form. In each case it is only when we regard the matter *qua* matter that we grasp any change. It is not the matter *qua* form that is changed. This either remains or is replaced by a succeeding form, but the matter, *in so far as* it is potential, is given the incomplete actualization of change. The matter, *qua potential,* is transformed. So the qualifying clause is very necessary. Without it we might suppose that form, already actualized, could be given another actualization, which would be a contradiction. It is not the wood *qua* wood that passes from potency into act (this is already in act), but the wood *qua* matter, and thus susceptible to further form.

Change is therefore the actualizing of the potential *in so far as it is potential.* Before the building begins, the house is only potential. When it is finished, the house is only actual. The change occurs in between. The actual building of the house is neither the actualizing of the perfected house nor the actualizing of the perfected wood, but the actualizing of a potency of this wood. Change, while it is going on, is always incomplete — on the way to something not yet there, precisely the imperfect *actualizing of a potency.*

If it were asserted that the same thing was both actual and potential *in the very same respect,* this would be a contradiction. But this is not asserted. The same *matter* (*not* form) is both actually wood in one respect and potentially a house in *another* respect. Until the house is finished, it is actually wood and potentially a house. At the last moment of the building process it is actually a house. There is no moment when it is both potentially and actually a house.

But even when one process is complete, the potency remains. Its insatiable capacity for further form is never filled, and sustains the ceaseless dynamism of nature. This incompleteness belongs essentially to all changing being, which is always ready for further perfection. Nevertheless stable modes of being emerge from the flux. It is now time for us to examine these modes of mobile being in order to arrive at a scheme of classification which may truly reflect their diversities and similarities.

To understand is to classify. Thought begins with the earliest efforts of the child to discern the similarities and differences of the objects of experience. As we grow older our horizon widens. We have to add new concepts. But our discernment also becomes more penetrating. Sometimes we see through seeming differences to grasp an underlying similarity, and vice versa. The world of nature is very rich and very confusing. The common insight of men grasps its major parts by a scheme of classification that is embedded in the structure of language and underlies all of our discourse.

The major categories of this scheme are often vague and ill-defined. New modes of being, hitherto not clearly focused, and borderline cases often throw it into confusion. But its basic insights cannot be ignored unless we are to assume that the way to understand ourselves and the things around us is hopelessly askew. If so, the chance of any individual philosopher's setting us right is very slim. We shall not adopt this scornful attitude towards the common reason of men. At no basic point shall we be forced to break with it completely. Our aim will be rather to build upon its basic insights, attempting to clarify them and refine them by means of the disciplined reflection of realistic thought.

This realistic philosophy has developed a technical terminology which it will be useful for us to understand. Thus the general traits which follow after being wherever it occurs are called *transcendental* properties of being. The most important of them are perfection of being, truth, and unity. The analysis of existence in general and this transcendental structure which always attends it, belongs to the discipline of metaphysics. In this book we shall be concerned with the changing being of our natural world. The basic kinds, or genera, of changing being are called *categories,* following the usage of Aristotle. It is with these categories of being that we shall be concerned in the present chapter. They fall into three divisions. First, there are those modes of being, substance, quality, quantity, and place, which determine special modes of change. Then there are those, action, passion, and time, which are involved in change. Finally, there are those, i.e., relations, which result from change. We shall now consider the categories in this order.

2. SUBSTANCE AND ACCIDENT

The most important of all the categories is substance. Whenever we name an individual or use the word "thing" we have this category at least vaguely in mind. What exactly do we mean? As the word substance implies, it is that which stands under, or supports, properties and accidents, and the changes by which these are gained or lost. Since we become aware of accidents like size, shape, and color, before we are aware of that which has them, it is natural for us to define substance in this way as that which supports accidents. But we must look for something more fundamental and peculiar to substance itself. What enables it to support accidents and properties? The answer will be evident if we think of the nature of change.

If something is to achieve an added perfection or accident it must already exist without the addition. Furthermore it must exist throughout the process by which the new perfection is gained. Otherwise it will not be changed. Finally, it must continue to exist after the accident has been gained without ceasing to be what it was. Otherwise it will not be perfected. The same will hold good of those privative processes by which something loses a perfection or accident. A thing can exist with or without the accidents which it supports. This should enable us to understand the realistic definition of substance which expresses its essential nature: *that which is capable of existing in itself*.[2] A star, a tree, a human individual are substances. On the other hand, there are many entities, like circular shape or greenish color which, though they are able to exist, cannot exist in themselves but only in something else. These are accidents. An accident may therefore be precisely defined as: *that which is capable of existing in something other than itself*.

From these definitions we may derive a demonstration for the real existence of substance which is a sufficient rebuttal to the many idealistic arguments which have been urged against this fundamental category. The demonstration is as follows: if anything at all exists, it must exist either in itself, in which case substance exists, or not. If not, then it must inhere in something else which exists in itself (i.e., substance), so in either case substance exists. The only escape from this demonstration would seem to involve nihilism— the dubious and contradictory assertion that *nothing exists*.

But we need not depend solely on such an argument for convincing proof of the reality of substance. We need only think of ourselves and our own responsible action to realize that we are not attributes or properties of something else. If so, we could not hold ourselves responsible for our acts, and praise and blame would be meaningless. Sense experience also provides us with abundant evi-

2 Aristotle, *Categories* 3A 7.

dence for the distinction between that which acts (the substance) and dependent acts and properties (accidents) in the field of sub-human existence. We know that the globular shape, the green color, the sighing sound cannot exist in themselves, but only in the tree.

We generally speak of accidents as dependent; of substance, as non-dependent or in-dependent, as though it lacked something positive possessed by the accidents (dependence). But this is only because we are more familiar with accidents, which are closer to sense, and therefore more readily known. We must not confuse the order of knowing with the order of being. In the order of knowing, accidents are known before substance. But in the order of being, substance is really prior to accidents and possesses a positive per-fection which they lack, namely, in-itself-ness or subsistence. As our definition indicates, this, not the supporting of accidents, is the es-sential mark of substance. Hence something might be substantial and exist in itself without supporting any accidents at all. We can-not conclude that the more accidents a thing possesses the more perfect it is, for even the least perfect substances may possess an indefinite number of accidents. The perfection of a substance must be judged by its capacity to exist and to act in itself, its degree of subsistence.

The most perfect substance would be one which was entirely complete in being and dependent upon nothing external in any way. Such a substance would exist and act by itself alone. It would be not only *in se* (in itself) but *a se* (by itself.) Descartes con-fused these two concepts, and defined substance as that which needs nothing else for its existence.[3] But this is the definition of perfect substance. On this basis no finite thing would be a sub-stance at all, as Spinoza consistently argued. But a thing whose existence is provided and sustained by external causes may still be an imperfect substance if the existence thus provided is existence *in itself*. Nevertheless as we move up from the lower to the higher levels of substance we can discern an increasing approximation to the completeness and autonomy of perfect substance, that which exists by itself alone.

Of course all the finite things which are directly observed by us

[3] *Principles of Philosophy,* Part I, Ll.

are imperfect and incomplete. But among them we can distinguish three general levels of increasing perfection. The things of inorganic nature are relatively vague and indeterminate in character. This is because their forms are so submerged in the potency of matter that they have been able to give it only a minimum of determination. Their limits are hard to fix, and their essential natures maximally unintelligible. Possessing this lowest degree of determinate being, their action is largely dependent upon external causes. They receive energy from the outside, store it up, and then release it in response to some external stimulus. They are substances which subsist, but of all natural beings they are the least autonomous.

When we turn to living things we find a higher level of completeness and autonomy. Even plants have all the perfections of a nonliving material thing, but something more in addition. They not only use their energy to act upon other things transitively, but to act upon themselves immanently in the processes of growth and reproduction. The small bud does not ripen into a fruit as a passive response to external influence, but as an active molding of the influences into a certain form. No external force can *make* the peach bud ripen if the intrinsic nature is not there to act. This greater degree of immanence in action implies a greater degree of immanence in being. The mobile organs of the animal and its perceptual activity enable it to achieve an even higher level of independence from external pressures. By sense awareness it can take account of external things before they impinge upon it, and use them for its own purposes.

It is not until we reach man that we find a subsistent substance of the highest possible material order. Through the faculty of reason, as we shall see,[4] he is able to assimilate intentionally the forms of all beings including his own, and thus to become a universal microcosm, a complete world in himself. This faculty is unmixed with matter and acts of itself without external material support. There is no power whatsoever that can force a rational man to think a thought or to make a choice that he himself does not will to make. Such immanent activity indicates a correspondingly higher level of subsistence in what we call the human person, "an

[4] Cf. ch. 19.

individual substance of a rational nature" (Boethius)[5] or "a distinct subsistent having an intellectual nature" (Aquinas).[6]

Of course this intellectual faculty is only one of the parts of the human person. The rest of his nature is material and passive. But in so far as these parts are brought under the control of reason the person as a whole may escape from external domination and act in the light of all being, seeking not only this or that determinate good, but the good in general, even an infinite good. Through rational activity it is in his power to attain this highest degree of evolutionary subsistence, which lies at the root of what we call the freedom of man and the dignity of human nature.

Having considered the nature of substance and accident, and three major levels of natural substance, we must now examine the different modes of change which are determined by these different kinds of being. We distinguish in our everyday speech between that more radical type of change in which a new substance comes into being and that less radical type in which the same substance gains or loses an accidental perfection. Thus when a new species of substance comes into existence we use the term "evolution," and speak, for example, of "the evolution of the horse from a small mammalian form in the Eocene Period." When a new member of an existent species comes into existence we use terms like birth and generation. We speak in a different way of accidental transformations. We do not say the educated man was generated from the uneducated, but simply that the man became educated.

Each of these processes is a hylomorphic transformation with two opposed superstrates and a material substrate.[7] But in generation the substrate is primal matter, and the positive superstrate is a substantial form which brings existence to the matter it determines. In accidental change the substrate is an individual substance, and the positive superstrate an accidental form. In our own case the two substantial transformations, birth, by which we come into being, and death, by which we cease to be, are clearly far more basic than the other changes to which we are subject. Thus we dread death, the loss of a substantial form, more than the loss of hair, hearing, sight, or any accidental form. All change is either sub-

[5] De duabus naturis.
[6] *Summa Theologica*, Part I, Qu. 29, Art. 3.
[7] Cf. ch. 13, § 6.

stantial or accidental, and this is the most fundamental distinction between modes of transformation.

Nevertheless, though it is clearly recognized by the native sense of mankind, it is often denied by sophisticated philosophy. On the one hand, there are those who insist that every change involves the emergence of something radically new. Every new form is a new thing, and every change therefore a substantial generation. If this is true nothing is ever the same, and all continuity is eliminated. At every instant a new thing replaces an old thing, only to be itself replaced at the succeeding instant. But this reduction of accidental to substantial change cannot be reconciled with established empirical facts. Is it not necessary to prepare the matter of any "new" technical object? Was not the house made out of the wood and brick now in it? In spite of accidental changes, are you not the same person you were a second, a minute, a year ago? Is losing one's hair to be classified with death? The facts indicated by these questions can be adequately recognized only by the distinction between substantial and accidental change.

It is not only possible to confuse accident with substance, but also to confuse substance with accident. Then every process has to be interpreted as the accidental transformation of a single underlying substance (monism) or of many such substances (atomism).[8] All things are essentially changeless. What we call the generation and destruction of new things are simply the modifications of a substratum which remains ever the same. But it is also impossible to reconcile this reduction of substantial to accidental change with recognized facts.

Was your birth the alteration of something other than yourself? Are you now the complex attribute of this? Do you perform your acts or is it rather something else which acts through you? Will your death be only an incidental modification of this thing or will it make an essential difference to you? What is the nature of this all-embracing substance? Is it essentially alive? Then all things, including stones and planets, are essentially alive. Is it non-living? Then all things, including plants and animals, are essentially dead. Has it a character transcending that of all the things we know? Then nothing is as we know it to be, and experience is a delusion.

[8] Cf. ch. 13, § 6.

Once again we must conclude that not all change is accidental, but that certain changes involve the emergence of a new substance that exists in itself. These are radically distinct from accidental change and possess certain peculiarities which we must briefly note.

If a new substance is to emerge, its form must be entirely different from what precedes it. This means that the old formal structure is completely destroyed and replaced by a new substantial form. What then underlies this radical change? Only the potency of primal matter. But this potency cannot exist without form. Hence we are led to ask about the status of this matter during the process of substantial change. Does it exist as something actual with no form at all or does it retain the old form for a short period while the new form is possessing it? Neither alternative is possible. Pure potency cannot exist, and the same substance cannot also be another substance at one and the same time.

Only one possibility remains. Generation and destruction are instantaneous. The passing away of one substance is the coming into being of another. At death, for example, the corpse comes into existence. Do both substances then exist at this instant? No! At this limiting instant the old substance has ceased; the new exists. When the corpse exists death has already occurred. How about the next preceding instant? There is no next preceding instant, for change is continuous. Between any two instants another instant may be found. At any instant preceding death, the matter is alive (cf. § 7, below).

The substantial transformation does not occupy an interval of time. It happens at an instant. But surely, it may be asked, such changes have a long antecedent history in the preceding form. Are there not many gradual processes leading up to death? Of course there are. Such changes are produced, however, by the disposing causes, not the perfecting causes.[9] They are accidental alterations in the living being. But the substantial transformation in which they culminate happens at an instant.

Such change occurs in three different modes, corresponding to the three different levels of natural substance. First, there are the material changes of inorganic nature, the physical and chemical transformations which occur throughout the course of cosmic evo-

[9] Cf. ch. 14, § 1.

lution. Then there are the accidental transformations of living organisms and the origination of new species which we call biological evolution. Finally, there are the more immanent, rationally tinged acts and interactions of human persons. The factors of awareness and choice which penetrate these changes and events give them a distinctive character which we recognize as human history.

These three distinct modes of change which occur in nature are a further indication of the existence of a vast plurality of different substances making up the world and determining by their natures radically different types of accidental change. What are these types? To what major groups do they belong? Let us now attempt to deal with this question in the remainder of this chapter.

3.   THE CATEGORY OF QUALITY AND ALTERATION

The word quality is sometimes used in a very broad sense to include any accident whatever. We are using it here in a stricter sense for a certain type of accident which intrinsically distinguishes and determines the substance to which it belongs. In so far as it is intrinsic it differs, as we shall see, from the last five categories. In so far as it distinguishes and determines the substance it differs from quantity. Furthermore the genus of quality has certain peculiar properties which are not found in any other accident. Certain qualities like pleasure and pain, hard and soft are contrary to each other. Such opposition is found in this category alone. Then many qualities are subject to intensification or remission, as an insight may be more or less clear, or a surface more or less intensely red. This property is also peculiar to the category of quality. Finally, qualities found the important relation of similarity. One thing is like another or unlike it because of some quality.

There are four major species of quality: habit, potency, passive quality, and finally shape and figure. Habit is wholly intrinsic to the substance and determines it either favorably or unfavorably toward the realization of its nature. Habits are either entitative, like health and disease, or operative, like the intellectual and moral virtues. These habits are fixed qualities found in certain operative potencies, but are not to be identified with them.

These active potencies are a second species of quality, which disposes the substance to operate or resist, for resistance is a kind of action. The two most important kinds of active potency are those, like heating, cooling, and other technical powers, which produce passions in external things, and the immanent powers, like reason and will, which dispose the agent to activities remaining within himself.

The third species of quality comprises the results of transitive action and alteration. To this species belong sensible qualities, like colors, sounds, and flavors, and the chemical and electrical qualities of inorganic nature.

The fourth species of quality includes the figures which terminate quantity, like spherical shape, triangular form, and the like. These are not subject to intensification and remission. We must now examine the mode of change which is determined by this ubiquitous category.

Of all the accidents, quality is closest to the essential form. The quality of a thing penetrates the whole of that which it qualifies, intrinsically determining it. Thus the deepest kind of change, which often prepares the matter for generation and always attends it, is alteration. The vegetable seed, for example, must be altered in the parent plant before it is capable of becoming a new plant, and its growth involves alterations in shape, color, hardness, and so on. The generation of chemical substances from one another is often attended by striking alterations. Thus the two colorless gases, hydrogen and oxygen, in becoming water, assume wholly different qualities, dictated as necessary accidents by the new substantial structure. In fact alteration is so closely associated with generation that it is often difficult in a given case to determine whether we are confronted with one or the other. This is particularly true of inorganic things, the essential natures of which are for the most part either completely unknown to us or known only vaguely through their sensible accidents.

We have already seen that generation is always from a privative superstrate to a positive superstrate. But in the case of alteration there is sometimes a passage, not merely between privative superstrates (which is true of all transformation), but also between actual contraries or opposites. Such a contrary is more than a mere privation. It is a *positive* species of the same genus, but as far as possible from its so-called opposite. To arrive at this opposite extreme the privation must first be reached, and then something further beyond. Such alteration between two opposites is peculiar to the category of quality.

Contrary qualities occur when some matter is susceptible not only to a positive, causal influence but to the privative cause as well. Thus our internal sense organs are not only susceptible to the filling of the stomach by feeling pleasure, but when it is empty, they respond in an opposite, *positive* way by feeling the pain of hunger. Water also responds, not only to heat by vaporizing, but to the absence of heat by the opposite process of solidifying. Thus opposite qualities arise, such as light and dark, warm and cold, hard and soft, tense and relaxed, sharp and dull.

Since the alteration between such opposite qualities is more extreme than ordinary transformations between a positive superstrate and its privation, such qualitative changes are often more striking to our senses than many of the other more fundamental kinds of change. That the same thing should be first solid, then vaporous, first light and then dark, impresses us more vividly in many cases than the less striking but more fundamental and radical transformation of generation from a deprived matter to a new substance. Only prime matter underlies such substantial change.

The same substance underlies two contrary qualities. It is able to be deprived of either, or to gain or lose either, by alteration. Hence the same substance may lack a quality altogether or come to possess it to a greater or lesser degree. Thus the gaining of a quality may take time and is not, like generation, instantaneous. Once gained, it may also be further intensified. A man may become more or less white. But he cannot become more or less what he is essentially—a man. Furthermore the same thing may be both heated and cooled or softened and hardened by opposed causes during the same period of time with some intermediate result. But the same thing cannot be both generated and destroyed all at once with some intermediate result. Here there is no possible intermediate. A substance must either be or not be at all.

It remains only to note the four chief varieties of alteration which correspond to the four distinct species of quality. First, there may be the gain or loss of a faculty like sight, for a power or faculty is a kind of quality belonging to the second species. Again, there may be the gain or loss of a fixed tendency to act—or habit—which is also a kind of quality. Indeed habituation is a peculiarly important mode of human alteration, produced by causes within ourselves. In the third place, there are physical processes of alteration, like warming and cooling, hardening and softening, lighting and darkening, and psychic processes in ourselves, like rejoicing and growing sad, desiring and avoiding, which are produced by external causes. Finally, in the fourth place, there are processes like shaping, bounding, circumscribing, and limiting, which achieve the termination of quantity in some qualitative shape or figure such as line, triangle, circle, sphere, and so on. In nature these alterations result from the generation of physical things, such as mountains and crystals, out of individual matter. But in geometry they limit, not the signate matter of individual things, but only the generalized matter of our mathematical imagination, and must be classified as accidental alterations of our minds.[10] These observations should enable us to grasp the nature of qualitative alteration and to distinguish it from generation.

4. Quantity

This category is a conspicuous and ubiquitous feature of the natural world. All material entities from the vast stellar galaxy to the invisible electron are spread out in quantitative dimensions. It is important to recognize that this category is an accident attaching to a substance on which it depends. Quantity cannot exist by itself (except as an abstraction, in the mind) . There must be something prior that is quantified. Hence growth or decrease is an accidental change. The child may grow bigger without ceasing to be. The same photograph may be enlarged. The same cigar may be diminished in size; the same mountain range worn away and decreased in height through erosion. Similarly, the number of material entities may be increased or decreased. In order to understand this mode of accidental change we must first briefly examine the nature of the accident of quantity. What is it?

In the first place, we must not confuse quantitative number with that more fundamental existential number which it presupposes. Every entity whatsoever is the single entity it is. A number

[10] Cf. § 4, below.

of such entities is certainly a multiplicity. But it is not necessarily a *quantitative* multiplicity. Quantitative number adds something more. Let us take an example. One man and one cat are not two men or two cats. They are two *animals*. Two animals and two trees are four *living beings*. If we add two rocks we do not have six living beings, but six *extended bodies*. From this we can see that quantitative number is always an accident *of something material* which is spread out in a certain order of succession, first one, then another, then another up to the last. Only material entities can be spread out in this way. If we added two immaterial entities to the previous six, we should have a multiplicity of utterly diverse existential entities, but we should not have a quantity of eight, since we could no longer bring them under a higher material genus subject to quantification.

From this we may draw the following conclusions. First, quantity presupposes existential multiplicity. Second, it presupposes a multiplicity of material entities which are necessarily subject to this accident. The accident itself is a spreading out of these entities in an order of succession, one following after another. Now let us attempt to distinguish this accident from the categories we have studied.

It differs from substance because it cannot, like substance, exist *in itself*. Every quantity is the quantity of *something else* (material) which is spread out or quantified. Even the pure mathematician, who abstracts quantity from the actual, material things of the world in order to study it alone by itself, has to conceive of a general or mathematical matter which he imagines to be spread out in quantitative order. Thus he conceives of different units ordered into various numbers. As quantitative units they are all the same. Nevertheless *they* are *numerically* different. Otherwise *they* would not constitute a multiplicity. They are units of mathematical matter subject to quantitative ordering. Similarly, he conceives of different geometrical figures such as lines, triangles, and the like. But he cannot conceive of them without the continuous mathematical matter out of which they are composed and which they terminate in different qualitative ways. Quantity is not a substance which can exist in itself. It is a necessary accident of material things. Hence change of quantity does not occur instantaneously, as substantial generation, but like the other forms of accidental change, requires an interval of time.

The accident of quantity differs from quality in that it does not distinguish or determine the formal nature of the thing but merely spreads it out in parts lying beyond each other. When a thing is altered, the whole thing is newly qualified and becomes different. But the very same thing may be greater or smaller without being newly qualified. Quality is like form and follows the formal nature of a thing. Quantity follows matter and spreads it out. Hence like matter, quantity is passive and is not, like quality, the source of activity. Thus, as we have seen, one contrary quality can act on its opposite to eliminate it or replace it. But quantities are never opposed in this way. Ten is not opposed to two, and one quantity will not destroy another actively. It may only be reduced to another passively by something external which adds or subtracts quantitative parts. Hence quantity is not subject to intensification or degree. Each quantity is just what it is. There is no such thing as more or less two, as there is more or less warm or soft or virtuous. Finally, as quality founds the relations of similarity and dissimilarity, quantity founds the relations of equality and inequality.

There are two species of quantity, the continuous and the discrete. The parts of the former are continuous. That is, they are all contained within the same limits as in a single line or plane surface. The parts of the latter are not continuous, as in the case of a number such as two or three. The units of which such discrete quantity is composed, are derived from the division of continuous quantity. Such units, even though they may contain no extension in themselves, are separated from one another and fall into an order of origination, first one, then two, then three, and so on. Hence they constitute a distinct species of discontinuous quantity.

It is impossible to reduce continuous quantity to a number of discrete units, and thus to undermine the distinctions between the two species, as Zeno and his followers have attempted to do.[11] Continuous quantity may be divided at an indefinite number of points but it is not made up of these points as elements. Between any two points there is something else, the matter which is given the

[11] Cf. Burnet, John, *Early Greek Philosophy*, London, Black, 1920, pp. 310–320.

order of quantitative extension. Why could not successive points be in contact with one another, and thus make up a continuous line? This is impossible, for contact is quite distinct from succession. Two points in contact would not be in succession: they would coincide. Hence a number of points in contact would not be a line: they would be a single point.

It is important to recognize the distinction between the abstract continuous quantity of the mathematical imagination, and the real, continuous quantity of things in *rerum natura*. These things have minimum quantitative parts which cannot be actually divided any further, whereas mathematical quantity is infinitely divisible by mental acts. In nature quantity is always found together with other sensible accidents, such as color, temperature, and resistance, in the prime matter of changing things. Mathematical quantity is isolated from all such accidents by an act of mental abstraction. Finally, when it possesses the general notion of quantity in this state of isolation, the mathematical imagination can divide it into unextended points or limits and can shape it into exactly bounded figures, like the circle and the straight line, which are not found in nature. Nevertheless nature does approximate them, for material things are really curved and triangular. Indeed the fundamental accident of extension is sensed by all the external senses. If this were not true we should never have gained the general notion of extension, and geometry would not exist.

Quantity determines a distinctive mode of change. Furthermore there will be as many distinctive modes of quantitative change as there are distinct species of quantity. As we have seen, these are basically two: continuous and discrete quantity. The terms *increase* and *decrease* apply more strictly to continuous quantity, whereas the increase or decrease of discrete quantity is more accurately expressed by the terms *addition* and *subtraction*. In nature there are two distinct processes of continuous quantitative increase. First, there is the increase of non-living things by the mere juxtaposition of new material parts, as the so-called growth of crystals. Second, there is the growth (in the proper sense of this word) of living plants and animals by the vital assimilation of new material parts into the living substance.

5. PLACE, POSITION, AND LOCOMOTION

Quantity separates the parts of a material thing and spreads them out in an order of origination. All natural substances are spread out in this way. Hence arise two further categories which are consequences of quantity but nevertheless distinct from it, as we shall see. By the *place* of a thing we mean, not its own surface, but the surface of the first containing body or bodies. When we move a book from one shelf to another there is no change in its intrinsic quantity or figure. Nevertheless it has changed its location, being now surrounded by different ambient bodies. So place is a mode of being distinct from quantity. It founds the relation of distance and indistance. Whether an object is near or far depends upon where it is, its place. This also determines a peculiar mode of change which we call locomotion, change of place.

Another mode of being, also derived from quantity and place but still distinct from them, is *position*. Thus a book turned upside down on the shelf may have the same intrinsic spread and occupy the same place as when it is right side up. Nevertheless we recognize an important difference. The whole book is in the same place but not the intrinsic, quantitative parts. Hence, as we say, the book has a different position (in the same place). A sphere may be rotating in the same place and yet its parts occupy different positions. Yet if the sphere does not rotate while it is being moved it may change its place without changing the position of its parts. Hence since the one may vary while the other remains constant, we must conclude that *place* and *position of the parts in place* are two distinct categories.

When the intrinsic, quantitative structure is exactly determined to its exact limits without reference to any ambient body, this is what we call the shape or *figure* of the thing. When we consider this with reference to other surrounding bodies, then it is *position*. The whole body considered with reference to what contains it, is *place*. If there were only two separate bodies existing in a vacuum with nothing surrounding them, they would still be placed in relation to each other. Each body would have a quantitative spread, and this would found a real relation of distance between them.

But if there were only one single body in the world, this would have no place whatsoever and its parts would have no position, though it would have figure and shape. Thus the universe as a whole has no place. Beyond its outermost limits there is nothing at all. With reference to these limits everything in the world has a determinate place and position, but it has no place and it cannot move. Material things within the world can move from one determinate place to another. Let us now examine this fourth major mode of change which we call locomotion, or change of place.

This is unlike growth and alteration in that it does not affect the intrinsic structure of a thing but only its inclusion or exclusion by other surrounding quantities (place). It is unlike generation in that it always occupies an interval of time. Places themselves are different but not opposed, though the motions from A to B and B to A are opposite, as are circular motions in a clockwise or counterclockwise direction. Since *places* remain even when occupied by different things, motion from one such place to another is easier to observe and to measure than alteration from a vanishing quality to another or even growth from a smaller size that no longer exists. Also, locomotion occurs as a condition of all the other kinds of accidental motion. It can occur without them, though they cannot occur without it. Hence it is the first, or primary, kind of accidental change and is used to measure all the rest. It is because of its readier measurability and its commoner occurrence that many, like Descartes, have come to think of it as the only kind of change.

This extreme view must be rejected on the ground of ubiquitous empirical evidence which shows that quantitative, qualitative, and substantial changes also occur. At the other extreme are certain philosophers who have argued against its existence. This view also must be rejected. But one of these opposed arguments raises important points worthy of study.

This argument was developed by the ancient Greek philosopher Zeno, the disciple of Parmenides. Locomotion, he said, is impossible because at each instant the moving arrow occupies a place equal to itself. But that which occupies a place equal to itself is at rest. Hence the arrow remains at rest. This interesting argument is known as the paradox of the flying arrow.[12] It may be answered in the following way.

It is true that at any instant the arrow must be at a determinate place. But being at a place at an instant does not mean that the arrow is at rest. To be at rest the arrow would have to occupy the same place for an interval of time bounded by two such instants. As a matter of fact the arrow at each instant is at a *different* position, which is precisely what is meant by being in flight. But we may say one instant follows directly after another. So throughout the whole time the arrow is merely at a position.

This commits the fallacy of supposing that motion is made up of instantaneous positions succeeding one another with nothing between. But there is always something between, namely, the flight. There is no next position immediately after what precedes. Another position may always be found between. This does not mean that the arrow *occupies* an infinite number of positions in making a finite flight, for as we have explained, *occupies* implies a state of rest. The arrow *goes through* an indefinite number of positions where it might have stopped but does not. Potency must not be confused with act.

Is there any *first* instant when the arrow may be said to be in flight? This question must be given a negative answer. Locomotion and the other forms of accidental change (growth and alteration) have *extrinsic* limits.[13] That is, they begin *from* a last instant of rest. But at this instant the arrow is resting, not moving. There is no *next*, succeeding instant at which motion begins. We must rather say that at *every* succeeding instant it is in flight until it comes to rest again. But at this instant also it is at rest, no longer moving. All the modes of accidental change begin and end with permanent states of rest, extrinsic to the motion.

We have now considered the fundamental category of substance and the four accidental categories of quality, quantity, place, and position. Each of these determines a distinctive mode of change. Substantial change is either the generation and destruction, or the evolution of new species of subsistent entities. Alteration is change in accidental quality. Growth and decrease are changes of quantity. Locomotion is the change of a whole material substance from one

[12] Cf. Aristotle, *Physics,* Book VI, 239A 10–239B 33.   [13] Cf. § 7, below.

place to another. When the intrinsic parts of a thing change their internal places within the substance, this is change of position. If this last is included as a special sort of locomotion we have four basic species of change: substantial, qualitative, quantitative, and locomotive.

We must now turn to three further categories which, though they do not determine distinct species of change, are nevertheless bound up with change in certain distinctive ways. These are action, passion, and time which we shall examine in this order.

6. ACTION AND PASSION

These two categories are bound up in an intimate way with the four modes of change we have been studying. As the iron filings change their place, they are being acted on by the magnet. As the water is altered from a liquid to a gaseous state, it is being acted on by the flame of the burner. The material things of nature are constantly acting and being acted upon to produce substantial, qualitative, quantitative, and locomotive modes of transformation. These ubiquitous modes of being are expressed in our language by the active and the passive voices. Natural substances are cutting, breaking, burning, pressing, pushing, and pulling other substances, which are being cut, broken, pressed, pushed, and pulled. The facts of experience show clearly that things are active and passive in such ways. Let us now try to analyze these modes of existence. How are they to be distinguished from efficient and material causation and from the categories of substance, quality, quantity, and place which we have just studied?

It is clear that action is intimately connected with efficient causation, but an exact analysis will show that the two must be distinguished. Action is a *part* of efficient causation in certain of its manifestations, but cannot be identified with it. Before the flame can heat the water, it must already be hot. Before the knife can cut the orange, it must already be exerting pressure. This *first act* of the efficient cause must already be inherent in an active agent before it can exert its effect on anything else. It is wholly intrinsic in the agent, and thus distinct from the second act which passes over into the patient.

It is *by* this category of action (the second act of an efficient cause) that the effect is produced by the first act. Both must be present in the efficient cause. But the first act is primary, and there-fore more essential. Indeed there are certain efficient causes, like the human intellect, which can produce their effects without the mediation of any transitive action passing into a patient. So we must conclude that action is a mode of being which belongs to certain efficient causes but which cannot be identified with efficient causation as such. A similar analysis applies to the material cause. Even before it is acted upon, it must be intrinsically potential to such action. The category of passion refers only to the actual recep-tion of the effect by intrinsic action, and is thus to be distinguished from the material cause as one of its parts.

Action (i.e., the second act of an efficient cause) and passion (i.e., the reception of an effect in a material cause) are both partly extrinsic. The cutting of the orange belongs to the knife as an ac-cident. But it also passes over into the orange which is being cut. This passion of the orange is really in the orange, but it is coming from the knife. Substance, quality, and quantity, on the other hand, are wholly intrinsic to a single being and refer to nothing outside. Place is not intrinsic at all, but as the first containing body is wholly extrinsic to what is contained. Furthermore it exercises no intrinsic effect on what is contained within. Action always exercises such an intrinsic effect, namely, the passion of being acted on. Hence we must conclude that action and passion are real modes of being distinct from the other categories. But are they really distinct from each other?

We have already discussed this question in connection with ef-ficient causation (Chapter 14, § 2), but certain points require further emphasis. The teaching of the teacher is not one process, and the learning of the student another.[14] There is only *one* process occurring, the change from ignorance to knowledge in the mind of the student. But this process has two distinct phases: its pro-duction by the teacher and its reception by the student. The activity of teaching is really in the teacher, supported by a knowledge (first act) which remains constant throughout the process. The process is really received in the student as a mode of being acted on (pas-sion). Hence though the process is one we must conclude that

[14] Cf. Aristotle, *Physics*, Book III, ch. 3.

teaching and learning are not the same mode of being. They occur materially *together* in the process of learning, but they are formally quite distinct phases of this process.

Action and passion fall into four major species corresponding to the four major kinds of change determined by the categories we have studied. Thus there are certain modes of action which are involved in the coming into being and destruction of substances. Another type of action brings forth qualitative alteration. A third type is involved in quantitative increase and decrease, and a fourth in locomotion and change of position. Hence though action and passion do not themselves determine a peculiar species of change, they are involved in every kind of material change. Since no material potency can actualize itself, there must be an extrinsic cause. This cause realizes its effect only through a transitive action which passes over into the patient and is received by it as a passion.

We must now turn to another ubiquitous mode of existence which is bound up with the four modes of change.

7.   TIME

Time is a mode of being which permeates every mode of change and to which we refer in a great variety of ways. All the verbs of our language are divided into tenses which indicate different modes of time. Sometimes we use prepositions in referring to the time *at* which or *through* which something happened. We also have an elaborate series of nouns, such as seconds, minutes, hours, days, weeks, months, years, and so on, to indicate periods of time. Like most phases of being which are important and ubiquitous, time is something extremely elusive and difficult to focus clearly by conceptual analysis. As we shall see, this is primarily due to a peculiar complexity in its structure.

This complexity becomes more apparent if we notice two different ways in which we refer to time. Sometimes, as when we are speaking about the dates of certain events, it is clear that we are thinking of something primarily mental and due to human enactment. The minute hand of the watch is really moving. The moon is revolving around the earth and the earth around the sun. But no one upon reflection really believes that seconds, months, and years actually exist in nature. Otherwise we could not explain the many different schemes for measuring time which have been invented by man. But sometimes, as when we say *the time is ripe* or *his time has come* or *time marches on,* we seem to be referring to a time which is inherent in the extra-mental change itself.

It is not surprising that this duality in our concept of time should be reflected in the views of two sharply opposed schools of philosophic thought. On the one hand there are those like Parmenides, Spinoza, and Bradley,[15] who hold that time is a sheer, mental figment, or construction with no basis in reality. On the other, there are those like Bergson [16] and his followers who hold that time is an extra-mental reality to which the mind contributes nothing save distortion and misunderstanding. The truth lies at neither of these extremes, but between them.

Time is the measure of change. As such it has something in it which is purely mental and not found outside the mind, as the piece of wood in front of me is not neatly divided into the inches and feet by which I measure it. But time is not a pure construction or fiction. It is founded upon something really exist'ng in the extra-mental change, just as the correct measure of the stick is based upon an extension really in the wood. Time is a certain mode of existence really present in external changes so far as they provide a foundation for the measuring concept in the mind. In order to understand this more clearly we must once more examine the nature of change, but now from a slightly different point of view.

The process of change is continuous up to its extrinsic term, when the change is over.[17] Thus the flight of the arrow proceeds without interruption until it hits the target, when it comes to rest. Of course the arrow goes through determinate, intermediate positions. But between these positions it is in a flight which passes away as soon as the intermediate term is reached. But even this term itself passes away as a new part of the flight begins. Both the intermediate and the terminating portions of a change are in constant transition. This is because the changing thing does not exist all at once but only successively, with further being constantly added to what has been.

This new being is added at the termination of the change. While

---

[15] *Appearance and Reality,* 9th impression, Oxford Press, 1930, ch. 4, pp. 33–37.
[16] Bergson, *Creative Evolution,* New York, Henry Holt, 1911, pp. 298–313, 329–345.
[17] Cf. § 5, above.

changing, the being is not yet actual but only in potency. While freezing, the water is not yet frozen. *When* frozen, the change is over. The change reaches actuality only at an instantaneous term. A new process may take its origin *from* this term. But this new process, not yet being at its term, is as yet only in a state of potency and not actual.

We must conclude that changing being can become actual only at an instantaneous *now* which is the term of a change already passed and the inauguration of a change about to be. Hence outside the mind, past and future are non-actual. All that is in full existence is a *now*, which realizes a past change and initiates a future still in potency. Of course, as we have already pointed out, the *now* itself no sooner comes into existence than it too passes away.

Finally, in extra-mental nature there is not just one great process of change going on which includes all the other changes. Since there are many changing substances, there are many independent processes of change, each having its own intrinsic structure. It is true that certain ones coexist and others do not. But they do not endure long enough to found any real relations. We cannot say that one actuality lasts *longer than* another, since outside the mind the past no longer exists. There is only a set of instantly actual entities which have already disappeared to be replaced by a new set. These successive actualities, existing at an instantaneous *now,* are the foundation for what we call time. But the mind must perform three operations before time can result, as the measure of change.

First of all, the mind must abstract the terminus of a process from the continuous, material matrix with which it is confused in nature.

Second, it must hold this in memory while it similarly fixes successive *nows* at regular intervals as it chooses—seconds, days, months, and so on. This series of remembered and projected *nows* is discontinuous and therefore unlike the actual processes of nature, which have successive termini, but always with a potential matrix in between. The dates of time have been freed from this matrix. They are not the motion itself but rather the number of the motion, and therefore able to measure it, or count off its emergent actualities.

Finally, the mind, making use of its capacity to remember the past and to anticipate the future (not actually in existence), can compare the number of one motion with that of another, and thus set up comparative relations (not existing outside the mind) between the duration of different motions and changes.

Hence time, the measure, is distinct from the change it measures in these three ways. Time consists of discontinuous *nows* which can be filled in with the continuous content of any actual process, whereas change consists of *nows* filled in with a continuous matrix peculiar to each actual process. Time includes both the number of an indefinite past and an indefinite future, whereas the extra-mental reality exists only at an instantaneous *now*. Time can bring any change of which we are aware under its measure, or, as we say, everything that occurs must happen in this single time. But such acts of comparison do not exist outside the mind. Here we have only a number of processes, each of which occurs only in itself, and not in any other.

If extra-mental reality consisted only of transient changes, the very limits of which were constantly passing away, it would have no permanent structure. So far, we have been examining such transient duration and its measure, which we call time. We must now note that permanent substance and accident terminate this transient change. This permanent structure also endures. *Transient being* endures by the addition of distinct existence. *Permanent being* endures by the conservation of one existence. Neither of these modes of being contains the whole of its existence all at once. Each involves a successive duration, either of one thing persisting or one thing succeeding another. Each is closely related to the other. Change may come to rest, and any resting thing may change. So both of these successive durations may be measured by time. We may count off the duration of a rest by the discontinuous dates of time, just as we can count off the duration of a process of change.

Bergson and others have justifiably called attention to a tendency to confuse time, the measure of duration, with space, the measure of quantitative extension. This confusion is manifest in the widespread habit of referring to time as a sort of "dimension" which can be counted off in regular intervals, like an indefinite geometric line. The pure measure of time, abstracted from the real duration which it measures, doubtless has this structure. It is thought of as an infinite line of time into which all events can be fitted and marked off by relations of before and after, just as a spatial dimension or space itself can be conceived as a great empty container with no end into which all the definite extensions of things can be fitted. But each of these, taken apart from the extra-mental things measured, and projected into the external world, is a sheer delusion. There is no such thing as a pure absolute time or a pure absolute space outside the mind. What really exists are different things each having a certain, individual duration and extension of its own.

When the measures of space and time are adequately conceived in relation to the real extensions and durations which they measure, there are important differences between them which cannot be ignored without grave confusion. Real extensions, in so far as they are stable and not in flux, coexist and endure. Hence they have real relations of distance between them and really contain one another. But real times do not coexist together in this way. Outside the mind time is divided into present, past, and future, which have no counterpart in spatial extension.

Furthermore in reality the past exists only so far as it is actualized in a present *now,* and the future exists only in so far as this present *now* is beginning it in potency. All that actually exists is a *present.* So there are no *real* relations between things existing at different times. There are only *mental* relations, which have a real foundation, so far as the mind accurately remembers what actually happened in a preceding *now,* no longer existent, or accurately anticipates what actually will be in a non-existent future.

Finally, each present *now* is ever passing, and except in the case of enduring entities which always change eventually, gives way to something different. Hence it is impossible for temporal events or enduring states to be *in contact* with one another, as spatial lines and planes. A change is terminated by a rest, but as we have noted (p. 339) the first instant is *extrinsic* to the change. By the time the change is finished there is no change. There is a last instant of rest, but at this instant the thing is not yet changing. Change occurs only beyond this instant. Furthermore one state of rest cannot be in contact with another, for a process of change must intervene between the two. Temporal states of rest and change succeed each other. Time cannot wait long enough for a contact to be established.

We must conclude that the category of time is sharply to be distinguished from spatial extension. Time is the measure of change, not the measure of extension. It is founded on the fact that natural entities do coexist and succeed one another in a certain order. But the mind, with the aid of memory and anticipation, chooses some standard process and marks it off in regular intervals, disregarding what occurs between the discontinuous numbers. Then it uses this series of numbers as a means of comparing and measuring the duration of other changes and periods of rest. Time, therefore, is a mental measure with a foundation in extra-mental reality.

8. RELATION

Having now examined the three categories of action, passion, and time which are bound up with all process, we must turn to a last and extremely important mode of being which results from all the four modes of change. The world of nature is full of relations. We have just referred to the temporal relations of *before* and *after* by which we measure the events of nature. But these relations, though they have a real foundation, are purely logical, since past and future have no extra-mental existence. The relations of distance and indistance, on the other hand, are not only founded on the enduring physical places of things but are themselves real. Causal action results in relations of dependence to which we refer by such terms as maker-of, builder-of, and author-of. The formal structure of things founds the real relations of similarity and dissimilarity which underlie the classification of categories we are describing in this chapter, as indeed they underlie any scheme of classification whatsoever. As we shall see, knowledge itself is a peculiar kind of relation of the mind to its object.

We commonly use the word "order" in referring to this important mode of existence. All material things are ordered to one another in certain ways. Let us now attempt to analyze the nature of relation with a view toward distinguishing it from the other categories with which it is often confused.

Relation is an accidental mode of being which cannot exist without some substance in which it inheres. But relation differs from the other accidental categories in referring its substance to something other than itself. Thus if my skin color is similar to yours, I have a relation of similarity to you. In this case I am the subject of the relation. The whiteness of my skin (a quality) is the foundation of the relation. Your skin color is the term of the relation. And my skin color as respecting yours is the relation itself. All real relations outside the mind possess these four structural elements.

The relation is formally caused by the foundation and the term. If these exist, the relation must exist. If either one of these passes away, the relation also ceases. In the case of certain relations, like similarity, there is always a *converse relation* answering back from the term to the subject. It is important to recognize that these *converse relations* are two, not one, relation "between" the two subjects. This can be seen clearly in the case of causal relations, for the relation father-of is not to be identified with its converse child-of. The reason for this is that each substance individuates and subjectivizes all its accidents. Hence my relation of similarity to you is mine, and your relation of similarity to me is yours. As we shall see, not all real relations have a converse.

Every real relation adds *some* new accidental being to the subject in which it inheres, though the difference between the foundation and the foundation *plus* the relation is very slight. Thus as the youth Phaedo grows taller, Socrates, without changing, may become shorter than Phaedo. Hence relation is the weakest of all the categories, making the least real difference to its subject. Nevertheless each relation makes some real difference though, like other accidents, it does not modify the substance essentially. In this sense all relations are external. On the basis of this analysis we can now distinguish relation from the other categories.

It clearly differs from substance and quality, which inhere absolutely within an individual entity without referring it to anything other than itself. It also differs in this way from quantity, which extends the parts *within* a subject up to its external limits but not beyond. Nevertheless a further question must be asked. Quantity extends the material parts in an "order" of priority, first one, then another. Why then is this not a relation between the parts which are quantitatively external to one another?

Here we must distinguish between two kinds of order: *originative* order, in which one element is prior, the rest posterior; and *relational* order, in which there is no such priority, but in which the foundation and term occur simultaneously. The relation does not arise from the foundation *before* it arises from the term. It arises from both together at once. Relational order, all of whose parts exist simultaneously, must therefore be distinguished from the originative order of quantity in which one part is prior to the next.

Relation is distinct from place for two reasons. First of all, both the place and the material body may exist, and yet the body may not be *in* the place. But if the foundation and the term both exist, the two must be *in* relation, wherever they may be. Second, the term of the relation does not "contain" the foundation within it.

The foundation of a relation does not pass over into the term or influence it in any way. Hence relation cannot be identified with action or passion. The agent and patient may both exist, and still there may be no action of the one on the other. But with the foundation and the term both in existence, the relation must arise.

Relation is not to be identified with the *successive* structure of time, for the diverse aspects of relational structure are *simultaneous*. Relation is thus distinct from the other modes of being. We must now turn to its major kinds.

First of all, we must refer to certain relational entities which are not strictly relations in the sense we have just described but which are unfortunately often confused with real relations. Thus there are *logical* relations set up by comparative acts of the mind but which do not actually exist in nature. The temporal relations between the present, future, and past belong to this large class. The relation of subject to predicate is purely logical and does not exist outside the mind. Indeed the mind may set up such a relation between any two entities whatsoever, whether or not there is any real foundation for the relation in *rerum natura*. Thus the mind may mentally relate substance and accident, though these are one entity in *rerum natura,* and no single entity can be related to itself. Nevertheless the mind may conceive one entity by two mental acts, and thus logically relate it to itself. In general we may say that if we find no foundation in reality which is distinct from the term, we may conclude that the relation is purely logical and not real.

There are, however, real relational entities in nature which nevertheless must be distinguished from relations in the strict sense. These are the so-called *transcendental relations,* like the passive potency of matter to be formed and the active power (first act) of the builder to build houses. These relative powers and capacities do exist in *rerum natura,* but they differ from relations in two ways. First of all, the foundation is the relation, as matter is a relation to form. In a real categorical relation, however, the two are distinct. Thus if I disappear, your relation of similarity to me will also disappear, but the foundation (for example skin color) will remain. In the second place, a *transcendental relation* may exist even without a term, though it is impossible for a strict relation to do this. Thus matter is related to a form of which it is capable even though the form does not exist; and the builder is able to build a house even though there is no house. These so-called transcendental relations are rather a certain kind of causal efficacy than relations in the strict sense.

Relations in the strict sense, which actually belong to the category we are studying, fall into three major groups: the equiparent, the mutual, and the non-mutual relations. The first (equiparent) is founded on the intrinsic, formal structure of things and always possesses a similar *converse* relation. Thus similarity is an equiparent relation, for if *A* is similar to *B*, *B* is also similar to *A*. Mutual relations are founded on efficient causal action. They possess a converse relation which is dissimilar. Thus *invader-of* is a mutual relation. The converse of this relation, *being-invaded-by,* is dissimilar. Finally there are non-mutual relations founded on extrinsic, formal causation which have no converse at all. Thus the idea of this chair is really related to the existent chair, its extrinsic, formal cause.[18] Of course we speak of the chair as being known. But this is a purely logical relation set up by the mind which corresponds to no real accident in the thing known. The chair does not suffer even the slightest accidental alteration when it is known. If so, it could never be truly known as it actually is. Many important relations, such as *picture-of* and *being-the-object-of-desire,* are non-mutual.

The failure to distinguish these different kinds of relational entity has led to important philosophical confusions. Thus when

[18] Cf. ch. 19, §§ 5 and 6.

logical relations are not sharply separated from real relations, it is easy to fall into the view that *all* relations are equally real. When the absurdity of populating the world with a host of logical entities dawns on the mind, this readily inclines the mind to skepticism, and we wonder whether *any* relations are real.

Those who focus on logical and equiparent relations are easily led to confuse the relation with its converse, and thus to think of a relation as a single bond, like a cord or string between the subject and its term. This mistake may be remedied by bringing mutual relations into focus, where it is clear that the relation is quite distinct from its converse, each inhering in a different subject.

The failure to recognize non-mutual relations as a distinct class has produced many tangles of so-called relativism. For example, if knowledge is viewed as a mutual relation we easily become confused and ask how anything may be truly known. As soon as we know an object, the object must gain a new converse relation to the mind. This will then change the object which is no longer the same. This new object must then be known by a new act, which will in turn breed a new object, and so on ad infinitum.

Finally, the failure to distinguish between the relation and the substance in which it inheres as an accident has led to the doctrine of *internal relations*. This view holds that when a substance is really related to other entities, these relations enter internally into its very substantial nature and make it essentially different.[19] When consistently held, it breaks down the independence of all finite substances and leads to a monism on the basis of which there is only one substance—the universe itself—and thus no real relations at all, for a relation must refer a thing to something other than itself.

Having now considered the nature of change, its sources and finite causes, and the different modes of being involved in change, we must now turn to the structure of this world as a whole. Is it capable of sustaining itself? Have all these different entities and modes of being brought themselves into existence? Are the finite material, formal, efficient, and final causes we have examined sufficient to account for the course of evolution? Has the material universe simply evolved of itself or does it require a first, transcendent cause?

[19] Cf. Bradley, *Appearance and Reality*, pp. 125, 347.

References

Recommended Reading

Aristotle, *Physics,* Book III, chaps. 1–3; *Categories,* chaps. 1–9.

Suggested Reading

1. For the modern dismissal of the Aristotelian definition of change, cf. Descartes, *Rules for the Direction of the Understanding,* Rule XII, near the end, in *The Philosophical Works of Descartes,* ed. Haldane Ross, Cambridge University Press, 1911, vol. 1, p. 46; and Locke, *Essay Concerning Human Understanding,* Book III, chap. 4.

2. On the distinction between substantial and accidental change, cf. Aristotle, *De Generatione et Corruptione,* Book I, chap. 4. For an influential attack on the concept of substance, cf. Hume, *Treatise of Human Nature,* ed. Green and Grose, London, 1874, vol. 1, pp. 533–544 (Book I, Part IV, Sec. 6).

3. For the definitions of continuity, contact, and succession, which are essential to an understanding of quantity (§ 4, this chapter), cf. Aristotle, *Physics,* Book V, chap. 3; Book VI, chaps. 1 to 231B 14.

4. For a difficult but illuminating discussion of the nature of *place* (§ 5, this chapter), cf. Aristotle, *Physics,* Book IV, chaps. 1–5.

5. On time, cf. Aristotle, *Physics,* Book IV, chaps. 10–14. For a critique of the tendency to confuse time with space (§ 7, this chapter), cf. Bergson, *Time and Free Will,* New York, Macmillan, 1928, pp. 75–139.

6. On relation (§ 8, this chapter), cf. Aristotle, *Metaphysics,* Book V, chap. 15; for a modern mathematical discussion, cf. Russell, Bertrand, *Introduction to Mathematical Philosophy,* London, George Allen & Unwin, 1920, pp. 29–63.

Chapter 16

THE FIRST CAUSE OF CHANGE

WE have now completed our study of the main structural facts which may be observed in the evolving world of nature. We have examined the nature of change itself, its principles and causes. Then we have classified the major kinds of change and the major genera of being which emerge in these. So far our procedure has been primarily descriptive, for change itself is evident to our senses, and its structure can therefore be directly elicited by a rational examination of the sensory evidence. Anyone, that is, anyone with a sound mind and normal senses, should be able to arrive at our preceding conclusions simply by opening his eyes and allowing his reason to play on what he sees, without indulging in prolonged deductive argument.

Now, however, we must raise a question which will lead us beyond the sensory evidence—is there a *first* or *uncaused cause* of the changes we see in nature? No such cause is directly observable by us. Every cause we can apprehend by our senses is a composite material being which, therefore, must be generated and sustained by other causes outside itself. An uncaused cause would have to be a *simple* being, but our senses not only have not, but can not observe any such cause, since their objects are material, and must therefore be compounded of matter and form. It is hopeless to look for sensory evidence or to expect natural science by itself to answer this question. Nevertheless it is a question which must be raised by any rational being who reflects at all seriously on the facts of evolution. What is the cause of evolution as a whole? Where did nature come from ultimately? Where is it going?

1. THE REALISTIC ARGUMENTS FOR THE EXISTENCE OF A FIRST CAUSE

There are three different answers which may be given to these vital questions. The first is the answer of *naturalism* which says that the evolutions of nature, observed by the senses, are able to stand by themselves, requiring nothing further for their structural completion. The material changes which we have been studying are all that there is to know. The second is the answer of *agnosticism* which says that there may be something beyond the evolutions of nature, but that, if so, we cannot know it. The third is the *realistic* answer of that classical philosophy on which our western culture so far has been based. According to this, the structure of evolution itself *requires* a non-changing being for its causal completion, though the nature of this being can be only imperfectly known by the human mind.

The decisive difference between the first and the third answers can hardly be exaggerated. They determine two modes of thought and life which are opposed in the most radical manner, as is abundantly illustrated by the great conflicts of our cultural history. For example, if the first answer is true, man is the highest being in the cosmos and there is no higher goal for him to achieve than to dominate subhuman things in realizing his material nature. On the other hand, if the third is true, there is a being in the cosmos higher than man, which it behooves him to know by the cultivation of his reason. If so, man should not only learn to dominate subhuman things by natural science and technique; he should also learn to control himself with a view towards achieving a higher purpose.

Agnosticism is theoretically independent of either answer, but since practical choices are unavoidable for a living man or a living culture, its practical effects tend to coincide with those of naturalism. Material needs are indisputably present for all those who live. The agnostic does not question these. Hence his skepticism is directed one-sidedly against the higher rational phases of culture, and its result is a practical drift into materialism.

Moreover, since we have learned at great cost the terrible effects of such materialism, not only in the overturning of individual life, but in the complete perversion of human culture, we must pay special attention to the structural reasons, gradually worked out in the history of western philosophy, which are capable of convincing any rational mind subjected to the requisite discipline, that the evolutions of nature, though unquestionably real, are not complete and do not constitute a world that is capable of evolving or existing by itself. Of course a single man or even a whole culture may for a time cling instinctively to a moral code demanding material sacrifice and self-control. But if his reason fails to grasp anything really demanding such control, it will be gradually weakened until, as we know, the structure of life is disintegrated, reason gives way to passion, and social order lapses into power politics. The reasons for trusting in realism rather than idealism and materialism are based on the traditional "arguments" for the existence of a first cause, some of which were formulated by Plato and Aristotle and all of which were carefully maintained, developed, and refined in the Middle Ages.

With the decay of philosophy in the late middle ages, these arguments were combined with non-realistic elements which eventually led to their distortion and neglect.

2. THE ONTOLOGICAL ARGUMENT

The most important intrusion into this body of realistic doctrine was the so-called ontological argument, first formulated by St. Anselm in the early middle ages. It was never defended by any classical, realistic philosopher, and was definitely rejected by Aquinas.[1]

Nevertheless in the period of modern philosophy, since the time of Descartes,[2] it has enjoyed a widespread popularity. This argument proceeds in a wholly a priori manner without reference to the facts of sense experience. According to it, the human mind possesses a clear and distinct idea of being and of perfect being. From this mental idea of that than which nothing more perfect can be thought, the argument attempts to deduce the actual existence of an extra-mental being. If this concept of perfection is *only* an idea we can certainly conceive of something greater and more perfect, namely, an actually existent perfection. But our concept is of an absolutely perfect being lacking nothing. Therefore the concept alone implies its actual existence. This argument, however, is subject to the following criticisms.

First of all, it ignores the distinction between mental and extramental existence. Even the thought of something exercising its actual existence outside the mind is still only a thought, which must be distinguished from real existence. From the former alone

---

[1] *Summa Theologica*, Part I, Qu. 2, Art. II.
[2] Cf. *Meditation* V.

we cannot deduce the latter. Hence the argument does not hold.

In the second place, the basic assumption of the argument that we have a clear and univocal concept of perfect being is subject to serious question. It is evident that we arrive at clear and distinct concepts only by means of a process of abstraction which always omits something. Thus the clear and distinct concept of humanity is gained only by ignoring the individual differences which distinguish this man from that man. The concept of being, however, omits nothing. Every universal mode of being, every individual trait or difference, is included within its vast scope.

This is sufficient to show that it cannot be put on a level with the other clear and distinct concepts of abstract discourse. If so, we should be able to define it in such a way as to distinguish it from what lies outside its scope. But nothing lies outside the scope of being. Hence it cannot be given a clear and distinct definition. But if we have no such concept of being, it follows that we have no such concept of perfect being. Hence the ontological argument cannot be accepted.

Nevertheless we do possess some sort of a concept of being. If it is not abstract, clear, and distinct, what sort of a concept is it? The answer is to be found in the notion of analogy, first suggested by Aristotle [3] and further developed and refined by later realistic philosophy. Being, together with all the other concepts of metaphysics, is an analogous concept. Instead of separating a certain phase from the total existence of an entity and then comparing other entities with this abstracted phase, the concept of existence ignores no phase but confuses all phases together in what it apprehends as the total existence of the entity.

It is an empirical concept which can never be completely divorced in our use of it from the objects of sense experience. The ontological argument is associated with an a priori mode of philosophizing which turned away from such objects and hoped to gain illumination from the endless manipulation of empty logical forms. This neglect of empirical fact brought with it a neglect of the realistic arguments for a first cause which have always appealed, not to concepts alone, but to the concrete data of experience.

This neglect must be ranked as one of the primary intellectual

[3] Cf. *Metaphysics* V, 6, 1016B 32.

phases of the recent cultural collapse in Europe. It is closely bound
up with the modern neglect of the philosophy of nature, for these
"arguments" are not a priori "proofs," but a posteriori completions
of the natural structures we have been studying. These structures,
once they are clearly grasped, require completion in certain ways.
No intellectual task is of greater importance in the revitalizing of
our culture than that of regaining an adequate understanding of
these different causal arguments by purifying them of the many
oversimplifications and outright distortions with which they have
been confused in modern thought. The conclusions we have so far
reached from our inductive or empirical study of natural phenomena should enable us to perform this essential philosophic task.

Thus we have reached certain conclusions, first of all concerning
the nature of change itself; second, concerning the composite material substance which emerges from this natural evolution; and
finally, concerning the whole, interdependent order of nature, maintained by all these evolutionary processes. Each of these natural
facts when examined closely may be seen to be incomplete and to
require completion by a first cause not directly observable among
the material phenomena of nature. There are also other phases of
the natural world which require a first cause,[4] but we shall choose
these three for special study.

3. THE ARGUMENT FROM CHANGE

This argument was first suggested by Plato.[5] Its principles were
clearly stated by Aristotle.[6] But it was first precisely formulated by
Aquinas.[7] It has been generally neglected in modern times because
of unclarity concerning the nature of matter and motion. The argument cannot be understood without the analysis of change which
we have presented in the preceding chapters, and the definition of
change to which this leads.[8] Change is the actualization of the po-

---

[4] For a condensed statement of five of these arguments, cf. *Summa Theologica*,
Part I, Qu. II, Art. III. We have chosen the first, third, and fifth of these for
study here. For a thorough exposition and commentary, cf. Garrigou-Lagrange,
R., *God, His existence and nature*, St. Louis, Herder, 1936, Vol. I; and Mascall,
E. L., *He Who Is*, New York, Longmans, Green, 1943, pp. 40–82.

[5] *Laws*, Book X.

[6] *Physics* VIII, ch. 5.

[7] *Summa Theologica*, Part I, Qu. II, Art. III.

[8] Ch. 15, § 1.

tential *qua* potential. Moreover change is a primary fact of nature which is now actually occurring. With this presupposed as a preamble, the argument itself becomes intelligible. It consists of two premises and a conclusion, which may be expressed as follows.

First Premise.   A change, like the locomotion of a brush, must be caused by something outside itself, like the hand, for otherwise it would be actual and potential all at once in the same respect, which is impossible. If the cause is itself changing, like the motion of the hand, then this in turn must be caused by something outside itself, and so on.

Second Premise.   But this regress of causes cannot proceed indefinitely. There must be a first, contemporaneous cause of change which is unchanging.

Conclusion.   The changes now occurring must have a first, unchanging cause which can be changed by nothing outside itself.

Every part of this argument, of course, may be questioned, but it is dubious whether these questions may be sustained. Thus certain thinkers like Bradley [9] have questioned the reality of motion and change. There is little point in trying to argue against the denial of a first principle directly evident to sense and reason. Such argument would inevitably rest on premises less evident than this. The only possible mode of reply must be put in the form of a *reductio ad absurdum*. We must be content to remind the reader that if change is unreal, so are all the objects of his senses, and himself as well.

The first premises will be denied by those who, like Descartes,[10] think of change as a determinate kind of entity which a thing either has or has not, as it is either triangular or it is not. If it is triangular then it will go on being triangular until some cause intervenes. In the same way, according to Descartes, once a thing has the character of change, it will go on changing with no external cause at all. But change is not a determinate mode of being or accident. If it were, it could be placed in one category. But this is not the case. As we have seen (Chapter 5), change permeates *all* the categories. As it occurs, it is a passage from the potential and

---

[9] Cf. *Appearance and Reality*, Part I, ch. 5.
[10] *Principles of Philosophy*, Part I, LXV; and Part II, XXV.

indeterminate to the actual. This cannot go on without the influence of something external which determines the matter in some definite way rather than in another. Potencies cannot actualize themselves. Houses are not heated without something to heat them. Murders are not committed without a murderer.

The second premise will be questioned by those who have fallen into the error of conceiving of the cause as though it preceded the effect in time. Why, they will ask, can we not conceive of a series of antecedent events stretching back indefinitely in time? We certainly can conceive of such a series, but this is not what is meant by cause. The murderous thrust did not first occur, to be subsequently followed by the murder of the victim. The real cause is contemporaneous with its necessary effect. It is this series of *contemporaneous* causes that requires a first member, for the influence proceeds from the cause *to* the effect. If there were no first cause capable of initiating the series, the influence would never be started and certainly would never reach an actual effect. The light in this bulb is sustained by energy in the wire, which is sustained by energy still further back, and so on. But if the wire is infinitely long and there is no first source having the energy to give, the light will cease. There must be a power plant with a generator, starting and sustaining the flow over the wire.

Many doubts arise concerning the conclusion. How, we may ask, can that which is changeless cause change? Is this not contrary to the evidence of experience? Are not the marks on the board caused by the motion of the chalk, and this by the motion of the teacher's hand? We may reply by turning the question. How can that which is itself still in flux have a determinate influence on anything else? Secondary instrumental causes may involve change. But they must be determined by a first cause that remains fixed throughout the process. What moves the teacher's hand? Is it not true that the first directing cause of this series must be a purpose which remains fixed throughout the process? If the teacher changed his mind in the middle of a sentence or forgot what he had started to do, would any determinate change be really effected?

The first cause of change must be changeless during the cosmic changes it effects. Why should it not change at other times? Because then it would not be the *first* cause for which we are inquiring.

Why should it not at least be able to change though not actually changing? Because then it must be held in rest by a still higher cause. The first cause must not only be changeless, but unchangeable, having no incompleteness or potency in its nature, but being wholly and perfectly in act.

4. THE ARGUMENT FROM CONTINGENCY

In addition to the fact of change, the empirical evidence shows us certain beings which come into existence and pass away. These contingent beings provide us with the empirical foundation for another argument. The principles of this argument, leading to a first cause which is necessary and simple, are found in Aristotle.[11] Aquinas gives a formulation of the argument in the *Summa Theologica*,[12] but there is some doubt concerning the precise reading of the text. As it is usually interpreted, it commits the fallacy of composition in arguing that because the things in the world are contingent, therefore the world as a whole is contingent. Hence we are here presenting a new formulation of this argument. By the word "composite" we mean anything consisting of intrinsic parts which are really distinct. By the word "contingent" we mean anything which, considered in itself, is only able to be, and therefore may either be or not be. By the word "simple" we mean lacking all composition, and by "necessary" we mean unable not to be. The argument consists of three premises and a conclusion.

First Premise.   Whatever is composite is contingent.

Second Premise.   Whatever is contingent must have an ultimate, necessary cause.

Third Premise. The world of nature is composite.

Conclusion.   Therefore the world of nature has an ultimate, necessary cause.

The first premise may be explained in the following way. Take the simplest case of composition, an entity consisting of two distinct parts x and y. x will account for the x-ness of the thing, y for the y-ness. But the whole thing consists of x and y together. What accounts for this? Not x, for this explains only the x-ness. Not y, for

11 *Post. An.* 92B 3 ff.; *Metaphysics*, Book XII, ch. 6.
12 Part I, Qu. II, Art. III, third argument.

this explains only the *y*-ness. Hence the togetherness of the two, the thing we are trying to explain, does not account for itself. The union of *x* and *y* (the thing) might be dissolved. This union is not necessary but only something that might either be or not be. Hence every composite is contingent.

The second premise asserts that every contingent being requires a necessary cause. Contingency is a special kind of composition, essence as against existence. A contingent entity is what we call a possibility (essence). It is able either to be or not to be. Thus anything which has evolved is certainly contingent, because at one time it does not exist. Then it exists. Hence it does not exist necessarily. There is nothing in the essence of the thing which demands existence. Its essence is only possible, not existence itself. Hence if such a contingent thing does actually exist, since it could not provide itself with existence, we may be sure that an external cause gave it existence. But if this cause also was contingent, it must owe its existence to an external cause. As we have seen, this sort of a contemporaneous, causal series must have a first beginning. Hence all contingent entities require an ultimate cause which is necessary. Such a cause must be simple, because as we have already seen (first premise), anything composite would be only contingent.

The third premise asserts that the world of nature is composite. This requires further explanation, owing to the ambiguity of the term "world." But unless we mean something absolutely simple, which not only never has changed but never can evolve, the premise will hold. This conception of nature is so fantastically out of accord with the facts of sense experience and the facts of science, that it may be discounted. If so, whatever we mean by "world," we mean something of a composite nature, and the premise must be accepted. It may be useful to show this in the case of a few more likely meanings of the term.

If we accept the view we have been describing, which is more in harmony with science and the common insight of man, we think of the world as made up of many diverse substances, each of which has come into existence by a process of evolution. Such a world will be composite in many different ways. In the first place, it will consist of diverse substances, each existing in itself. The togetherness of these entities requires an explanation. Furthermore each of these substances is a hylomorphic compound, including the matter out of which it has evolved and the formal nature distinguishing it from other entities. The matter does not require the form, for it has existed under other forms, nor the form the matter, for other individuals of the same species can be found. This togetherness therefore requires an explanation. Since all the entities are compound and contingent the whole world is also compound and contingent, for the whole is simply all the parts.

But even though we reject this realistic picture of the world the more plausible alternatives will still satisfy this third premise. If we take the atomistic view,[13] and hold that the world is ultimately composed of tiny units which remain ever the same though entering into combinations to make up the more complex entities, such a world is still composite. There are many distinct atoms together. This requires an explanation. Furthermore each atom is itself composite, for it possesses, not only certain traits in common with different atoms, but also other traits which distinguish it as an individual from the rest. This hylomorphic composition in each atom [14] requires an explanation.

We may take a monistic position and hold that the world is only one substance and that what we call new entities are merely the accidental modifications of this substratum. But even this means a composition of substance and accident which is not self-explanatory. Unless we are prepared to assert that the facts of nature are completely determined and that it would be contradictory for any such fact not to exist and that possibility and change are unreal, this third premise stands.

The conclusion then follows necessarily from these premises. The first cause cannot be something contingent, receiving its being from an external source. It must exist necessarily, and thus lack every kind of composition, form-matter, substance-accident, and essence-existence. Its nature must be such as to include existence within it. Only then would it not require external causal support and be in a position to give being to contingent entities. Such a necessary, simple, first cause is required by the world of nature whether its existence stretches back indefinitely in time or whether it had a first

---

[13] Cf. ch. 13, § 6.
[14] Cf. ch. 14, § 6.

beginning. In either case it will be something composite, and thus require a necessary, first cause without any complexity attaching to its nature.

5. THE ARGUMENT FROM THE ORDER OF NATURE

The first argument starts from the empirical fact of change; the second, from that of the composite substances resulting from change. But all these substances taken together make up a single structure which we call the universe or cosmos, and which possesses a perfection of its own, that of persistent order. This persistent order has been at least dimly recognized since the very dawn of reason on earth, and it has provided a material foundation for those earliest half-formulated arguments which convinced men that there must be a higher, intelligent cause for the transformations of nature. The greatest philosophers of classical and medieval thought, including Plato, Aristotle, and Aquinas, have recognized the cogency of this type of argument and even skeptics like Hume have been forced by the very facts to grant it some cogency.

The world of nature is evolving and changing; so it must contain a principle of indeterminacy or potency which we have called matter. This matter is the substratum out of which the whole of nature has emerged and is emerging. Without such a principle evolution would be impossible, for the forms of nature are discontinuous.[15] Therefore matter was in nature at its very inception, and must remain as long as nature endures.

The indeterminate potency of matter is insatiable and never filled. It can always be other than it is or even lose its structure. The matter now formed into man may decompose into dust, and the dust into the elements. Now it is a garden. In five years it will be a brier patch. The material substratum of nature is potential, not actual. It does not of itself require one order rather than another, or indeed any order at all, unless it is acted on by further determinate causes. The fact that there is such an order founds a third argument with two premises and a conclusion, as follows.

First Premise. Causes which are non-intelligent but productive of an orderly effect are ultimately determined by a first, intelligent cause.

[15] Cf. ch. 13, § 3.

Second Premise. The causes of nature are non-intelligent but productive of an orderly effect (i.e., the cosmos).

Conclusion. Nature, therefore, must be ultimately determined by a first, intelligent cause.

Many inferences drawn by common intelligence as well as by science illustrate the truth expressed by the first premise. Imagine that you are walking in the woods and suddenly hear a whirring sound followed by a sudden impact. You stop and watch a flight of arrows successively impinging upon the bull's-eye or very close to the bull's-eye of a target some distance away. You do not attribute this to chance. Such non-intelligent causes as bowstring and tightening of muscles at once spring to your mind. But you do not stop there. The *ultimate* cause is an intelligence, which guides these subordinate agencies to a foreseen goal. In such cases this inference usually may be verified by direct experience of the archer. There are other cases, however, where such verification is not possible. Nevertheless the inference is not questioned and often plays an important role in scientific procedure.[16]

Orderly effects such as the stone heads of spears, pottery, and other paraphernalia are found in caves and rock strata. The anthropologist at once recognizes that such orderly artifacts did not make themselves. He does not attribute them to chance coincidence. He recognizes at once the causal activity of cutting and molding implements. But he does not stop there. The ultimate cause was an intelligence directing these non-intelligent implements to a foreseen orderly goal. Not only is this true, but from such evidence a great deal more is inferred concerning the nature of primitive cultures and primitive men long dead, with whom no anthropologist ever has had, or ever will have, any direct acquaintance. We do not question these inferences to Neanderthal man and Cro-Magnon man as figments of anthropologists' imaginations. Indeed we should not, for the principle on which they are based is altogether sound. It is the principle stated in our first premise. But once having accepted the principle we must be ready to apply it to similar instances.

[16] Cf. Thompson, W. R., (F.R.S.), *Providence, The Maritain Volume,* New York, Sheed and Ward, 1943, pp. 229–246.

Why must we accept this principle? The answer involves the first roots of causal theory. An efficient cause must itself be determined to exert some one effect rather than another. Otherwise it will produce no effect at all. What then can determine an efficient cause? There are two possibilities. One is that it may be determined by another efficient cause of a material order forcing it to act in a definite way. But this only postpones the ultimate issue. What then determines *this* force? We must discover some other kind of cause or no ultimate answer will be found. What other kind of cause can govern efficient action? Only some cause of an immaterial or ideational order. Thought alone can ultimately guide action to a determinate end. Hence all determinate effects must be ultimately traced to such a final source or they must remain unexplained.

The second premise will, of course, be questioned by those who deny that nature is an orderly effect, as well as by those who admit an order, but think that this can be explained in the 19th-century manner as the result of chance variations and natural selection. Let us now examine these objections from a present-day point of view.

Those who deny that there is any order of nature are up against very stubborn facts even at the lowest level of inorganic nature. The highly indeterminate entities of this level show a certain uniformity of behavior which can be expressed in natural laws. It is true that within these limits their behavior shows wide variations. Nevertheless the limits are there. An electron does not act like a protozoan. It acts in a generally uniform way. Unless this were so science would be impossible.

Furthermore the higher living organisms are dependent upon this inorganic order as well as upon one another. Plants are dependent upon the earth, the sea, and the atmosphere. Animals are dependent upon plants for their food. Human nature depends in myriad ways upon all these subordinate orders. We could not live without carbon and the peculiar structure of the carbon atom, or without water and its peculiar characteristics. This interdependence of diverse factors certainly constitutes an orderly effect which we recognize by the use of such terms as *cosmos* and *universe* to describe the world we inhabit. If it were a pure chaos we should certainly not be here to describe it.

But is this not a very imperfect order? How about fires, floods, earthquakes, eruptions, and explosions which take such a fearful toll of the things of nature? As we have seen,[17] accidents of this sort do and must occur in any world capable of evolution. Such a world must contain the indeterminate potency of matter which may produce coincidences of this sort when acted on by diverse secondary causes. But these coincidences are the exception rather than the rule. If not, neither we nor any other stable entities would exist at all.

Since the time of Hume's *Dialogues Concerning Natural Religion*,[18] questions like the following are often raised in this connection. What kind of order is this? Is nature not imprudent and wasteful, wantonly pouring forth millions of caterpillars in order to get one butterfly? A human manufacturer would soon be bankrupt by such inefficiency. The answer to this anthropomorphic objection is that the author of nature is not a human manufacturer. The intelligence back of nature is not interested simply in the production of one limited article such as butterflies, but the whole order in which one part is dependent on other parts. Thus caterpillars not only produce enough butterflies to preserve the species, but also provide food for other living things, including certain birds.

Is this not cruel and unjust to the butterflies? Would they not be much better off if left to themselves to increase and multiply? They would not be better off. If left to themselves they would increase and multiply to such a degree that they would soon consume all available food and would be left to the slow death of starvation on a vast scale. Is it not better that a balance of nature should be maintained in which one species supports another and each is preserved to play its subordinate function in the whole? Such questions can of course be multiplied indefinitely. If we reflect upon them seriously we may confirm our basic human insight that we inhabit, not a chaotic pluriverse, but a single cosmic order or universe.

How about those who grant all this, but still follow our ancestors of the 19th century in insisting that this order can be explained simply by chance plus the effect of adaptation and natural selection? How does this theory look today?

It looks very different from what it did to the Darwinian enthu-

17 Cf. ch. 14, § 4.
18 Part XI.

siasts of the 19th century who regarded it as a *clavis universalis,* capable of unlocking all the secrets of evolution. This view has not been able to withstand the careful criticism which has been directed against it in the light of recent scientific evidence. Natural selection is still regarded as an important factor in adapting living forms to specialized environmental conditions. But it is no longer thought to be the cause of radical steps in evolution. Forms which are extremely well adapted to a specialized environment are by this very fact ruled out from the main stream of evolutionary development.

Thus the early fish, whose sensitive feelers were gradually turned into paddles, became perfectly adapted to the special environment of the open ocean, and lost all plasticity.[19] The ancestors of the amphibia were rather those less well-adapted creatures who kept fumbling with the ocean floor and who maintained a certain generalized plasticity. Similarly the horse,[20] by becoming well adapted to a speedy running life on the plains, lost the flexible digit which was the key to higher mammalian development. The ancestor of man was not distinguished by any peculiar physical trait or structure. He seems to have been rather a new experiment in plasticity and generalized adaptability.[21] It is through such non-specialized and flexible forms that the main stream of evolution has taken its course.

To what, then, shall we attribute this advance? Not to the selection of random variations. This has been on the whole a conservative factor which has produced, not advance, but inflexible stability like that of certain forms which became so well adapted in the Cambrian period that they have suffered no major change down to the present day.[22] In fact chance cannot offer us an intelligible explanation.[23] If we focus the whole picture at once without becoming lost in minor detail, we gain a distinct impression of a sort of cos-

[19] Heard, G., *The Source of Civilization*, London, J. Cape, 1935, pp. 66–74.
[20] Opler, M. E., Fact and Fallacy Concerning the Evolution of Man, *Phil. and Phen. Research*, Vol. 7, p. 639.
[21] Opler, M. E., Fact and Fallacy Concerning the Evolution of Man, *Phil. and Phen. Research*, Vol. 7, No. 4, June 1947, pp. 640–641; cf. Haldane, J. B. S., *The Inequality of Man*, London, Chatto and Windus, 1932, pp. 92–93.
[22] Lecomte du Noüy, *Human Destiny*, New York, Longmans, Green, 1947, pp. 81–99, for an illuminating statement of these facts by a modern biologist.
[23] Cf. ch. 14, §§ 4 and 5.

mic purpose. Working up from the earliest living matter, experimenting now with this now with another form, breaking in where a groping flexibility leaves room for further advance, always with a next step in view, we watch it building up to the creature man.

We now see that the great mistake of the earlier defenders of finalism was to focus on special adaptations of special structures and special organisms. Here the picture is not so clear. But in the grand strategy of evolution taken as a whole, the impression of purpose or antichance, as the scientist may prefer to call it, is unmistakable. Here is something with a constant aim throughout the periods of geologic time. Here is a sustained, orderly effect which justifies the inference to an intelligent cause.

When we turn to the sequence of human history, which began with the first human civilizations approximately five thousand years ago, this impression is even more clearly confirmed when we are enabled to grasp it as a whole with the aid of such a work as Toynbee's *Study of History*. Through the rise and disintegration of human cultures we see the same penalization of mechanical adaptation and the same fostering of flexible advance towards a rational end.[24] Here also a sustained orderly effect is impressed upon us with an even sharper clarity, if we do not lose the forest for the trees.

But this rests upon a biological basis and this on a physical basis. The part cannot be an order without an order of the whole as well. The world is a cosmos, an orderly effect. If we agree with science in holding to the principle expressed in the first premise, we must draw the inference expressed in the conclusion.

This inference leads to *some kind* of intelligence, certainly not a human intelligence. In the first place, it is clear that the knowledge guiding such a vast enterprise must be far more penetrating and sweeping than any science available to man. The power required for its establishment and maintenance belongs to an order transcending any that is humanly accessible. This becomes clearer when we remember that the greatest triumphs of human art and ingenuity have been gained only at the lowest, natural level over objects which are very sluggish and possess only a minimum of spontaneous activity. But the order of nature is also maintained at higher levels where secondary causes with a high degree of self-

[24] Cf. *A Study of History*, New York, Oxford Press, 1947, pp. 326–336.

activating power must be guided and controlled without reducing them to the level of mere passive, physical instruments. This is more evident in human history, the highest level of natural change, where the peculiar powers of reason and free-choice are at work. Yet the most recent research has verified the fact that even here we can glimpse an intelligible pattern unfolding.[25]

We cannot grasp these facts without grasping that the powers presiding over nature, whatever they may be, are not primarily interested in the imposition of a rigid order on inert natural subjects, but rather in the eliciting of a rational order from free and spontaneous agents. We get this impression of a sort of fumbling experimentation and watchful waiting even at the higher levels of organic evolution, where many species have been allowed to cut themselves off from the central current by over-adaptation. It becomes even more vivid at the level of human history where we see civilization after civilization committing suicide as the result of freely chosen sluggishness and cultural crime.[26] Time seems to be a matter of almost no importance. This indicates a presiding intelligence not restricted by human temporal limits. It suggests something which cannot be understood as a mere material craftsman, but as a governing power that is capable of foreseeing, eliciting, and guiding the free choices of free agents. Such a power cannot be adequately conceived along anthropomorphic lines. It clearly belongs to another order.

In trying to follow through the implications of these inferences to a first cause, we must thus give up all concrete images taken from our experience which can only lead us astray. We must rely on reason alone. The disciplined results of realistic thought will be of the greatest service to us in avoiding the grave dangers of anthropomorphism in reflections of this kind.

6. The Nature of the First Cause

We have now examined three arguments based upon facts of experience which demand causal completion. These arguments require a first cause that is immobile, necessary, and intelligent. At first these traits seem to be disconnected. We certainly do not under-

[25] Toynbee, A. J., *A Study of History,* chs. 1, 2, and 5.
[26] Cf. *op. cit.,* chs. 13–16.

stand anything as long as we see in it only a jumble of incoherent attributes. We understand it clearly only when we gain some insight into its most basic characteristic from which the rest may be seen to follow, as for example, we have come to see that human rationality is more basic than the color of the human skin. This basic character is the essence of a thing. So let us now ask concerning the essential nature of the first cause. What is its most fundamental character, from which, once it has been grasped with some degree of clarity, all the rest may be seen to follow?

Different schools of thought have given divergent answers to this question. The later Platonic schools, following the line of thought suggested by our first argument, have identified the essence of the first cause with goodness. The Scotists have chosen infinity. Others, following the line of thought suggested by the third argument, have selected intelligence as the essential character, attempting to derive all the rest from this. The followers of Descartes have selected freedom. It has been shown, however, that there is an even more basic trait from which these and other attributes may be deduced. This trait may be more clearly revealed by pursuing a little further the reasoning suggested in our second argument.

This argument proceeds from the empirical fact of contingency. All finite beings have come into existence. No contradiction is involved, as Hume asserted, in thinking of any such thing as non-existent.[27] This shows that they may either exist or not exist, that their essence is distinct from their existence. Such contingent beings therefore cannot explain themselves. They require a first, necessary cause to give them that existence which they cannot give themselves. But now let us ask in virtue of what trait a being may be said to exist necessarily. There is only one way of answering this question. It must be because the essence of this being is existence itself.

Such an entity will not *participate* in an existence coming to it from some external source. It will itself *be* existence. If we ask why such a being exists we need not refer to any external causes. We must answer that it already *is* existence. Hence its non-existence would be a contradiction. It is unable not to exist, and thus exists necessarily. The reason for this is that its essence is indistinct from

[27] Hume, *Treatise of Human Nature*, Book I, Part III, Sec. III.

its existence. The clear recognition of this basic fact goes back at least to St. Augustine.[28] The essence of the first cause is existence.

From this, all the other attributes may be deduced. As we shall see, being as such implies no necessary limitation or restriction. Hence it lacks all potency and is immobile. The results of the first argument are explained. Being fully in act, it lacks no perfection and is infinite. Since intelligence is a mode of being, this may be deduced, and the results of the third argument are also explained. Free acts arise from intelligence as their source, for they require deliberation. Hence the capacity for free activity may also be deduced from this essential character. Finally, since its very nature is to exist, no external cause is required. It could not cease to exist without ceasing to be what it is. It exists by itself (*a se*) necessarily, and the results of the second argument are explained. Everything that we have so far discovered about the first cause can be accounted for in terms of this most basic trait. Hence we must conclude that existence is its essence.

Let us now attempt to list all the attributes that may be deduced from this essence in an orderly way. These attributes fall into two major divisions: those conceived as *entitative,* and those conceived as *operational.* This is due to the fact that in all finite entities with which we are directly acquainted there is a distinction between the entity itself and the various operations by which this entity is perfected. Thus in the case of human nature we distinguish between the man himself and his essential traits of animality and rationality, and the various acts by which he attempts to perfect himself, or in technical language, between the *entitative* traits and the *operational attributes.* In dealing with the unique case of the first cause our intellect is forced to make a similar distinction, though as we shall see, it is not wholly appropriate. Let us first turn to the entitative attributes, which we conceive as belonging to the being of the first cause.

7. THE ENTITATIVE ATTRIBUTES OF THE FIRST CAUSE

The first of these is *simplicity.* This can be proved in the following way. As we have already seen, any composite entity is contingent. But the first cause is necessary and non-contingent. Hence

[28] *De Trinitate* V, 2, 3; and *De Civitate Dei,* XI, 10.

it must lack all composition. Anything which is actually undivided is one, even though it is capable of being divided. Thus the chair on which I am sitting is one as long as its various parts are not separated. But they can be separated. Anything composed of parts has the potency to be reduced to these parts. The first cause, however, lacks all potency (cf. the first argument). Hence it is not only one in the sense that it actually lacks division. It is perfectly one in the sense that it cannot be divided. This is the attribute of simplicity which must be attributed to the first cause in a special sense. It is not only undivided but indivisible.

From simplicity we can then deduce the important attribute of *transcendence*. As we have seen (§ 4, above), all the finite entities of the natural world are composite. They are all contingent, which means that their essence is distinct from their existence. They are made up of the matter from which they have evolved, and form. They are spread out in material, quantitative parts. They are composed of substance and accident. But the first cause lacks all composition of any kind. This means that it must exist by itself in separation from them, even though its influence may extend to all of them. Nevertheless the pantheistic notion that the first cause is combined or fused with them, must be absolutely rejected. If it entered into composition with any such being or with all of them to make up some sort of new whole, it would suffer a change, and thus cease to be what it is. But this is impossible, for the first cause lacks all potency for change (§ 3, above). Lacking any capacity for composition, it is utterly separate from the finite things of nature and must exist apart from them.

Here we must notice a certain difficulty. If the first cause lacks all composition whatsoever, how then can we go on attributing different attributes to it? Justice, for example, is different from mercy. If we then attribute both to the first cause, are we not forced to recognize some composition in this being? Here we must recognize a certain distinction connected with the limitations of the human intellect, that between *what we conceive* and *our mode of conceiving it*.

Thus we conceive of material entities by universal concepts. But this does not entitle us to infer, with some of the followers of Plato, that what we are conceiving is a set of universal concepts. In the same way we must conceive of the first cause by modes of apprehension which are diverse from one another. But this does not justify the inference that what we are apprehending is composed of these diverse modes. In this case what we are apprehending possesses all the diverse perfections we attribute to it, but in a higher, eminent mode of absolute simplicity.

Does this not mean that we are distorting the facts by our piecemeal mode of apprehension? Not if we are aware of this imperfection, make allowances for it, and take pains to correct it. We have to apprehend the unitary essence of man by two distinct concepts, that of animality and that of rationality, which are logically distinct. But in the individual man, Peter, they are not two but one. Nevertheless this does not lead to any distortion, for we combine the two concepts together in a unitary definition which we identify with the single entity in the judgment, *Peter is a rational animal.* Thus we correct the piecemeal mode of apprehension, and no harm is done.

We may make a similar correction in the case of the first cause, when we clearly recognize its eminent simplicity, which stands above the diverse attributes by which we apprehend it. Then no harm is done. These perfections are actually present in the object we are studying. But in this object they exist in an indivisible unity which transcends our piecemeal mode of apprehension. If we remember this we shall fall into no distortion as we go on attributing further properties to the first cause.

We must now turn to the attribute of *perfection.* This may be also deduced from the results of the second argument. That whose essence is being itself, can lack no positive perfection, for every perfection is some mode of existence. All of these are contained under existence itself, which transcends any finite or limited mode. From this we may deduce the attribute of *infinity,* or the lack of any limitation in the first cause. Potency is a limitation or imperfection of being, not yet fully being that which it is able to be. We may also conclude from the first argument that the first cause lacks all potency,[29] and from this deduce that it is fully in act, or to use the Latin form of an Aristotelian expression, *actus purus.* This is a positive way of expressing the non-finiteness or infinity of the first

[29] Cf. this chapter, § 3.

cause. It will help us to avoid confusing this positive infinity with the negative, imperfect infinity of prime matter which is able to be actualized by an indefinite number of forms. The first cause is not infinite in this sense. It is infinite in the positive sense of lacking any imperfection of unrealized capacity, and being *pure act.*

From this we may deduce that the first cause is *good,* for by goodness we mean that which realizes the capacities of a finite nature; by evil we mean the privation of any such realization. But lacking all potency and being fully in act, the first cause lacks any privation. Possessing every higher perfection of being in an eminent mode of simplicity, it must, therefore, be judged as perfectly or eminently good. Of course this eminent goodness must be distinguished from the good of man or the finite goods that realize the nature of any subhuman creature. Nevertheless there is a connection between the two. The good of a creature, though finite, is nevertheless *some* mode of active existence. Hence it bears a similitude with tne unlimited being of the first cause. We may conclude that every creature, in seeking what is actually good, is seeking after something akin to the eminent being of this cause.

From infinity we may also deduce the attribute of *omnipotence.* The power to give being to external things is a perfection which we possess with important limitations. The first cause, however, being pure act, must possess this power to an unlimited degree, i.e., the capacity to bring things into existence out of nothing. In fact it is only with reference to such a power that the ultimate origin of nature can be explained. This power, however, does not mean the capacity to bring contradictory entities into existence, as Descartes and his followers have held. Does this then mean a limitation of omnipotence, something, that is, that the first cause cannot do? No, because a contradictory entity is impossible, nothing at all, and the power to create nothing is not a positive power but a privation.

From the creative power to give existence to possible entities, we may also infer the so-called *immensity* of the first cause, the power to be everywhere present, where being is given and sustained. It is important to note that the first cause possesses these powers of creativity and immensity as necessary attributes. The acts of actual creation and that of being ubiquitously present among created things, however, are not necessary attributes. As we shall see, they may or may not exist, for there is nothing to compel the first cause to exercise his powers of creation. This act was due to a free and voluntary choice.

Finally, we come to the two attributes of *immutability* and *eternity*. The first may be derived from the results of the first argument, which leads to the conclusion that the first cause is without potency (§ 3, above). Change is the actualizing of the potential.[30] Hence since it lacks potency, we must infer that the first cause is immutable. This means more than a mere state of rest or factual absence of change. It means the absence of any *capacity* to change, immut-*ability* in the exact sense. From this may be deduced the attribute of *eternity*—the perfect possession of being all at once.

We have seen that time is the measure of a successive duration in which being is successively added to being.[31] Eternity is the measure of a non-successive being which is possessed all at once. Furthermore change is realized only at a limiting instant which itself passes away. Eternal being is realized perfectly at an instant which does not pass. The first cause therefore possesses the whole of its being at an eternal now which is not succeeded. This also involves a radical distinction from the successive being of transient entities. We can gain no sensible image of such existence. Nevertheless we can rationally grasp it and understand that it is necessitated by the immutability of the first cause.

At this point the reader may complain that we have lost all contact with the world of experience and are indulging in speculative adventures which cannot be verified by any direct observation. In a sense this is true. This being is immaterial like the human mind, and therefore cannot be observed by any sense. But the reader also believes in many other things which cannot be verified by direct sensory observation, at least if he has any confidence in the results of modern science. Electrons, protons, and neutrons have never been directly observed. Furthermore we are assured that any attempt to visualize their structure by concrete images must lead to serious distortion. Nevertheless the existence of such entities and their peculiar properties may be conceptually grasped and ration-

[30] Cf. ch. 15, § 1.
[31] Cf. ch. 15, § 7.

ally deduced by causal inferences from what is directly observed. The same is true of the theory of the first cause we have just presented.

Here again anthropomorphic images will not help us. We must trust to reason alone and its causal inferences. When we leave all subjective prejudice behind and follow these inferences through, we are led to a first cause whose essence is existence. In working out its peculiar structure we must abandon familiar experience and rely on rational deduction alone. Viewed in this light the theory is not so much an anthropomorphic figment (for surely it is further from common experience than the theory of the electron) as a triumph of deductive inference. Its attributes are much stranger than those of the electron. Nevertheless they are connected with the observed facts by the inexorable chains of reasoning we have tried to suggest.

The primary attributes of the first cause are absolute *indivisibility, transcendence, infinity, perfection, omnipotence, immensity, immutability,* and *eternity.* Unless we can show an error in the deductive reasoning or in the description of the basic facts, we must accept them. Now we must turn to the operational attributes of the first cause.

8.   THE OPERATIONAL ATTRIBUTES OF THE FIRST CAUSE

These are conceived by us as acts performed by an already existent nature. We have already pointed out that such a distinction cannot actually exist in a non-composite being, which is its activity, and therefore has no capacity for further perfection. Nevertheless the perfections which we conceive in this imperfect way are actually contained in the eminent unity of the first cause. So if we make due allowance for our mode of apprehension, a sound understanding of them will give us additional knowledge concerning this being. Indeed the agelong argument and discussion concerning the supreme intellect and the supreme will, have clarified their nature in certain important respects and have thrown much needed light on human nature which possesses these faculties in an imperfect way. It is appropriate, therefore, that we should briefly summarize the results of these discussions before we turn to an analysis of human nature in the next section.

The most fundamental of these operational attributes is *intelligence*. That the first cause possesses this perfection is proved directly by the third argument. But a more illuminating demonstration arises from a consideration of the nature of intelligence. This will become more evident if we contrast it with the nature of matter.

We have already noted how matter restricts the forms with which it unites to the limits of a single individual, and thus produces that cosmic loneliness which we find everywhere in the material world.[32] We have also noted how this cosmic loneliness is overcome only through the intervention of intelligence, which is able to lift the forms of nature from their isolating, material matrix into a universal status which can be communicated from one mind to another. Matter is necessarily spread out in quantitative dimensions. Concepts have no size and weight. Material entities are in constant flux and never reach a fully determinate state. Concepts, once they are clearly grasped, are definite and not subject to further change.

Matter makes things incommunicable; mind makes them communicable. Matter quantifies; mind frees from quantity. Matter sets everything in motion; mind produces what is immobile and determinate. That which works in these ways against the influence of matter must be recognized as immaterial. Indeed this is evident if we reflect upon the act of understanding which, though it is some form of union, nevertheless is clearly not any sort of material union. When the physicist knows something about a vapor he is in some way united with the vapor, but he does not become physically vaporized. When the anatomist knows something about bone structure he is in some way united to bone, but he does not become ossified. Intelligence is immateriality, and the more an entity is free from matter, the higher is the level of its intelligence.

We have already seen that the first cause, being utterly non-composite, must be completely free from matter.[33] Therefore it must be intelligent in the highest degree. We have also shown on other grounds that it is non-quantitative and immutable, two attributes attaching even to the limited reason of man. When we reflect upon these facts we can see the sense in which rational insight, even in the restricted modes known to us, can provide us

[32] Cf. ch. 14, § 6.
[33] This chapter, § 4.

with important clues concerning the nature of the supreme being.
It will do this if we succeed in developing a concept of immaterial,
or intelligent, being which is free from the limitations of human
reason.

These limitations are primarily two. First of all, our intelligence
works in a piecemeal manner.[34] We cannot clearly grasp a being as
it is altogether at once. Before we do this we have to split it up
into different aspects which are more or less intelligible to us as
we take them one by one. Then we have to piece them together
again by propositions and inferences. It is only after this discursive
process that we are then sometimes able to grasp the whole thing
as it is. But the eternal being of the first cause precludes any such
process of discursive reasoning. We must suppose that, in contrast
to us, it must grasp things no matter how complex they may be, all
at once in an instantaneous flash of insight. Furthermore since it
lacks all potency, we must reject the idea that it has to go through
any passage from a state of ignorance to a state of knowledge, like
the learning process in man. All objects of knowledge must stand
clearly before it in an eternal now.

The second limitation of our knowledge is even more fundamental. As an evolutionary being, every individual human person
is a material substance, isolated by his matter from every other substance and carrying on a host of incommunicable, material processes
private to himself. The faculty of reason and the discursive processes
of rational insight are only accidental phases of his existence.[35] It
is true that by these immaterial processes he can assimilate other
forms and thus overcome his cosmic isolation, thereby communicating with his fellows and engaging in common activity with
them. He can even gain some understanding of his own nature and
lift himself partially into that clear and stable existence which is
the gift of intelligence. But he must also exist materially. Hence
this process can only be a partial and incidental phase of his existence. A man *has* intelligence. He cannot *be* his intelligence with
the whole of himself.

But as we have seen, the first cause has no matter or potency in
his being. Furthermore he lacks the composition of substance and

[34] Cf. ch. 19, § 2.
[35] Cf. ch. 17, § 3.

accident. Hence we must reject the notion that his understanding is only a phase of his being. He must not only *have* intelligence; he must *be* this intelligence. Our knowledge is always characterized by a diversity between the object which can be known and the faculty which can know it, though this diversity is constantly being overcome by the attainment of actual knowledge in which the faculty *is* the object known. In the supreme intelligence, ever in a state of act, there is no such diversity whatsoever. This intelligence is the being which is known, and this being is the intelligence knowing it.

Thus if we wish to find the closest approximations to that extraordinary existence which broods over our cosmos, we must turn to the contemplative life of man, and the voluntary choice and aspiration which follow along after it, and share in its immateriality. Though suggested by both Plato and Aristotle, the founders of realistic philosophy, this truth has been widely recognized since the time of Augustine, who sharply formulated it in the light of Christianity. According to him, the scriptural doctrine that man is made in the image of God must be taken in this sense.[36] The most suggestive clues to the life of the supreme being are therefore to be found in the experiences of prayer, contemplation, and heroic sacrificial action. Though these experiences have no doubt been most clearly exemplified in the lives of the great creative personalities of human history, they are open to every man.

The primary object of the supreme intelligence must be the being with which it is identified. This is what Aristotle must have meant by his reference to the divine self-contemplation (*noesis noeseos*).[37] But such knowledge must include a knowledge of the divine, creative power. This must be conceived by us as having two subdivisions. First, there must be an insight into all the *possible* entities which might be brought into existence, analogous to the pure theoretical insight of man.[38] In the supreme being this has been called *the knowledge of simple intelligence*. Such knowledge of possibilities, being derived from the omnipotence which is a necessary attribute of the first cause, is necessary as well as immutable.

[36] Cf. *De Trinitate* XIV, 8.
[37] Cf. *Metaphysics,* Book XII, ch. 7.
[38] Cf. ch. 5, § 2.

But then in addition there must be a knowledge of those possibilities which have been chosen for realization in the order of
their succession, analogous to the practical knowledge of man.[39]
Such knowledge, since it rests upon a divine choice which cannot
alter, is immutable. But it is not *strictly necessary*, like the knowledge of eternal possibilities. It is only *hypothetically necessary*,
that is, necessary on the ground of a free choice, immutably made.
We must reject the view that would deny such knowledge to the
first cause, for this would imply that He was not wholly aware of
what He was doing and would introduce a crucial imperfection into
His nature.

In order to avoid this inconsistency we must therefore defend the
thesis that the governing cause holds before Him in an eternal *now*,
the complete knowledge of what has been, what is now, and what
will be, even those contingent choices of free human individuals
who do not as yet exist for us. This, of course, suggests certain difficulties, particularly that of reconciling this necessary knowledge
with the freedom of man. To this crucial difficulty we may suggest
the following answer.

Suppose I have a friend who is sorely tried by a situation to which
he may respond either by committing a subtle crime of theft or by
refusing to commit the crime and falling into financial straits.
From my present temporal standpoint this is a future act which
may turn out either way depending upon his exercise of choice.
As such, I cannot now know what this future contingent act will
be. From the point of view of such a passing present neither can
the first cause know.

But we must now recognize that there is another way of regarding this event. Even for us, after the event has happened, it loses
its contingency and can be known with certainty. Suppose my friend
resists the temptation. This event is still a contingent event, but
it is now determinate and can be known. What to us appear as
future events, are present in this determinate mode of existence to
the first cause. He sees them, not as future and indeterminate, but
as present and determinate, as they will be to us if we live to see
them.

But how can the same thing be both future and present? Is this

[39] Cf. ch. 3, § 1b.

not a contradiction? That which is temporally future cannot also be a temporal present. But there is no reason why they both should not be present before another kind of present, the eternal now of a perfect intelligence, which of course we do not possess.

But then if all things are present before this intelligence, is it not ignorant of the future and the past? No, because we also are before him with all our temporal limitations, our memories of the past, and our anticipations of an indeterminate future.

But if this future event is known from all eternity with certainty and necessity, does this not mean that the event has lost its contingency and is now really determined and necessary? It does not mean this. A contingent event does not lose its contingency even after it has happened, though it may be certainly known by us. Thus the free choice of my friend, having happened, is known by me with certainty as a free act for which I congratulate him.

In this way the contingent acts of men are known in their full determinacy as free acts by the divine intelligence. Time is like a long caravan the members of which can see only what is directly before and behind. But the eternal present is like a high eminence unattainable to us, from which the whole caravan, the full gamut of time, can be taken in at once with perfect clarity.

That the first cause acts purposefully or voluntarily follows from the third argument. This can also be understood by an analysis of the meaning of "will." By this word we refer to a mode of action which does not arise automatically from either external or internal, material causes, but which is governed and guided by rational awareness. A voluntary act is one which is preceded by deliberation, and thus joined with reason. Now we have seen that the first cause is intelligence. It is also perfect act. Hence it is an identity of reason and activity, or voluntary in an eminent sense.

From this we may deduce that the first cause is personal, for a person, according to the definition of Boethius,[40] is an individual substance of a rational nature, that is, a being existing in himself, with intellect and will. The first cause more than fulfills this definition, for he exists not only *in* Himself but *by* Himself as well. He is eminently rational and perfectly in act. Hence He is a personal being, and we are justified by philosophical argument alone in

[40] *De duabus naturis.*

referring to Him as a person by the personal name God and by personal pronouns rather than the neuter forms we have so far been using.

9.   THE FREEDOM OF GOD AND THE FREEDOM OF MAN

Are the acts of this personal being necessary or free? The great medieval controversies concerning this question brought the concept of freedom for the first time into sharp focus and resulted in certain conclusions which shed light, not only on the nature of the first cause, but on the nature of man as well. The most important of these was the insight that freedom cannot be identified either with any sort of necessity or with mere indeterminate caprice.

No will is free in the sense that it can will anything without limitation. Every will is constrained by a moral (not a physical) necessity to some good which is its final end. Far from being inconsistent with freedom this attachment to a necessary end is the foundation of all genuine freedom. Man, for example, does not become free by ceasing to will the life of a man and trying to live like a snake or baboon, if indeed this is possible. The first cause also is not free in the sense that He can cease to will His own being and to rest in this perfection. This He must do necessarily. But is this the whole of freedom?

The Arabian philosophers of the Middle Ages, under Neo-Platonic influence, tended to answer this question in the affirmative, at least so far as God was concerned. They made no distinction between the immanent activity of God in willing His own existence and the extrinsic, creative activity by which the finite world was brought into being. Hence both were regarded as equally necessary. Just as God must sustain Himself in being, so by a necessity of nature He must pour Himself forth in external manifestations. The world is thus conceived along Neo-Platonic lines as an inescapable emanation or series of emanations from the first cause. This view, however, is subject to three very serious objections.

In the first place, it means that God is not free, for though freedom cannot be identified with complete indeterminacy, it certainly does involve an element of indeterminacy. And freedom is a perfection which exists at least to a degree even in the subordinate creature, man. To deny any freedom of choice to God, therefore, is inconsistent with the divine perfection. In this respect He will be reduced to a lower level even than the subordinate creature, man.

In the second place, it will mean that God is dependent on something other than Himself. Without the world He cannot realize a necessity of His nature. This is even more obviously inconsistent with the infinite perfection of the first cause.

Finally, the view has pantheistic implications, for if the world necessarily emanates from the divine nature, it is hard to resist the conclusion that it is intimately entwined and fused with the divine being. But this is inconsistent with the simplicity and transcendence of the first cause we have considered.[41]

It was in seeking an answer to these difficulties that the great doctrine of the freedom of God was first clearly formulated by the medieval Christian philosophers, especially by Aquinas.[42]

The notion of necessity must first be focused before this doctrine can be understood. Necessity means being determined to one thing and one thing alone. We can distinguish three kinds. First, there is necessary determination by an extrinsic, efficient cause. If a stronger person forces my fingers to pull the trigger, I am not free but acting under necessary constraint. God, of course, is not subject to any such necessity, since He is the first cause and cannot be acted upon by what He has Himself brought into being and sustains.

Second, there is necessary determination by an intrinsic, natural cause. Thus plants are constrained by a natural necessity to grow upward, to put out leaves, and so on, and a hot object tends to radiate heat. There are two reasons why such action cannot be consistently attributed to God. In the first place, as we have seen, He is rational and this rationality permeates all his action. Such rational action is never automatic. In the second place, if God acted in this way He must have produced something infinite and like Himself in nature. Not only was this not the case, but we can see that it was impossible, for two perfect beings imply a contradiction. One or the other would have to possess something which the other *lacked*.

Third, there is moral necessity, the intrinsic determination to an act demanded by reason. Thus if my reason tells me that an act is good and all other alternatives are less good, I am under a moral

---

[41] This chapter, § 7.
[42] *Summa Theologica*, Part I, Qu. 19.

necessity to perform this act. If the creative act is interpreted in this way, following Leibnitz and other modern thinkers, then God is not free, for such acts are morally determined to one. Was God acting under moral necessity in creating an external world?

We cannot answer this question in the affirmative without denying the perfection of God. This is the crucial point to be seen. The essence of this being is existence, under which all modes of being and perfection are contained. If we say that such a being would be better with something else in addition, we are denying His unlimited goodness. We are conceiving of Him in an anthropomorphic manner as imperfect and needing something more to be perfected. We are no longer thinking of God but of a finite being seeking to realize itself and requiring to be sustained by an external cause. Unless the whole argument of this chapter is fallacious we must reject this notion of a finite God, which explains nothing, but itself requires an ultimate explanation. The first cause was under no moral necessity to create a world. Such a world could add no perfection not already contained in the divine infinity. It could add more beings—not more being. This leaves only one possible alternative. The world did not come into being through any necessity: it was the result of a free act of choice.

This does not mean that the world was uncaused. The acts that we ourselves freely choose are certainly caused by us, or they would not be subject to praise or blame and we should not be able to regard ourselves as responsible agents. But they are not caused by a necessary cause, determined to one effect alone. The will, governed by rational apprehension of an end that is genuinely good, is confronted by different alternatives, either of which might reach the end. The creation of the world presented such an alternative to the first cause. It was not necessary for the realization of his ultimate perfection.

On the other hand, we must not suppose that it interfered with this perfection. Through an act of creation the ultimate perfection could be manifested by a great diversity of creatures. This is good, but not in any sense that would rule out other possible alternatives. For complete goodness was already in existence. So without compulsion it was freely chosen in accordance with reason, though not necessitated by reason. In the same way we are often presented with alternatives, either of which may enable us to realize our ultimate end. In such cases if we act wisely, we choose in accordance with reason, though we are not necessitated by reason. Thus the world is due neither to rational necessity nor to any irrational caprice. It is due to a free act of choice, like all truly free acts, made with the approval of reason and deliberation.

But how can human beings perform such free acts if they are at the mercy of an omnipotent, first cause whose purposes must be fulfilled? Are we not faced with a dilemma? Either we are free and sometimes choose wrongly, in which case the divine purpose is frustrated, or we are always made to choose in the proper way, in which case we are not really free. This ancient dilemma first posed by the Stoics and Skeptics of the Hellenic civilization and repeated by many modern skeptics including Hume,[43] may be answered by making use of certain important distinctions and doctrines developed in the course of the history of realistic thought. We shall not be able to explain this answer in detail. It may be possible, however, to explain some of the critical distinctions on which it rests and to suggest its major outlines.

We must note, first of all, that the dilemma does not regard free choice itself as a value falling within the scope of the divine purpose, but only as a disruptive factor which might upset the well-laid plans of a human artisan, with only limited time and power at his disposal. Such anthropomorphism, however, is open to serious suspicion. It is quite clear that we are not dealing with a human economic or engineering enterprise, but rather with an agency of an entirely different order, having unlimited time and power at its disposal. The very fact that man has emerged at the culmination of the evolutionary process shows that voluntary action, the free choice of good, is a major concern of this agency. Furthermore we can understand why this is so, for we ourselves in our rational moments set a very high value on freely chosen acts of sacrifice and devotion.

Do we not admire more a courageous act that is freely chosen than the same act performed under some external compulsion, such as the fear of ridicule or disgrace? In this we are correct. Freely chosen activity is more valuable than automatic behavior. If God

[43] Cf. Dialogues Concerning Natural Religion, Part X, *Treatise on Human Nature,* ed. Green and Grose, Vol. 2, pp. 439–440.

had been satisfied merely with the latter, man never would have appeared upon the scene. He alone among all the creatures of nature is capable not only of doing what is good, but of understanding what is good and choosing to perform it for its own sake. But this carries with it necessarily the possibility of his failing to exercise these immanent faculties. As a matter of fact it is perfectly clear that he has so failed, and has thus brought evil and disorder into the world in a way which must have been foreseen by the first cause. Is this cause then responsible for evil?

Certain theories of divine determinism have argued in this way, but in doing so they have ignored the distinction between causation and permission. For example, even we would not judge that an administrative officer in delegating certain powers to a subordinate whom he knows to be capable of carrying them out, and then sustaining him in office, is the cause of his free misuse of these powers. Similarly, the first cause, by sustaining man as a free being, permits him to misuse this freedom. But this is not the same as *causing* the misuse. Indeed, as we can clearly see, the misuse is punished by natural sanctions; it always brings further evils in its train. A bad act is always punished by a tendency to perform further bad acts. Does this not mean that God from all eternity singled out certain individuals, perhaps the mass of mankind, to suffer such punishment? This is the deterministic conception.

If God willed all men to be saved then the facts show that this will has been frustrated. Therefore we must assume the alternative that from eternity he has willed certain men to be punished. This gruesome doctrine, however, ignores another vital distinction between what has been called the *antecedent* and the *consequent* will.

Imagine a human judge before whom a prisoner has just been brought for judgment. What is the initial, antecedent attitude of the judge? If he is fair-minded, it is certainly not one of biased condemnation. On the whole, he wishes the prisoner well and hopes that he will prove innocent. This is his antecedent will. If, on the other hand, the evidence shows that the prisoner is guilty of a crime, he will decree the just punishment. This is his final, consequent will in the light of all the particular circumstances.

Similarly, in the case of the first cause, we must distinguish between His antecedent and His consequent will. Antecedently, He wills in general that all men are to choose correctly. They have been endowed with all the necessary faculties and instruments for a proper choice. They can be prevented from this only by a pride and lethargy they may freely bring upon themselves. If they do this by their own choice, then by a final, consequent will, a just punishment is imposed upon them. But does this not mean that good has been conquered by evil in the world?

To this we may answer that the "world" is something very vast and very rich, with many realms concerning which we know little or nothing, and with a history not yet closed. But we do know enough to see that this suggested conclusion does not necessarily follow. All men do not misuse their freedom. Free devotion and sacrifice have been revealed in history. Furthermore we can see that goodness is sometimes brought out of the most terrible acts of cruelty and oppression, as the heroism and martyrdom of resistance has been brought out of the excesses of tyranny. This should enable us at least to glimpse that omnipotence which is not only able to govern the automatic action of non-rational things by necessary causes, but the acts of rational beings by eliciting causes which bring good out of evil without the use of dictatorial power. We know abstractly that such omnipotence is possessed by the first cause. Here we see it at work in the concrete flux of history. Nevertheless must we not admit that at least the antecedent will to save all men has been frustrated?

This question is based upon an assumption that the manifestation of human love and devotion exhausts the purposes of the first cause. Once more we must guard against the anthropomorphic foundations of this assumption. God's purpose in creation was to manifest not only His freedom and rationality, but all the other attributes as well, including justice and mercy. These are made evident with poignant clarity by the maintenance of a natural order which inflicts unmistakable punishment on lethargy and pride, and by the constant offering of corrective assistance to those in the deepest misery. It is to these further attributes that we must now finally turn.

It is clear that certain qualities essential to the perfection of human nature cannot be attributed to the first cause even in an analogous sense. Since He is not subject to material passions requir ing rational control, it would be absurd to think of Him as characterized by temperance.[44] Since He does not have to fight against opposing obstacles, we cannot attribute courage to Him, though the immutability of His decrees may bear some analogy to a certain aspect of this human virtue.[45] If there is room for any distinction of persons within the divine nature there may be something analogous to friendship. But this question would carry us beyond anything that can be shown by reason alone. Since friendship involves equality and reciprocity,[46] a relationship of this sort between God and any creature is out of the question. But something analogous to the other outwardly directed virtues of generosity, justice,[47] and mercy must be attributed to the first cause.

Underlying all of these, is that joy in active being and that free bestowal of it upon others for its own sake which is no longer adequately translated by our word "love." We glimpse it in that uncompelled, creative action by which being is freely given to the finite creature; in that distributive justice by which all that is required for its realization is offered to each; and finally in that unfailing mercy by which aid is freely poured forth for the correction of faults and defects. This love must not be confused with desire or concupiscence, which implies a need or defect and which is moved by something able to fulfill it. The divine love is not passively aroused by anything intrinsically lovable in the object. It is something purely active, which presupposes nothing in the object, but freely bestows value upon it. This outpouring of benevolence arises from no lack, but is rather the manifestation of a perfection that already exists.

If the creature is loved, not for his own sake, but for the sake of something in the agent, does this not imply egotism? If a man carries out an act to show how good *he* is, this is vanity, but not if he acts for the sake of manifesting what is really and finally good. Benevolent action is that which wills good to the object. It does not necessarily regard the object as better than the good which is willed. The teacher who takes delight in imparting the truth to a few stu-

[44] Cf. ch. 6, § 2.
[45] Cf. ch. 6, § 1.
[46] Cf. ch. 11, § 2.
[47] Cf. chs. 7 and 8.

dents or even to only one, and who rejoices in the truth more than in the student, is not thereby guilty of egotism. In the same way the first cause is not moved to will goodness to the creature for the sake of a perfection not yet possessed. But rather He wills this to the creature because of joy in a perfection already possessed from pure benevolence, with no hope or desire for reciprocal gain or return. This pattern may be at least dimly discerned in the highest examples of human generosity.

We must now conclude our outline of the arguments by which realistic philosophy has deduced the existence of a first cause as well as certain of its attributes. This knowledge is fragmentary and incomplete. There are many more things that we need to know. It is also hazy and analogous, general and abstract, for concrete sensory images are of no help in grasping what is immaterial. Nevertheless the human mind can form an analogous concept of being which is broad enough to include even this within its transcendental scope. Hence we are able to gain a confused and shadowy understanding of the first cause in relation to its effects. For any further insight into the intrinsic life of this being, we must turn to a higher light than that of human reason, which can take us no further.

But in spite of the weak and hesitant character of this light, its faltering illumination must not be despised. When properly focused and utilized it can assure us of the existence of a first cause belonging to a higher order of being than man. In this way theoretical reason, when pushed to its furthest, metaphysical limits, provides a potent antidote for that human pride and arrogance which is perhaps the most insidious source of cultural disintegration.[48] When applied with discipline to the difficult task of analyzing the nature of this primal being, it has shown itself capable of yielding the conclusions we have outlined in this chapter.

These disciplined discussions and conclusions have shed considerable light on such obscure concepts as unity, goodness, reason, will, and freedom which must be utilized in any disciplined attempt to study the complex structure of human nature. It is to this task that we must now turn our attention.

[48] Cf. ch. 12, § 1.

REFERENCES

Recommended Reading

Aquinas, *Summa Theologica,* Part I, Qu. 1–20.

Suggested Reading

1. Most of the arguments used by modern naturalists and agnostics may be found in Hume's *Dialogues on Natural Religion,* ed. Green and Grose, London, Longmans, Green, 1874, Vol. 2. A very influential, skeptical classification of the classical arguments (into ontological, cosmological, and teleological) is found in Kant, *Critique of Pure Reason,* Transcendental Dialectic, Sec. III, A583, B611 ff. A sounder treatment of these arguments is given by Garrigou-Lagrange, R., *God, His existence and nature,* St. Louis, Herder, 1936, Vol. 1, and by Mascall, E. L., *He Who Is,* New York, Longmans, Green, 1943, pp. 57–82.

2. For criticisms of the ontological argument, cf. Aquinas, *Summa Theologica,* Part I, Qu. 2, Art. 1; Kant, *Critique of Pure Reason,* Transcendental Dialectic, Sec. IV, A592, B620 ff.; and Maritain, J., *The Dream of Descartes,* New York Philosophical Library, 1944.

3. For a first statement of the principles of the argument from change, cf. Aristotle, *Physics,* Book VIII, chap. 5. For a classical exposition of the argument, cf. Aquinas, *Summa Theologica,* Part I, Qu. 2, Art. 3. For modern commentary, cf. Garrigou-Lagrange, R., *God, His existence and his nature,* Vol. 1; and Mascall, E. L., *He Who Is,* New York, Longmans, Green, 1943, pp. 40–45.

4. For the principles of the argument from contingency, cf. Aristotle, *Posterior Analytics* 92B 3 ff. and *Metaphysics,* Book XII, chap. 6. For a classical statement of the argument, cf. Aquinas, *Summa Theologica,* Part I, Qu. 2, Art. 3. For modern commentary, cf. Mascall, E. L., *He Who Is,* pp. 46–52.

5. For the argument based on the order of the universe, cf. Plato, *Philebus* 30; Aristotle, *Physics,* Book II, chap. 8, and *Metaphysics,* Book XII, chap. 10; Aquinas, *Summa Theologica,* Part I, Qu. 2, Art. 3, argument 5; and Hume, *Dialogues Concerning Natural Religion,* Part XII. For recent commentary, cf. Garrigou-Lagrange, R., *God, His existence and nature,* and Mascall, E. L., *He Who Is,* pp. 54–56.

6. On the nature of the first cause, cf. Plato, *Republic,* Book II, 381; Aristotle, *Metaphysics,* Book XII, 1072B 4 ff.; Aquinas, *Summa Theologica,* Part I, Qu. 3; and Garrigou-Lagrange, R., *The One God,* St. Louis, Herder, 1944, pp. 156–204.

7. For the entitative attributes, cf. Aristotle, *Metaphysics*, Book XII, chap. 7, 1073A 4 ff.; and Aquinas, *Summa Theologica*, Part I, Qu. 3–11.

8. For the operational attributes, cf. Aristotle, *Metaphysics*, Book XII, chap. 7, 1072B 13 ff.; and Aquinas, *Summa Theologica*, Qu. 14–22.

9. On the question of freedom, cf. Aquinas, *Summa Theologica*, Qu. 19; and Garrigou-Lagrange, R., *The One God*, pp. 487–728.

THE HUMAN PSYCHE AND ITS
FACULTIES

HAVING examined the material, changing world, its causal structure, and the inferential conclusions concerning a first cause to which this structure leads, we turn now to a study of the finite creature man which will occupy us for the remainder of this work. Man is a topic of peculiar interest to us, because of the fact that we ourselves are human. But there are also other reasons connected with the central, intermediate position of man in the cosmos. On the one hand, he is a physical offspring of nature who, as we know, has developed continuously from the prime matter which underlies the whole of cosmic evolution.

As a material being, he is subject to change, to chance, and individuation, like all other natural entities. In him all the categories, or modes of changing being, are exemplified. He supports qualities like color, shape, virtue, and vice. The matter of which he is composed is spread out quantitatively and occupies a place among the other extended entities of the natural world. He acts upon these surrounding entities and suffers from their action upon him. His being is measured by time and ordered to other entities by many relations. He undergoes the four modes of change to which all natural being is subject. He is brought into existence and passes away by the substantial changes of birth and death. As long as he exists he is subject to qualitative alteration, quantitative increase and decrease, and motion from place to place. In him, therefore, the whole structure of material nature is epitomized.

But on the other hand, he is distinguished by the possession of an awareness and intelligence which marks him off from all other natural entities. This distinctive part of human nature is immaterial, and men can use it to identify themselves with remote, external things from which they are materially quite distinct. Such knowledge, being immaterial, can be shared with other men, whose bodies are quite separate, to overcome that cosmic loneliness which isolates each material individual from every other. Furthermore it makes men aware of different possibilities of action among which they can freely choose, instead of merely responding to external stimuli in ways determined by their physical nature.

In the exercise of human understanding and choice, we glimpse something of a higher order which is also present in this remarkable, composite being. He is not only a material organism, but an immaterial intelligence. Hence all that man has been able to learn of the first, immaterial source of existence by pushing his reason to its farthest limits, is also relevant to the understanding of man.[1] In him, not only the structure of material nature, but that of immaterial being, also is epitomized.

In this sense the composite being of man is a microcosm in which the material and the immaterial meet together in a restless unity, the misery and grandeur of man. Pascal has compared man to a fragile thinking reed (*un roseau pensant*),[2] a comparison now made much more pertinent by recent astronomical knowledge. Inhabiting a tiny, minor planet in a corner of the physical cosmos, this miserable creature maintains a precarious and fleeting existence amongst the overwhelming, material powers of nature, on which he is dependent in innumerable ways. Considered from the purely material point of view of physics and astronomy, man is a creature of almost unbelievable insignificance. What is his magnitude compared with that of a galaxy? What is his life when measured in terms of light years? Subject to the myriad devastating forces of nature, he can be destroyed by a drop of water, a bubble of air.

The grandeur of man lies in another field of being altogether. In spite of his physical insignificance he alone knows his fragile nature and apprehends his situation. In him alone the whole vast realm of blind unconscious force and extension is lifted into the being of rational awareness. In him alone nature comes to know itself. This is the dignity and grandeur of man.

The extended physical aspects of human nature are sensible and

---

[1] Cf. ch. 16, especially §§ 5 and 8.
[2] *Pensées, Grandeur et Misère de l'Homme,* XII.

can be observed and studied by the sensory techniques employed by the special sciences. These sciences have made important contributions to an understanding of certain subordinate aspects of man and his behavior. But the higher, immaterial aspects of human nature, his intellect and will, are not sensible and cannot be studied by such techniques. No one has ever measured the length and shape of a human thought. No chemist has ever weighed the science of chemistry on his scales. No one has ever looked at a free choice of man through his microscope or spread it on a microscopic slide. And yet these are the ruling, guiding factors of human conduct so far as man really acts like a man. Hence in order to understand human nature as a whole and human action, another technique, not limited to sensory apprehension, is required.

Fortunately, in addition to sense we possess the faculty of reason, which is not restricted to the apprehension of material, extended being. We cannot touch or taste or smell or see an idea; but we can understand it. Hence with the aid of sense and reason together, we may hope to gain some understanding of human nature as a whole and of that human activity by which this nature seeks to perfect itself. All men possess some such knowledge, at least in a vague, incipient form. The attempt to clarify such knowledge, to test it, and order it in a careful way, has resulted in a certain discipline, the science of man as a whole, or as we shall call it, in accordance with present-day usage, philosophical anthropology.

This discipline, which has been pursued by realistic philosophy throughout the course of western history from the days of the ancient Greeks, is divided into two primary parts: the study of man and his behavior in general, philosophical anthropology proper; and the study of man and his behavior in the concrete, the historical sciences. These last fall beyond the scope of this work, which must restrict itself to the discipline of philosophical anthropology proper. It is to this task that we now turn.

1. The Human Psyche

Man is a natural entity or substance. As a substance, he exists in himself, supporting faculties and accidents of various kinds. As a natural substance, he has evolved continuously from something else which has been slowly prepared by the reception of prior forms for the final, distinctive form of man.[3] Since that out of which an entity has developed remains within the entity, though under a new form, the existent human individual has a composite, hylomorphic nature. On the one hand, he is the prepared matter which, as such, is only capable of being man; and on the other hand, he is the human form, which discontinuously distinguishes him from all other entities by rationality, the soul or psyche.

Since we can clearly distinguish the body from the soul which animates it, there are three ways in which we may regard a living man. First, we may concentrate upon the formed body which is the matter of a man. This is indeed an essential part, but if we regard it as the only essential part, we easily fall into a materialistic view which dismisses rationality as a mere accident. As we shall see, this view is not borne out by the facts. Second, we may concentrate upon the differentiating form of man, the rationality which distinguishes him from all the other creatures. This also is an essential part, but if we regard it as the only essential part, we easily fall into a spiritualistic view which dismisses the material body as a mere accident. This view also is not supported by the facts.

Nevertheless each of these views has won many adherents. Throughout the course of western thought there has been a conflict between those who have held that man is essentially a physical body to which conscious awareness is attached as a peculiar accident or epiphenomenon, and those who have held that man is essentially an immaterial consciousness to which the body is attached as a mere vehicle or accident. In its more extreme forms materialism has even gone so far as to maintain that thought itself is purely physical, and has sought to identify it with individual changes or disturbances in the central nervous system or other organs. On the other hand, in its more extreme forms spiritualism has gone so far as to maintain that the body is psychical in character, and has sought to identify it with psychic appearances having no independent existence apart from the mind.

Both of these views when consistently formulated are far removed from the common insight of mankind, which tends to regard the human person as something more than a physical organism, though its concepts are not worked out with great precision and accuracy.

[3] Cf. chs. 13, § 4, and 15, § 2.

Nevertheless it refuses to reduce the human person either to purely material or to purely immaterial categories, taking a middle position between these two extremes. This third position has been carefully formulated, refined, and defended by realistic philosophy since the time of Aristotle. According to it, man is a hylomorphic being,[4] having two essential parts: an organized, material body, and a rational life which animates it. As in the case of any other evolutionary entity these are not two independent things joined together in an accidental unity, but two constitutive principles of one thing, each of which is able to exercise its functions only with the aid of the other. Let us now attempt to state this view with a precision and care which may help us to clarify our own concepts. Since human nature is a form of life, it will help us first of all to study the Aristotelian definition of life.

The Latin word for that which animates an animal body is *anima*. This is usually translated by the English word, *soul*. In recent times, however, this word has gained certain spiritualistic implications which raise doubts in the mind of the modern reader. We shall therefore use the word *psyche,* taken from the Greek, where the word had no such implications. By psyche, we mean simply that which makes any animal body live while the animal is alive. The human psyche means that which makes the human body live and act like a man, and which is certainly separated from it at death. How are we to define life in general? According to Aristotle, it is *the first act of an organic body able to live.*[5] What does this definition mean?

Some forms may be able to exist alone without matter. But natural life is an evolutionary form which requires matter in order to exist. Hence the definition of life includes something strictly speaking outside of it, namely, the physical body, which is able to live. Spiritualism is rejected. The life of man requires a body, a special kind of a body with different parts or organs capable of acting intrinsically on one another (an organic body). Otherwise it would be internally homogeneous like a rock or a crystal, and unable to nourish itself or move itself through the action of one organic part upon another. The actual matter of life is always such an organic

[4] Cf. ch. 13, § 6.
[5] *De Anima,* Book II, 1, 412A 30.

body. The remote matter, as we have seen, is that ultimate potency which underlies the whole sequence of evolutionary change. The soul of man cannot be defined without reference to such matter; hence spiritualism is impossible.

The psyche is the form or act of such a body, because matter is actualized only by a determinate form. Life is to its organic body as the structure of an axe is to the iron and wood of which it is made. But here we must notice a most important difference. The iron and wood remain essentially what they are (iron and wood) even after they have been given the form of an axe. This form actualizes a secondary, accidental capacity of the iron and the wood to sustain accidents. It does not actualize a first capacity of matter to be under this or that substantial form. But life is not the second act of something that already exists. It is not an accidental but a substantial form.[6]

This is what is meant by the first act, that which first brings matter into existence as a substance which can then sustain accidents. Before a human being can sleep and eat and move and perform the second acts of life, he must already be alive in that first act of matter which makes him a living person. This first act came into being with the person and remains in act as long as the person lives, even when he is asleep, or as we say inactive (in second act). Even when a person is sleeping or resting or vegetating, he is performing these second acts as a man. This first act of being the person we are, is always in act. It cannot be discontinued without destroying the very being of the man.

The psyche is therefore the formal structure, the most important part of certain natural substances which exist in themselves. In man this formal structure is a composite whole consisting of several formal parts. Human nature includes the form of *physical substantiality* which is able to spread out its matter in an order of quantitative parts. In addition it must include the structure of *life* which produces certain differentiated organs and supports the faculties of nutrition, growth, and reproduction. It must also include an *animal nature* supporting the faculties of sensation and locomotion. Animal matter, which is possessed by these generic forms, is not yet man; but if it is not already given a further non-rational determina-

[6] Cf. ch. 15, § 2.

tion, it is capable of being endowed with the peculiar form of man, that of rationality, which is able to support the immaterial faculties of intellect and will. Hence materialism is also rejected.

All this is implied in the realistic definition of the living creature man, the *rational animal*[7] which explicitly states only the proximate genus (animal), and the final difference (rational). This complex form of human nature is not four complete forms (physical substantiality, life as such, animality, and rationality) accidentally united, but four partial forms (physical, living, animal, rational) united essentially into the single substance of man. In the extramental substance they are united into one being, possessing these different levels of perfection all at once. The human mind may analyze them out and distinguish them from one another. But in the existent person they are indistinct, but virtually distinguishable. His animality is not one thing, his rationality another, and his substance still another. His substance is corporeal, vital, animal, and rational. Nevertheless it possesses all these perfections in a single composite unity.

In the case of an artificial substance like an axe, the accidental form is superimposed on a matter like wood and steel, which retain their natures in the axe, and even after the axe is destroyed. But the body of a man is not an independent substance merely acting in a human way. It is from the very first a human body dominated by the nature of man. So after death the body no longer remains a human body, as the iron of the axe remains iron even when it is no longer an axe. From these facts we must conclude that the form of man is a natural, evolutionary form which dominates all of its parts and holds undisputed sway over the primary matter from which it has emerged in the process of organic evolution.

But after the axe shape is removed, the iron is able to become an axe. Similarly, the dead body contains prime matter which is able to be possessed by the form of a man. What then, one may ask, is the difference between the two cases? We may answer by pointing out three major differences.

First, the iron can be artificially made into an axe without undergoing any further intermediate transformations. It is the proximate matter of an axe. But the prime matter of the dead body is only the

---

[7] Cf. Aristotle. *Politics* 1253A 10.

remote matter of a man. Before becoming a man it would first have to lose almost all the formal determinations it possesses and then regain another set in the proper order, material substance, life, animal and rational.

Second, since shape is only an accidental quality of the iron, it can be turned into an axe without any transformation of its essential nature. The transformation of a dead into a living body, on the other hand, would involve many such essential, evolutionary changes.

Third, axe-making can be performed by the external action of human art alone without the active cooperation of the iron and the myriad causes of nature. But the essential transformations involved in the passage from non-living matter to man require, not only the cooperation of the matter, but the active cooperation of the whole order of nature and its sustaining, efficient causes as well. All this is involved in Aristotle's brief reference [8] to the distinction between such an instrument as an axe, and a natural body.

2. THE MIND-BODY PROBLEM

We must now consider a certain problem which has called forth much speculation in modern times, the so-called mind-body problem. Human nature seems to consist of two very different things— on the one hand, the material body which is made up of extended, physical parts, and the mind which is immaterial and not made up of extended parts with a certain size and shape, but rather of unextended thoughts (such as that of justice, triangularity, and so on). What then, we ask, is the relation between this immaterial mind and the material body? How can something material act on something immaterial, as when the physical energy of a blow produces a mental effect. Where does this energy go? How can the physical influence the non-physical? What link binds them together?

Is it then that there are two trains, a train of physical events and a train of thoughts, each running along parallel to the other but neither one influencing the other? This runs counter to clear evidence of the fact that the mind *can* influence the body. In addition it seems to destroy the unity of the man, who is not two entities running parallel, but a single, individual entity. We may adopt the

[8] *De Anima* 412B 12.

theory of interactionism defended by Descartes and assert that man is two substances, an unextended mind and an extended matter, each of which is able to act upon the other. This view, however, would also seem to destroy the unity of the human person, who is clearly not two substances but one. The only other solutions would seem to be that of materialism which reduces the mental to the physical or that of spiritualism which reduces the physical to the mental. But these both run afoul of the disconcerting empirical evidence which clearly reveals both body and mind in man. Is there any way of arriving at a different view which will escape these difficulties? The realistic analysis of hylomorphic substance [9] provides us with such an alternative view.

As we have seen, the living body and the life that animates it are not two entities joined together in some mysterious way, but *one, single, material entity,* constituted by two distinguishable but inseparable parts—matter (the body) and form (the psyche). Matter cannot exist by itself, for it is indeterminate potency. It can only exist when this potency is given specific determination by form. The bronze matter of the ring cannot be, without being some shape or form. Hence we need not inquire what third thing binds together the bronze and the circular shape in a bronze ring, for matter, or potency, and form are *immediately* joined together, the former being precisely the latter in potency. It is just as absurd to ask what binds together or relates the living body and the life which actually animates it. Matter is by itself a relation to form.[10] The germ cells from which life originates must already be alive in potency, or they could never become actually animated.

Man has evolved from a natural matter. His form is new and different, or things would have remained as they were and there would have been no evolution. His proximate matter must have preceded man, or the evolution would not have been continuous. Just as the individual man proximately originates from germ cells potentially able to receive his individual nature, so did the new species man proximately originate from a preceding, proximate, animal matter, actually brute but able to receive this new specific nature. What we call the individual, human body is the actual matter of human life,

[9] Cf. ch. 13, § 6.
[10] Cf. ch. 13, § 5, p. 291; and § 4.

What we call the individual soul, or psyche, is simply the form that animates it, or brings its vital potency into act. One of the derived parts or faculties of this rational psyche is reason or mind, which though it cannot operate without material conditions, is nevertheless in its own operations immaterial in character.

Our thoughts *as such* have no particular size or shape. They are not triangular or circular. They do not *as such* move about from place to place. Nevertheless we do not have to conclude with Descartes that the mind never moves at all and that, for example, when you fall downstairs, your mind does not fall with you, being an immaterial substance, or a thing that thinks. The mind is not a thing which can act or fall by itself alone, but the immaterial accident of a material thing, namely, a man. If the substance *as a whole* moves, the accidents, even the immaterial accidents, move with it—though it is the substance that moves, not the immaterial accidents as such. Thus once we understand the distinction between matter and form, and that between substance and accident, the mind-body problem offers no insoluble difficulties for a realistic, evolutionary philosophy.

There are a good many misconceptions which lead us to raise the mind-body problem in an exaggerated manner that must defy any rational solution. We must be content with a brief discussion of five of these, in which we shall rely heavily on the treatment of change we have presented in the second and third chapters.

The first of these misconceptions is a false intellectualism which leads us to assume that what we conceive by two separate concepts must exist as two separate substances. We have already noted a case where this assumption is apt to lead us astray.[11] There are many other instances. Thus the convexity of a snub nose can be conceived apart from the nose, but in reality the two are one single nose. In a similar manner it does not follow that because we can conceive the rational part of the psyche in isolation from the animal part, the two exist apart. Outside the mind, in nature, they exist as phases of a single entity.

A second misconception is the tendency to regard the immaterial operations of the mind as capable of functioning all alone without the cooperation of sense, imagination, and their physical organs. As

[11] Cf. ch. 16, § 7, pp. 372 ff.

a matter of fact, as we shall see,[12] cooperation from the physical senses is always necessary.

A third fallacy is that of confusing matter with certain quantitative forms and of thus ignoring its insatiable capacity for further forms. The animal body is then easily regarded as a finished thing rather than as a partially formed matter ready to receive further determinations. As a matter of fact there are many such determinations even apart from the final differentiating form of reason. The neglect of these is a fourth misconception which has had a great deal to do with dualistic statements of the mind-body problem.

On this view man is conceived as an extended, physical body on the one hand, and as a pure, immaterial mind on the other. But this leaves out the other intermediate determinations which lie between these two extremes of psychic structure, a most important misconception. Man is not only a physical body and a mind. In between these he is also a living body which nourishes, grows, and reproduces itself, and an animal body which senses, moves, and desires. It is this whole composite structure of ordered forms, one resting on the other, which finally reaches its climax (dependent upon all the rest for its exercise) in the rational form which produces the psychic faculties.

The failure to distinguish this rational part of the psyche from the faculties is a fifth misunderstanding which plays a role in the widespread dualistic view of human nature. The faculty of understanding is quite separate from other physical faculties of nutrition, growth, and so on. But it must be formally caused by some ruling, formal element in the psyche itself which is always in act. This is united with, not separate from, the other formal elements in that single structure which is the nature of man.

But is it necessary to distinguish this substantial form from the various faculties and powers? This question has been thoroughly discussed in the history of realistic philosophy. Let us now try to summarize the results of this discussion.

3.   THE PSYCHIC FACULTIES

The human psyche is the form of a natural substance, man. It gives the underlying matter a determinate structure which we call

---

[12] Cf. ch. 19, § 4.

human nature. It determines the matter and makes it human, but it does not eliminate it. Hence the concrete entity is still dynamic and unfinished. This union of material indetermination with formal definiteness is expressed in what we call active tendencies. Because of its material basis a natural tendency is vague and indeterminate. It is open to many different alternatives and may become canalized in this way or that. Nevertheless because of its formal basis it is not wholly indeterminate. Each tendency has a certain character that makes it tend in a certain general direction rather than in another.

The ultimate source of this determinacy is the substantial form of the entity, its nature. The ultimate reason why an acorn tends to grow is the formal nature that is present in it. The ultimate reason why an infant tends to act in a human way is the human nature that has gained possession of the matter of which it is composed. In this way the human form or psyche not only operates as a formal cause, but as an efficient cause, producing movements, and also as a final cause, giving these movements a certain, determinate direction.

Since the form of man is complex it is the source of many different tendencies which become apparent in the acts performed by concrete men. These acts belong to five major groups. Wherever human nature is found, one also finds tendencies of these five kinds: towards nutrition, locomotion, sensory awareness, rational apprehension, and appetite of various kinds. The universality of these tendencies shows that they have their first source in human nature itself, the substantial form of the individual man. But this form, though complex, is one, and remains always in act as long as the person is alive. But the active tendencies are quite distinct from one another and need not always be in act. This suggests that the *proximate* source of each tendency is a certain faculty or power, a necessary accident of the human psyche. Let us now examine the reasons for this conclusion.

Some voluntaristic philosophers have held that it is unnecessary to distinguish between the psyche and its various acts, maintaining that the soul *is* its eating, feeling, desiring, thinking, and so on; and that a man *is* what he does, literally making himself by his various acts. But two sets of facts make this view unacceptable. In the first place if it were true, all the acts of a man would be essential to the man and it would be impossible to say that he was a man unless he were desiring or thinking, for example. But this is defi-nitely false. The man remains essentially a man even though he is not desiring or sensing or thinking, for example, when asleep. In the second place if this view were true, we should have to suppose that the man changed essentially whenever he experienced a new sensation or a new thought. But this also is definitely false. From infancy to old age he remains the same man in spite of all the acci-dental changes he experiences. These changes do not destroy the man or bring a new man into being. Hence they must be regarded as accidental in character. Man perfects himself. He does not make himself.

However, a further question arises. Why should we not agree with Ockham [13] and others that the psyche itself, though distinct from its acts, nevertheless *immediately* produces its accidents, eating, feeling, desiring, moving, and thinking, without the mediation of distinct faculties? Is it not simpler to suppose that the psyche *as such* is able to perform all these different acts? An examination of the question will show that this "simpler" view does not accord with the facts.

If the psyche flowed immediately into its various acts, it would itself be a capacity of sensing, thinking, and so on. But a capacity is specified or essentially determined by its act or end. The power to heat is defined by the actual heat in which it terminates, the power to sense by the act of sensation, and so on. Hence if the psyche were immediately capable of its acts, it would be formally specified by nutritive and sensible objects *outside itself*. Though it is com-pleted by acting on such objects, it is not specified by them, but rather in itself absolutely.

Furthermore the psyche can lose a whole faculty like that of sight and still remain essentially what it is. Also, this determining nature of the psyche cannot be a mere capacity or group of capaci-ties, for a living man is not merely something like a seed which is *able* to live, but something always *actually alive* as long as it exists. In addition this *first act* of the living body is always one and the same. But the potencies are very different. No one, for example, could confuse the material capacity to digest physical food with the immaterial capacity to understand, the assimilation of form without matter.

[13] Cf. ch. 1 § 9.

For all these reasons, therefore, we must conclude that the psyche which continues to animate the body as long as it lives, must be distinguished from the five major faculties of human life, none of which is always active and some of which may be lost without the cessation of life. These faculties complete the psyche as *necessary* accidents and are formally caused by it as soon as it is brought into existence. Their efficient causes are the same as those which produced the new individual substance, but they achieve this effect only through the mediation of the substantial form, as Samson brought down the temple only by first breaking the pillar. Thus the faculty is necessarily caused by the substantial form but is formally distinct from it, as the number three is necessarily odd but formally distinct from odd (since only one number is three, but many numbers are odd). Each of these faculties is able to act in a certain way under certain conditions, and thus to complete or to perfect the living substance which already exists.

Certain of the five major faculties we have enumerated are divided into important subdivisions. The vegetative faculty includes the three subfaculties of nutrition, growth, and reproduction. The faculty of sense includes both the internal and the external senses.[14] Reason includes both theoretical and practical understanding.[15] Appetite has two major subdivisions: first, the initial, natural impetus emanating from the substantial form, and thus not a separate faculty, which lies at the root of all human action; and second, the faculties of cognitive appetite, which are elicited by sensory or rational awareness.[16]

Most of these faculties operate in a material manner. Hence they belong to the whole concrete man of soul and body together. But two of them, reason and rational appetite, do not operate in a material manner. Hence they belong to the psyche, though they cannot be brought into action without the cooperation of other physical faculties. These two faculties, reason and will, are of peculiar interest to philosophical anthropology for three reasons. First, they constitute the most distinctively human part of man. Every other phase of human nature is shared with the animals. Second, they are the

[14] Cf. ch. 18, §§ 2, 3, and 4.
[15] Cf. ch. 3, § 1.
[16] Cf. ch. 20, §§ 1–3.

"guiding" or "governing" faculties, not in the sense that they always govern, but in the sense that human life cannot be lived in an adequate or natural manner unless these distinctive faculties guide the rest. Third, the acts of these faculties are immaterial, and thus impervious to the measuring techniques of sensory science. They must be studied, therefore, if at all, by a philosophical discipline which is able to employ rational analysis alone without the aid of quantitative measurement.

The subordinate faculties of locomotion are of little interest to this discipline. They have a purely instrumental importance and are subject to sensory examination and physical explanation. With respect to the nutritive faculty and its subdivisions we may also be very brief. In man this faculty maintains the existence of the individual, material entity, brings it to its proper size, and provides for the reproduction of progeny, thus preserving the species and providing the material foundation for human life on the earth. It nourishes itself, not through external juxtaposition, but through an internal assimilation of the food by means of the digestive system and its complex subordinate agents. It grows in quantity to certain internally determined limits by the assimilation of more food than is required for mere survival. These processes are analogous to those which, as we say, *feed* and increase inorganic entities, as the rainfall feeds and increases the river system. But in vital nutrition and growth the causes lie *within* the organism, external factors being only necessary conditions. In the inorganic world, on the other hand, the causes of maintenance and growth are external.

This vital immanence becomes especially clear in the case of reproduction. External agencies such as eruptions and convulsions of the earth can produce new river systems. But living organisms use the superabundance of assimilated matter to prepare certain parts by which they reproduce themselves. Life alone produces life. These preserving or nutritive functions, of course, belong to the concrete human being. Therefore their organs and operations may be observed by the senses and by the instruments of anatomy and physiology. But so far as their operations are not merely the operations of man, but genuinely *human* operations, they cannot be exhaustively understood without the philosophical techniques which are alone capable of grasping the directive, cognitive faculties of human nature.

As is the case with other animals, the basic lower senses of touch, taste, and smell are primarily concerned with nutrition. That which nourishes is moist or dry, hot or cold, sweet or bitter, and odoriferous. Hence a mobile animal capable of procuring its own nutrition must be sensitive to these properties. By touch primarily and by all the senses accidentally, we feel pleasure in that which satiates a need, and pain in that which lacerates or burns or frustrates us. Thus we not only tend, like non-living things, to predetermined ends, but to many things which we feel by sense to be pleasant and away from many others which we feel by sense to be painful or frustrating. We rightly distinguish this from the tendencies of non-living things as *desire* or *appetite*.[17]

In addition to the fundamental lower senses, man possesses also the higher distance senses of sight and hearing which disclose the qualities of sound and color pattern. These qualities are not essentially connected with the nutritive properties of external things and are of less direct relevance to basic vital needs. But they are connected with other more fundamental properties of things in the external environment, and hence they vastly extend the range of sensitive cognition and the scope of the appetition determined by this awareness.

4. The General Nature of Cognition

Sensitive cognition is partly physical and partly immaterial or cognitive. So far as it is conditioned by physical organs and changes, it is open to the sensory techniques of physiology and physiological psychology. These are capable of describing the complex detail of the various sense organs and the physical agencies and processes which physically influence them. But they cannot gain access to the cognitive aspect, the essential aspect of feeling itself or sensation. Hence from this point of view sensation itself remains an insoluble mystery. Physical vibrations of the tympanum and electrical phenomena in the central nervous system, no matter how complex they may be, are not the same as an *awareness of sound;* and vibrations of the atmosphere are not the same as the sound of which we are aware. Several generations of materialistic epistemology have been utterly unable to convince us that the yellow which we see is nothing but light vibrations of a certain wave length or colorless quanta

[17] Cf. ch. 20, § 1.

of energy. Sensing a colored object is conditioned by such measurable changes, but it certainly involves something more. This can be understood only by a philosophical technique not restricted merely to the measurable quantitative properties of things.

Sensing is a kind of awareness or cognition. Having one's eye colored blue is not to be *aware of* blue. Having one's head vibrate is not to sense sound. The physical presence of something in something physical is not knowledge, though it may condition knowledge. So we must ask first of all what cognition or awareness is. Certainly it is *some* kind of presence. But what kind?

I become aware of what I did not know before. Gaining awareness is a process, but what kind? (1) Physical change always involves some matter already formed (for instance, cold) which is capable of receiving some opposite form (for instance, heat). This process involves the elimination of the privative form (cold) as well as the assimilation of the new form (heat). (2) In this process the matter does not become the form itself, but becomes united with it in a *third entity* which is neither the one nor the other, but a combination of the two. (3) Also we must notice that the form of the matter is numerically distinct from the form of the cause. Thus the heat of the hand is a different heat from that of the fire which warms the hand.[18] Now if we look carefully at the process of acquiring knowledge we shall see that it is quite distinct from physical change in all these three respects.

First of all, we can *feel* warm without first feeling cold, and vice versa. Sensing is a process which does not necessarily involve the destruction of an opposite form in the assimilation of what is sensed. The faculty is free from physical determination and ready to receive any of a large range of forms. This is not so clear in the lower senses where there is a greater dependence on physical change and where we do sense heat much more sharply, for example, when preceded by cold. But in the higher senses of hearing and sight, this freedom from material change is very evident. We do not have to hear a low sound to hear a high sound. We can see red without first seeing green. The sense faculty, though requiring a physical cause, is immaterial and therefore ready to move at once into any form within its range without the prior destruction of a contrary.

18 Cf. ch. 14, § 1.

In the second place, we tend to think of a cognitive faculty as a sort of matter which is able to be physically changed by the object, in the sense that it is impressed by a new form, as the hand is impressed by the heat from the fire. But if this were the case we could never know anything as it is, but only a third thing resulting from the union of the form with the matter of the mind faculty. But so far as we *know,* we do not make any *new,* material entity, but assimilate the form or nature of the thing exactly as it is. This shows that noetic assimilation cannot be the *physical reception* of an impression.

Finally, in the third place, we cannot regard the known object of which we are aware, as the exclusive efficient cause of our awareness of it, for such a physical cause, as we have seen, can at best produce only something similar in an alien, physical matter. When I *know* the heat of the fire I must assimilate something that is formally identical with the heat outside the mind. If I only know something similar to the thing I can never know the thing at all and, indeed, can never step outside of the mind to discover whether anything there is similar or not. Thus in the sensing process there is no longer any formal distinction between the sense quality which is acting and the sense being acted upon, as in physical change, for as Aristotle points out, though what *can* sound and what *can* hear are two very different things, "the actual sounding of the sound and the actual hearing of the sound are *one* actuality." [19]

From this we must conclude that noetic presence is quite distinct from physical presence or subjective inherence with which it is so prevailingly confused.[20] What is physically inherent in me as the result of external, physical causes alone, belongs to me and can never give me knowledge of anything outside of me. Hence to confuse a *sensible species,* like the color yellow, with a physical impression, produced by external vibrations or similar causes, leads us into a subjectivism or solipsism which makes any understanding of the facts of knowledge quite impossible. If to know an object were merely to be physically influenced by that object, every physical thing would know. We must therefore at the very outset recognize the existence of an *immaterial* mode of presence in which it is a

[19] *De Anima* 426A 15.
[20] Cf. ch. 19, § 1.

case, not so much of an external cause making something physically present in me by a material impression, as a case of an internal act of the knowing faculty making an external object noetically present before me by an immaterial species.

We must conclude that what we call knowledge is a mode of existence quite distinct from that physical existence which we so easily sense as soon as we open our eyes, and therefore so easily conjure up in our imaginations. Each material thing physically or subjectively possesses its own nature or form, and physically or subjectively receives the influences of other material agents upon it. These influences, or impressions, are individualized and subjectivized by the physical recipient. Noetic existence is entirely different.

A *noetic* recipient is no determinate form or physical substance. If it were, it would individuate all the impressions it received into its own subjective nature. The noetic recipient must therefore be a pure, indeterminate potency. Such a recipient will receive the form of something outside it *objectively,* or precisely as it is in the external thing, without physically assimilating it and making the form subjectively its own. What is physically present is localized in the matter of this thing. What is noetically present is not so localized, but present objectively or intentionally as the nature of something other than the receiving species. The physical impression *by which* we receive a physical influence has a definite size, and shape, and position. But the noetic impression *by which* we know is an immaterial species, representing the form of something other than itself.

It is through their possession of these extraordinary, cognitive faculties that the higher animals, by sensory awareness, and more especially man, through sensory and rational awareness, are able to overcome the subjective isolation that necessarily attaches to all material entities.[21] Such beings can unite themselves only with those forms and modes of being which are physically inherent in them at a given time. They are thus restricted to the physical dimensions of their matter and are isolated both in space and time from all those entities with which they cannot come into physical contact. The past is absolutely beyond them, since it is dead and gone. The

[21] Cf. ch. 14, § 6.

future is also beyond them, since it is non-existent.[22] They are separated from all the other physical beings which exert no influence upon them. Even when such an influence is received it is at once subjectivized and individuated by the material recipient, so that there is no possibility of genuine union with the other entity as it is in itself. Each material entity is united only with itself, dwelling within its own restricted limits, completely cut off from the rest.

But through cognition this cosmic loneliness is actually overcome. The facts show that even the animals through sense alone can become aware of external entities, and thus unite themselves with things from which they are physically separated. They are able to enjoy, not only their own material forms, but the forms of other entities as well. This indubitable fact cannot be explained in physical terms alone, for things which are physically separate cannot be *physically* united. But cognition is a fact. By sensory cognition the animals can become cognitively united with things which exist at great distances from them. By rational cognition man can become united in this way with all things.

Through his understanding of causal sequences he can make the past and the future noetically present, though they are not physically present. The farthest reaches of the cosmos are open to his understanding, even the immaterial knowledge of his fellow men. In this way man can overcome the cosmic loneliness and subjectivism which he shares with all the other material creatures and can become (noetically) all things. The physically insignificant, human individual possesses this amazing capacity, and it is the source of what we call the dignity of man. From this possession of rational insight proceed all the distinctively human operations: science, historical knowledge, prediction of the future course of events, rational control over nature, and cooperative action with his fellows which can be achieved through rational understanding and agreement alone.

The most important task confronting any anthropology is to explain these extraordinary facts. But they confront us with a basic issue. Are we to abandon those materialistic prejudices which arise from our greater familiarity with extended physical things and try to grapple with these non-material facts of cognition? Or are we

[22] Cf. ch. 15, § 7.

going to cling to our prejudices and try to disregard or distort the facts? If we are empiricists we shall try to shake loose from our prejudices and really follow the facts.

Let us, then, turn to an examination of the three most important faculties of human nature, sensory awareness (Chapter 18), rational awareness (Chapter 19), and finally the appetites called forth by these modes of cognition (Chapter 20).

REFERENCES

Recommended Reading

Aquinas, *Treatise on Man, Summa Theologica,* Part I, Qu. 75–78; and Aristotle, *De Anima,* Book II, chaps. 1–4, 12 to 424B 3.

Suggested Reading

1. Aquinas, *Treatise on Man, Summa Theologica,* Part I, Qu. 75; Aristotle, *De Anima,* Book II, chaps. 1–2; and Plato, *Phaedo* 91–95.
2. Aquinas, *Treatise on Man, Summa Theologica,* Part I, Qu. 76; Aristotle, *De Anima,* Book II, 412B 6–9, 313A 3–9, 414A 4–29. For a statement of the dualistic position, cf. Descartes, *Meditations* VI. For parallelism, cf. Spinoza, *Ethic,* Part III, Prop. I–II.
3. Aquinas, *Treatise on Man, Summa Theologica,* Part I, Qu. 77–78; and Aristotle, *De Anima,* Book II, chaps. 3–4.
4. Aquinas, *Treatise on Man, Summa Theologica,* Part I, Qu. 78, Art. 3 and Qu. 85, Art. 2; Aristotle, *De Anima,* Book II, chap. 12 to 424B 5; and Plato, *Phaedo* 65–66.

Chapter 18

SENSORY COGNITION

IN the preceding chapter (§ 4) we contrasted physical assimilation with noetic assimilation. The one results in a new hylomorphic entity, the other in nothing new at all except the elevation of something already existent into a new level of immaterial presence. Bearing this distinction in mind, we must now turn to the more rudimentary type of human cognition which involves both a physical and a noetic assimilation bound together in one. This is the process we call *sensing* or *feeling*.

Sensing is a mode of awareness or cognition. In sensing we assimilate the form without the matter *objectively*, thus becoming aware of something as it is—external to the physical subject of the awareness. But this does not mean, in the case of sensation, that physical influences from the object are not also necessary. For example, the physical warmth of the fire must physically heat my hand if I am to feel its heat, but feeling the heat is not the same as having my finger burned, or the burning stick would also feel, which is absurd. The physical influence received in the skin is not the sensation of heat but the medium by which this is carried to the sense organ under the skin. Moreover as for the actual sensation it is an act of the temperature sense which is resident in the sense organ, which abstracts the form of heat from the physical changes of the skin medium, and thus makes the heat of the fire noetically present as long as the fire keeps influencing the organ. We must therefore distinguish five factors in any sensation.

1. FIVE FACTORS IN THE STRUCTURE OF SENSATION

These five factors are: first, some quality capable of producing a similar physical effect on some transmitting medium in contact with the sense organ; second, the transmission of the physical species to the organ via the medium; third, the abstraction of this form from its matter by the sense faculty in the organ; fourth, the sensible species thus abstracted (the sound middle C, the color yellow, the taste of sweetness) ; and fifth, the material object which is made immaterially present, or known, by this species. If we omit any of these essential factors the facts of sensory awareness slip through our fingers.

If we try to get along with the first, second, and fifth, alone, i.e., with physical causes plus the physical effects in the organ, we have an impression subjectively inhering in the organ which is at best only like the external quality, and therefore not knowledge but only physical assimilation. This kind of an explanation is best called *representationalism*. It was held by Suarez, Descartes, and many of their modern followers. It is open to two objections. First, according to it, we can never know the object at all but only something supposedly similar to it representing it in the mind. But how can we ever jump out of our minds to compare them with what is outside, and thus establish any similarity? In the second place, how do we know the impression which inheres in us? Either its *physical* presence is its *noetic* presence, or it is not. If we say the former we cannot explain two sets of evident facts. The first is that a nonliving thing, like a stick of wood, in which heat is physically present, certainly does not sense the heat. The second is that many qualities, like ultraviolet light, may physically inhere in us without our sensing them. So we are forced to admit that the mere physical presence of the impression in us does not constitute knowledge. But then we have simply postponed the whole problem and have not explained it at all. Representationalism is impossible.

Some epistemologists have jumped to the other extreme, omitting the first and second factors altogether and trying to get along with the third, fourth, and fifth, alone. The mind, they insist, can know external objects just as they are, without any mediation at all. The sense faculty all by itself immediately identifies itself with any sensible object. But this view is open to a whole range of objections. First, why then should we not sense everything with any sense, though the facts are that each sense senses only one kind of thing, as vision, color; and hearing, sound. We also know that there are many things in the external world which we do not sense at all, like ultraviolet light. Second, many facts point to the causal dependence of sensation upon physical influences emanating from the object. For example, we cannot see colors at night. Finally, if it is simply the nature of sense to be aware of anything as it is, why should our senses give us only partial perspectives of things which are so often the occasion for erroneous judgment, as in the case of motion, size, and the other common sensibles. This view cannot account for the relativity and deceptiveness of sense.

Sensation necessarily and essentially involves all five factors. First of all, there must be a quality physically inhering in something external, as the colored paint inhering in the wall. Then secondly, this quality must be physically transmitted and impressed on the sense organ, as light energy impresses the retina. Third, the faculty of sight, while so acted upon, must be capable of abstracting the form of the impression from the matter, inasmuch as the retina not only is physically affected by the red light from the wall, but also assimilates the redness, or what we call *the color red,* without assimilating the paint in which the red exists outside the eye, and the vibrations, or quanta of energy, by which this form of redness is transmitted to the eye. Fourth, there is the sensible species, or form of redness itself, quite distinct from the physical changes and vibrations. It is *by* this sensible species that we see the external red wall, for this form, not being materialized, is formally identical with the red of the wall and not merely a supposedly similar representation. Finally, in the fifth place, there is the object which is seen by this species, the wall *qua* colored.

The relation between the activated sense organ and its object is not merely one of similarity. If so, we could not distinguish sensing from being materially changed, since any matter, in being changed, assimilates a similar form. But now the relation is the peculiar noetic relation of identity. As Aristotle says [1] "the activity of the sensible object and that of the percipient sense is one and the same activity." This assimilation of the form itself is knowledge or awareness. We do not become physically colored, but *by* the sensible species, we *sense* the color on the wall. By clearly recognizing these five factors we can solve the traditional difficulties concerning sensation and develop an intelligible and coherent explanation which may, indeed, prove surprising to a materialist, but neither surprising nor astounding to one who will think seriously of the actual facts. Let us consider some of these difficulties.

[1] *De Anima* II, 425B 27.

For example, one may object that this is merely a restatement of the ancient view that external objects are constantly peeling off little replicas of themselves and transmitting them to our sense organs through various media. Is this view not absurd?

Some of the ancient materialists did hold a view of this sort, that full-fledged images of things were emitted in this way and finally impressed physically on a sense organ. This view is absurd, but the realistic theory differs from it in two vital respects. In the first place, it holds that what is transmitted is not a tiny quantitative replica of the thing, but some quality (like color or sound) carried by physical energy to the organ. In the second place, it does not identify the sensation with the physical reception of this qualified energy, but rather with the abstraction of the quality from the energy by the sense faculty. This view is not absurd.

At this point the modern materialist will be apt to object that what is transmitted to the sense organ is not a color, a sound, or a fragrance, but rather colorless photons, soundless air vibrations, or tiny odorless particles of matter. The colors, sounds, and odors are merely the physical effects of these on the sense organ. Outside the mind there is nothing but a colorless, soundless world of quantitative structure, measured by science. This popular view, however, is subject to very serious difficulties.

In the first place, how can that which is purely quantitative and lacking all quality cause quality? Non-A cannot cause A. This is impossible. So we are forced to the conclusion that when purely quantitative influences impinge upon the purely physical sense organ, there is a sudden creative welling-up of the sounds and colors we think we sense in the external world. Of course they are only subjective. The surface of the water is really there; the blue color is in me. But unfortunately the surface is inextricably entwined with the color. So far as the basic facts of sensation are concerned the surface is certainly where the blue is. So if we erroneously suppose that the blue is a mere creative construction, there is no reason for supposing that the surface also and the quantitative structure of things, are not also creative constructions.

Materialism, if it is consistent, must lead to complete subjectivism. Then all sensory knowledge will be undermined, including the quantitative information of science which rests ultimately upon sensory observation. The only way of avoiding this impasse and of defending scientific knowledge, is to accept the view that the so-called secondary qualities are just as real and as independent of the mind as the so-called primary qualities, though they are more superficial and not so fundamental in the actual constitution of things as are the primary. The blue surface of the water is really there. This quality is transmitted to the sense organ through the intervening medium.

But if this is so, one may say, then the surrounding media will be full of qualities such as colors, sounds, and odors. Is this not absurd? Not unless our whole experience of things is basically askew. Do we not experience the stained-glass cathedral as full of colored light? Do we not hear the thunder rolling in the clouds? Do we not become aware of the scent which pervades the whole garden? Before they reach the sense organ these qualities are of course physical, that is, they are borne by the material media they characterize. But the physical light in the room is really yellow, the air vibrations really sounding, and the rose particles in the garden really scented, even when no sense organ is present. Quality exists in the extra-mental world, as well as the quantitative structure measured by scientific techniques. The sense faculty is able to separate the quality from the matter which bears it, and to feel it as yellow, as sounding, or as fragrant.

All our information concerning the external world must come to us through the senses. This objective information is divided into the following three major classes. First, there is what we actually or strictly sense by each sense. But this is divided into two subclasses: (1) what we sense *immediately* and (2) what we sense *through some mediation,* or as the result of sensing something else. Then, there is (3) what we sense only by accident or association. We shall now consider each of these divisions, starting first of all with (1), viz., the proper, immediate object of each sense.

2. The Immediate Object of the External Senses

As we have already noted, all sensation involves both a physical and an immaterial reception of the species in the organ. These two modes of reception determine two distinct types of sensation, according to whether one or the other preponderates. The matter which is subject to physical alteration of one kind is also subject to the opposite kind. The hand can be heated or cooled. The tongue can be sweetened or soured. There are two extremes and a mean state. The matter is susceptible to such an influence and is constantly being moved up and down from one condition to the opposite, or lapsing into quiescence, if there is no change.

As Aristotle points out, the more rudimentary lower senses are more closely connected with such physical change. Thus the temperature sense can feel hot or cool by contrast with the preceding state. There is a certain physical mean, deviations from which can be felt. But if a deviation persists it can no longer be felt and is confused with the mean. It is the *change* to a certain form or state that we feel, rather than the state itself. Since this physical change is *in* the organ, these sensations are more subjective than objective. The species is only partially abstracted from the matter and is still confused with its subjective vehicle. Thus the flavors we taste are closely associated with two opposites, sweet and sour. The sense stands at a normal mean which may be upset. We taste a change to sweet rather than sweetness itself, and the sweet taste cloys or vanishes after a short time. The taste is subjectively felt to be localized in the mouth. This is true of touch, the fundamental sense, whose organs are spread throughout the body and which always senses its object as physically localized pressure on a certain determinate part. This is also true to a lesser degree of smell.

When we come to the higher distance senses of hearing and sight, however, we find that the intentional, objective element preponderates—being clearly disassociated from the physical alterations which we do not feel at all except in the case of very violent stimulations. Normally the action of the object is not sensed, and the sensation itself not localized. This is because the intentional species of the object is more clearly and sharply received apart from the matter. A sound or color is not opposed by a contrary between which the sense continues to oscillate, but we either sense or we do not. No opposite has to be removed before we can assimilate a new species, for the indeterminate potency of sense has become more free from material conditions. The mean is a *psychic* mean, almost free from any material determinacy, which can be upset only by destruction of the organ.

This immaterial, and therefore indeterminate, potency is actu-alized at once into a determinate species of sound or color without any obtrusive physical change. The species is received rather than a motion to the species. Hence we can go on hearing the same sound or seeing the same color without any diminution of awareness such as is manifest in temperature feeling. Finally, this relative freedom from matter makes vision manifestly the most objective of the senses. Since the pure immaterial species is received, we no longer localize it in the retina. This is true to a lesser extent of hearing.

It is now necessary to recognize the following senses, each with its own proper object. First, there is touch, which apprehends pres-sure or physical resistance; second, the temperature sense, also widely distributed through the body, whose object is hot and cold; third, taste, localized in the tongue as a special development of touch, which apprehends flavors; smell, localized in the nasal passages, which apprehends odors; fifth, hearing, an objective sense, whose object is sound; and finally, sight, the highest and most ob-jective of all the external senses, whose proper object is color.

Since sensation necessarily involves first of all the physical action of something external impinging on the sense organ, the immediate (though incomplete) object of sense is always this physical impres-sion plus its resulting *species impressa*. As a physical impression it is in the organ. As a psychic impression (species) it is a representa-tion or image of something outside. Thus in the case of touch, this immediate object of sensation is physical warmth somewhere in the skin, plus the species representing it. In the case of taste it is a combined chemical and psychic effect brought about by substances in the saliva, when they reach the nerve endings which connect with the brain. In the case of hearing it is the sound plus the vibrations in the ear which touch the acoustic nerve. In the case of vision it is the color pattern which is physically spread out on the retina.

As Aristotle pointed out, following Plato,[2] these immediate ob-jects of sense are infallible—as so received. To deny them is to deny an evident fact. It is stupid to tell a man with a bitter taste on the tongue that he has no such taste, or to dispute with some-one seeing yellow as to whether he is seeing yellow. To possess the sense of taste is to possess the ability to discriminate between sweet

[2] Cf. *Theaetetus* 152.

and sour. To be mistaken in discriminating is simply not to possess the sense at all. But we can go even further than this.

What is received in the sense organ is not only a *physical,* inherent effect of the cause, but a psychic species, formally identical with the form of the contemporaneous cause, and hence an adequate image of this cause. Thus the lower senses cannot be mistaken in their awareness of the proper objects which act contemporaneously upon them. The wood now pressing my finger is really hard; the sugar I now taste is really sweet; and the rose I smell is really fragrant. In the case of vision and hearing, whose objects often lie at great distances and which act on the sense by a long series of intermediate, transmitting agencies, I can be sure that the sound now acting on my ear is really sounding and the color pattern now impinging on my retina is really yellow as I sense it.

Here two contrary mistakes are to be avoided. I must not fall into sensationalism and suppose that the pure yellow I sense exists in the air outside my eye precisely as I sense it, for outside my apprehension it exists materially in a different way, inseparably combined with the light energy of which it is only a distinguishable aspect. But on the other hand, I must not fall into materialism or subjectivism and suppose that the yellow is only in me and that the physical light is not yellow at all and the rose not really fragrant. The fragrance of the air may not be an important phase of the physical structure of the air. The meteorologist may therefore ignore it and pass it by. But it is really there for all that. The wood now pressing my finger is really harder than the wood now pressing my other finger, and the surface of the rose is really red.

The external senses are trustworthy with respect to their immediate, *proper* objects. They apprehend certain surface qualities of the physical things that act on them. But we must carefully note the crucial distinction between the *immediate* object of these senses and their *mediate* object. It is most important at this point to recognize that noetic immediacy is not to be identified with physical inherence or even with physical contact with which it is often confused.

Immediacy is an epistemological term. It refers to that object which is apprehended directly by the faculty without its first having to apprehend another object. In this sense of objective immediacy the proper object of each sense is immediately apprehended. But every sense requires a medium through which a quality is physically transmitted and a psychic or sensible species by which the extramental object is apprehended. This gives rise to certain questions.

Is this true of touch, we may ask? Is the skin not in direct physical contact with what we touch? So in this case at least, is it not true that sensation is reduced to physical contact? This is not true. As Aristotle first pointed out,[3] the skin is not the organ of touch but rather an internal medium, spread like an elastic membrane over the body through which external pressures are conveyed to the sense organs inside. If being pressed were the same as the feeling of pressure this pencil would now be feeling my finger pressing it. This of course is absurd. The organs of touch in my finger not only receive a sharp physical pressure, but they can also separate the quality from the physical impact and feel the sharpness of the pressure. But here another question arises.

Is not the separated, psychic species just as much *in* the organ as the physical impression? Why then is the psychic species a representation of something else, whereas the physical impression is not? Here is the answer. To the degree in which the psychic species is freed from the individuating matter of the receiving organ, it is no longer the physical form of this material subject alone, but equally the intentional form of the object now influencing the organ. Hence it represents the latter.

Does this then mean that the sensible species is a pure, universal form freed from all material conditions whatsoever? No, a pure universal species is never attained by sense. Such a faculty can free a received quality from its own matter, and thus receive it objectively and intentionally rather than subjectively and materially. But it cannot free this quality from the physical conditions with which it is objectively connected. It is not the color alone that acts on the medium and then on the eye, but the colored apple, having a certain size, a certain shape, being in motion or at rest, and lying at a certain angle from the eye. Sensory abstraction is not powerful enough to free the species from all these other forms with which it is materially combined in the object. It always apprehends a concrete cluster of mediate properties together with its immediate ob-

[3] *De Anima,* Book II, 423A 6 ff.

ject. It is to these *mediate* objects of sensation that we must now turn.

3. The Mediate Object of the External Senses

Since the qualities which we sense immediately do not exist all alone by themselves but only as the qualities of physical bodies in the world of nature, we cannot sense these qualities without also becoming mediately aware of certain physical traits which always sustain them. The most important of these are continuous quantity, divided quantity or number, place, change of place, rest, figure, and position. Every physical body possesses the intrinsic attribute of extension. This extension lies in some *place* surrounded by other extended bodies. The body either remains within this place or changes its place by locomotion. The extension must be terminated by some definite shape or *figure*, and its parts must be ordered in some position relative to one another. No external sense can apprehend its proper, immediate object without also becoming aware of certain of these underlying traits, which are the common objects of all the external senses, and are therefore called the *common sensibles*.

Since the time of Locke it has become customary to refer to these as *the primary qualities*, and to what we have called the proper objects as *the secondary qualities*. This usage should now be abandoned, as it is connected with the assumption that the primary qualities of size, shape, etc., are primarily *sensed* exactly as they are in the thing, whereas the secondary qualities are merely subjective constructs. Thus Locke held that sensations of the primary qualities are "resemblances" of something really in the extra-mental thing, whereas sensations of the secondary qualities do not resemble anything outside the mind at all.[4] The first part of this assumption is definitely false and the second, if true, must lead to an unmitigated subjectivism which is incompatible with the existence of knowledge.

Hence it is better to steer clear of these materialistic and subjectivistic connotations by referring to fundamental, extensional properties, so far as they are sensed, as the "common sensibles," because they are sensed by all the external senses in common. As

[4] *Essay Concerning Human Understanding*, Bk. II, ch. 8, 15 ff.

over against Locke, the realist maintains that these properties are not directly and immediately apprehended by sense but only indirectly and very imperfectly through the mediation of the proper sensibles. This conclusion is verified by three lines of evidence.

First, if the extensional properties were the proper object of any sense, this would either be one sense or many. But neither alternative is possible in the light of the actual evidence. If they are the peculiar object of one sense, we must ask which one? Not touch, because we also *see* size and shape. We can even *hear* a great tidal wave rushing towards us and distinguish it from a small one. Are they then the proper object of all the different senses? This is impossible, for two senses with the same proper object would be one and the same sense. We must conclude, therefore, that the common sensibles are not the proper object of any sense but that they are rather sensed by all through the mediation of the proper objects.

Second, there is the evident fact, ignored by Locke, that these common sensibles are improperly or delusively sensed. I see the round penny as an ellipse. Even touch cannot inform me infallibly as to whether my train or the one next to me in the station is really moving. But it is impossible for a sense to be mistaken with respect to its own proper immediate object. If anything is to be apprehended at all something must be infallibly apprehended as its proper or peculiar object. But no single sense apprehends these extensional properties infallibly. Hence they are not the proper object of any sense.

One may argue that color is inseparable from surface, that color cannot be sensed without surface, and that therefore the latter is as much a proper object of sight as is the former. But the answer is that surface can be apprehended in abstraction from color, as witness geometry, which studies extension without considering any color at all. This shows that we are dealing with two properties which are *formally* distinct, though no doubt materially inseparable in the physical thing.

Finally, in the third place, we may argue from what we know of the composite structure of the physical thing. Extension is intrinsic to the thing. It is also passive and of itself inactive.[5] Nevertheless it underlies all the superficial properties and acts of the

[5] Cf. ch. 15, § 4, pp. 334–335.

body. A physical thing must be first spread out in quantitative parts before it can support qualities or powers or acts of any kind. Our senses must be physically influenced by such superficial properties in order to become aware at all. Hence they must apprehend these surface qualities first and then, through them, gain a secondary but not infallible awareness of the more basic extensional structure. What is primary in the order of knowing is secondary in the order of being, and vice versa.

We cannot see color without also seeing the surface on which the color is physically extended. We cannot sense a sound without also sensing the direction from which the sound comes, and whether it is moving (like the buzz of an airplane motor above us) or at rest. The object I taste is in my mouth, and nothing can press against me without being spread over a certain continuous surface with definite limits. But though I do actually sense these extensional traits, I do not sense them *immediately,* but only *mediately* by means of the proper object of each sense.

Thus I see extended surfaces only by first seeing the color of the surface, *pure* quantity or extension being utterly invisible. Also I feel the round shape of the bowl of my pipe only by first feeling its resistance to touch. There is an extended body of air always stretched over the skin of my hand. But I cannot *feel* this unless a movement of air presses it against my skin. Only those shapes which are attached to physical bodies, capable of exerting pressure upon me, can be felt by touch.

Thus the sense of touch is of no value to the geometrician, who studies abstract shapes apart from the sensible matter in which they naturally inhere. He grasps this pure geometrical structure by reason and imagination, not by sense. If any single sense could do this, quantity would not be apprehended by any of the other senses except by accident, as we see (by accident) the sweet sugar. But as a matter of fact we *do* sense quantity, number, motion, and the other common qualities by all the senses, though not *immediately* as sight sees color and taste tastes flavor, by abstracting the property to which it is susceptible. We sense these common qualities *mediately,* through the different effects on our sensations of their proper qualities. These felt differences are the common qualities.

Here we must remember that no quality can act without that which sustains it, and the proper qualities, like color, flavor, and so on, are invariably sustained by common sensible qualities. Hence a large and a small patch of the same color affect sight differently, and a moving sound and a resting sound affect hearing differently; impressing a different species. We sense these differences in the impressed species, and thus actually sense the common qualities through the mediation of the proper qualities. But this *mediated* sensation is not infallible.

Very often the proper qualities do not correspond to the common qualities underlying them, which we sense only through the former. Then we may receive a so-called erroneous impression. A real quantitative discontinuity may be covered up by painting over interstices to give the appearance of continuity, and a genuine continuity may be made to look discontinuous by a difference of surface color. Since magnitude affects sense only by the way in which it physically affects the sense organ, it will be apprehended, not as it is in itself, but only in relation to the organ. Thus a large entity at a great distance exerts only a small influence on the organ, and will be apprehended as small. A penny in itself round, but sending an elliptical bundle of rays to the eye, will be apprehended as an ellipse. An object really at rest, but moving in relation to the organ, will be apprehended as moving, and so forth. The common qualities in general are never apprehended as they are in themselves but only as they physically affect the sensitive organism in relation to its magnitude, position, and motion. This occasions many erroneous judgments and leads to the widespread view that all sensation is relative, and therefore deceptive. But such a conclusion is not necessary.

As we have seen, the proper qualities, though very superficial and unstable, are really sensed as they exist in the thing. That which we sense most accurately is least important in the structure of the thing, whereas that which is more important and more stable in the thing we sense least adequately. But the situation is by no means hopeless, for all the senses in common, sense the common sensibles. Therefore with respect to them, one sense may be used to correct the relative apprehensions of another. Thus by approaching the distant object and touching it, I can discover its true size and shape.

By the kinaesthetic sensations from my muscles I can usually tell whether it is I or the thing that is really moving.

Far from forcing us to abandon our natural realism this relativity of the common sensibles really confirms it, for were we actually condemned to a necessary subjectivism, we should never be aware of this fact and would certainly never be able to correct it, as we clearly are, by further experience and the use of one sense (particularly touch) to check another. Each sense, unless diseased, gives us an infallible awareness of its proper object. All the senses together give us an adequate awareness of the more important common sensibles.

4. THE INTERNAL SENSES

a. THE COMMON SENSE. Sensation is a kind of change, or the actualization of a capacity. As we have seen (Chapter 16, § 3), nothing is capable of moving itself, for this would require the same thing to be both actual and potential all at once, a contradiction. Hence the capacity to see color must be actualized by some color distinct from itself, and in general we can say that no sensation clearly senses itself. But we certainly do sense our own sensations. For example, we sense that we are seeing or not seeing; we feel ourselves to be hearing. Not only this, but we are able to distinguish the yellow color we are now seeing from the bitter flavor we are now tasting. This is beyond the capacity of either of the two senses alone, for sight sees only color, and taste tastes only flavor. For these two reasons we must recognize the existence of a *common sense* distinct from the external senses, but intimately bound up with them.

This sense apprehends the sensations of the other senses, so far as they are actually affecting the subject here and now. In doing this it also senses the harmony or disharmony of the object with the apprehending faculty, pleasure or pain in the case of the lower physical senses, beauty or ugliness in the case of the higher distance senses of sight and hearing. It is true that every cognitive act, including that of sense, is attended by a vague and imperfect awareness of itself. But the external senses are unable to turn to their own acts as objects, and so to become clearly aware of themselves. Thus we must distinguish between the external sensations, the pleasures or pains completing them and the *clear* awareness of these feelings provided by the internal, *common sense.* The failure to make this distinction has led certain modern idealistic anthropologists to deny unconscious sensations and unconscious pleasures and pains. But this denial is countered by many phenomena discovered and rediscovered by modern schools of psychology.

As the Aristotelian tradition has emphasized, it is perfectly possible that certain sensations and tendencies and the feelings attending them, may never reach the *common sense,* because of interrupted communication and the direction of attention elsewhere. Such sensations therefore may never be clearly felt. With increasing anatomical knowledge it has become clear that the seat of this common sense is in the brain. The external sensations are carried by nervous currents to this central seat, where they are felt by a central awareness, which senses the external sensations and distinguishes them and their various objects from one another.

b. FANTASY.   In addition to the common sense, man, in common with other animals, possesses another internal faculty of extreme importance, *fantasy,* or imagination. This faculty performs three functions. First, it is susceptible to any sensations received by the common sense which it is able to preserve as permanent dispositions within itself. Secondly, it is able to recall them, or reproduce them, even when their objects are absent. Such images may be internally excited by physiological disturbance, by habitual association, and, in man, by the will.

This ability to represent any sense object even when absent clearly distinguishes fantasy from the external senses and the common sense, which act only when their objects are physically present, and indicates that it is a higher faculty with a higher degree of immateriality. Nevertheless in spite of this greater independence from external, physical action, its object is always singular and concrete, never universal. Hence it is a faculty of sense not reason, with which it is unfortunately often confused.

In the third place, fantasy is able to combine sensations together and to separate them into new combinations, never actually sensed together. In this way it is constantly completing our partial sensations into complete *perceptions,* as when we actually *sense* only the front of a house but with the aid of imagination and the store of images gained in past experience, we actually *perceive* the sides and back of the house which we do not sense except *by accident* (i.e., with the aid of another faculty).

A large part of what we now call *mental training* consists in teaching our fantasy to provide us with imaginative constructions which really accord with the nature of things, for since they are not produced by the physical object itself, they may of course be false. Such false images are either *illusions,* which complete a sensed object in an erroneous manner, as when I perceive a night shadow as a specter; or retinal spots, as spots in the sky; or *hallucinations,* which are complete in themselves, as in dreams.

In waking hours when our faculties are functioning normally, the common sense is able to distinguish the operations of one faculty from the operations of another, but when the common sense is dulled by sleep or by the action of drugs, it no longer functions clearly and is unable to distinguish external sensations themselves from their fantasies. Such *hallucinations* occur rarely in waking life unless our apprehensive faculties are completely deranged. Perceptual illusions, on the other hand, are very common. They are the price all animals pay for the possession of an imaginative faculty under their own control. But the advantage far outweighs the disadvantage.

A plant is unable to learn new habits, but runs through a predetermined cycle of acts. But an animal, first gaining sensory awareness of external objects and storing them up in the imagination, learns to respond to them even when they are not physically present, and thus greatly to extend the range of its appetites and active adjustments to the world around it. In human education nothing is more important than the training of the imagination under the guidance of reason, the highest apprehensive faculty, to form true pictures of man himself; of the most important objects in the world; and of the world itself. By this means the range of our sensations is enormously extended and their partial and distorted perspective corrected to correspond with the actual nature of things.

One of the main functions of what we now call the *fine arts* [(*mimetic arts,* according to the ancients) is to guide this process of image-formation in line with the truth. When properly trained in this way the sensitive imagination needs only a slight, sensory cue to provide a much more complete and accurate picture of the real situation than sense alone could ever provide. Without such images quickly supplied by fantasy, the higher faculty of reason would be helpless, because it is from such images that reason abstracts its universal concepts. What we often call *thought* is not intellect alone but the abstractive faculty of reason, which shines like a light on the stream of fantasies constantly supplying it with material objects to think about.

c. THE ESTIMATIVE FACULTY AND MEMORY. The congruence between each sense and its appropriate object results in the pleasure which crowns its activity. But all animals, in addition to this, have an internal faculty which is able to grasp the agreement or disagreement of the object with the whole nature of the animal, its helpfulness or injuriousness. Thus the bird, as we say, *by instinct* knows how to build its nest; and certain insects by this *estimative faculty* know how to paralyze their prey instead of killing it, so that it may be preserved as food for their larvae. This estimative capacity is not acquired but results from the nature of the species.

Animals also possess the faculty of *sensitive memory,* which is quite distinct from the capacity of fantasy to reproduce an image. By memory we become aware of a single, sensible thing as having been sensed before. We recognize the thing as already cognized. The images preserved in fantasy are not preserved in any such order of before and after. They can be imaginatively reproduced without being remembered. The most important feature of memory is its selectivity. The animal *remembers* only those images which represent something useful or harmful to itself.

It is this subjective reference which necessitates the order of *before* and *after,* for the activities of the natural organism succeed one another in time, and what is useful must therefore be brought into relation with this succession of acts. Memory is a treasury, not of sensory images, but rather of *estimations* of what has been harmful or advantageous to the animal. They are called internal, because they do not apprehend these things as they are in themselves but only pragmatically as they fit into our internal feelings and foster or frustrate our internal subjective life.

In man, instinct is always further elaborated by rational cogitation, which is able to devise further means supplementing instinctive estimation. The possession of the higher faculty of reason also enables man to supplement sensitive memory, which happens all at once without voluntary control, by the higher activity of *reminiscence,* which, under the guidance of reason and will, seeks *voluntarily* to recover what has fallen from memory.

5. PERCEPTION AND SENSORY ILLUSION

Each sense is restricted to a *proper* object of its own. Thus we *see* color, we *hear* sound, and we *taste* flavors, and so on. But as we have noted, there is also in man and the brutes a faculty (imagination) which is able to preserve and to reproduce these psychophysical impressions, or images, when their object is physically absent and some other is physically present. My sense impression of the white object now before me is an image identified with something other than itself, though I tend to ignore its presence as long as the object is physically before me. Hence I readily acquiesce in the view that there is only the object plus some physical impression received in the sense organ. When however this physical change can be excited by the imagination without any external influence at all, then the psychic character of the disturbance is evident, for it refers to something other than itself. Therefore it is correctly recognized as an image, and the faculty which calls it up as the imagination.

When sugar is seen, the imagination tends to reproduce the sensation of sweet, which was in the past experienced with the vision. When as the result of long experience such diverse sensations become firmly associated, so that one is at once invariably supplied with the image of the other, we speak as though one and the same sense were apprehending both objects. Thus we say that we *see* the *sweet* sugar or the *hard,* yellow wall, and that we touch the *fragrant* rose. Of course we do not *see* the sweet or the hard either properly or mediately. What is at once given by a distinct, apprehensive faculty is sensed only *by accident,* and a vast amount of what we ordinarily say we *sense* is really only *perceived* in this way by association.

For example, it is only by accident that I sense objects as existing wholly external or independent of me. As we have seen, all sensation involves the physical transmission of an external influence to the sense organ. What I sense, strictly speaking, therefore, is neither external nor internal, but rather an internal psychophysical image of something outside. Thus it is only *by accident* that I hear the external violin.

What I hear strictly speaking is the psychophysical sound image of a co-present pattern of physical sound outside, now acting on my ear. But in past experience I have learned to move my head slightly, noting the position in which the sound is most intense and thus judging the direction from which it comes. Also I have learned to associate such sounds with other visual and tactile patterns. It is only by correlating all this independent past experience together, that by accident I perceive the sound as coming from the violin outside me, and learn to distinguish *by accident* between the sound of the violin and the sound in me as I hear it.

The apprehension of the external object as such at a distance from me is attained only by the correlation of independent sensations of visual accommodation, touch, and so on. Also, as we have seen, I sense only a continuous, relative motion. The motion of the thing independent of me is again, strictly speaking, not sensed but only perceived by accident. The causal structure of things— potency, the substantial form, the efficient action of one thing on another, and the relation of means to end (final causation) —are *strictly* apprehended by reason alone. Hence it is only by accident that we sense the capacity of the wood to be burned, the living man standing before me, the influence of the knife in cutting the orange, and the orange as a means of satisfying hunger.

Each sense apprehends its proper object infallibly and the common sensibles only relatively. But with respect to what it apprehends *by accident* an external sense may be completely mistaken. Thus I may apprehend the whiteness of the object before me, its oblong shape in relation to my eye, and may remember my previous apprehension of the sweet taste of sugar. But the combination of these two apprehensions, in my sensing *by accident* that this white object is *sugar,* is in no sense infallible. It may be only a piece of pasteboard. But this by no means justifies the conclusion that our external senses are therefore completely untrustworthy. If I were mistaken in my apprehension of sweetness and whiteness, I could never be mistaken with respect to their combination in any

given instance. A mistake is always a synthesis of infallible apprehensions combined by accident.

Thus I sense a tiny pattern of light now acting on my retina,
and I know what a star is. But my sensation that this light is now
coming to me from an existence star many billions of miles away is
an accidental combination of the sensation with associated knowledge, which may very well be mistaken, for the star may have
ceased to exist. But if I did not actually apprehend the light acting on my retina and if I were altogether ignorant as to what a
star is, I could not be mistaken. I would simply apprehend nothing,
and no apprehension is not a mistaken apprehension.

The failure to distinguish accurately between sensation *proper*
and sensation *by accident* (perception) is a primary cause of that
skepticism concerning the external senses which is so widespread at
the present time. As a matter of fact the occasional occurrence of
sensory errors gives no legitimate ground for any such basic mis-
trust of the senses.

Sensory errors fall into two major groups: (1) those with *physical* causes (sensory errors) and (2) those with *psychic* causes (perceptual errors).

1. The first group includes three classes of sensory error.

a. There are errors due to a simple failure of some sense, either
temporary as in snow blindness or permanent as in color blindness.
Such failures are not "errors," strictly speaking, but privations (a
lack of the sense). Nevertheless they may occasion erroneous perceptions, or illusions, and erroneous perceptual judgments, if the
privation is only partial as in the color-blind and if its presence is
unknown. These errors may be corrected by retraining the imagination and judgment.

b. There are errors due to physical disease of the organ, as the
jaundiced eye sees yellow, and the fevered hand feels everything
cold. Reason easily recognizes these. They are of course corrigible
by physical treatment.

c. The most troublesome variety of *physically* caused errors involves the transmitting medium, which may cause error in the three
following ways:

(1). By the protracted length of time required for transmitting
the species to the organ. Thus the star, which has disintegrated before its light reaches the eye, is perceived as present.

(2). By disturbances in the transmitting medium which alter the species, as smoke makes the pillars writhe, or the atmosphere makes the stars twinkle.

(3). By the divergence of two or more transmitting media which alter the species, as in the case of the bent stick under water.

These errors may be corrected by touch if the object is accessible. They may all be understood and corrected by rational apprehension as soon as their nature is understood.

2. Psychic errors fall into two groups.

a. *Illusions,* in which something actually sensed is perceived *as* something else, as in the case of stereoscopic vision. These are caused either:

(1). By normal habits of perception, as in the meeting of the railroad tracks or in the Muller-Leyer illusion or in the feeling of two pins with the fingers crossed. These can be corrected only by an appeal to reason or to an independent sense.

(2). By peculiar subjective interpretation, as fear complexes and the like, which can be *corrected* by retraining the imagination.

b. *Hallucinations,* in which nothing is actually sensed, or very little, by the external senses. Images in the imagination are taken for external sensations, the common sense being too benumbed or befuddled to distinguish the acts of different faculties. Hallucinations are caused either:

(1). By natural causes, as dreams.

(2). By the soporific effect of drugs or external agents on the common sense.

Hallucinations are always corrected by a return to the normal state of the internal senses. A clear understanding of the complex causal structure of sensation reveals the possibility of such errors as these, but gives no ground for any general philosophical distrust of the senses. Such skepticism usually expresses itself by the raising of such questions as: How do I know that the whole external world is not a great hallucination? How do I know that life is not a dream?

As a matter of fact the raising of such questions and the difficulty experienced by many in answering them in a manner convincing to themselves, is a genuine tribute to the amazing accuracy of our imagination and noetic capacities. As we have seen, the physical presence of something in matter is not the same as the immaterial presence of something before a noetic faculty.[6] Many things may be physically inherent in me and around me, like millions of neutrons, of which I may have no cognitive awareness at all. On the other hand, with the aid of reason and imagination I may make a dead person noetically present to me, who is not physically present at all. When I am not befuddled and my common sense is working normally, I can easily distinguish these two modes of presence and the different faculties involved. I can tell the difference between thinking about someone and seeing the person physically before me.

The external faculties of sense with the aid of perception are able to bring into cognitive awareness only what is physically present. I am aware of the storm that is actually raging outside my window, and I see the typewriter that is physically here before me. Ordinarily my sensory awareness corresponds with amazing exactitude to certain phases of what is materially existent around me. This is normally true even of the images constantly supplied by my imagination to supplement the attenuated cues provided by the external senses. These images constantly bring hidden aspects of surrounding physical things into my awareness.

It is only because of this amazing accuracy of our sensory faculties that we sometimes trust them too far and fall under the influence of an illusion, supposing that because something is noetically present it must be physically present. Thus under the influence of fatigue or drugs the common sense may lose its ability to distinguish between the imagination working by itself alone, as in a dream or hallucination, and the imagination working with the external senses, and confuse pure noetic presence with physical presence.

But this is in itself a great tribute to the accuracy of the imagination and its remarkable capacity to coincide with physical presence. If it generally deceived us it would take more than weariness to make us confuse the two. It is only because of our great noetic power that we run the risk of illusion and hallucination. If it always deceived us we should not trust it at all and should fall into no delusions. But then of course we should be restricted like vegetables to our own subjective matter and would know nothing whatsoever. Illusion is the price that any organism must pay for

[6] Cf. ch. 17, § 4.

the possession of free cognitive faculties, like reason and imagination, which can lift things into cognitive presence even when the things are not physically there to act upon it.

But here the skeptic may raise a further question. You tell me, he will say, that my external senses bring things that are physically present outside me into a cognitive presence. But how do I know this? How do I know that there is anything physically present at all? I put my hand down to what you call the table. I press against it, but perhaps this is merely my own sensation.

All right, let us argue the matter. What is it you say you are touching? Are you touching your own sensation of touch? This is not even good grammar. It is certainly not in agreement with any sound analysis of the facts. Any such analysis will show that every sensation of the fundamental, external senses is *of* something distinct from itself. When I touch the wood of the table, there is of course something in my finger, but not only this. There is the feeling in my finger *of* something external pressing. This primitive datum cannot be questioned without ignoring the nature of the sensations we actually have. As to *what it is* precisely that is pressing my finger, there may be real doubt, but not that there is something external. This is an original datum of sense.

But suppose I am not convinced, the skeptic may say. Show me some argument which will demonstrate the existence of an external world.

There is no argument of this sort. The premises of any such argument would have to be derived from sensory evidence, like every image of fantasy and every concept of reason. If this evidence is denied no argument is possible save a reduction to the absurd. Thus we can show the skeptic that if he is consistent he will be reduced to solipsism, and not even to this, for the awareness *of* self is also an intentional awareness of something *other*. If this intentional reference is denied sensation will be denied, and we must simply abandon all knowledge and lapse into the vegetative state.

But the skeptic will still probably maintain that he is not convinced. Suppose I have lapsed into the vegetative state, he may say. How can I be convinced of an external world? Is there any way?

There is a way. Open your eyes and use your senses. If these cannot convince you, nothing can. But their constant, self-evident testimony to the existence of external things may be reinforced and clarified by two lines of argument. First, there is the fact that we cannot make or provide ourselves with external sensations of our own making when we are in an unbefuddled state. On the subjectivistic hypothesis we should be able to do so. But though I can imagine something pressing against me when there is nothing there, I cannot sense something unless it is really there, and unless I am already befuddled, I can distinguish between sensing and imagining.

Second, there is the basic fact of the intentionality of all sense, which is invariably of something other than itself. This is not an additional inference tacked on to a unitary sense datum but a primordial factor in any sense datum. It cannot be denied without denying sensation itself. These two lines of argument, however, it must be noted, cannot demonstate the primitive, given fact of sensation. Only having sensation will do this. Careful analysis and argument may clarify and illumine this self-evident fact. They cannot replace it.

6. SENSATION AND ITS CAUSES

We have now completed our description of the sensitive faculties. The most fundamental of these are the external senses, for the other sense faculties merely preserve, combine, or elaborate the awareness of external things which comes through these first of all. Let us now recapitulate by giving an account of the causal structure of sensation and a final definition.

Sensation is a kind of cognition. Its function, or final cause, is to assimilate the nature of what lies outside the organism. How is this achieved? What is the efficient cause of sensation? Here much confusion reigns at the present time. The materialist claims that the efficient cause is the physical influence or impression of an external thing, which is simply received in the organ as a physical alteration. Thus he confuses sensation with the physical assimilation of an accident in the organism and cannot explain how sensation is a knowing faculty, capable of assimilating what lies outside itself objectively as it really is. The idealist, on the other hand, claims that the efficient cause is wholly intrinsic to the organism, refusing to admit the reception of any extraneous influence. He confuses knowing with a kind of making or creation, and he also cannot explain how we know anything outside us as it is.

These one-sided views leave us only with an organism confronted by its own subjective accidents, and the question then arises as to whether we really know anything at all or, indeed, as to whether any external world exists. This so-called problem of knowledge cannot be answered, once it is raised in consequence of a faulty explanation. It can be avoided only by offering a correct explanation of the complex fact of knowledge—the true function of epistemology. A correct explanation of its complex, efficient cause, which is neither wholly internal nor wholly external, is of crucial importance.

This efficient cause is partly internal. To this extent we may agree with the idealist. Unless we are to accept the exaggerated and fantastic thesis of panpsychism (that all things sense), we must agree that sensing involves a mode of activity that occurs within the living animal. The sense organ of such an animal has within it a capacity which, once it is actualized, is able to abstract the pure species of what alters it and to receive this pure species intentionally as long as it is physically altered. Unless an animal had within it some capacity of this kind it would be physically or solipsistically locked up inside itself and its own individual accidents, and could never sense or become aware of anything at all. It would remain restricted, like a plant or an inorganic thing, to its own substantial nature and its subjective accidents. Sensing involves an immanent, vital activity of the living animal as an instrumental, efficient cause. But this is not the primary, efficient cause. Here the idealist is simply wrong. The immanent act of sensing cannot actualize itself. It must be brought into action by prior, efficient causes.

A vast amount of evidence, which the materialist is quite correct in regarding as essentially relevant, shows that the activity of sensing is efficiently caused by the physical reception of influences or impressions from a medium which is in turn affected by the quality of something external. We cannot *touch* unless something exerts pressure on the skin. We cannot *see* unless light impinges upon the retina. We cannot *hear* unless air vibrations are received in the tympanum. Such impressions must be subjectively received. Here the materialist is right. He is very wrong, however, in supposing that the transmitted impression is wholly without quality and that sensing is indistinguishable from physical alteration.

As we have seen, the impression of sense is psychophysical in character. It is both the physical reception of an alteration in the hand, the pattern of light on the retina, the vibrations of the ear, and the resulting psychic reception of the impressed species alone without matter, the feeling of pressure, the color yellow, and the middle-C sound. This immaterial *species impressa* is identical in form with the external quality, and thus enables the faculty to know it as it is. Without the final abstraction of such an immaterial species we could not distinguish between sensation and physical alteration, and all material things would sense. Also we must realize that this species is not the object of knowledge, *that which* is known, but rather *that by which* we know the external object. Unless the faculty, which in itself must already be able to reach out to external things, is informed by some such species, it is impossible to understand why it should know one thing rather than another or why, as is evident in the case of sense, it should cease to know as soon as the external thing disappears and ceases to supply the species.

We must therefore conclude that the efficient cause of sensing is essentially threefold. The primary, efficient cause is the physical alteration of some surrounding medium by the quality of something external. The second, subordinate, instrumental cause (which may be further subdivided when there are several transmitting media, as in the case of the bent stick under water) is the physical action of the medium on the psychophysical sense organ. The third, subordinate, instrumental cause is the abstraction of the species by the psychic faculty. Sensation is the effect of these three efficient causes and cannot be properly understood without them.

The *formal* cause of sensory cognition is twofold. The *extrinsic,* formal cause is the heat or color or sound or flavor inhering physically in the external thing. But the sense faculty cannot know this unless it is represented vicariously in the faculty by an immaterial species. This species is therefore the *immanent,* analogous, formal cause of the sensing process.

Sensing is a mode of cognition. It is not a mere alteration, but the immaterial assimilation of form without matter. Since however this psychic assimilation cannot occur without the physical alteration of the organ, it is subject to those material conditions which govern the alteration of this organ. If it is not altered no sensation will be produced. If it is altered the intensity of the alteration and other quantitative factors (the primary qualities) of the process, will modify the sensation. The material cause of sensation is the physical organ of sense.

We may define sensation, therefore, as *the objective apprehension of certain, external qualities, combined under material conditions in the sense organ with other qualities.*

References

Recommended Reading

Aristotle, *De Anima,* Book II, chaps. 6, 7, and 12; Book III, chap. 2, and chap. 3, 427B to end; and Aquinas, *Treatise on Man, Summa Theologica,* Part I, Qu. 78, Arts. 3 and 4, and Qu. 85, Art. 6.

Suggested Reading

1. *De Anima,* Book II, chaps. 6–7, and *Treatise on Man, Summa Theologica,* Qu. 78, Art. 3. For an influential statement of the subjectivist view of sensation, cf. Locke, *Essay,* Book II, chap. 8, 7 ff. For a further development of this into an epistemological monism, which identifies the sensation with the thing known, cf. Berkeley, *Principles of Human Knowledge,* 25, and 86 ff.

2. *De Anima,* Book II, chap. 6, 418A 7–418A 17, and *Treatise on Man, Summa Theologica,* Qu. 78, Art. 3, Obj. 1, and answer. For an influential treatment of sensations and ideas, as though they were non-intentional entities or accidents "within the mind," cf. Descartes, *Meditations,* Meditation III, first six pages.

3. *De Anima,* Book II, chap. 6, 418A 17–20, Book III, chap. 1, 425A 14– chap. 2; and *Treatise on Man, Summa Theologica,* Qu. 78, Art. 3, Obj. 2, and answer. For the modern theory of primary and secondary qualities, cf. Locke, *Essay,* Book II, chap. 8. For an idealistic critique of this theory, cf. Berkeley, *Principles of Human Knowledge,* Sec. 9 ff.

4. Aquinas, *Treatise on Man, Summa Theologica,* Qu. 78, Art. 4, and

Obj. 2. On the common sense, cf. Aristotle, *De Anima,* Book III, chap. 2. On fantasy, cf. *De Anima,* Book III, chap. 3, 427B 7–chap. 4.

5. Aquinas, *Summa Theologica,* Qu. 85, Art. 6, and Qu. 17, Art. 2; and *De Anima,* Book II, chap. 6, 418A 20–27, and Book III, chap. 3, 428B 17–429A. For an expression of radical, philosophical distrust of the senses, cf. Descartes, *Meditations,* Meditation I. For an idealistic attempt to explain illusion in terms of future prediction alone, without reference to intentionality, cf. Berkeley, *Principles,* Sec. 28 ff.

6. *De Anima,* Book II, chap. 12; and *Treatise on Man, Summa Theologica,* Qu. 84, Art. 1. For a radically different view of the nature of sensation and its causes, cf. Locke, *Essay,* Book II, chap. 1, 23 ff.

Chapter 19

RATIONAL COGNITION

ALL men are at least vaguely conscious of the fact that they possess a higher faculty (reason), and distinguish thinking, understanding, and reasoning from feeling and sensing. We are aware that animals possess sense organs and sensation, but we do not attribute speech and understanding to them. We are also aware of the fact that although science is impossible without sensory observation, it certainly involves something quite distinct from sense. Hearing this and seeing that, is not the same as understanding *what it is* we hear or *what it is* we see. We can hear with perfect accuracy the words of a foreign language and still not understand the words.

The mere accumulation of sensations does not necessarily involve the acquisition of understanding. People may travel through the world and gather up a vast accumulation of individual experiences, and still have little understanding of what they have seen, felt, and imagined. All this is true, but we must not be content simply to fall back on common-sense opinion. We must examine the evidence more closely and seek to determine more exactly the distinguishing mark of this higher mode of apprehension. This mark is *immateriality*.

1. THE IMMATERIALITY OF REASON

As we have seen, sense is restricted to odors, flavors, colors, and other qualities, always apprehended under certain material conditions. I cannot sense color as such, but this particular color, spread out on a certain surface, having such and such a particular size and shape. Human thoughts or ideas are certainly not so restricted. First of all, they are not limited to any determinate objects. I can think, not only of odors, flavors, and colors, but of the invisible and intangible substances underlying them. I cannot touch or see the humanity of my friend but I can apprehend this by my thought. In fact there is nothing whatsoever that I cannot make the object of reflection. Matter is a certain mode of being, not being itself. It exists under certain quantitative conditions, not others. Therefore a faculty like sense, which can be actualized only by material influences, has a limited range of apprehension. For instance, no sense can clearly apprehend itself. But the faculty of reason can apprehend being, under which everything whatsoever, whether it be sensible or insensible, must fall.

In the second place, sense cannot achieve the universal. What I see is *this* long, yellow shape lying here and now before me. This is even true of the imagination, for although I can imagine *a* pencil lying somewhere else, beyond the range of my vision or at some future time, it must be some individual pencil at some particular time. What I remember is also some particular occurrence, like the death of a friend at a particular place and a particular time. Sense is chained to those forms which can act physically on a material medium. These are always forms in a material substratum which may either continue or be replaced by others equally individual and contingent. But by my mind I can apprehend the universal, necessary nature of a pencil, what a thing must be to be a pencil at *any* particular place, and at *any* particular time, not the death of this or the death of that, but the universal and essential nature of death itself.

These differences point to a faculty, free from those material conditions which restrict the range of sense, and unlimited in scope. The most extraordinary fact about human nature is that it is marked off from all the other natures surrounding us by the possession of the immaterial and therefore unrestricted apprehensive faculty called reason.

You will find it hard to sustain any doubt you may have concerning this fact if you will closely reflect on a further fact which is so familiar that we seldom give it much attention. This is the fact of the communicability of thoughts. Whenever you argue or converse with a friend you are sharing meanings which are not only similar but absolutely identical. When he says *pencil,* you must know exactly what he means. An image that is only similar will not enable you to understand and to discuss intelligibly the very same subject matter. If you are arguing with him about the moon, it must be the very same moon you are both discussing in terms of concepts that are identically shared. If not, you will be discussing something really different, even though only slightly different, and you can never agree or even disagree, for disagreement is not mere difference, but rational difference concerning the very same thing.

Here one may raise a question. Is it really necessary that the two parties to a dispute have the very same thing in mind? Is there not a possible alternative? Suppose they have two similar things in mind. Then so far as their thoughts are similar they will agree. So far as they are different they will disagree. Is anything more than this required?

Something more is definitely required. In the first place, they would never be able to ascertain that their thoughts were similar unless they shared the same, identical concept of similarity. Even if we grant this for the sake of the argument the proposed explanation will not work. If my thought of a single object A is only similar, and therefore partly different from your thought of the same object A, then one or the other of us (or both) is mistaken, and we are neither in agreement nor in disagreement, for we are thinking about two different things. Unless both parties are referring to the very same entity, disputation is impossible.

This primary fact of human communication and argument is in itself enough to show the universality of thought and therefore its radical difference from all the sensitive faculties. Sensations and images cannot be shared. Your sensation of sweetness, when you taste the sugar, is yours, and mine is mine. I cannot possibly transmit my private sensation to you unless by another distinct faculty I can universalize this sensation and form a concept of it, as it is in general. Without such a faculty of reason or understanding no discourse or argument would be possible. But we all know that genuine agreement and disagreement do occur among men. They do transmit meanings from one to another. They do argue and dispute. Hence in addition to sense we possess *another* apprehensive faculty, capable of grasping the universal and necessary natures of things.

Think now for a moment of these objects of our thought. The integral object of sense is a composite, material object which is in flux even as I sense it. The light on the surface of the pencil is flickering as I see it; the airplane which I hear is moving even now as I hear it. It is this whole, composite, changing thing that I sense. But my concepts do not change in this way. I can never repeat a single sensation again. But I can think the same thought over and over. Science and knowledge, once achieved, are changeless and fixed. In fact if it were true of thought as it is of sensation, that my thought is in a process of flux as I think it, I could not think or achieve any stable truth at all. If my concept of triangle changes as I think it, then certainly no geometrical demonstration will be possible, or even any fixed concept of any stable "it" at all.

This is enough to show an essential difference between the faculties of thought and sensation. I sense the composite, material, triangular wood before me here and now. This certainly is changing as I sense it. But by reason I abstract from what is particular and changeable in this thing and apprehend something in it which is indifferent to change. Concepts are abstract and changeless. Of course we attain concepts by a process of learning. But the concepts we attain by this process do not move and grow like physical things. Fluidity and change are admirable in subrational realms. Nothing more can be expected of them. But in the realm of mind they are signs of privation and immaturity.

A question may be raised at this point. If concepts are universal and changeless so far as they are actualized, then all men ought to think the very same things and express themselves in the very same way. But this is altogether out of line with the facts. Men certainly do not think the same things, nor do they express themselves in the same way. Consider the tremendous diversity of human language.

In answer, we may point out that the world is a very rich place, containing an indefinite number of different things to think about. Hence certain groups, living in particular environments, may focus their attention on certain things which are ignored by other groups living in different environments. But when two groups think about the same things they arrive at the same concepts to some degree of clarity. The verbal symbols by which these concepts are expressed vary endlessly according to the habits of different languages, but the concepts are the same. Otherwise it would be impossible to translate from one language to another.

What is material is quantitative, always restricted to some individual entity here and now, and finally ever-changing. But as we have seen, thought is not quantitative, not individual, and finally changeless.[1] The necessary conclusion from these evident facts is that understanding, or rational apprehension, is an immaterial operation requiring an immaterial operator, since the mode of operation always follows the nature of that which operates. Only that which is in itself hot can heat another thing. Only one who in himself already knows can teach another. The thoughts or operations of the human understanding are immaterial. Therefore the mind or understanding of man is in itself immaterial. This is the conclusion to which we are necessarily led.

This conclusion, however, is opposed by the widely diffused materialism of our time which defends the truth of the view that thought is to be identified with complex physicochemical changes in the nervous system, determined by physical influences emanating from within and without the organism. This view, however, is self-refuting, and ultimately unintelligible.

How am I to understand the materialism that is being defended as true if it is physically changing as I try to think it? As soon as I think it, it has changed or moved to something else. How can the materialist transmit any such individual current in his brain to another brain with currents of its own? In what strange mockery is he indulging when he defends this individual motion in his brain as universally true? All he is doing is reacting physically to physical stimuli in a manner determined by the quirks in *his* brain. But the quirks in *my* brain are different. Truth, as distinct from fixed obsessions and prejudices, is precisely what is not so determined. As soon as we discover any signs of physical influence, such as some emotional disturbance, back of a theory asserted to be true, we at once discount it as a complex or prejudice. When the naturalist asserts that all theories have such physical causes, he is then condemning his own theory as a mere irrational obsession or prejudice. Does he assert his own view to be really true? He is then involved in an evident contradiction. Thought is something immaterial and free from material conditions and determinations. Of course this does not mean that true understanding, because it lacks physical causes, lacks all causes and is therefore purely indeterminate and capricious. As we shall see, it is necessarily caused by the nature of that which is understood and by operations of the noetic faculties.

[1] Cf. ch. 16, § 8.

The view is self-contradictory and therefore absurd. Thought is something immaterial—free from individual conditions and determinations.

This conclusion is implied by the actual facts we have been examining as well as by many further facts. It is also implied by the very nature of knowledge, if this structure is carefully examined. As we have already seen,[2] to know something is in some sense to assimiliate that thing into the mind. But it cannot be any physical process of assimilation by which the mind is physically changed by some external, material cause, because in any such process the mind and the new form physically imposed upon it would combine to form a new composite, individual entity—the material mind plus a new quality that is physically assimilated into itself. But knowledge does not result in the formation of any such new entity.

To know is to know something precisely as it is formally, apart from knowledge. There must be not merely a *similarity,* but an *identity* between what is in the object and what is in the mind. Otherwise knowledge is impossible. One may question this, of course. Why, we may ask, does the mind have to be identical with its object? Suppose I do not know the thing as it really is in itself, but only something similar. Then at least I partly know the thing so far as it is similar. Why is this not an adequate account of knowledge?

It is not an adequate account for the following reasons. First of all, if I can never know the thing as it really is by a noetic identification, I shall never know anything beyond my idea with which I can compare it, to find out whether or not it is similar. Second, how do I know my idea as it really is, if a mental act can never be identified with what is other than itself? I shall not be able to know my idea but only something similar, and not even this but only something similar. No knowledge will be possible.

If I can know an *idea* by perfect identification, then there is no reason for denying that I can know external things in the same way. Such knowledge involves identity, a mode of assimilation in which no new, third, composite entity is formed. Such a non-composite assimilation must be non-physical or immaterial in character.

We have already seen that since sense is a genuine form of cogni-

2 Cf. ch. 17, § 4.

tion, there must be even here an immaterial assimilation. But it is definitely restricted by material conditions. Sensation is psychophysical in character, involving a physical as well as an immaterial, abstractive, efficient cause. The higher, apprehensive faculty of understanding is completely and unrestrictedly immaterial, and therefore requires no particular physical organ. If it did, we should notice intensity and strain in this organ when confronted by intensely knowable objects, as intense light blinds us and terrific sounds damage the eardrum.

But as Aristotle remarks, thought about highly intelligible objects, far from wearing out the mind and making it less able to think, on the contrary sharpens the mental faculties and makes them more able to think less intelligible objects.[3] This is because the mind, unlike sensation, is immaterial and therefore separable from the body. But modern science, we are apt to say, teaches that we think and reason with the brain and that injuries to the central nervous system interfere with mental processes.

Modern science teaches no such thing. Questions concerning the general nature of knowledge lie beyond the province of any of the special sciences. To which of the sciences does the study of science belong? Can the chemist make a chemical analysis of the science of chemistry? of physics? of biology? Knowledge once it is acquired is immaterial. Hence it cannot be quantitatively weighed and measured. How long is the science of physics? How much does the science of chemistry weigh?

The nature of knowledge is a philosophical question which requires philosophical techniques for its investigation. The processes of acquiring knowledge and of expressing it, require the cooperation of external and internal senses, which are physically centered in the brain. Hence it is not surprising that brain lesions and other injuries to the central nervous system, interfere with these processes. The realistic view of knowledge we are presenting does not require us to deny any fact that is known to science. But in addition to these particular physical facts, discoverable by the special techniques of the quantitative sciences, it must also recognize the amazing fact of science itself.

But how are we to understand such a faculty? Precisely what does

[3] *De Anima* 429A 31 ff.

it apprehend? How does it operate? How are these immaterial operations related to material things in nature? We cannot hope for any
aid from special sciences employing special techniques of sensory
observation, for what is immaterial lies completely beyond the
range of sensory observation. You cannot see or taste the number
three. You cannot observe your concept of justice through a microscope. Reason alone is capable of apprehending her own immaterial operations. Let us then turn this higher faculty reflexively on
itself and see if it cannot achieve some clarity in understanding, first
its object, and then its immaterial mode of operation.

2. THE OBJECT OF KNOWLEDGE

There are two ways in which a form may be received. The first is
the material mode of reception, by which all transitive, physical influences are assimilated. Thus the brick materially receives the heat
of the sun, and the canvas receives the colors spread out upon its
surface. This mode is called subjective, because the form retains no
independence or otherness but is completely amalgamated with the
receiving subject. The second is the immaterial mode of reception
by which all knowledge is assimilated. Thus when I see a color, I
certainly receive the form of the color but not as the canvas physically receives the paint. There is no subjective amalgamation of the
form with the material recipient. The form is received objectively,
precisely as it is in the external thing, retaining its independence and
otherness. Every noetic faculty has such an object.[4]

Reason is a noetic faculty. Hence it has a certain kind of object
(formal object) which it holds before itself. My ideas are entita-
tively mine. They modify my substantial being as accidents of a peculiar kind. But the forms they bring before the mind are not subjectively in me. The rock structure I understand is not physically
inherent in me. It is objectively or intentionally present as an object over against my subjective being. The very same thing that
exists physically or subjectively in itself can also exist non-physically
or objectively before the knowing faculty. The distinctive function
of man is precisely to bestow this peculiar, cognitive mode of being
upon the material things of nature. If reason is such a cognitive

[4] Cf. ch. 17, § 4.

faculty distinct from sense, it must have a formal object which is distinct from that of sense. What is this formal object?

In attempting to answer this question we are apt to be confused by two difficulties. The first is that in most cases the object of reason is materially the same as the object of sense. The astronomer is trying to understand the nature of the planets whose motions he observes through his telescope. The biologist is trying to understand the nature of the cell he observes through his microscope. I may be trying to understand my own human nature which I also *feel* in many ways through the external and internal senses. That which I understand, therefore, seems to be the very same thing as that which I sense, and I seem unable to distinguish the two faculties. This difficulty is further accentuated by a second, the fact that reason is clearly unable to function at all without some sensory apprehension.

We are all aware of the great advances in modern natural science resulting from the telescope and microscope, which extended the range of sensory observation. We all know that it is no use trying to explain the nature of color to a congenitally blind man, and we recognize the truth of the ancient dictum that where sense fails, science also must fail. Are we not then forced to the conclusion that science and knowledge in general concern the very same material entities that impress our senses? But two faculties which concern the very same *formal* object are really one and the same.[5] Are we not then forced further to the conclusion of sensationalism, that the ideas or concepts of reason are nothing more than sensations or images of the imagination?

On this view reason is the same as sense, and we are reduced to an extreme skepticism or nominalism,[6] which holds that all reality, whether in the mind or out of the mind, is individual and unrepeatable. Certain philosophers, unwilling to deny the basic fact of universality, which as we have seen, is involved in all intelligible discourse, have tried to defend a mitigated nominalism or conceptualism,[7] according to which all reality *outside the mind* is completely individual. *Inside the mind*, however, according to the con-

[5] Cf. ch. 17, § 3.
[6] Cf. § 3, below.
[7] *Ibid.*

ceptualist, genuine universal concepts are found. Sense alone has the power to apprehend individual external facts. But once apprehended, the mind then universalizes these facts and formulates general hypotheses by combining them and separating them in logical discourse. When the so-called problem of *induction* is raised and we ask how a universal hypothesis or theorem can ever be verified by individual, contingent facts, many answers are given in terms of the so-called laws of probability and the uniformity of nature.

But no one of these answers is sufficient. Why should even a general law of probability hold of utterly contingent facts? How can we be sure that nature is going to repeat herself? How from the sensory fact that one swan or two billion swans are white, can we jump to the universal and necessary conclusion that *all* swans are white? At least, you may say, the conceptualist can observe that *this* swan is white, and the next, and so on. Yes, provided he already knows the universal essence of *swan* and the universal essense of *white*. But how does he know these? By noting certain similarities among certain animals—that they have wings, long necks, and so on. Of course he can do this if he already knows the universal essence of *animal*, that of *similarity*, that of *wing*, and that of *neck*. We cannot sense these. Hence the conceptualist can give no intelligible account of how we come to know them in the first place.

How can we explain this? Only by first recognizing the presence of formal structure in nature and then by recognizing the capacity of the intellect to abstract this form even from a single instance, freeing it from everything which materially restricts it to this instance or that, and seeing it in its naked universality. Sense cannot do this, for it apprehends only a cluster of accidents bound together in some individual matter. But there is no science of the individual. So in order to explain science we must recognize another faculty with a distinct, formal object—the universal form freed from every irrelevant individuating trait with which it is materially associated.

The non-individual object of reason is sharply distinct from the individual object of sense, and there is no way in which the former can be reduced to the latter. A billion individual men will not produce the abstract essence of humanity, any more than a billion mice will ever produce a man. The object of reason is *sui generis* and irreducible to sense. Here we may interrupt with a pertinent question.

Why can it not be that the object of reason is a group or class of sense objects? Such a class consists only of the individuals making it up. In this case we should not have to assume any distinctive object of reason.

But in this case we should also have no class, for a class is not merely a number of individuals. It is made up of all those individuals *of which* a universal essence may be predicated. This cannot be achieved by sense. We do not touch or taste classes. But you may say, the act of predication is something purely arbitrary and mental. Outside the mind there is only a number of individual entities, no classes at all.

This is precisely the view of conceptualism which must lead to skepticism concerning scientific knowledge. Some classes are purely arbitrary, with no foundation whatsoever in reality. All predication, even that which is true, is purely mental. But this does not mean that all knowledge is a purely mental construction with no basis in extra-mental reality. Individual entities in nature may be really *similar* to one another. The intellect may then abstract this form and truly predicate it of the members of the class. In this case what we universally predicate of the members is actually present materially in each of them, unless we have made a mistake.

Conceptualism may be defined as the attempt to explain how reason can function without apprehending any *peculiar object of its own,* distinct from that of sense. But the problem of induction then arises and shows that such an explanation is impossible. Confronted with this problem the conceptualist must either intellectualize sense or sensationalize reason. In the first case, he will confuse the object of sense with an essence and fall into an exaggerated realism, thinking of individual, material things as clusters of universals. In the second, he will think of reason merely as the faculty of making unverifiable assumptions and guesses about the individual, material objects which sense alone apprehends. This must lead him into some sort of pragmatism or skepticism.

The basic fallacy lies in a failure to see that sense and reason are *distinct* faculties, each with a *distinct object of its own.* Rational cognition cannot be explained unless it actually apprehends some object distinct from that of sense. But if we are not to construct an artificial world of separate Platonic universals apart from the material things of sense, how are we to answer the crucial question as to *where* this object is and *what* it is? This brings us back to the original difficulty. Let us now attempt to answer it.

The object of reason is precisely *where* the object of sense is. It is precisely something implicit in the material thing, either its essence or the essence of some one of its accidents. *In the thing,* this essence and its innumerable accidents exist all together in a matter which restricts or individualizes them. It is this composite, material whole which is apprehended by sense, neither the orange as such nor the yellowness of the orange, but the concrete, yellow orange with all its sensible accidents confused together. The object of reason is *materially* the same but *formally* distinct. That is, what I understand by reason is precisely the essence of this concrete, sensible object, the orange *itself* or the yellowness *as such,* with everything irrelevant or extraneous omitted. Is it necessary to fall back on a distinct faculty of reason for this, you may ask. Can I not sense yellowness as such through vision alone? The answer is *no.* No one has ever sensed yellowness as such or the color yellow by his sense of sight alone. What we sense is always *this* yellow color of *this* large orange, in *this* light, at *this* distance from me, and so on. The color yellow is an abstract universal, freed from everything formally irrelevant to it. Such an abstract essence can be apprehended by the abstractive faculty of reason alone.

Reason apprehends the very same thing (materially) which sense apprehends, but it grasps something in this thing (formally) which sense cannot grasp, either the essence alone by itself or the accident alone by itself. The object of reason is not another *thing* existing separately from the sensible thing. It grasps this very thing or some accident of it *abstractly as it is in itself,* with nothing else added or subtracted. Sense cannot do this, because it always grasps a concrete manifold, materially confused together.

Such material unity is founded on the indefinite capacity of prime matter to receive any number of variegated and utterly unrelated forms. The senses apprehend only such material unities. Reason apprehends formal unities. When it is functioning with analytic exactitude it concentrates upon these and frees itself from sensory examples. But it may also achieve this only to a minimum degree and fall back upon sensory illustrations and sequences to take the place of formal analysis.

It is of the greatest importance to distinguish these two modes of thought—the material, so characteristic of the childish mind; and the formal, so characteristic of the adult mind. The former makes a constant appeal to the senses, always pointing to concrete examples and cases and apprehending confused clusters of forms without being able to separate them one from the other. The more mature, formal mode of thought, though it starts with concrete examples, nevertheless always attempts to grasp the universal essence of what is presented to it and tries to resolve confused, material unities into abstract, formal unities.

Thus we can distinguish the two objects from each other without being forced to hold, with the Platonic realists, that the two objects exist apart from each other as two materially different things.[8] But while asserting that the two objects exist only as one sensible, material thing, we still maintain that they are distinct phases of the thing and are not forced to reduce the one faculty to the other. Reason is a noetic faculty quite distinct from sense, though it grasps an aspect of the sensible thing abstractly, and therefore cannot operate until sense has supplied it with a confused manifold from which it can abstract the essence. But if reason proceeds abstractly in this way, leaving out certain phases of the thing, does it not then give us only a partial and distorted view of what is really there?

The answer is that a *partial* apprehension is not necessarily a *distorted* one. Thus we do not say that a single sense distorts the object, because it does not apprehend what another sense apprehends. I can truly see the whiteness of the sugar without tasting its sweetness. In the case of any complex object $a + b$, I may apprehend a alone or b alone, without any distortion, *so long as I do not deny the existence of the other element.* The abstraction of reason neither asserts nor denies the existence of that from which it abstracts. Hence it does not distort. But then at least must it not be admitted that it is partial or inadequate? Reason may grasp various aspects

[8] Cf. § 3, below.

of the object one by one, but sense alone grasps them all together as they really are in the thing.

This again is a mistaken inference. Before a composite entity $a + b$ may be grasped *adequately* as a totality, its parts must first be grasped adequately, and sense cannot do this. It apprehends, not the articulated, structuralized whole in which the parts are clearly distinguished as they are in the thing, but only a jumbled version of the whole in which the parts are confused with one another and the whole. Hence whether our aim is to grasp any part of a thing or any whole thing or indeed anything at all, we must conclude that reason alone is capable of grasping it *as it really is in the thing,* and that it is without qualification the higher, apprehensive faculty.

Having considered the object which reason apprehends, we must now turn to those rational operations by which this object is apprehended. We have already concluded that the mind understands by universal concepts. We must now ask more specifically what these universal concepts are, how they are related to extra-mental entities, and how they are produced by the mind, or more summarily, what is a universal and how is it caused. This problem must be answered by any adequate theory of knowledge. In the history of western thought, it has been called *the problem of universals.* First, we shall examine three non-realistic ways of answering this problem, noting the strong and weak points in each theory. Then we shall present a realistic theory of rational knowledge. Finally, in the third place, we shall attempt to show how this realistic theory, not only corresponds to the factual evidence, but also escapes many of the serious difficulties which attach to the other views.

3. NOMINALISM, EXTREME REALISM, AND IDEALISM

The nominalist [9] is a consistent materialist. He holds that there is no evidence for the existence of immaterial universals outside the mind, and concludes that all being is material and individual. The universal exists neither outside the mind nor in the mind. What are commonly called concepts or universals, in his view, are really mere words or physical disturbances of some kind in the organism. Some nominalists, like Ockham, accept the fact that these sounds or nervous changes do in some way intend or refer to external en-

[9] Cf. ch. 1, § 9.

tities, but they have never offered any clear explanation of how a physical entity can thus transcend its individuation. These peculiar disturbances, according to the nominalist, are produced, like sense impressions, by physical agencies which are either outside or within the organism. Thus reason tends to be reduced to sense.

The strongest phase of this nominalistic theory is its recognition of the basic fact of individuation. This is certainly sound. There is no evidence for immaterial concepts or essences floating about in the material world. Every extra-mental entity is individual and restricted to its own quantitative boundaries. Here the nominalist is on very firm ground.[10] But when he insists that concepts are also individual sounds or accidents, he falls into difficulty. How is such an entity to become identified with something external, physically quite distinct from itself? How is the fact of communication between minds to be explained?

These are certainly facts. If he accepts these facts the nominalist cannot consistently hold to his physicalist theory. If he rejects them he has rejected rational understanding and discourse. What is he doing when he explains and defends his own theory as true? Is he merely making noises? Why then should we pay any attention to him? Is he merely having brain disturbances and laryngeal articulations? Then we can only pity him, and wait until he is able to communicate with us and argue intelligibly.

Extreme realism lies at the opposite pole from nominalism. It holds that universals exist both in the mind and outside the mind as well. The facts of discourse make it plain that universals exist in the mind. Since these universals give us genuine knowledge about extra-mental reality we must conclude that universals also exist outside the mind. This is the extreme realist position. In the history of thought, it has been expressed in two distinct forms.

According to the first, there is a special "realm" of universals, existing outside the mind in separation from the individual, material things which are measured by space and time.[11] According to the other, now represented by the school of neo-realism, there is no special "realm" of universals, but the individual things of nature are themselves made up of universal quantities, qualities, and rela-

10 Cf. ch. 14, § 6.
11 Cf. ch. 1, § 3, p. 16.

tions.[12] In this extreme form the view approaches that of strict idealism, which also mentalizes the whole external world in a similar manner. As to the origin of universals, the extreme realist has to maintain either that they are already innate in the mind or that the mind receives them from the outside in a completely passive manner without any activity of its own.

Extreme realism is indubitably on firm ground when it asserts the existence of universal concepts in the mind. It is also certainly correct in insisting that we do gain knowledge concerning extra-mental realities by this means. The universal concept must have some basis in the changing world of nature. These are its strong points. But when it goes on to maintain that universals exist outside the mind exactly as they exist within the mind, this view falls into serious difficulty.

There is no evidence whatsoever for any special "realm" apart from the physical beings of nature. If these things are reduced to clusters of universals then matter is denied, and we have no way of accounting for the evident continuity of change, the indeterminism of chance and accident, and the basic fact of individuation.

Furthermore, the realist explanations of the origin of ideas are full of difficulty. There is much evidence to show that knowledge is not innate in the mind but that it has to be acquired with the aid of sense experience. Certainly the mind is not wholly passive in this acquisition of knowledge, which proceeds by propositions and arguments. It is difficult to hold that concepts, propositions, and syllogisms, the units of discourse, occur in material nature and then somehow migrate into the mind in some mysterious way.

The idealist holds an intermediate position, that universals are immaterial entities, constructed or created by the activity of the mind and existing in the mind alone. But idealism has expressed itself in two distinct forms, the conceptualism of Kant and his followers, and the strict idealism of the absolute idealists.[13] According to the conceptualists, there is an extra-mental world of things in themselves which may be directly given in sense experience or may not be knowable at all. But concepts are constructed or made by the mind for pragmatic purposes of adjustment and convenience.

---

[12] Cf. ch. 13, § 5.
[13] Cf. ch. 1, § 11.

They have no foundation in the unknowable reality of things in themselves. According to the absolute idealist, there is no such realm. Mind is the only ultimate being there is, and the concepts constructed by mind exhaust the whole of reality. This view has now sunk into decline, but conceptualistic idealism, often merging with certain degrees of nominalism, is at present a most influential doctrine.

The soundest phase of this doctrine is its insistence upon the activity of mind in the processes of knowing. Here it is on very firm ground. Thinking is certainly more than the mere development of basic ideas already innate in the mind or the mere passive reception of something migrating in from the outside. Concepts are never found outside the mind. Propositions do not grow on trees. Syllogisms do not lie beneath the ground. Mental being is distinct from extra-mental being. Here the conceptualist theory is very sound.

But when it attempts to interpret mental activity along material lines, as the making or molding of some new entity not in existence before, the theory becomes most dubious. Knowing is not to be confused with making. The caterpillar makes its cocoon, but it does not thereby know anything. The stomach makes food out of what enters the digestive tract. It does not know. At this point the conceptualist is subject to the criticism of the extreme realist that he has ignored the extra-mental foundation for knowledge, broken the bond, which must exist in some form, between knowing and that which is known, and reduced the mind to a sort of pragmatic machine shop.

Is there any theory of knowledge which can incorporate the strong points in each of these theories but avoid the weak points? Such a theory must agree with nominalism in recognizing that all extra-mental entities are material and individual, but must reject the fallacy of nominalism in denying universal concepts in the mind, and thus destroying knowledge and discourse. It must agree with extreme realism and absolute idealism in seeking a basis for knowledge in extra-mental reality, but must reject any mentalizing of the world of nature. It must agree with conceptualism in recognizing the activity of the mind in knowing and the distinction between mental and extra-mental existence, but must at the same time reveal some bond between the mind and external reality. Is there any theory of this sort? Such a theory has been developed and critically refined by realistic philosophy in the course of its history. Let us now attempt to explain it.

4. THE REALISTIC THEORY OF UNIVERSALS

The realist agrees with the nominalist that everything outside the mind is material and individual, but he recognizes the existence of universals in the mind. He agrees with the extreme realist that knowledge is not a mental creation or construction and that it must therefore have a foundation in extra-mental being, but he refuses to identify this foundation with something universal or mental in character. He agrees with the conceptualist that the mind is really active, not passive in the process of understanding, but he refuses to identify this activity with that of molding or making anything new. According to the realist, this activity is rather an abstractive activity which, as we have seen, involves the separation of a certain formal nature from everything irrelevant with which it is materially combined.

Any material existent can be separated in this way and brought before the mind. For example, my senses may make me aware of this individual, human being now in the room. They do not make me conscious of his humanity, his height, his weight, his pale complexion, the color of his hair, the sound of his voice, but of all these different formal natures confused together in this material individual. The senses do not falsify reality. They apprehend their proper objects as they really are *in the individual thing,* i.e., as concreted together with what is formally distinct from them. But they do not apprehend them as they are in *themselves,* man as such, *the* color yellow, and so on, apart from everything formally irrelevant to them.

Sense does not give us a false view of reality but a confused and fluid, material view, rather than a distinct and stable, formal view. This we achieve by reason alone, which can separate each nature from everything with which it is confused and apprehend man as such, extension as such, color as such, and so on, each alone as it is in itself. The extra-mental nature, when thus abstractly considered by a mental act, is called "the absolute nature." When we raise the philosophical questions: *what is this thing you are talking about?*

what is man? what is color? what is the precise definition of any entity? we are seeking for the absolute nature of the thing.

This absolute nature is not a universal. It is what Plato called the pure idea, all alone by itself (*auto kath auto*), in a state of utter solitude, apart from everything not contained in it essentially.[14] The first act of understanding is to bring such a solitary nature before the mind, to make it intellectually, non-physically present. This absolute nature is not a universal, certainly not a construction. It exists, amalgamated with many other forms in the extra-mental individual, which may be grasped in this confusion by sense. It is not a universal either, for it has not yet been compared with other individuals of which it may be predicated.

It is an absolute nature or neutral entity which is neither individual nor universal. The ultimate, simple units of discourse, or categories, which we have studied (Chapter 15), are such neutral entities. When I think of quality or quantity or man as such, this is not an individual object, for I have abstracted from all individual determinations. Neither is it a universal, for I am not thinking of this nature as related to the individuals from which it has been abstracted. What then is the universal, and how does it arise?

It is not a separate thing existing by itself, as both extreme realists and idealists suppose. It is a *relation*. The foundation of this relation is the absolute nature, or category. Once the mind has brought any form into such a state of solitude, it can be compared with the concrete individuals from which it has been separated by the mind. When, as the result of such a comparison, the absolute nature is seen to be present in these individuals as well as in an indefinite number of other possible individuals, it is then a universal concept, identically related to any number of singular instances. This universal relation exists only in the mind, for the abstract consideration of an absolute nature and the comparison of it with a multitude of subordinates, are *mental* acts which occur nowhere else.

This distinction between the abstract nature, or category (not yet a universal), and the mental relation of universality, enables us to avoid any idealistic mentalizing of extra-mental nature. When I predicate *man* of Socrates, Plato, and an indefinite "class" of men, I do this by setting up a relation of universality in my mind. But

[14] Cf. ch. 1, § 3, p. 15.

what I predicate of Socrates and so on is not this mental relation but the absolute nature *man* which is perfectly capable of existing outside the mind with further individual determinations. The absolute nature is thus the link which exists both outside the mind materially, and inside the mind immaterially.

Once isolated in this way it may be mentally related by the relation of identical predication to the material things in five different ways, the five kinds of universal relation; as their genus, difference, species (genus and difference together), necessary accident, or contingent accident. These five universal relations, or *predicables,* exist only in the mind. What is related by these relations, the absolute natures or *categories,* and the individual entities, exist outside the mind in *rerum natura.* The critical part of this logical procedure is the bringing of the absolute nature into a noetic presence before the mind. What faculties are responsible for this vital act?

Unless we are to adopt the theory of innate ideas on a priori grounds we must follow the evidence which strongly indicates that all rational knowledge is acquired. First, we do not know. Then we know. This passage from ignorance to knowledge is manifested in many ways throughout the whole course of human life from infancy to senescence. We call it the learning process. How is it to be explained?

Since no process arises out of nothing we must suppose, first of all, a completely indeterminate capacity, the *possible intellect,* which at the start knows nothing but which is able to know all things. This primary, noetic capacity bears an obvious analogy with prime matter but differs from it in three ways.[15]

First, prime matter cannot exist alone without any form. But the intellectual capacity can exist in a state of pure indeterminacy before any knowledge is actualized in it. Indeed whenever we begin to examine any question rationally, we must recapture this pure indeterminacy of the possible intellect, free from every alien, material influence, and ready to be determined solely by the structure of the thing as it is in itself.

Second, prime matter receives forms subjectively by merging them with itself in a new composite whole which is neither the form alone nor the matter alone, but both together, and hence suscepti-

15 Cf. ch. 13, §§ 4 and 5.

ble to further change. The possible intellect, on the other hand, receives the forms objectively, precisely as they already are, without the formation of any third composite entity, and hence when the reception is complete, not susceptible to further change.

Finally, in the third place, prime matter is restricted to the reception of certain forms which require matter for their existence. It cannot receive the forms of immaterial entities. The possible intellect, on the other hand, is absolutely unrestricted. It is able to apprehend being itself, and therefore all forms whatsoever, even the forms of immaterial entities, like reason and its immaterial acts.

But as we have seen, no potency can actualize itself. Hence we must now ask what it is that actualizes this indeterminate faculty of the possible intellect. Since it is evident that no one else, no other being can do our thinking for us, this must be something within each human individual. Since it must be capable of actualizing or "impressing" the possible intellect, it must be already in act or active. Hence it has been called the *active intellect*. This is like a light, ever actively shining and ready to illuminate any object brought within its range, elucidating whatever is intelligible and "impressing" its absolute nature, or "intelligible species," on the possible reason.

This immaterial power does not act transitively on any external matter to make it into something different from what it was before: the astronomer makes no alteration in the solar system by knowing it. Neither does it mold any internal matter into something other than it was before, since it acts on the possible intellect which was nothing determinate before. Ever in act, it can illumine, or bring into abstract intelligibility, whatever is brought within its range. But what is brought within its range, and how?

This brings us to the role of sense and imagination in rational knowledge. They provide us with material objects to think about, bringing such confused clusters of forms within the scope of reason, so that its light may shine upon them. Through their instrumentality we are provided with something to understand. Sense offers us forms and qualities clustered together in the matter which is able to act efficiently on the material sense organs, but not on the immaterial, possible intellect. Imagination, by reordering these clusters, can further prepare them, so that at a moment's notice it can provide reason with a suitable object for illumination.[16] Then the active reason abstracts some nature from this object, frees it from all irrelevant determinations, and impresses it upon the possible intellect. This impressed species is what we call an idea, or ultimate unit of discourse.

Once the possible intellect has been impressed with these intelligible species or absolute natures, it can compare them and contrast them with one another. With the aid of sense and imagination it can also compare them with the individual entities from which they have been abstracted, and discern the various universal relations of identity which obtain between the abstract natures and the concrete instances. Thus by judgment and reasoning, it may analyze a concrete entity into all its intelligible components and combine these together precisely as they are combined in the thing itself.[17] These processes (judgment and reasoning) are the objects of logic, which studies those mental processes of combination by which we know reality, and make it immaterially present before the mind precisely as it is.

This is the realistic theory of the nature of knowledge. Let us now contrast it with the other views we have previously examined.

5. REALISM VS. OTHER THEORIES OF KNOWLEDGE

This realistic theory agrees with nominalism that all the things of extra-mental nature are material, changing, and individual. This dynamic world of nature is left intact. In this respect realism can accept all the affirmations of materialism and naturalism. It disagrees with them, however, in insisting that the empirical facts of human insight and communicable discourse must be recognized. Immaterial concepts must be recognized and explained. Sense and imagination play a subordinate role in their derivation. But beyond these, the purely immaterial, rational faculties are required. Even sense and imagination cannot be adequately explained in purely physical terms, for they involve an identification with things which are materially quite distinct. This mode of immaterial presence is more strikingly evident in rational understanding, because of its unrestricted scope. The affirmations of nominalism and naturalism

[16] Cf. ch. 18, § 4b.
[17] Cf. ch. 5, § 2a.

are correct as far as they go. But their negations must be rejected as inconsistent with evident facts, and even inconsistent with the assertion of their own doctrines as intelligible to other minds and true to extra-mental existence.

The realistic theory agrees with extreme realism that universal, immaterial concepts exist in the mind, though it rejects the view that they are innate. It also agrees with extreme realism in holding that these concepts must have a corresponding basis in extra-mental reality. If we know at all, we must know something as it really exists, apart from our mental acts of knowing. But realism rejects the notion that this involves the existence of universal entities outside the mind and the consequent etherealization of nature. There is no empirical evidence whatsoever to support this view.

Mental existence before the mind is not to be identified with subjective, physical existence in matter, though the very same formal nature can exist in both ways. It is this form, or absolute nature, which constitutes the bond between mind and matter. The very same category can exist subjectively in matter, and objectively or intentionally before the mind. Hence knowledge can be explained without imagining any special realm of essences or attempting to mentalize the natural world of space and time. In this respect realism also diverges sharply from strict idealism, which fails to preserve the distinction between the mental and the extra-mental.

At this point realism finds itself in close agreement with conceptualism, which holds that concepts exist only in the mind, and not outside. Instead of leaving this chasm unbridged, however, and the problem of induction wholly unexplained, the realist offers an explanation grounded on evident facts. In the light of these facts he rejects the Kantian thesis that knowledge is to be interpreted as a constructive or molding activity by which something new, not in existence before, is created. This is a materialization of knowledge based upon a false analogy. To know a thing is not to change it in any way. It brings no new thing whatsoever into existence. On the other hand, this does not mean that the mind is passive in attaining knowledge. Here also realism is in agreement with conceptualism. But instead of being a constructive or molding activity, the first basic operation of the mind is to separate each formal element of the extra-mental thing from other entities with which it is materially confused, and to bring it into a noetic presence before the mind precisely as it is. In its second operation of judgment the mind may then recombine it with those other elements precisely as it is combined in the thing.

In this way it may be seen that the realistic epistemology includes the strong points of the other theories and escapes the major difficulties which confront them. But any theory must be finally tested, not by other theories, but by the facts themselves. This realistic theory claims to be in agreement with evident facts of human experience which show that the rational assimilation of external realities, physically quite distinct from us, does occur in man. This theory offers an intelligible explanation of these facts. The only way of finally testing it is to look at the facts themselves. In order to help the student in this process we shall conclude our discussion by suggesting an analogy.

6. Concluding Analogy

So far we have considered different aspects of the knowing process one by one. Let us now attempt to grasp them all together synthetically and in brief. We shall be greatly aided in this if we can discover some easily imaged physical process whose phases are related to one another in a manner similar to that in which the phases of the knowing process are related. The process of photography does provide us with such an analogy. It is true that every element of this process is physical and material in character, and hence quite different from the immaterial elements of knowing. Nevertheless the two sets of distinct elements are related similarly, so that photography provides us with an instructive analogy to knowledge which may be of aid in enabling us to understand its complex structure as a whole.

Think of the flashlight-camera apparatus functioning in a gloomy chamber, where the shapes and patterns of surrounding objects are plunged in obscurity, just as the forms of the objects surrounding us are plunged in the vagueness and indeterminacy of matter. Then the flashlight suddenly illumines the hazy scene, as the active reason illumines a concrete image or sensory scene. The shapes and patterns of these objects, really inherent in them but not seen, are at once rendered clear and distinct, and impressed on the camera film by the light. In the same way the forms and natures of material things, really inherent in them but not understood, are rendered clear and distinct by the active reason, and impressed on the possible intellect.

The geometrical impression on the film is in one way quite distinct from the geometrical shape of the object. One is in the camera; the other is in the matter of the thing. But nevertheless the two patterns are formally similar (*not identical*). In the same way the *species impressa* in the mind is in one way quite distinct from the nature inherent in the material thing. One is in the mind; the other is in the matter of the thing. Nevertheless the two forms, though existing in different ways, in two different substances, are formally identical.

Then think of the elaborate process of developing the film, and touching up the prints and combining them into a panoramic picture. This takes place in darkroom and studio far away from the original object. It involves various peculiar chemical processes which have nothing to do with anything in the original object. Yet the fully developed print may be an accurate replica of the thing! Think of the analogous process of logical reflection, in which the ideas already impressed on our minds are developed into clear definitions and then combined into true judgments of the complete nature of the composite entity. All this takes place in the mind, far away from the original object. It involves various peculiar logical processes which have nothing to do with anything in the original object. Yet the fully developed *species expressa* and judgment may be a formally identical replica of the thing itself. By these logical processes true knowledge is attained, *not* of the processes, but of the very thing itself.

The extreme realists and neo-realists, who think of universals as really inherent in things, commit an absurdity analogous to that into which we should fall if we were to suppose that the chemical solutions, used in the darkroom to develop the picture of the room, were actually inherent in the room. On the other hand, the conceptualists and idealists who see that universals are only in the mind, deny any foundation for them in reality, and therefore think of understanding as a kind of *making* process. They commit an absurdity analogous to that into which we should fall if we became so obsessed with the intricacies of the film development process, that we forgot about the original exposure, insisting that the whole of photography lay in the darkroom and confusing the development of a negative with the making up of something new that had no archetype at all. As a matter of fact such *idealistic* or *creative* picture making would contradict the essential nature of photography, which lies neither in making up anything new nor in the unfolding of something already innate in the camera, but rather in assimilating the geometrical pattern of some external archetype.

This archetype is not fundamentally changed in taking the picture. The change is *in* the camera. The picture is relative to its archetype. The archetype is not relative to the picture. In the same way knowing is an assimilation of the form without the matter. The change is *in* the mind, *not* in the thing. This thing goes on existing just as it is whether known or not, as a man remains just what he is whether his picture is taken or not. Our knowledge is essentially relative to that which is known. But that which is known is not really relative to our knowledge of it. We could go on elaborating the analogy further, but this is enough to give us a sense of the knowing process as a whole, from which we can grasp its essential, causal structure.

It is an immaterial process of assimilation which, like all processes, involves that which is acted upon (the possible intellect) and that which acts upon it (the active intellect). The primary, efficient cause of the process is the active reason; the instrumental efficient cause is the imagination, which actively provides a concrete object to be rendered intelligible. The extrinsic, formal cause of understanding is the form of some external thing existing in matter. The intrinsic, analogous, formal cause is this *same* form existing in abstraction from matter in the possible intellect. What then is the final cause?

Here we must distinguish the proximate from the remote, final cause. The *proximate, final cause* of knowing is simply to know being, as completely as is possible, that is, first of all to know the facts; then every formal, efficient, and final cause as it is in itself; and finally to express these causes in the actual order of their operation—first causes first, and second causes second. In other words, it is the reasoned facts that we are working toward, not merely the experienced facts, materially confused in sensory presentation; but nevertheless be it remembered that the former are the very same facts as the latter!

Of course the material cause can be known only indirectly in relation to the other causes, but in this way it may be understood. However, it is more important to control matter than to understand it, which brings us to the *remote, final cause* of knowing. This is to achieve human happiness—the domination through concrete action of matter by form, of man and the world he inhabits by reason. Such is the nature of knowledge, the governing faculty of man and the highest and most extraordinary of all the processes of nature.

We must now turn to the conative, or appetitive, faculties of human nature which naturally follow the modes of apprehension we have been considering.

REFERENCES

Recommended Reading

Plato, *Phaedo* 78–82; Aristotle, *De Anima*, Book III, chaps. 4, 5, and 6; and Aquinas, *Treatise on Man, Summa Theologica*, Qu. 75, Art. 2; Qu. 79, Arts. 1–4; and Qu. 85, Arts. 1, 2, 5, and 6.

Suggested Reading

1. Plato, *Phaedo* 78–82; Aristotle, *De Anima*, Book II, 413A 3–8; and Book III, chap. 4 to 429B 4.
2. Aristotle, *De Anima*, Book III, chap. 4, 429B 4–B 22, and chap. 7, 431B 12–chap. 8; and Aquinas, *Summa Theologica*, Qu. 84, Art. 1; and Qu. 85, Art. 1, and Objs. 1 and 3.
3. For a modern statement of nominalism, cf. Berkeley, *Principles of Human Knowledge*, Author's Introduction, especially Secs. 12, 13, 15, 20, and 24. On extreme realism, cf. Montague, W. P., *Ways of Knowing*, New York, Macmillan, 1925, chap. 4, Secs. 1–4. For a statement of conceptualism, which lacks any reference to the absolute nature and thus leads to an unbridged chasm between the concept and the extra-mental reality, cf. Locke, *Essay*, Book III, chap. 3, especially Sec. 11, and Book IV, chaps. 7 and 9. For a more recent defence of the conceptualist point

of view, cf. Lewis, C. I., *Mind and the World Order,* New York, Scribners, 1929.

4. Aristotle, *De Anima,* Book III, chap. 5 and chap. 6–430B 6; and Aquinas, *Treatise on Man, Summa Theologica,* Qu. 79, Arts. 1–4; *Concerning Being and Essence,* tr. Lecky, G. G., Appleton, New York, 1937, chap. 3.

5. Aquinas, *Treatise on Man, Summa Theologica,* Qu. 84, Arts. 3, 4, and 6.

6. Aquinas, *Treatise on Man, Summa Theologica,* Qu. 85, Arts. 2, 5, and 6.

Chapter 20

THE APPETITES

SINCE all finite creatures possess a principle of potency or imperfection in their essential constitution,[1] they tend in some way, or strive according to their nature conatively towards that which can perfect them (the good). Even non-living things, which possess no apprehensive faculties, naturally tend or incline toward that to which their nature makes them susceptible. This general tendency is then externally specified by the particular causes acting upon them. Creatures like man which are endowed with cognitive faculties not only possess a general natural inclination to what is good for them, but also internally specified modes of this general inclination, elicited by their knowing faculties. Thus every concrete human appetite is a complex to which natural inclination contributes one element, and some knowing faculty, another.

It is very important to distinguish these two factors which are present in all actual desire. Knowledge, as we have seen, is always assimilative. It absorbs something outside us into the knowing faculty. Desire, on the other hand, is outward going. It passes from ourselves to something external or beyond us. Such a general tendency to all that is good belongs to us by nature. This natural urge is the root of all definite human desires. But these desires become definite only through the mediation of a cognitive faculty which directs this natural urge, already present, to some specific object. Hence they contain both a natural and a cognitive conation.

If we ignore the cognitive factor we fall into a one-sided voluntarism, which looks upon appetite as an independent faculty, entirely separate from reason, and denies the possibility of all eliciting, rational control. If, on the other hand, we ignore the natural conative factor, we fall into a one-sided intellectualism, which looks upon appetite as a mere automatic consequence of cognition without any freedom of its own. This theory is refuted by the well-

[1] Cf. ch. 13, §§ 4 and 5.

known fact of incontinence, or lack of control, which certainly involves an appetitive factor quite distinct from cognition. In the light of these facts we must conclude that human desire is always a compound of natural urge, together with cognitive specification, and that human nature cannot be adequately perfected without the harmonious integration of these two distinct but inseparable factors in a soundly elicited appetition.

In man there are three cognitive faculties capable of determining our basic natural appetition in three basic modes of elicited desire. First, there are sense, imagination, and the mode of calculation which takes these as its standard.[2] Second, there is the instinctive, estimative faculty, and the mode of calculation which takes this as its standard.[3] Finally, there is the rational faculty which alone, as practical reason, can properly specify the ultimate good for man, the necessary means to this ultimate good, and finally the contingent means. Let us now consider the three modes of human appetition elicited by these three distinct modes of cognition, in the order named.

1. Sensory Appetition

Every human being runs up against certain particular, sensible things which foster his activity, therefore yielding pleasure, and others which frustrate it, therefore yielding pain and discomfort. Images of both are then reproduced in the imagination which governs his desire or sensory appetite. He habitually seeks those things which have given him pleasure in the past and habitually avoids those things which have given him pain. How does he decide whether a given object will be pleasant or painful? By referring to the images of past experience stored up in his imagination. Any object resembling a pleasant image will be regarded as really pleasant by nature, and therefore desirable. On the other hand, anything resembling a painful image will be regarded as really painful by nature, and therefore undesirable. Thus sensible apprehension of concrete entities, through the imagination, elicits fixed modes of appetite. These modes of appetition will be as sound and trustworthy as the sensory apprehension which elicits them. But, as we

[2] Cf. ch. 18, § 4b.
[3] Cf. ch. 18, § 4c.

have seen, sensory apprehension is not wholly sound and trust-worthy.[4]

In the first place, it apprehends only certain superficial, acci-dental qualities of things, never their essential nature. Hence two objects which are sensibly similar, as two speeches intoned in a simi-lar rhetorical manner, may be judged to be similar, though really quite distinct with respect to the essence of what they are saying. Also, two speeches that really say the same thing may be judged to be altogether different simply because of the diverse ways in which they are intoned, one being pleasing, the other displeasing to the ear. Thus without the aid of more accurate apprehensive faculties our imaginations are apt to construct fantastic images based on what is merely accidental to the objects themselves—thinking of a good speech, for example, as something intoned with a certain modulation of voice, irrespective of what is really said. Such imagi-native delusions will then elicit an array of opinion, a set of likes and dislikes, and a mode of practical calculation which are bound to lead us wide of the mark.

Opinion is a mode of theoretical apprehension which follows the sensible appearance rather than the real nature of things. Whenever we jump to a conclusion that something is really as it seems to sense and imagination, without careful rational analysis, we have an opin-ion that may be true or false. Thus if something has given us pleas-ure, we tend to form the opinion that it is really good, and may allow it to influence us subjectively in the formation of other opin-ions or prejudices. Such a biased structure of belief, based upon subjective interest rather than the facts, may then call forth a biased set of likes and dislikes.

As Aristotle says,[5] opinion is quite distinct from desire. Opinion is produced by the theoretical faculty, though without adequate examination of the evidence. It ranges over the whole of being. We may have opinions about the Great Nebula in Andromeda, the center of the earth, and things which are non-existent or even im-possible. But we have likes and dislikes only for a restricted range of objects which it seems possible for us to attain. Opinions are true or false. Likes and dislikes are good or bad. They eat into our char-

[4] Cf. ch. 18, § 5.
[5] *Nic. Eth.*, Book III, ch. 2, 1112A ff.

acter and make us into the kind of human beings we really are. We easily forget our opinions and soon find new ones to take their place. But our likes and dislikes, once formed, constitute a fixed part of our material being and are extremely hard to get rid of. Opinions are theoretical. Likes and dislikes are practical.

But in spite of this difference they exert an important influence on each other. The opinions we form about what is good and bad call forth likes and dislikes, and these likes and dislikes may lead us to accept or reject certain opinions without adequate examination. Once such a biased structure of opinion and desire is established, it may become a fixed obsession and lead whole lives and communities to their destruction. Hence it is of the utmost importance that all those who have anything to do with the training of children (i.e., all human beings), and the children themselves as soon as possible, should have sound and trustworthy knowledge of what is really good and really evil, or at least sound opinions on these subjects. Otherwise unsound opinions will call forth unsound desires and characters, each re-enforcing the other in an ever intensifying vicious circle.

Since the concrete images which elicit such opinions follow no particular order of before and after, and appeal only to a restricted, habitual appetite rather than to our nature as a whole, it is possible for our unguided imagination to harbor two opposed images side by side, each eliciting an opposed set of likes and dislikes in utter disregard of the other. Thus the undisciplined fantasy, on the one hand, will conjure up delightful images of the fruits of saving and productive toil, while, on the other, it will devise even more blissful pictures of spending orgies which dissipate these fruits. Unless these images can be corrected and subordinated to some overarching purpose supplied by a higher faculty, the desires will fall into mutual conflict and the personality, as we say, will be split apart until one of the opposed tendencies succeeds in ruthlessly repressing the other, with the result that the man becomes a miser or a wastrel. When such a deluded fantasy gains complete ascendency it may invert the whole natural order of appetition, enslaving it under some fixed idea or obsession.

So it behooves us to watch very carefully over the images and pictures which fill our imagination. If they are not constantly corrected by reason and brought into essential agreement with reality, they will split our desires into isolated fragments and turn our nature upside down, leading us to subordinate ends to means and to reject the better for the worse. Fortunately, in common with the other higher animals, we possess another mode of sensory appetite which may act as an ally of reason in the critical organization of desire.

2. Irascible Appetite

As we have seen,[6] human nature possesses another mode of cognition, the estimative faculty, which together with memory elicits a more stable type of striving or struggling for more distant and arduous objects than those of the appetites. This estimative capacity, which corresponds to what we call *instinct* in animals, is able to apprehend the agreement of certain particular sensible objects, not merely with a particular, conative tendency, but with our human nature as a whole. Since our individual nature is changing successively in time, these estimations are not merely preserved in isolated phantasies, but are remembered by the distinct faculty of memory as having occurred in a temporal order.

Hence unless the whole order of life is inverted they fit into an order of remembered images which is more stable and integrated than that of our compartmentalized phantasies. Such a stable organization of remembered utility, therefore, elicits another mode of striving which is distinct from sensory appetite. This mode of striving is connected with other experiences extending back much further into the past, and aims at an end lying in a more remote future. Hence it is able to struggle against arduous obstacles for which we have no appetite whatsoever, and thus often falls into conflict with such appetite and the more isolated phantasy directing it.

Irascible aspiration, as Plato first called it, is visible in the animals which, following the guidance of their estimative faculties, will often fight for food and for their young, subjecting themselves to pain and suffering for which they have no appetite. Children and men will similarly fight for some particular, arduous goal or victory which they esteem as useful on the basis either of social tradi-

[6] Cf. ch. 18, § 4c.

tion or of individual memory, subjecting themselves to sufferings and deprivations for which they have no appetite or interest at all.

This mode of appetition is naturally superior to short-range appetite and can greatly assist the rational faculties in controlling the desires, in order to achieve that complete activity which is the natural aim of human life. But here an objection may be raised. Men do terrible things in fits of rage for which they are later very sorry when they think about them. In such cases the irascible element would seem to be very definitely opposed to reason. What then is meant by referring to them as allies?

Note the time interval indicated in the statement of the objection. Rational repentance comes "later," when reason first begins to function. Then we become angry at our irrational anger. The irascible element is thus not simultaneously opposed to reason when reason is present, though in the absence of the latter it may lead us astray. As a matter of fact it is impossible for us to become enraged at anything which our reason clearly tells us is just or to become ashamed of anything which our reason tells us is sound and wholesome. Imagine concrete cases and test this thesis for yourself. This is the evidence that shows the natural alliance between these human tendencies.

Why then, we may ask, does reason later on condemn the irascible part? It does not do this if its judgment is enlightened. Repentance does not concern only a part of the man, and leave the rest guiltless. When a person really repents, he repents for the whole of himself, especially his guiding faculties of intellect and will. We sin, not only through our sensuous appetites, but through our minds and wills as well. Indeed these are even more to blame, for their lethargy was the primary, privative cause of the evil. The lower faculties merely tried vainly to fill a gap left by the inactivity of the higher. But by themselves they cannot be relied upon. Appetite may be deluded by pleasure and pain. Irascible striving is less unreliable. Nevertheless it cannot be relied upon to give us guidance which is ultimately sound and trustworthy.

In the first place, this mode of aspiration is not guided by any rational apprehension of what human nature really is, but only by an estimate of particular utility. Unless reason clarifies its goal, directing it into a genuinely natural course, it easily falls into confusion, and fantasy may usurp this function. In this case human nature is apt to be confused with some minor aspect of itself, and the whole order of means and end distorted and inverted. Even if this does not happen the estimative faculty by itself cannot achieve any concept of the human good in general, but only judges some particular, sensible good as good for this individual or this particular society. Hence it is apt to be led astray by purely accidental sensory resemblances. Some individual object may resemble what has been truly useful in the past, and yet be essentially diverse, as the peace of appeasement may superficially resemble genuine peace, though containing the hidden seeds of war and slavery. Also an individual object which strikes the senses as something entirely new and unique, may yet be essentially the same as what has been experienced before, as some ancient philosophical error is often dressed up in new language to masquerade as a great original contribution to philosophy.

Only the higher faculty of reason is able to make the crucial distinction between essence and accident on which all accuracy of insight and soundness of aspiration must ultimately depend. The traditional aspirations of a community and the deeper habitual urges of an individual can be maintained in a stable, natural condition only when concrete estimations are purified by rational criticism, and the desires which they elicit are subordinated to rational choices of the will. Let us now turn to this highest mode of human conation.

3. RATIONAL APPETITE OR WILL

By sense we apprehend a particular good, relative to this or that sensitive faculty. By estimation we apprehend a particular good, relative to this or that individual nature. By neither of these faculties can we apprehend what is good in general. Reason alone achieves such universal cognition of what is in itself good, apart from all irrelevant accidents. This superior mode of cognition elicits a superior mode of appetition—voluntary aspiration or will. But how, we may ask, can anything be good in itself? Has it not been stated that goodness is the perfection or completion of some nature? Is it not therefore true that such goodness is restricted to the nature it perfects? Is it not then relative to this nature?

We must answer by accepting the first part of this objection, but denying the second. Any good that is realizable in the world of nature is finite, limited, and therefore restricted. The human good is restricted to man, and therefore lacks many perfections. This does not mean, however, that it is relative in the proper sense of this word, which means a reference to something beyond. The dynamic nature of man tends to its completion, reaches out for what is good, and is thus relative to it. But the good, once realized, is a rest of this tendency in itself, and thus not relative. The good is not relative to the interest or tendency, but the tendency is relative to that completion in which it can come to rest, which is good in itself, though still, no doubt, restricted and finite.

This is denied by those who think of good as relative to appetite and define it as any object of any interest. According to this theory interest is viewed as something fixed and non-relative which bestows goodness on those neutral entities which become related to it. These entities and perfections are in themselves only potentially good. This potentiality is actualized only when we take an actual interest in them. Thus a thing may gain or lose its relative goodness as our interests fluctuate, but the interest as such is always good, and the source of goodness in things. This subjectivist theory is based upon an ultimate confusion of actuality and potentiality. It is false for the following reasons.

First, every interest is relative to something good in itself which will give it rest and stability. We cannot become interested in anything which does not at least *seem* good. The interest is potential and relative to what can complete it, and thus bestow goodness upon it. The good is actual, not relative, or we could not rest in it. It is not the interest which actualizes the good, but the good which actualizes the interest. Thus we cannot strive for something purely potential (I do not want a *potential* steak) but only for that which is actual and complete in itself. Finally, it is absolutely false that good things lose or gain their goodness because of the fluctuations of our appetites. A foundling child does not become valueless because no one is any longer interested in it. Things remain good in themselves whatever our interests may be. These goods may be accurately and clearly known only by the faculty of reason.

First of all, reason apprehends metaphysical or transcendental goodness, which extends as far as being itself, for all existence is the perfection of some nature. Hence the study of this belongs to general metaphysics, and we shall not consider it now. What we are interested in here is a second kind of universal good, the good for man, that which perfects not this man or that, but human nature as such. Since man is a rational animal he is noetically related to being; therefore all positive existence is relevant to his perfection. The order into which all entities fall, simply *qua* existing, is the object of metaphysics, the theoretical or metaphysical order. But the order into which all entities fall, *qua* perfecting human nature, is the object of ethical science, the practical or moral order. What is this order?

The governing principle of this order on which all else depends, is the end of man, the full perfection of our nature. Since human nature is not simple but complex, this perfection will have many phases. Regarded *formally,* the end of man consists of all those entities and modes of being which, by reason of their general intrinsic nature, perfect the being of man. Each of these is an intermediate, formal end. All of these *universal* entities, taken together in the order of their importance, constitute the formal, final end of man. All the *particular* objects in which these are to be found constitute the *material,* final end. Regarded *subjectively,* the end of man consists in the resting of every human faculty in that which perfects it, or brings it to full activity. The realization of each faculty is an intermediate, subjective end. The realization of all of them, taken together in their natural order, is the subjective, final end of man.

Suppose you are striving to become generous. This is then the object of your aspiration. But this object can be regarded in two ways, formally and materially. We may regard generosity abstractly, irrespective of what particular acts are generous. This is the formal, objective end. But no man can ever achieve a formal or universal end. No one can be generous in general. He must find this formal end in certain concrete objects, say the giving of this money to this man. This is the material, objective end. The rest of his aspiration in such an object, once achieved, is the subjective end. Our striving does not cease when it achieves completion, nor does its object lose its value, as is now widely supposed. Our striving rather reaches its climax and enjoys the perfection it has achieved.

Every man has at least some vague notion of this final end for the sake of which he is living his life, though this notion is often only imperfectly conceptualized and mixed with much irrelevant, accidental matter derived from sense and phantasy. Unless such admixtures are constantly purified by rational criticism the ultimate end is apt to be confused with what is only an apparent end, really only a means, and the aspiration elicited by this misapprehension completely inverted. Thus the primary task of all moral philosophy is to clarify so far as possible and to determine accurately the ultimate perfection or activity of our nature. The whole of metaphysics, philosophy of nature, and psychology or anthropology are directly relevant to this clarification, which cannot be adequately achieved except in the light of these purely theoretical disciplines.

The end is the first source of all moral reflection, just as the first premises are the first source of all theoretical demonstration. Theory then proceeds to discover middle terms by which the universal conclusion to be demonstrated can be connected with these necessary premises. In a similar way the second step in moral reflection is to discover the necessary middle terms or means by which human nature in its potential or imperfect state can be actualized or connected with its end. When this beginning and this end are clearly apprehended, the whole complex structure of the necessary, intermediate means comes at once into view.

Thus the undeveloped individual cannot attain the different virtues or intermediate ends, which perfect different aspects of his nature, without undergoing the necessary process of learning and habit formation. This process cannot be made available to every individual in a given society, its common good cannot be achieved, unless the various arts and techniques of possession, production, distribution, and human therapy are maintained in their proper or natural order in that society.[7] The precise definition of these necessary means and the accurate determination of their relative position with respect to one another, is the second essential task of moral philosophy, strangely neglected and confused with the third, following task, by the medieval tradition of Aristotelian philosophy. This third task is to help individuals choose freely and prudently those particular, contingent means which may lead this or that individual to his final goal.

[7] Cf. ch. 12, § 3.

The general nature of the human end is necessarily determined by human nature, and the general means required to achieve this end are necessarily determined by the end. So we may well ask, therefore, in what sense our wills are free. Of course we are "free" to confuse the real end with an apparent end and to misconceive the necessary means leading to this goal. Many thinkers have confused such misunderstanding with genuine freedom. But this is itself a serious misunderstanding. It implies that we cannot become free without misconceiving our proper end, and thus inverting the whole order of life. But surely genuine freedom is not an imperfection which distorts our nature, but rather something very precious which perfects it. Furthermore this view opposes freedom to rationality in such a way that one excludes the other. According to it, we cannot act rationally without losing our freedom, and we cannot become free without losing our rationality.

But it is quite clear from the facts that these goods are not opposed in any such exclusive manner. A man can be both rational and free. In fact the more carefully we think of the matter, the harder it will be to see how a man can be one without the other. We must conclude, therefore, that genuine freedom cannot lie merely in misconceiving the ultimate end. This may be a *sign* of freedom, but it cannot constitute real freedom. We must ask once more wherein our freedom truly lies. The end is determined by nature. Necessary means are determined by this end. If our wills are free there must be something else embedded in the essential structure of the human act. There is something else.

We must not forget that we are material entities, not existing in general, but here and now, under restrictive, material conditions.[8] Since action always follows the mode of existence, and a thing always acts as it is, we cannot act in general for a general good. We must always act *in particular, here and now,* for a *concrete and particular good.* We cannot reach out for a universal steak but only for *this* steak. I cannot get the steak without reaching for it. This is a necessary means to this end. But I may reach more or less rapidly, with two hands or with only one. These are not necessary means but *contingent* means, for I may achieve the end whichever of these I choose.

[8] Cf. ch. 14, § 6.

This is a trivial example, but it illustrates the important fact that with respect to every end, there are both necessary and contingent means. With respect to the former, I am not really free, but with respect to the latter I am free to choose. Such choices of contingent means constitute the genuine freedom of the will. The human will is determined with respect to the end and the necessary means to the end. It is undetermined with respect to the contingent means. Hence the more clearly we can discern the ultimate, natural end of man, and the more determinately we can strive for it, the less is our danger of becoming obsessed with contingent things which are of less importance, i.e., the freer we shall be.

The third task of moral philosophy is to cultivate so far as possible the virtue of prudence which enables us to choose wisely in the contingent situations confronting us, those non-necessary means to our ultimate goal which will most effectively take us from where we are to this end. Freedom can be maintained only by the constant exercise of this virtue, which includes two factors: (1) a clear understanding of the ultimate end, our own situation, and the necessary means to this end and (2) constant deliberation and choice of the concrete, contingent means leading us to this end. Freedom is lost (1) by falling into confusion concerning the ultimate end and the necessary means leading to it and (2) by failing to deliberate and plan about concrete courses of action leading us here and now towards the end.

Such is the nature of will, or rational appetition. Reason alone, of our several apprehensive faculties, is able to grasp the universal and essential nature of man, and the universal and essential nature of that which perfects him. Hence reason elicits that mode of voluntary aspiration which is alone capable of bringing man to the goal for which his nature has predestined him. Nature has also determined a goal for the other creatures, but since they cannot reason, she has also determined for them the various means by which they must for the most part achieve this goal. To man, of all the natural animals, she has given the mysterious power of rational insight by which he can grasp his nature and its end.

Hence to man alone she has also given the attendant freedom to determine his own means of attaining the end which he can grasp —the power not merely to be perfected, which the other creatures have, but to realize and to perfect himself. Only reason can grasp an end, for an "end" is always relative, and reason alone can apprehend relations. Only reason can grasp the means to the end, for this is relative to the end. Hence, while the other animals are determined to act for a certain end, they cannot rationally understand or assimilate this. They are determined to embrace certain means to this end, but they do not understand these acts as means.

Man alone is free because he understands his end, as such, and the necessary means to his end. Furthermore he is free, because he is left to devise and to choose his own contingent means, meeting his own individual circumstances, making his own way through the mazes of concrete, human history, towards or away from that ultimate goal of perfection which every man and every woman at least dimly understands. This voluntary, free aspiration, or will, is the highest mode of appetition which is prescribed by the law of our nature to rule over estimative and sensory appetite, and indeed over every active tendency in our nature. Only in this way can men really take over their own lives and achieve the goal for the sake of which they were brought into existence on this earth—the human living of human life.[9]

4. The Relation of Will to the Other Faculties

The natural appetition of man follows immediately upon his nature. It is neither sensory nor voluntary, but the common root of both. It is not at one time in potency and at another time in act, for as long as the nature exists at all it must necessarily tend to its perfection. Sensory appetite and will, however, do not immediately follow nature, but are elicited by cognition. They are special modes of natural appetition, each of which may exist in a purely potential state. A man must always be tending in some manner to his perfection. He need not always be actually willing. Such an act of will is elicited from natural appetite by rational cognition. Hence the structure of voluntary action is a composite one, involving both appetite and reason united in an intricate structure to which we must now turn.

Will is an active tending to some specific end, an elicited inclination to such good as is apprehended by the intellect. Hence it must

9 Cf. ch. 2, § 1.

include an *active* factor of tending, or exercising, provided by appetite, and a *specifying*, or determining factor provided by intellect. But each of these factors is further subdivided. Altogether we can discern 12 distinct aspects of this complex structure.[10]

1. The first aspect of voluntary aspiration is *the simple apprehension by the intellect of some good*. What then moves the intellective power to act? Not will, because this must be elicited by a preceding intellective act. We must answer *natural appetition*, which necessarily follows the subjective nature of man, tending subjectively to actualize every natural faculty, including intellect.

2. As soon as the intellect apprehends something good (capable of perfecting our nature), a nisus, or indeliberate tending to this good, is elicited in our natural appetite as the second phase of voluntary activity. This is no longer natural appetition but natural appetition elicited by rational apprehension of the good, namely, *wish*.

3. The third phase of voluntary action is *practical judgment* by which the will, already aroused, applies the intellect to the task of judging whether the good is really able to be gained, and is here and now a genuine good capable of perfecting my nature as it is. There is no point in seeking what is really impossible or, though good for human nature in general, is not good for me in my peculiar, and possibly abnormal circumstances. But is it really impossible for me or is it just that I fear the effort and the change involved?

If the object is really perfective of human nature, and therefore intrinsically good, then indeed my circumstances must be most peculiar and in fact diseased, if it is not good for me. These are the questions which practical judgment must decide. On the whole, it can be said that practical reason is least unsound when it gives the least weight to individual fears and foibles, and is least likely to judge that any genuine good is impossible for the agent.

4. The process of judgment is apt to involve considerable oscillation between opposed judgments. When the final judgment of the practical intellect is that the object is really possible for the agent, then the will is determined to tend towards this end through the requisite means. We shall never actually attain any goal, except by

[10] Cf. ch. 3, § 1c.

sheer luck, unless we really intend it. This phase of intention is the fourth phase of rational conduct. We no longer merely wish for the object, but actually intend to attain it for ourselves.

5. Through intention the intellect is then determined to deliberate concerning the means of obtaining the intended end, for we do not deliberate about mere wishes. We deliberate only about what we really intend. This crucial process of *deliberation* involves the discovery of middle terms capable of connecting ourselves, in the particular situation encompassing us, with the intended goal, just as theoretical reasoning involves the discovery of middle terms capable of connecting some conclusion to be proved with evident premises already known. But it is not the same. As we have seen, one of its terms is particular and individual, all the middle terms are relative to this term, and the whole process is governed by a concrete intention to arrive at the goal. Hence one may be a good theoretical investigator and a very bad deliberator, and vice versa.

6. Deliberation is carried on primarily by the intellect, which alone can grasp relations and middle terms. But unless the will, on its side, really follows its intention with a *consent* to follow the means discovered by deliberation, the whole process will collapse into a mere disguised daydream. How lovely it would be if I first did this; then I could do that; and I might do this; then I might arrive at the end! Such an imagined chain of possible means is not an actual process of deliberation, for it is only half intended and therefore a case of what we now call wishful thinking. The *active consent* of the will to follow the means discovered in deliberation is the essential, sixth phase of voluntary action.

7. By virtue of this appetitive approval or consent of the will, which commits it actually to adopt some means to the intended end, the intellect is then moved to examine alternative sets of means with a view to determining which is more apt in the case at hand. Since we do not act in general but always individually in a "situation" fraught with the infinite, accidental detail attaching to all that is concrete, the deliberative faculty may always lay out different courses of action, each of which will lead to the end.

So far as it fails in this essential deliberative function, an opportunity for the rational control of action is lost, and the agent falls into slavery to externally controlled appetite. This also may happen when the intellect is too ingenious in devising means and becomes so fascinated with its own constructions that the process is never terminated by a clear-cut decision. This *decision* as to which means is the best in the given situation is essential to the preservation of human freedom. Two opposed dangers are to be avoided.

On the one hand, we must not become so obsessed with the need for rightness in the means, as to confuse this with the end. The value of the means is a derivative value, derived from the value of the end. Therefore Kant and his followers are mistaken in their attempt to separate rightness from goodness. No means is right which does not lead us to a good end, and the rightness of the means is wholly dependent on the goodness of the end.

On the other hand, we must not become so obsessed with our need for the end, as to ignore the rightness of the means, and to regard any means as right which brings us to the end, irrespective of how we get there. The end does not justify the means in the sense in which this phrase is usually taken. The end justifies the *right* means, that is, any means which does not involve an evil greater than the good of the end to be attained.

Here it is peculiarly important to remember that every virtuous act is a part of the final end of man,[11] whereas external transitive powers over things and possessions have only an instrumental value in so far as they enable us to act rationally. Hence the attainment of some such external instrumental good as an end can never justify a vicious or irrational action on our part. This is already to confuse a means with an end, for the action by which we perfect ourselves is more valuable and important than any number of external possessions.

That means is more right than another, which, in the given situation here and now, offers richer opportunities for the active perfection of my nature and of all those in the human community (the common good) . In case of conflict between the individual good and the common good, the latter is preferable, as the whole is by nature more important and more valuable than the part.[12] The *intellectual discrimination of the better means here and now* is an essential seventh phase of the deliberative process.

[11] Cf. ch. 2, § 1.
[12] Cf. ch. 9, § 3.

8. But it does not complete the aspiration. We all know that it is possible for the practical intellect to decide that one means is better than another, without affecting our action. So we must add an eighth, further stage. The will must accept this decision of the practical intellect and choose the preferable means before the others. This is *the act of free choice.*

9. By virtue of this choice the intellect is then moved to *command* the execution of the chosen means in accordance with the ancient dictum: *sapientiae est ordinare.* Reason alone can grasp the whole situation in its intricate totality—the final end together with the necessary steps it demands, and the preferable contingent means to this end. Hence it is the function of reason to issue the final command to action—*the imperium.*

10. The tenth following phase is action itself—the active use by the will of all the other human powers and faculties together with their external means which lead to the end. This is that *voluntary, active employment of means to the end* by which alone our rational nature is perfected.

11. But there can be no active use without something passively being used. So corresponding to this active use by the will there is, in the eleventh place, *the passive effect of this in the intellect, senses, and motive powers.* These subordinate powers are used by the will in such a way as to actually apprehend the concrete means and to actually employ them here and now for the attainment of the end. If these subordinate powers are not properly tempered (by virtue) to such use, they will not do as they are commanded, and the end will not be attained.

12. Finally, in the twelfth and last place, there is the crowning act of rest or enjoyment in the end. Contrary to a widespread misconception this is no mere feeling or emotion of internal sense, but the final act of the will, which is to rest in the congruent object of its endeavors. Of course this may be attended by sensuous pleasure and delight, so far as sensuous appetite has been properly tempered and subordinated to the control of reason and will.

It is also a mistake to agree with the widely held doctrine that all enjoyment is *esthetic,* all striving *moral.* Men strive intensely to achieve esthetic ends. They also enjoy many good things which are not esthetic, like the conquest of a vicious enemy. The esthetic and the moral each has a distinctive end and a distinctive mode of striving. The good is something we strive to possess and enjoy when we *have* it. The beautiful, on the other hand, is something we strive to apprehend (or construct for the apprehensive faculties) and to enjoy when we *contemplate* it.

All of these twelve phases are essentially involved in the intricate structure of a *voluntary* act. If every faculty makes its proper contribution at the proper time, in the proper manner dictated by nature, the act will then be naturally sound, or virtuous—i.e., wise, prudent, just, courageous, and temperate.[13] It will be *wise* so far as the intellect (in the light of an accurate, synthetic, and theoretical insight into being) truly apprehends the end of man (aspect 1), and adequately judges the possibility of its attainment (aspect 3). It will be *prudent* so far as the practical intellect accurately deliberates the necessary and contingent means (aspect 5), adequately distinguishes which among the contingent means is most apt and fit (aspect 7), commands their use here and now (aspect 9), and reflects on each stage of the concrete act in obedience to the command of the will (aspect 11).

The act will be *just* so far as the will, in the first place, concerns itself with its natural end, which can be apprehended by the intellect alone in the light of an all-encompassing, theoretical wisdom, loving it (aspect 2), intending it (aspect 4), and finally enjoying it (aspect 12); and in the second place, concerns itself with the necessary and proper means to this end, consenting to use only such means as can be distinguished by the intellect (aspect 6), choosing the better and more appropriate means (aspect 8), and finally using these means so as to give to each thing its due (aspect 10).

The act will be *courageous* so far as this active use (aspect 10) fails to be overcome by opposition and struggles on to its goal in spite of all difficulty. It will be temperate in so far as all the subordinate faculties without hesitation or rebellion subordinate themselves to the command of reason in their passive use by will (aspect 11).

Each of these four cardinal phases of virtuous action is dependent upon the rest, and no one can fully exist by itself in separation from the others. Furthermore nature dictates a definite hierarchical

---

[13] Cf. ch. 5, § 1.

order in which each faculty is subordinated in a certain way to another. We must now examine this order more closely with a view toward discovering more exactly how one faculty moves another.

As Aristotle pointed out, one faculty can move another subordinate faculty either despotically or politically, depending on whether the subordinate faculty has or has not an alternative, independent mode of action. If it has not, then it is from the very start at the mercy of the higher faculty which controls it despotically, as the body is despotically ruled by the soul which animates it. If the lower faculty has access to an alternative, independent mode of operation, then the higher faculty must win its control politically by processes of habit formation, as the will must win control over sensory appetite by the gradual development of discipline, which may be opposed by sluggishness and rebellion.

This ever present possibility of appetitive insurrection leads many to conclude that there is no natural basis for the claim of the higher faculty to rule the lower, just as in the analogous field of politics, the ever present possibility of revolution leads many to conclude that there is no natural, but only an arbitrary, or conventional, basis for social order. This is a great mistake. The "independence" of the lower faculties is not due to any lack of natural authority on the part of the higher, immaterial faculties, but rather to their peculiar immanent mode of operation, which distinguishes and dignifies our nature as free men.

But this also enables us not to use them if we do not choose, and thus to provide the lower faculties with a spurious "independence." No external force, no matter how vast or overwhelming it may be, can *make a man change his mind* or alter his voluntary decision without his consent. These immaterial faculties are immanently actualized. Hence it rests with the individual alone whether they are to be finally actualized or not. If an individual will not think or choose, no external power can make him do so.

But the lower, sensitive faculties are not so completely within our control. Their "independence" from reason is really a dependence on external causes. If these faculties are present at all, then external objects presented to us will force us to see and to hear. Thus images can be forced upon our imaginations, and our sensuous appetites manipulated and controlled. In fact they must be so controlled either by chance or by external manipulation, unless the higher faculties intervene, in accordance with the demands of nature. But this demand can be met only by our own immanent action. Nature demands that we think and choose freely, and of ourselves win a political control over the rest of our nature by the free establishment of a second nature, or system of habits, penetrating into every phase of human life, which accords with the governing insights of reason.

Our *first nature* is simply presented to us at birth. But this nature necessarily demands for its fulfillment a *second nature* of habits which can be realized only by ourselves alone, under the higher faculties of intellect and will.[14] Freedom lies precisely in the establishment of such a second nature. The failure to establish it and the consequent "independence" of the lower faculties, is not freedom at all, as we so erroneously suppose, but its precise opposite, self-subjection to the slavery of external, material force and tyranny. But how are the different faculties subordinated to one another in this free order of second nature? First of all, which of the two highest faculties is really dominant over which?

We cannot give a simple answer to this question. Each faculty dominates the other despotically in a certain respect. But each is also independent of the other in a certain respect. Hence the harmonious perfection of these two powers, the most crucial factor in the perfection of human life, is a free or immanent process of habit formation in which, as in a naturally ordered human community, each citizen dominates another in his own proper sphere in order to establish a political union to which each makes a free contribution.

The human act is like a hylomorphic compound in which the intellect provides the formal, specifying elements, and will the moving power. Thus intellect despotically dominates will in *specifying* the precise nature of its end and the means leading up to the end, for the will cannot begin to actualize itself until the intellect presents it with something specific to seek. But once aroused, the will despotically dominates the intellect as it dominates all the other faculties in *efficiently causing* their exercise or quiescence. Thus the intellect cannot act unless the will sustains its action. But

[14] Cf. ch. 3, § 2.

the will itself cannot act except for some end specified by the intellect. If the actual end, dictated by nature, is properly specified from the beginning, then each faculty will reenforce the other. It is only by submitting to the insights of reason that the will can act at all. It is only by submitting to will so specified that reason can be maximally sustained in action.

But whereas each naturally sustains the other in this way, we can note a certain natural priority of intellect to will, for the former must first be brought into action by the nisus of human nature itself before the will can be aroused at all. Also, the final cause of voluntary aspiration must be constantly presented to it through the mediation of rational cognition, and the final cause, being the cause of all the causes, is prior to efficient action. In spite of this natural determining priority of intellect to will, we must note a balancing factor on the side of will—its greater inclusiveness.

This arises from its concrete character. The whole perfection of the intellectual faculty is included as a desirable good within the concrete order of practice or execution, whereas the whole practical order is not included within the intelligible order of understanding, which abstracts from the particular and contingent. This is why Plato's practical philosophy achieved a more sweeping synthesis than Aristotle's more accurate but less inclusive theoretical philosophy.[15] But with the whole classical tradition of philosophy, we must acknowledge *the natural priority of intellect to will and the supremacy of wisdom over all the other virtues.*

In the light of this we can also see that the acts of government, which play a role in social life analogous to that played by the will in individual life, through the possession of supreme, efficient power, are naturally dominant over every material phase of social life and even over its intellectual phases so far as these involve efficient action. At the same time these acts of government are nevertheless in themselves naturally subordinate to the *specifying* influence of the higher intellectual arts of education, pure science, and philosophy.

That form of voluntarism which defends will as the highest human faculty is really advocating just such a tyrannizing of individual life as the dreadful social tyranny which we know results from

[15] Cf. ch. 1, § 3.

allowing governmental power to dictate what is taught in the schools. An irrevocable law of nature demands the general supremacy of the specifying, finalizing, theoretical order over the practical order of means and ends.

In aspects 1 and 2 of the voluntary act (pp. 481–482) the intellect exercises a despotic control over will, for we can wish only for those goods which reason apprehends. But throughout aspects 3 to 9 (pp. 482–485) its control over the will is not despotic but political. The judgments, deliberations, and discriminations of the practical intellect may be ignored, overridden, or simply prevented altogether by a rampant, untrained will taking the bit into its own teeth. During the actual execution of the act (aspects 9 to 12, pp. 485–486) the will despotically governs the passive exercise of reason and its own willing of the means, but exercises only a political control over the instrumental action of the subordinate sensitive faculties, since these faculties, as we have seen, are capable of falling into fixed dispositions under external irrational control.

This is true of both irascible and sensory appetite, though as Plato clearly noted, the former is a natural ally of practical reason and is far less likely to fall into subrational slavery while the higher faculties remain active even to a slight degree. As Plato also pointed out, one of the most remarkable facts about our nature is the surprising inability of the irascible power to bring itself into open opposition with reason and will. It is psychologically impossible for a man to become genuinely angry at an injury done to him which his reason tells him is really deserved, and therefore rational and just. We cannot go on struggling and hoping for what our reason tells us is really hopeless. We cannot feel genuinely ashamed for something which our reason tells us is truly natural and sound.

This irascible power in our nature can become corrupted only on the condition that reason and will are themselves already corrupted. Hence the first step in the establishment of a dictatorship must be the control of propaganda and education, by which practical reason can be inverted and confused. It is only on this condition that our hopes, fears, angers, shames, and other irascible tendencies, which follow the best insights we have, will prove malleable to the tyrant's decree.

But this is not true of the lower sensory appetites. They are further from the immaterial rational powers and much more likely to fall under "independent" external domination. When this happens they are capable of openly resisting the commands of reason and will. Some uncontrolled act yields us momentary pleasure and leaves an alluring image in our phantasy, which leads us to further repetitions of the act. Each repetition makes us more susceptible until, as we say, we have been "conditioned," or in more technical language, an *immobile disposition* has been formed. The only way of avoiding such susceptibilities to external control is to acquire the passional virtues which, as we have seen,[16] dispose our sensory appetites to harmonize with will, and the practical reason directing it. But without these passional virtues our appetites and feelings no longer eagerly follow the will but sink into apathy or open rebellion against it.

The human will is commonly imaged as a mere efficient force or "power" which is most clearly manifested at such times of conflict in forcefully repelling or "repressing" the rebellious appetites. In a similar way the state is misconceived as mere executive "power," which exercises its control only by forcefully repelling or repressing factional rebellion. In both cases this is a great delusion. The breaking out of open rebellion, even though it be "repressed," is an indication of lack of control rather than of control.

Force alone is a temporary measure which never penetrates to the root of the difficulty. In spite of violent temporary defeat, an insurrection will break out again unless the misconceptions on which it is based are corrected. Genuine political control is really manifested, not so much in the use of armed force, as in those less sensational measures of legislation and persuasion which lead all lesser aims into harmony with the central purpose of community life.

The "political" control of the individual human will over the subordinate appetites is exactly analogous. It is really manifested, not so much in the repression of rebellious desire, as in the less sensational measures of planning, deliberation, and imaginative persuasion which take account of every aspect of human nature and bring them all into harmony with the central overarching purposes of individual life. As a matter of fact when some appetitive disposition breaks away from rational control, the will cannot act upon

[16] Cf. ch. 5, § 3; and chs. 6 and 7.

this appetite directly but only through the mediation of the images governing it. What we call "repression" is a matter, not so much of eliminating the appetite, as the alluring image which elicits it.

An alluring image necessarily calls forth desire. In order to get rid of the latter we must forget the former. Disordered appetite is caused by disordered imagination and opinion. Such a chaotic imagination can easily become obsessed with some lurid fantasy. Unless the will intervenes by moving the disordered faculty to think of something else (repression), it may become immobilized in what we call a "fixed idea," which may secretly govern our actual behavior even when we seem to be thinking and doing other things. Then rational freedom is lost, and the whole order of life is finally inverted.

The will may postpone such a catastrophe by acting directly on the imagination, leading it to replace the dangerous fantasy by another of a less irrational character. This is why it is of fundamental importance that every imagination be supplied with a rich array of persuasive images, derived from literature and the other so-called fine arts, ordered in accordance with the natural demands of practical reason, and capable of arousing appetites which re-enforce the deliberate choices of the will.

But as long as any wandering images remain unassimilated into this rational order, even though temporarily forgotten or suppressed, there is always the danger of rebellion and the loss of freedom in slavery to an *immobile obsession.* This danger can be finally overcome only by rational analysis of the image itself which, with the aid of satire and irony, may first win an indifference to its mesmeric power over appetite and then may finally achieve reconstruction in line with an overarching, rational purpose.

Unless this purpose is kept clear by theoretical insight and supported by compelling images and appropriate habits of feeling and impulse, the will itself may not only lose control over appetite but may itself become perverted into an instrument for the realization of interest. This most complete and terrible inversion of human nature, as Aristotle pointed out,[17] is much worse than mere lack of control, for it infects, not only the lower, subordinate portions of human nature, but its ruling faculties of intellect and will as well.

[17] *Nic. Eth.* VII, ch. 9.

Of course sensuous appetite cannot directly influence the immaterial will. But it can affect the will through the mediation of the intellect, which apprehends the goodness of all things, including that of sensuous appetite, and sensuous pleasure. When other higher goods are not clearly focused, our practical reason can direct the will to this *satisfaction of interests* as the highest end of man.

Human nature will then be confused with those chance interests which merely happen at a certain time to obtain, though many of them may be purely incidental or due to tyrannical manipulation. Those who take this position no longer think of the good thing as inspiring the interest because it is good, but argue that anything is good if someone is interested in it, no matter who, precisely because of his interest. Thus human action is derationalized, subjectivized, and materialized.

The highest goods, which are really capable of satisfying the highest capacities of our nature, are confused with those material objects which satisfy sensuous appetite. The qualitative distinction, which makes certain good things *intrinsically* better than others, is lost sight of and replaced by a purely material or quantitative judgment of more and less. The complete or good life, in which every capacity of our nature is perfected in the true order of its importance, is confused with the purely quantitative ideal of satisfying as many interests as possible. Human freedom is neglected or passed over altogether, for the ability of reason to elicit sound aspirations and prune away or subordinate interests is denied, and man has to be regarded as the slave of those particular interests which at any time he may happen to have. Interest replaces reason as the ruling human faculty, and the practical intellect is degraded into a useful instrument for devising clever plans and means by which as many interests as possible may be satisfied.

Such theories as these, when put into practice, degrade our highest immaterial faculties and invert our human nature to the maximum degree. Will is reduced to appetite—reason to an instrument. Instead of rationally determining the ultimate good and then ordering the rest of our nature to this natural end, reason prostitutes itself to the service of the lower appetites, following rather than guiding, "rationalizing" rather than justifying. Human degradation can sink no lower.

5. THE WORLD OF NATURE AND MAN

We have now finished our presentation of the realistic theory of the natural world, its natural evolution, and its highest product, the creature man. Our study began (Chapter 1) with an outline of the history of realistic philosophy from the time of the Greeks to the present day. This philosophy is realistic in holding that we inhabit a world sustained in being by causes which are independent of human opinion and desire. It is rationalistic in holding that the structure of this world, including the nature of man, may be known by the mind as it really is. Finally, this philosophy holds that such theoretical knowledge may give trustworthy guidance for the direction of human life, both individual and social. After examining this realistic, practical philosophy (Part I) we entered upon the task of explaining its essential, theoretical doctrines concerning the natural world and man.

We have now completed this task. In Chapter 13 we examined the change which permeates all natural being and the hylomorphic structure which is possessed by any changing entity. In Chapter 14 we considered the causes of natural change, the formal cause which unites with the matter of any concrete entity to make it into the kind of being it is, the efficient cause which moves the matter into its form and sustains it in being, and the final cause which determines the moving agent to act in a determinate way. In addition to these we also examined that material potency which is the most elusive of all the causes and which is ultimately responsible for the ubiquitous dynamism, indeterminacy, and individuation of nature.

In Chapter 15 we turned to the different modes of being, or categories, which are involved in the natural processes of change. Four of these (substance, quality, quantity, and place) themselves determine distinctive modes of change. Three of these (action, passion, and time) characterize any process. One (relation) emerges as a result of change.

In Chapter 16 we studied certain empirical arguments for an invisible, first cause which have been formulated and defended by the great realistic philosophers. We then examined the nature and attributes of this first cause, so far as they could be deduced by reason alone without the aid of direct sensory observation.

Our conclusion was that basic sensory facts, such as the first existence of finite entities, the constant evolution of natural entities, and the order of this change, could not be accounted for unless we follow the common insight of men and the more exact philosophical expression of this insight, in inferring the existence of a first cause whose essence is existence. It can then be shown that such a being is absolutely simple, perfect, immutable, intelligent, freely active, immaterial, and therefore not directly observable by us. With this first cause the existence of the world and its ordered processes becomes intelligible. A pattern can be vaguely discerned. The processes of inorganic change are the basis for the higher and more complex process of organic evolution. At the core of this latter process there has been a nucleus of living substances, which have resisted the tendency toward adaptation to a special environment, and have retained their flexibility. From this nucleus higher forms have constantly emerged, until the climax has been reached in man.

Human nature has been the object of our study in this second section. Though physically insignificant and powerless this remarkable and paradoxical offspring of nature, man, is endowed with an immaterial faculty of apprehension which enables him to penetrate to the farthest reaches of material nature and beyond, and thus noetically to identify himself with all things. We began our study of this extraordinary creature in Chapter 17 with an examination of the psyche, or soul, and its various faculties. This soul, or formal structure of a human being, cannot be regarded as the accidental property of anything else. It is rather the first act, or substantial form of a living, material being, that underlies all of its operations and faculties as their first, formal cause.

This form contains subsistence (the capacity for self-existence), corporeity, vitality, animality, and rationality within itself—all bound together into a single structural unity. The last three traits produce special faculties with special organs for the performance of vital functions. These are the vegetative functions of nutrition, growth, and reproduction, the animal functions of sense and locomotion, and the rational functions of intellect and will. The soul itself, as an incomplete or dynamic form enmeshed with matter, has a natural subjective tendency to complete itself through the acts of all these faculties.

The function of philosophical anthropology is to gain an over-all picture of man as a whole, and especially of those guiding, immaterial faculties of intellect and will which are not open to the sensory methods of the physical sciences. Hence we passed very rapidly over the corporeal nature of man and the vegetative faculties. In Chapter 18, however, we undertook a more careful study of sensory cognition and its composite, psychophysical structure. We took up the external senses, the internal sense, imagination, memory, and the estimative faculty.

By these faculties we attain a partly sound, but partly relative, apprehension of certain modes of external being as they are confused together in individual entities. They are unable to abstract each mode of being from others with which it is materially confused and to apprehend it exactly as it is in itself. Nevertheless in spite of illusions and hallucinations, a careful examination does not justify any thoroughgoing philosophical distrust of the senses. They give us an awareness of external reality which is limited and confused but not basically false. When crowned by the more exact insight of the higher apprehensive faculty of reason and purified by its critical judgment, this awareness is expanded and clarified in the penetrating perspectives of knowledge.

In Chapter 19 we turned to this highest faculty of reason, by far the most extraordinary capacity which is found anywhere in the natural world. Depending upon sense and the whole physical organism to supply it with objects for reflection, this faculty nevertheless possesses a peculiar apprehensive power of its own. This power consists in an ability to identify itself immaterially with any formal nature, exactly as it is, in abstraction from everything with which it may be materially confused in sense or imagination. Once such an abstract nature is grasped, it may be compared with other individuals, and thus identified with them as a universal concept. In this way the nature may be apprehended, not merely as it exists in *this* material example, but universally as it must be anywhere in *any* example. Thus the range and exactness of knowledge are magnified and intensified.

In Chapter 20 we turned to the active, dynamic aspect of human nature. This nature, like that of any hylomorphic entity, is a tendency to express itself in every mode of action possible to it. But this subjective tendency cannot be adequately fulfilled without the guidance of the cognitive capacities of sense and reason, each of which elicits special forms of active tendency, or appetition, under their own control. Because of its unique capacity to grasp all things, including itself, reason must become the supreme guide of human conduct if the natural end of man is to be achieved.

But reason alone is a purely apprehensive faculty which has nothing to do with action. It can become a guide for conduct only when working in union with the conative tendency it elicits. This union of reason and tendency is what we call *will*. Many desires and appetites for concrete objects are elicited by sense and imagination. Many irascible, struggling tendencies are elicited by the estimative faculty. But freely chosen, voluntary acts are elicited by the faculty of reason, which can apprehend all that is good for man. Working in cooperation with these active tendencies, it may then specify the will in such a way as to do justice to every phase of human nature in an ordered pattern of life.

The most essential feature of human life, as it is actually lived, is the struggle of the intellect and will to gain control over all the manifold, subordinate aspects of our complex, material nature (cf. Part I). Human history, both that of individuals and that of human civilizations, presents us with an ever varying series of concrete pictures, but the essence of the picture is always the same. Men are faced with different concrete challenges in different material situations. They meet these challenges by different modes of passive response and sometimes by chosen action. The basic challenge is always the same.

Will this amazing polymorphic creature, physical and mental, material and immaterial, individual and universal, come to exercise his highest immaterial faculties intensively enough to guide his material life by the immaterial light of reason and science? Such control has never been more than very remotely approximated even by great human individuals, still less by human societies. It never will be more closely approximated in the concrete, unless men first gain at least enough insight to grasp rationally what such control would be like, what a really human life would be.

The importance of describing the natural life of man, that life which nature herself has made possible by endowing him with im-

material faculties of reason and voluntary choice, was seen long
ago by the Greeks, who inaugurated the science of ethics, the study
of human life not as it is, not as it has been, not even as it will be,
but as it *ought to be*—as it would be if man realized fully the capacities of his nature. What would human life be like if man ceased
drifting in passive response to material influences? What would
happen if he voluntarily took over his life and directed it in accordance with the real nature of things, as they can be grasped by
reason? We have considered the realistic answer to these questions
in Part I.

REFERENCES

Recommended Reading

Plato, *Republic*, Book IV, 434–441; Aristotle, *Nicomachean Ethics*, Book I,
    chap. 13; and Aquinas, *Summa Theologica*, Part I, Qu. 80–83, and
    Prima Secundae, Qu. 10–17.

Suggested Reading

1. Plato, *Republic* IV, 434D–438; Aristotle, *Nicomachean Ethics*, Book I,
    chap 13; and Aquinas, *Summa Theologica*, Part I, Qu. 80, and 81 Art. 1.
    For a more detailed account of sensory appetite, cf. *Summa Theologica*,
    Prima Secundae, Qu. 22–39.
2. Plato, *Republic*, Book IV, 439–440; and Aquinas, *Summa Theologica*,
    Part I, Qu. 81, Arts. 2 and 3; cf. *Prima Secundae*, Qu. 40–48 for a fuller
    account.
3. Plato, *Republic*, Book IV, 439 and 441; Aristotle, *Nicomachean Ethics*,
    Book III, chaps. 2 and 3, Book VI, chap. 2; and *Summa Theologica*,
    Part I, Qu. 82, Arts. 1–3, and Qu. 82; cf. *Prima Secundae*, Qu. 8–10.
    For a reduction of all human motivation to appetite or passion, and
    a denial of "will" and "freedom," cf. Hume, *Treatise of Human
    Nature*, Book II, Part III, Secs. I–III.
4. Plato, *Republic*, Book IV, 434–441; Aristotle, *Politics*, Book I, 1254B–B
    12, and *Nicomachean Ethics*, Book I, chap. 13, and Book VII, chaps.
    1, and 4–6; and Aquinas, *Summa Theologica*, Part I, Qu. 82, Arts. 4–5;
    cf. *Prima Secundae*, Qu. 11–18, for a detailed discussion of judgment,
    intention, deliberation, consent, choice, and so on. The student will
    find an influential defence of the radically opposed view that reason
    has no influence on human appetition in Hume, *Treatise on Human
    Nature*, Book III, Part I.

Glossary of Technical Terms

ACCIDENT. That which exists not in itself but only in some substance as its property or attribute.

NECESSARY ACCIDENTS, like the faculties of digestion and reason in a human individual, are caused internally by the substantial form.

CONTINGENT ACCIDENTS, like sun tan, are produced by external causes acting on the substance. Hence they may be lost without the destruction of the thing itself.

ANALOGOUS CONCEPT (ANALOGY). A concept by which the broader metaphysical modes of being, such as being, unity, matter, etc., are grasped in terms of a minimal, proportional similarity. Even though *A* is dissimilar to *B* and *C* to *D*, the *relation* of *A* to *C* may be similar to the *relation* of *B* to *D*. Thus one thing may be quite dissimilar to another, as may also their existences. Yet as the first is to its existence, so is the second to its existence. In this way existence and other metaphysical concepts of a very broad scope may be grasped not by a *univocal concept* (q.v.) but analogously by an *analogous concept*.

A POSTERIORI KNOWLEDGE. Knowledge which is gained only with the aid of sense experience. According to the realistic theory, all knowledge is a posteriori in this respect.

APPREHENSION, *see* COGNITION.

A PRIORI KNOWLEDGE. Knowledge which is supposed to be achieved by the mind alone without any dependence upon sense experience.

The existence of such knowledge is defended by extreme realists and conceptualists. It is denied by nominalists and modern realists.

ART. The disciplined cooperative pursuit of a subordinate natural end of human life. The different arts fall into three major divisions—*noetic, poietic, politic* (q.v.).

BY ACCIDENT. If a certain trait *B* is related to an entity *A* in such a way that *A* cannot possibly exist without *B*, then *B* is *essential* to *A*.

But if *A* and *B* are formally distinct, though found together in the same matter, the association is said to be *by accident* or coincidence.

Thus if a man's primary intention is to make money but he is also found to be honest, this second trait is *accidental* to the first, for money can also be made without honesty. The two traits are not essentially related. Neither one *requires* the other. Their association is a mere coincidence in the same matter which happens *by accident*.

CAUSATION. The diffusion of being from one entity to something distinct from itself. Thus matter provides a substratum to form, and form gives its own specific determinacy to matter. These are the two *intrinsic* causes of a concrete natural substance. But there are also two *extrinsic*

499

causes. An active tendency in one entity can move another as its efficient cause, and an idea can diffuse its specificity to a tendency as its final cause. These four modes of causation—material, formal, efficient, and final—are described in Ch. 14.

CHANGE. The actualization of that which is potential, so far as it is potential. Thus the actual vapor in the clouds possesses the potency to be condensed by cool air. The actualization of this potency is the process we refer to as *raining*. Cf. Ch. 15, §1.

CIRCULAR ARGUMENT. An argument in which the conclusion merely repeats in other words what is already asserted in one of the premises, e.g., all men must die because they are mortal.

COGNITION (NOETIC ACTIVITY). The act by which one being may unite itself with another being from which it is materially or existentially distinct.

Thus the physicist may *know* the liquid (become one with it) without becoming *physically* liquefied. Cf. Ch. 17, §4.

CONCEPTUALISM. A theory which holds that universal concepts are constructed or created in the mind, but that everything outside the mind is individual and unique. This fails to account for the fact that our concepts actually do apply to natural objects and leads to the so-called problem of *induction* (q.v.).

CONTINGENT. That which is capable of being otherwise (opposed to the *necessary*, q.v.).

CONTRADICTION, LAW OF. Being is absolutely exclusive of non-being; it is impossible for the same entity both to be and not to be at the same time in the same respect.

DEDUCTION. The process of argument or *syllogism* (q.v.) by which the mind passes from universal knowledge already achieved to a different conclusion which is either universal or particular. The process by which the mind passes from sensory cognition of the individual here and now to universal knowledge is called *induction* (q.v.).

DESIRE (APPETITE). The active tendency of animals which is elicited by *sensory cognition* (q.v.).

EFFICIENT CAUSE, FIRST ACT AND SECOND ACT OF. The efficient cause is that which influences some external matter to bring it into a determinate form, as the acts of the carpenter make the rough wood into a chair. This efficient cause can exist at two levels of activity.

In its *first act* the efficient cause is an active power, a structure of habits in the mind and muscles of the carpenter which makes him able to make a chair.

In its *second act* this cause passes over into the wood and exerts its necessary molding effect.

After this effect has been achieved, the cause remains in its *first* act. The carpenter is still *able* to make a chair, even when not actually making one.

ELICITED DESIRE. All natural entities are endowed with a tendency to complete or activate their forms. In addition to this, animals endowed with cognitive faculties have further active tendencies elicited by cognition. Any desire for a *known* object is *elicited*.

EPISTEMOLOGY. The science which attempts to explain the actual phenomena of human knowledge and to determine its general scope.

ESSENCE (ESSENTIALLY). The various determining traits that a thing must have to be at all, and without which it cannot be, make up its *essence* or possibility.

Thus to be understood and desired for its own sake belong to a truly generous act *essentially*. That it involved a gift of such and such magnitude in this case was only *by accident* (q.v.). Generosity did not necessarily require this.

EVIL. *Evil* is not *privation* (q.v.) in general. In this case all finite entities would be *evil*, for they are all deprived of something which they lack. But when a thing lacks something required by its nature for its proper perfection, this is *evil*. Thus lack of sight is not *evil* for a stone. It is *evil* for a man.

EXISTENCE. The last perfection which brings a determinate possibility or essence (q.v.) out of its causes and places it *in rerum natura*.

EXTREME REALISM. The theory that universal concepts exist not only in the mind but outside the mind as well, either as elements of which "physical" things are composed, or as inhabitants of a special realm of *essences* apart from the physical world. Cf. Ch. 19, §3.

FACULTY. The quality in an entity which makes it *capable* of performing certain acts even when these acts are not actually performed. Thus a man who is not blind has the faculty of sight even when his eyes are closed.

The *faculties* of a natural entity are usually *necessary accidents* (q.v.) caused by the substantial form or nature, which is always *in act* as long as the entity exists.

FINAL CAUSE. In the most general sense, that which determines efficient action to work in one way rather than in another. In this sense, the material nature of any material entity would be a final cause. It is the nature of the oak tree which makes the acorn grow.

In a stricter sense, final cause means that which *ultimately* must determine efficient action. This is an idea of what is good. Such an idea can elicit voluntary desire, a form of efficient causation, and specify it. Unless we are to attribute all things to a blind efficient cause, or fall into an infinite regress of efficient causes each determining the other, we must assume the existence of a first ideational or final cause.

FIRST NATURE. As opposed to the *second nature* (q.v.) acquired by cognitive animals in a process of habit formation, the *first nature* is the original, formal structure which specifically determines a material entity to be of this or that kind.

This *first nature* comes into existence with the entity itself and endures as long as the entity endures. It necessarily causes a tendency toward further perfective action. This is called *natural desire* (q.v.).

FORM. A mode of existence which is definite and distinct, and thus unlike matter which is vague and indeterminate. The major kinds of *form* include substance, quality, relation, and the others listed in Ch. 15.

FORMAL OBJECT. The *formal object* (as opposed to the material object) of a noetic faculty is the aspect of real existence with which the faculty is capable of becoming immaterially identified.

Thus when I see this blue pencil, the material object of my visual faculty is the whole, material pencil including much besides blue. The formal object is blue color.

FREEDOM. Present only where reason is present, and always involves two factors. (1) The free act is spontaneous, arising from within the agent without external constraint. (2) The free act involves a factor of indeterminacy or free choice by the will among various alternatives presented by reason.

GOOD (VALUE). The object of all tendency, appetite, and desire. All things tend to what is good, and seek after it according to their nature. But we cannot seek without seeking *something*. What do all things seek? The actuality or *perfection* (q.v.) which will complete and fulfill their nature. The good is *perfection* of being so far as it is the object of tendency or desire.

HABIT. A fixed quality of the will disposing it to deliberate and act in a certain way.

HUMAN GROUP. A number of human beings united by common love of a common good which is rationally apprehended by each individual. Cf. Ch. 9, §2.

HYLOMORPHISM. The doctrine that all natural entities (including man) have emerged from an evolutionary process and therefore include in their nature a matter (*hylé*) from which they have evolved, and a form (*morphé*) which gives them a determinate structure marking them off from other species. Cf. ch. 13, §6.

IDEALISM. The philosophical theory that being must be identified with the noetic being of an object before the mind.

IMAGINATION. A faculty which stores up the psychophysical images received by the external senses, excites them in the physical absence of their external objects, and separates and combines them in new configurations.

IMMANENT ACTION. As opposed to *transitive action* (q.v.), an *immanent act* is one which remains in the agent, perfecting him alone and not passing over into something external. Understanding, for example, is an *immanent act*, making no change in anything external to the mind.

IMMATERIAL BEING. Forms existing in matter are spread out quantitatively, individuated, and subject to quantitative change. This is called material existence.

Certain forms can be given existence without first entering into such a combination with matter. They are neither quantitative, individual, nor subject to quantitative change. Such existence is called *immaterial*. Cf. Ch. 19, §1.

INCARNATION, DOCTRINE OF THE. The central dogma of Christianity according to which God has entered the material events of human history *in the flesh*.

INDIVIDUAL. That which is undivided from itself and divided from all other entities. Cf. Ch. 14, §6.

INDUCTION. The process of abstraction by which the mind frees the form of a natural object from its material individuating traits and gives it an immaterial universal being before the mind.

When this process of abstraction is confused with that of making or constructing, as by the conceptualist, the so-called *problem of induction* arises. Since we actually observe only a number of individual men, not *all*, how can the mind *construct* a concept which will apply, as all our concepts do, to *all* possible instances?

INTENTIONAL (INTENTIONALITY). The peculiar reference or relation of a sensation or a concept to that *of* which it is the sensation or concept.

Thus the concept *man* refers *intentionally* to the human nature (including the notes of rational, animal, living, material, and substance) which is possessed in common by all individual men.

KNOWLEDGE, *see* COGNITION.

LAW. The rational ordering of means to the common good of a community.

LOGIC. A science concerned with the way in which *intentional* (q.v.) concepts must be ordered together in propositions and arguments so that they may express the truth. Since all concepts are intentional, *logic* has two branches: *formal*, which concerns the true order of concepts; and *material*, which concerns the true order of objects of concepts.

MATERIALISM. The philosophical theory that being must be identified with material being which is always individual, and spread out in quantitative dimensions.

MATTER. A mode of existence which is incomplete because of its indeterminacy or lack of form. Before it is actualized it must be given a determinate structure or form. Things are material so far as they are incompletely existent or potential, and only *able* to receive some formal determination not yet actually received. Unless matter were present in the world of nature it would be impossible to account for the continuity of change, and for the ubiquitous facts of chance and individuation. Cf. Ch. 13, §§4 and 5.

MIDDLE TERM, *see* SYLLOGISM.

NATURAL DESIRE (TENDENCY). As opposed to *elicited desire* (q.v.), *natural desire* is the original urge to further action which arises from the first formal nature of an entity. Each thing tends to act according to its nature. Fire burns; a plant grows. In cognitive animals this *natural tendency* may be taken over and modified by *elicited desire*.

NATURAL LAW.   The universal pattern of action required by human nature *in general* (not in the concrete) for its completion or perfection. Cf. Ch. 2, §2.

NATURAL SELECTION.   The Darwinian explanation of natural evolution by "spontaneous variations" which first happen to arise, and a stable environment which first happens to be stable. Given these chance factors, the unadapted forms will be weeded out and the adapted forms will survive. Cf. Ch. 16, §5.

NATURE.   1. The determinate *form* (q.v.) of a material entity so far as it causes the entity to tend or act in a certain definite way.

2. The word *nature* is also used collectively to indicate the whole world of material entities, each tending by reason of its *formal nature* to complete itself.

See also FIRST NATURE and SECOND NATURE.

NECESSARY.   That which is unable to be otherwise. The following kinds of *necessity* are distinguished:

1. Strict—the absolute incapacity to be otherwise.

2. Hypothetical—the incapacity of a choice or an act to be otherwise once it is chosen or performed.

3. Natural—the incapacity of the effect of natural causes to be otherwise, unless there is the coincidence of some opposing cause made possible by the indefinite potency of matter.

4. Moral—the incapacity of an act to be otherwise *if a certain goal is to be obtained.*

NOETIC ART.   All men have the capacity to know things as they really are in themselves. The cooperative endeavor to perfect this knowledge so far as possible is *noetic art*. Cf. Ch. 10, §3a.

NOMINALISM.   The theory which denies that immaterial, universal concepts exist either outside the mind or in the mind. Mental concepts have to be interpreted as individual, material responses in the nervous system, or physical sounds. Cf. Ch. 19, §3.

PASSION.   A fixed quality of appetite and imagination producing a tendency to respond in a certain way to perceived objects. Cf. Ch. 5, §3a and b.

PERFECTION.   A thing is *perfect* so far as it has emerged from the incompleteness of potency, in which all finite entities begin, and possesses the complete activity required by its nature for its proper perfection. Only the *perfect* is desirable or *good* (q.v.) .

POIETIC ART.   All men have a capacity to make the material instruments which are required for the living of human life. The cooperative realization of this capacity to produce the material instruments for a human community is *poietic* or *making art*. Cf. Ch. 10 §2c.

POLITIC ART. All men have the capacity to deliberate, plan, and choose their way of life. The cooperative endeavor to realize this capacity in order to attain the common good of a whole community is *politic art.* Cf. Ch. 10, §3b.

POSITIVE LAW. The contingent means chosen by a given community in its particular circumstances to achieve its common good.

POTENCY. Incompleteness of being as opposed to actuality, or completeness of being. There are many kinds, of which *matter* (q.v.) is one.

PRACTICAL SYLLOGISM, *see* SYLLOGISM.

PRIVATION. The presence of any finite form in matter involves the absence of others. An entity is said to be deprived, in the most general sense, of all those actualities which it does not actually possess.

RATIONAL COGNITION. The knowledge of existence as it must be universally, through an abstract, cognitive identification with its essence. Cf. Ch. 19.

REALISM. The name given to a certain philosophic way of thought first inaugurated by Plato and Aristotle, developed and refined in the Middle Ages, and still living at the present time. This view includes three basic theses: (1) the world is made up of substantial beings really related to one another, which exist independently of any human opinions or desires; (2) these substances and relations can be known by the human mind as they are in themselves; and (3) such knowledge can offer sound and immutable guidance (the law of nature) for individual and social action.

SECOND NATURE. As opposed to the *first nature* (q.v.) with which every material entity is originally endowed, noetic creatures possess a *second nature* or structure of habits elicited by cognition.

This *second nature* is of peculiar importance in man. Human freedom is realized to the degree in which our *first nature* is taken over by *second nature.*

SENSORY COGNITION. The knowledge of an individual, material entity through a cognitive identification with certain qualitative *accidents* (q.v.).

SOLIPSISM. The view that an individual man can know only his own subjective states and accidents. It is usually caused by a tendency to explain knowledge in terms of the limited categories of physical change and causation.

SUBJECTIVISM. The view that the objects of knowledge inhere as physical accidents or impressions in the knowing subject. It is caused by materialistic habits of thought which lead us to suppose that forms can be given existence only by physical causes which impress them on matter. If this were true, *subjectivism* would be inescapable. Cf. Ch. 17, §4.

SUBSTANCE. That which exists in itself and not in something formally distinct from itself as a property or accident. This individual tree, this animal, and this man are natural *substances.* The weight, the skin color, and the intelligence of this man are his accidents.

An artificial substance such as an engine or a pen is really a number of natural *substances* combined together in an accidental structure imposed by human *art* (q.v.).

The form and the matter, and the integral parts of a substance, such as the brain and the heart of a man, are not accidents. They are substantial parts, or incomplete *substances*. Cf. Ch. 15, §2.

SUBSTANTIAL FORM. The first act of any material entity which determines its matter, causes its necessary faculties and accidents, and finally gives it a constant tendency toward further completion.

SYLLOGISM. That process of thought by which the human mind can pass from something already known and expressed in propositions to something else not yet known and expressed.

It is based on the principle that two entities which are identified with a third are themselves identical. Thus if B is C, and A is B, then A is C. In this case B is C is the *major premise,* A is B is the *minor premise,* and B is the *middle term.*

In the *practical syllogism,* a given act is related to a desirable end through an instrumental middle term or *means.* Thus if ferrous foods alleviate anemia, and this is a ferrous food, it will alleviate anemia.

TRANSCENDENTAL CONCEPT AND MODE OF BEING. Certain concepts refer only to restricted modes of being, this kind or that. The *transcendental concepts* refer to modes of being which belong to anything whatsoever that exists at all in any way. The most important *transcendentals* are existence, unity, truth, something, and goodness.

TRANSITIVE ACTION. As opposed to *immanent action* (q.v.), *transitive action,* like pushing, pulling, heating, and cooling, does not remain in the agent but passes over into something external to give this an added existence.

UNIVOCAL CONCEPT. A concept by which some phase of existence may be grasped abstractedly apart from other phases with which it is combined *in rerum natura.* Man, animal, color, two, and most of the restricted concepts of common speech are *univocal.* More inclusive concepts, like good and unity, are *analogous* (q.v.).

VICE. A habit which is not in accord with the law of nature.

VIRTUE. A habit which is in accord with the law of nature. Cf. Ch. 5.

WILL. The active tendency in man which is elicited by *rational cognition* (q.v.)

Name Index

Albert the Great, 25
Alexander of Hales, 24
Alexander the Great, 17, 18
Anselm, 355
Aquinas, Thomas, 25–27, 128, 137, 198, 199, 227, 327, 355, 357, 360, 363, 383
Aristotle, 16–21, 24, 25, 26, 46, 53, 71, 84, 90, 91, 104, 107, 113, 116, 122, 128, 129, 130, 131, 135, 137, 138, 140, 141, 142, 143, 144, 145, 146, 148, 150, 159, 167, 173, 214, 226, 243, 244, 247, 248, 249, 250, 252, 266, 278, 288, 302, 314, 320, 323, 338, 355, 356, 357, 360, 363, 379, 398, 409, 415, 418, 419, 421, 447, 471, 487, 489, 492
Augustine, 22–23, 128, 180, 199, 258, 371, 379
Averroes, 24
Avicenna, 24, 300

Bentham, J., 51
Bergson, H., 293, 343, 345
Berkeley, 31, 32, 33, 283, 290, 303
Boethius, 327, 381
Bonaventura, 25
Bradley, F. H., 284, 290, 343, 351, 359

Descartes, 29–31, 290, 303, 321, 325, 338, 355, 359, 370, 374, 401, 414
Dion, 12
Dostoievsky, 129
du Noüy, Lecomte, 313, 367

Epicureans, 21

Garrigou-Lagrange, R., 357

Heard, G. 367
Hegel, 33
Hermias, 17
Hume, 31, 32, 51, 283, 363, 366, 370, 385

John of Rochelle, 24

Kant, I., 32–33, 48–51, 303, 456, 463, 484
Kierkegaard, S., 34

Leibnitz, 31
Locke, 31, 32, 283, 303, 321, 422, 423

Marxists, 285, 289
Mascall, E. L., 357
Mill, J. S., 51–52, 303
Morgan, Lloyd, 293

Ockham, William of, 27–29, 31, 454
Opler, M. E., 367

Parmenides, 284, 338, 343
Pascal, B., 393
Payne, Thomas, 217
Plato, 10, 11–16, 22, 23, 25, 26, 46, 53, 104, 110, 116, 137, 139, 144, 167, 173, 179, 180, 197, 199, 214, 218, 244, 252, 264, 266, 355, 363, 372, 379, 419, 473, 489, 490
Plotinus, 21, 22
Proclus, 21

Scotus, Duns, 27–28, 51
Sellars, R. W., 293
Sextus Empiricus, 21
Siger of Brabant, 24
Smuts, J. C., 293
Socrates, 9–11, 253
Speusippus, 17
Spinoza, 31, 343
Stoics, 21, 44, 45, 49
Suarez, 28, 29, 414

Thompson, W. R., 364
Toynbee, A. J., 51, 195, 203, 259, 368, 369

Urban IV, 25

Victorinus, 22

William of Moerbeke, 25

Zeno, 335, 338

Subject Index

Absolute nature, 459–460
See also Categories
Accident, 324 ff.; accidental vs. essential cause, 305–306; always present in nature, 308–309; and causation, 307 ff.; confused with substance, 328; science seeks to eliminate, 309; sense cannot abstract from, 421–422, 452; vs. responsibility, 89–91; vs. virtue, 58
Action, 340 ff.; and efficient causation, 340–341; distinct from nature of finite entity, 376; distinct from passion, 341–342; extrinsic, 341; follows mode of existence, 479; four species of, 342
Agnosticism, 354
Alteration, 331–333, 339
Analogy, 356; attacked by Scotus, 27–28, 291; matter understood by, 290–291
Anatropé, *see* Inversion
Anger, *see* Indignation
Anthropology, 393–394; concerned with reason and will, 405–406; reveals no antisocial men, 176; use of final causes, 364
Appetite, 109–110; as faculty of soul, 403, 405; classification of, 110 ff.; controlled by moderating virtue, 114; corruption of, 490–491; distinguished from inorganic tendency, 407; guidance of external, 132 ff.; guidance of internal, 116 ff.; irascible, 473 ff.; natural ally of practical reason, 490; natural vs. elicited, 469–470, 481–482; sensory, 470 ff.; three forms of elicited, 470
Apprehension, *see* Cognition
Arts, 103 ff.; correction of, 233 ff.; inversion of, 262 ff.; natural order of, 266 ff.; noetic, 211–215; poietic, 221 ff.; politic, 215–221; two divisions of, 104
Atomism, 292–293, 362

Authority, 188 ff.; corruption of, 196; democratic, 208–209; despotic, 208; in noetic groups, 213–215; in social disintegration, 230–231; makes common action possible, 193–194; subordinate to members, 198, 216; three functions of, 194–195; under law of nature, 217
Autonomy, 325–326
Avarice, 155

Barbarism, 262
Being, *see* Existence
Business, 230, 240–241

Capital, 225 ff.
Cardinal virtues, 97–98; in Aquinas' philosophy, 26; Plato's view of, 13
Categorical imperative, 49
Categories, 322–323; classification of: action, 340 ff., passion, 341–342, place, 337, position, 337, quality, 330 ff., quantity, 333 ff., relation, 347 ff., substance, 323 ff., time, 342 ff.; Aquinas' view of, 26; Aristotle's view of, 18; Kant's theory of, 32; vs. universals, 459–460
Causation, 297 ff.; and responsibility, 82–83; formal, 298–299; in philosophy of Aquinas, 26; in philosophy of Aristotle, 18–19; modes of, 305–307; necessity of, 299–300; results in relations of dependence, 347
Cause, 302, 304; accidental vs. essential, 305–306; actual vs. potential, 306–307; by accident, 307 ff.; contemporaneous with effect, 82–83, 303–304, 359; four kinds of, 302, 304; sought by all discursive reasoning, 101, 299–300
Central sense, functions, 426–427
Chance, 307 ff.; cannot explain orderly effects, 364–365; in Darwinian theory, 312–313; not uncaused, 315; suddenness of, 312

508